The A. B. SIMPSON Collection

VOLUME I

The
A. B. SIMPSON
Collection

VOLUME I

• Includes A Larger Christian Life •
Cross of Christ • The Fourfold Gospel •
Walking in the Spirit •

A L

ISBN: 978-1-6673-0616-2 paperback
ISBN: 978-1-6673-0617-9 hardcover

Table of Contents

Cross of Christ 9

The Fourfold Gospel 97

Walking in the Spirit 173

A Larger Christian Life 311

Contents

Cross of Christ

- Chapter 1. THE KALEIDOSCOPE OF THE CROSS 10
- Chapter 2. UNDER THE SHADOW OF THE CROSS 18
- Chapter 3. THE BRAND OF THE CROSS 26
- Chapter 4. THE UPLIFT OF THE CROSS 35
- Chapter 5. ENEMIES OF THE CROSS 42
- Chapter 6. THE CROSS AND THE WORLD 50
- Chapter 7. VOICES OF THE RESURRECTION 58
- Chapter 8. SEEKING THE LIVING AMONG THE DEAD ... 68
- Chapter 9. THE POWER OF THE RESURRECTION 77
- Chapter 10. AFTER-EASTER-DAYS 85

The Fourfold Gospel

- Introduction 98
- Chapter 1. CHRIST OUR SAVIOUR 100
- Chapter 2. CHRIST OUR SANCTIFIER 112
- Chapter 3. CHRIST OUR HEALER 123
- Chapter 4. CHRIST OUR COMING LORD 135
- Chapter 5. THE WALK WITH GOD 151
- Chapter 6. KEPT 162

Walking in the Spirit

Chapter 1. LIVING IN THE SPIRIT 174
Chapter 2. WALKING IN THE SPIRIT 180
Chapter 3. PERSON AND ATTRIBUTES OF THE HOLY GHOST 186
Chapter 4. OFFICES AND RELATIONS OF THE HOLY GHOST 191
Chapter 5. EMBLEMS AND ASPECTS OF THE HOLY SPIRIT 197
Chapter 6. THE SPIRIT OF LIGHT 206
Chapter 7. THE SPIRIT OF HOLINESS 220
Chapter 8. THE SPIRIT OF LIFE 231
Chapter 9. THE SPIRIT OF COMFORT 243
Chapter 10. THE SPIRIT OF LOVE 252
Chapter 11. THE SPIRIT OF POWER 263
Chapter 12. THE SPIRIT OF PRAYER 278
Chapter 13. COOPERATING WITH THE HOLY GHOST 287
Chapter 14. HINDERING THE HOLY SPIRIT 296

A Larger Christian Life

Chapter 1. THE POSSIBILITIES OF FAITH 312
Chapter 2. THE JOY OF THE LORD 328
Chapter 3. FILLED WITH THE SPIRIT 344
Chapter 4. THE LARGER LIFE 358
Chapter 5. ISHMAEL AND ISAAC; OR, THE DEATH OF SELF 373
Chapter 6. "MORE THAN CONQUERORS" 388
Chapter 7. GRACE ABOUNDING 400
Chapter 8. FROM STRENGTH TO STRENGTH 414
Chapter 9. GOD'S MEASURELESS MEASURES 425
Chapter 10. SPIRITUAL GROWTH 439
Chapter 11. ENLARGED WORK 452

Cross of Christ

By
A. B. Simpson

A. B. SIMPSON

Chapter 1.
THE KALEIDOSCOPE OF THE CROSS

"And the people stood beholding" (Luke 23: 35).

What varied thoughts and feelings moved the hearts of those who stood that day beholding the cross of Calvary! We can perceive the cruel heartlessness with which the Roman soldiers drove the nails and reared the cross, interested only in getting their share of the petty spoil for which they cast lots. We can conceive of the fiendish ferocity with which the rulers and chief priests gloated over the agony of their victim and felt themselves at last avenged. We can comprehend the heartbreak with which those loving women looked upon the helpless anguish of the One in whom they had so much believed. We can realize something of that mother's grief as she recalled the words of Simeon thirty years before, "Yea, a sword shall pierce through thy own soul also." We can imagine that Peter, gazing from afar upon the tragedy, would have given worlds to have taken back that last dart with which he had pierced his Master's heart, but realized that now he should see Him no more. And we know something from the narrative of the awe and veneration with which the Roman centurion gazed upon the preternatural signs which accompanied His death and exclaimed, "Truly this was the Son of God."

And so they stood beholding. And all through the ages generations after generations have turned their eyes to that central cross as it has loomed larger and loftier above all other spectacles in the vision of the human race. Once more Christ is set forth before us, crucified among us, and faith and love once more stand beholding. As we gaze upon that scene so old and yet so ever new, it seems as if that cross appears like some vision in a kaleidoscope. With every turn that holy Scriptures as they present to us some of these varied phases of the cross of Jesus.

A Death Scene

Death is always an impressive spectacle, but this was no ordinary death. Here was a man who did not need to die, but One who chose to die, One who came to die, One whose supreme mission was to die, One over whose cross each of us can write, "He died for me."

A Crucifixion

This is more than an ordinary death scene for He "became obedient unto death, even the death of the cross." Crucifixion was adopted by the Romans as the severest form of capital punishment. It was the most agonizing and it was the most shameful of all deaths. What agony was endured as every muscle was strained to its utmost tension, as the helpless body hung by its own weight from lacerated flesh and bones, slowly dying from sheer anguish with no vital organ wounded, and as the crucible of pain burned up by slow degrees life's last powers of endurance. How pitiful was the cry of the crucified Savior as it was foreshadowed in the prophetic Psalm: "I am poured out like water, and all my bones are out of joint: my heart is like wax; it is melted in the midst of my bowels. My strength is dried up like a potsherd; and my tongue cleaveth to my jaws; and thou hast brought me into the dust of death" (Psalm 22:14,15).

And what shame was suffered as He hung there, crucified between two thieves. He was treated not only as one of them, but worse than either. His very name was blotted out of the family records at Bethlehem, and He was looked upon by men and even treated by His own Father as if He were the worst and vilest criminal that ever lived or died.

A Murder

"Him ... ye have taken, and by wicked hands have crucified and slain." "Whom ye have delivered up, and denied him in the presence of Pilate, when he was determined to let him go" (Acts

2:23; 3:13). It was a judicial assassination. He was God's martyred Lamb, and our martyred Master.

A Voluntary Sacrifice

Jesus said of His own death, "The good shepherd giveth his life for the sheep." "I lay down my life for the sheep .... I have power to lay it down, and I have power to take it again." He gave Himself for us. "No man taketh it from me, but I lay it down of myself" (John 10:14,15,18). As He hung upon that cross, even death could not come till He said, "It is finished," and bowed His head, as if beckoning death to come, and "gave up the ghost." Was there ever a death like this? Human nature flees from death as the worst of all evils. But here was a Man who from the beginning to the end of His life had one supreme object - to lay down His own life for the sake of others.

A Baptism

"I have a baptism to be baptized with; and how am I straitened till it be accomplished" (Luke 12:50). It was ever present to His thoughts. It was ever calling Him to the cross. It was ever coloring every act and object of His life. It was ever casting its shadow over His consciousness so that He died a thousand deaths before He even approached the cross.

A Passion

"He showed himself alive after his passion" (Acts 1:3). Literally, the word passion means suffering. But it conveys the idea of intense suffering, suffering that involved His inner as well as His outer being, His soul and spirit as well as His rent body. It is true that "He poured out his soul unto death."

A Travail

Travail is considered the severest form of human agony, and thus represents in the most emphatic light the excruciating anguish of the Savior's death. But it speaks of more than agony. It has in it the silver lining of hope and life and promise. It is the birth pang of a new creation. "She remembereth no more the anguish, for joy that a man is born into the world." And so there was a joy even in the Savior's agony, and already the promise came to Him, "He shall see his seed, he shall prolong his days, and the pleasure of the Lord shall prosper in his hands. He shall see of the travail of his soul, and shall be satisfied" (Isaiah 53:10,11)

A Decease

They "spake of his decease which he should accomplish at Jerusalem" (Luke 9:31). Decease is more than death. It means an outgoing, a departure, and carries with it the idea of a future life and a continued activity. So He changed the sphere of His existence and passed through the gates of death to a higher and more glorious ministry.

A Planting

"If we have been planted together in the likeness of his death, we shall be also in the likeness of his resurrection" (Romans 6:5). This figure has an added charm in the beautiful conjunction of the Easter season and the Spring when all nature is alive with illustrations and types of the new creation. The figure of planting is very different from that of burying. It is not a grave plot, but a garden. You do not drop the lifeless remains of some loved one into the gloomy grave; you simply put away a living seed with the confidence that it will bloom forth in beauty in shoot and bud and blossom and fruit. And so the death of Christ was just a glorious planting, and every time we die with Him, we are just making a great investment, from which we are going to reap some day a hundred fold. Let us not be afraid to let the "corn of wheat fall into the ground and die," for "if it die, it bringeth forth much fruit."

A Lifting Up

"As Moses lifted up the serpent in the wilderness, even so must the Son of man be lifted up" (John 3:14). "When ye have lifted up the Son of man, then shall ye know that I am he" (John 8:28). "And I, if I be lifted up from the earth, will draw all men unto me" (John 12:32). The cross of Christ is intended for the eyes of the whole world. Let us lift Him up by our testimony, by our love, and in our adoring praise and worship until all the world shall stand beholding.

An Offering

The idea of an offering is something that pleases God. In Christ He beheld for the first time with perfect satisfaction the consecration of a human life. Even if no sinner had ever been saved it still would have been an offering well pleasing to God, "for a sweet smelling savor."

A Sacrifice

A sacrifice is different from an offering. It carries with it the idea of sin to be expiated, of substitution for the guilty, of atonement for the transgressions of men. So Christ died for sinners that they might not die, and suffered "the just for the unjust, that he might bring us to God" (1 Peter 3:18).

A Great Victory

On the cross He met Satan and overthrew him. "Having spoiled principalities and powers, he made a show of them openly, triumphing over them in it" (the cross) (Col. 2:15). And so we are said to overcome by the blood of the Lamb.

An Example

"Christ also suffered for us, leaving us an example, that ye should follow in his steps... who, when he was reviled, reviled not again; when he suffered, he threatened not; but committed himself to him that judgeth righteously: who his own self bare our sins in his own body on the tree, that we, being dead to sins, should live unto righteousness" (1 Peter 2:21,23,24). The crucifixion was a great object lesson of submission, gentleness, meekness and self surrender. "He is brought as a lamb to the slaughter, and as a sheep before her shearers is dumb, so he openeth not his mouth" (Isa. 53:7). Christ's death is much more than this; but let us not forget this also amid the suffering and trial through which we follow Him.

A Ransom

Christ's death was the meeting of the conditions of that great covenant which the Father had made with His Son ages before, promising eternal life to all for whom He should pay this costly price. And now the price has been paid, the redemption accomplished, and the heirs of the covenant may come and claim as much as that blood is worth.

A Reconciliation

At Christ's cross God and the sinner can meet while Christ stands between reaching out one pierced hand to the Father and pleading, "Father, forgive them; for they know not what they do," and the other to sinners and beseeching, "Be ye reconciled to God."

A Revelation

"God commendeth his love toward us" not by talking about it, but by doing something which proves it and commends it as no words could ever have done, "in that, while we were yet sinners, Christ died for us" (Romans 5:8).

A Pledge of the New Creation

Christ's cross is the pledge of the new creation, for there old humanity died in the person of the seed of the woman, and new humanity was born in the person of the second Adam. And now, as we identify ourselves with Him we are counted dead with Him to the curse of the law, to the dominion of the carnal nature, to the very center of our physical being and to the extent of the future resurrection itself. The reason I am justified is that the old sinner is dead with Christ, and I am no longer he, or liable for his sins. The reason I have victory over the power of sin is that in Christ I am dead to sin and I need no longer fear it or obey it. The reason I claim my healing in His name is that He has borne the liabilities of my body, and I can lay them over on Him who died for them. And by the same reason I am already anticipating the coming resurrection and triumphing over the fear and power of death. "If any man be in Christ, he is a new creature: old things are passed away; behold, all things are become new. And all things are of God, who hath reconciled us to himself by Jesus Christ" (2 Cor. 5:17,18).

An Inspiration

"For the love of Christ constraineth us; because we thus judge, that if one died for all, then were all dead: and that he died for all, that they which live should not henceforth live unto themselves, but unto him which died for them, and rose again" (2 Cor. 5:14,15).

> I've got a word in my heart like a fire,
> That will not let me be;
> Jesus the Son of God, who loved
> And gave Himself for me.
>
> If He'd loved and died for some one else;
> For Peter or blessed Paul;
> If He'd loved and died for men like these;
> One wouldn't have wondered at all.
>
> But 'twas for me that Jesus died,
> For me and a world of men;
> Just as sinful, and just as slow
> To give back His love again.
>
> Did'st Thou love and die for a man like me?
> Then, Master, I will take
> More thought for the perishing souls I meet
> If it's only for Thy sake.

Identification

The cross of Christ demands from each of us identification. It is of no use to us unless we make it our own and enter into His death and resurrection. "Reckon ye also yourselves to be dead indeed unto sin, but alive unto God through Jesus Christ our Lord" (Rom. 6:11).

> When Jesus died on Calvary,
> I, too, was there
> 'Twas in my place He stood for me
> And now accepted, even as He
> His righteousness I share.

Chapter 2.
UNDER THE SHADOW OF THE CROSS

"This do in remembrance of me" (Luke 22:19).

This inscription placed by the hands of the Master over the Feast of Love might well be made the watchword of our whole Christian life. The Lord's Supper is a sort of microcosm, or miniature, of the believer's life, and over every moment, every word and every action we may well inscribe, "Do this in remembrance of me."

After good Archbishop Darboy had been murdered by the Paris Communists, they found upon the walls of his dungeon the sketch of a rude cross, with these four words marking its extreme dimensions: height, depth, length, breadth. To his devout spirit the cross seemed to measure the love of God and the grace of Christ in its height and depth and length and breadth.

The arms of that cross are wide enough to cover every need and every experience of our daily lives. Its foundations are deeper than our deepest sorrows, and our loftiest heights of rapture can never reach above its heavenly altitude. It is God's measure not only of His love, but of our lives.

The medieval saints used to erect, in the center of the market square of every town, a simple cross, so that it came to be known as the Market Cross; and it may still be seen in many of the older towns of Europe. The simple and beautiful idea was that the cross should dominate all the business of earthly life, and that all transactions, interests and concerns should ever be under that shadow of the cross.

"Under the shadow of the cross" -- how much this phrase suggests of sweetness, sacredness and practical consecration. Perhaps you are wearing a gilded cross upon your bosom, dear sister. Does the heart that throbs beneath it beat true to its holy meaning? Are the words that come from that throat, whose necklace is clasped by the symbol of His gentleness and suffering, in keeping with the cross you love to wear? Are the habiliments of your person and the habits of your life suggestive of Him whose only marks of honor were the thorn rents, the spear gash and the blood drops of agony on Calvary?

Let us contemplate the cross in its practical relation to our actual Christian life.

Refuge for the Sinner

When the sinner comes to the deep and awful sense of his guilt and peril, what refuge can he find apart from the cross of Calvary? "Thus far did I come, laden with my sin," wrote Bunyan, telling the story of the sinner's refuge. Then as the strings broke and the burdens rolled away, there came the joyful song of praise,

"Blest Cross! Blest Sepulcher! blest rather be
The Man that there was put to shame for me."

Refuge for the Tempted

When temptation comes and the newborn soul has found its first stumbling stone, what can bring deliverance and victory but the cross of Calvary? And oh, what new light comes as the soul begins to fully realize that Christ has purchased for it not merely a brief reprieve or a new probation, but a complete and everlasting vindication. Our sins have not only been forgiven, but obliterated; in fact, they have ceased to be our sins and have been assumed by the great Sin Bearer, and we are henceforth as free from liability for them as if we had never sinned! In the death of Calvary we have died, and we stand before the judgment and the high court of heaven in the position of those who have paid the full penalty for sin already and who, looking up in the face of heaven, can say, "Who shall lay anything to the charge of God's elect? It is God that justifieth. Who is he that condemneth? It is Christ that died, yea rather, that is risen again, who is even at the right hand of God" (Romans 8:33,34).

A. B. SIMPSON

Salvation from the Effects of Sin

Sometimes our past comes back again like great ocean billows threatening to overwhelm us. It is then that the cross rises as a mighty barrier and breakwater, even as rocks resist the billows around their shores, and we find that instead of reaping the harvest of our evil sowing, there is One that has reaped the wretched issue for us and we are free. We do not have to pass through the processes of natural law or pay the full penalty which sin exacts in the present life; but we may claim complete deliverance from the wreck of body and brain, and from temporal conditions which might justly have been our heritage, and go forth into a life as glorious and free as if we had just dropped from heaven, the new creation of infinite love.

Sanctification through the Cross

When we come to the great conflict with inbred sin we find once more that the cross has made provision not only for our justification but also for our sanctification. We do not have to fight alone the demon of depravity in our own hearts or slowly build up out of the wreckage of the past a holy character. But we find that the old man, as well as the old deeds, was crucified with Him, and that it is our privilege to lay off the nature of self and sin and put on the very nature and life of Christ Himself "who of God is made unto us wisdom, and righteousness, and sanctification, and redemption" (1 Cor. 1:30). And as the process of grace goes deeper and reveals to us yet undiscovered depths of corruption, we shall find that the cross is deeper still and that with every new revelation we may continue to put off" the old man with his deeds and ... put on the new man" in a loftier resurrection life, as step by step we come to "know him, and the power of his resurrection, and the fellowship of his suffering, being made conformable unto his death" (Phil. 3:10).

Healing through the Cross

Still further we slowly learn that the shadow of that cross touches our mortal frame, that our very bodies have been redeemed, that our liability to sickness because of sin has been canceled by His death, that we may lay over our sicknesses and infirmities upon Him who bore them, and that we may take His resurrection life for every physical need of this mortal frame. "He was wounded for our transgressions, he was bruised for our iniquities: the chastisement of our peace was upon him; and with his stripes we are healed" (Isa. 53:5).

Fellowship with His Cross

Much of our life contains suffering and trial and the shadow of the cross is also here. Looking upon our trials as unmeaning accidents, the blow of fate, the luck of evil fortune, or the cruel wrongs of men and women is so different from taking them from our Father's hand as the cup of His loving discipline and as the fellowship of our Savior's cross! How we have striven sometimes with some tremendous sorrow, and have refused to bow our head as it grew darker and more dreadful and as the iron of despair entered our nerveless soul. Then at last a sweet message from the heart of God the Comforter has breathed the prayer of faith and submission, "The cup which my Father hath given me, shall I not drink it?" How the clouds melted away, and like a benediction there have fallen upon our hearts the precious words, "These things I have spoken unto you, that in me ye might have peace. In the world ye shall have tribulation: but be of good cheer; I have overcome the world" (John 16:33). And again the echo has fallen upon our ears, "Think it not strange concerning the fiery trial which is to try you, as though some strange thing happened unto you: but rejoice, inasmuch as ye are partakers of Christ's sufferings; that, when his glory shall be revealed, ye may be glad also with exceeding joy" (2 Peter 4:12,13).

Ah, but you say, "People caused my sufferings." Well, did not people cause His? And that is the very thing which makes your fellowship with His cross complete. But again I hear you say, "Yes, but I am innocent of the things they say; I am misrepresented, lied about and persecuted." Was not that the very glory of His cross? Are you going to throw back on Him the burden which He has left for you to share? Yes, it is true that we may "fill up that which is behind of the afflictions of Christ... for his body's sake, which is the church" (Col. 1:24). You can never share the wrath of God for sin; that He bore alone. But He has left for you to carry with Him, "the fellowship of his sufferings." An old legend tells us that when He met Simon Peter fleeing from Rome to escape the fiery wrath of Nero, He asked him, "Whither goest thou?" Peter frankly answered and told of his flight, and then asked in turn, "Lord, whither goest Thou?" The answer came, "I am going to Rome to be crucified a second time, because My disciple Peter has run away from his cross." It is no wonder that Peter turned back from his flight and hastened with downward head to follow his dying Lord. Let us also return and follow the Crucified.

> Must Jesus bear the cross alone?
> And all the world go free?
> No, there's a cross for every one,
> And there's a cross for me.

But it will cease to be a cross when we are sweetly conscious that He is bearing the other end, and that we are suffering with Him now and shall yet be glorified together.

Beloved, surely we may say, as we think of all these things, "God forbid that I should glory, save in the cross of our Lord Jesus Christ by whom the world is crucified unto me, and I unto the world" (Gal. 6:14).

> The cross, it takes our guilt away,
> It holds the fainting spirit up;
> It cheers with hope the gloomy day
> And sweetens every bitter cup.

The balm of life, the cure of woe,
The measure and the pledge of love,
The sinner's refuge here below,
The angels' theme in heaven above.

Our Attitude to Others through the Cross

The cross is also practical and powerful in its influence upon our ministry for others, our relation to the world and our work for God. How differently we would think, speak and judge concerning our fellow Christians if we lived more under the shadow of the cross. A Christian lady once asked, "How can I be delivered from the spirit of censorious judging and severe speaking of the faults of others?" In that moment came to me a revelation of the Lord Jesus Christ bearing the sins of others and taking them upon Himself. For us then to put our hands upon them is really to crucify Him afresh and demand that He should suffer again for the things that He has already borne. The revelation was so unspeakably vivid that it came almost like a shock and whatever effect this truth may have had upon the heart and life of the friend in question, the writer will never forget the awful light in which it seemed to place the sin of uncharitableness, censoriousness and evil speaking. Is not this covered by such texts as this, "Who art thou that judgest another man's servant?" "Who shall lay anything to the charge of God's elect?... Who is he that condemneth? It is Christ that died." Beloved, let us think and speak and love henceforth under the shadow of the cross.

Our Attitude to the World through the Cross

The apostle declares that through the cross he has been crucified unto the world and the world unto him. Is this true of us? Do we look upon this world as the enemy that murdered our Lord? Can we join hands with it in its Christless pleasures and godless ambitions any more than a sister could dance with the ruffian that had murdered her brother? The world crucified our Christ and to us henceforth it must be recognized as our foe. Indeed, by the death of Christ we have died to the world and are counted as men that have passed out of it and then come back to it in a second life as God's sent ones, commissioned to represent the Master here. We cannot do this if we stoop to the world's level. It is from our heavenly place of identity with Him that we may expect to lift it to the higher level.

The cross in the market place! Oh, what a difference it would make if the cross of Calvary dominated all our business dealings, all our social amusements, all our pleasures and all our plans! Avarice would not dare claim its graft. Pleasure would blush in its mad revel before that vision of Him who came not to seek enjoyment or gain, but rather to lay down His rights and give up His very life, not only as an example of righteousness, but as a sacrifice of love.

The Cross – the Inspiration of Zeal and Sacrifice

And oh, how poor our sacrifices and services for our Master and our fellow-men appear under the shadow of the cross! "He died for all, that they which live should not henceforth live unto themselves, but unto him which died for them, and rose again" (2 Cor. 5:15). The cross is the only inspiration of true benevolence, sacrifice and zeal for the salvation of men and the salvation of the world. If its mark has been placed upon us, then we are not our own; we are bought with a price, and all we are and have belongs to Him, and the great sacrifice is little to give to Him.

A contemporary journal stated that during the last winter of the war in Manchuria the Japanese emperor, learning of the sufferings of his soldiers from the awful rigors of the Russian winter, was so distressed that he refused to allow the fires to be lighted in his palace and he spent that winter in fellowship with the sufferings of his heroic army. Such was the spirit of Jesus when our race was in peril. Heaven could be to Him no longer heaven, but down from the seats of glory He hastened to share our sin and save our world. Oh, surely, we might watch with Him one hour, and count it joy to share the fellowship of His love by sacrifice and service for the salvation of men! Are we doing this? Has the cross put its mark upon our ministry, upon our gifts, upon our personal labors for Him and for the perishing around us and the heathen in more distant lands? Well may we cry when we think of such love:

> Oh, for a passionate passion for souls!
> Oh, for the pity that yearns!
> Oh, for the love that loves unto death!
> Oh, for the fire that burns!

No Cross, No Crown

What significance will the cross have in connection with the crown? Beloved, if anything is true, this is true, that there will be nothing in heaven that does not have the mark of the cross upon it and has not passed through death and resurrection. Even the very earth and heavens must pass away, and a new heaven and a new earth emerge. There shall be no joy, there shall be no glory, there shall be no crown for us there that did not come from some surrender, some sacrifice, some renunciation, some crucifixion here. God help us, therefore, to stamp upon all our life below and our crown above the passion sign of the cross.

Chapter 3.
THE BRAND OF THE CROSS

> "From henceforth let no man trouble me: for I bear
> in my body the marks of the Lord Jesus" (Gal. 6:17)

The word marks in this text is translated by Rotherham, "brand marks." The world describes a mark that has been branded into the flesh, and suggests the idea of the cruel practice of certain nations in branding political offenders in the face with a badge of dishonor which never could be erased. The Greek word literally means "a stigma," and suggests a mark of reproach and shame. The apostle says that he bears in his body to branded scar which identifies him with Christ and His cross.

The kind of mark which he refers to is made plain by the verse almost immediately preceding, "God forbid that I should glory, save in the cross of our Lord Jesus Christ, by whom the world is crucified unto me, and I unto the world" (Gal. 6:14). It is the cross of Christ which is the object at once of His shame and His glory. Let us look first at the marks of the Lord Jesus, and then at their reproduction in His followers.

The Cross Marks of Christ

He was always overshadowed by the cross which at last He bore on Calvary. His life was a life of humiliation and suffering from the manger to the tomb.

His birth was under a shadow of dishonor and shame. The shadow that fell upon the virgin mother could not be removed from her child, and even to this day only faith in a supernatural incarnation can explain away that reproach.

His childhood was overshadowed by sorrow. Soon after His birth, He was pursued by Herod with relentless hate. He spent His early childhood as an exile in the eland of Egypt, which had

Cross of Christ

always been associated in the history of His people as the house of bondage.

His early manhood was spent in toil and poverty and He was known all His later life as "the carpenter's son." A modern painter represents Him as under the shadow of the cross even in the early days at Nazareth; as He returns from a day of toil with arms outstretched with weariness, the setting sun flings the shadow of His figure across the pathway, suggestive of a dark cross.

His life was one of poverty and humiliation. He had nowhere to lay His head, and when He died His body was laid even in a borrowed tomb.

He was rejected and despised by the people among whom He labored. "He came unto his won, and his own received hem not" (John 1:11). His work was, humanly speaking, a complete failure, and when He left the world He had but a handful of followers who had remained true to His teachings and person.

His very friends and companions were of the humblest class, rude fishermen and common people without culture and, indeed, often without the ability to appreciate their blessed Master. Coming from the society of heaven, how H must have felt the strange difference of these rude associates; and yet, never once did He complain or even intimate the difference.

The spirit of His life was ever chastened and humble. The veil of modesty covered all His acts and attitudes. He never boasted or vaunted Himself. "He shall not strive, nor cry; neither shall any man hear his voice in the streets." (Matt. 12:19), was the prophetic picture which He so literally fulfilled. He sought no splendid pageants, asked no earthly honors; and the only time that He did assume the prerogatives of a king, He rode upon the foal of an ass and entered Jerusalem in triumph as the King of meekness rather than of pride.

Perhaps the severest strain of all His life was the repression of Himself. Knowing that he was Almighty and Divine, He yet held back the exercise of His supernatural powers. Knowing that with one withering glance He could have stricken His enemies and laid them lifeless at His feet, He restrained His power. Knowing that He could have summoned all the angels of heaven to His defense, He surrendered Himself to His captors in helplessness and defenselessness. He even surrendered the exercise of His own will, and drew from His Heavenly Father the very grace and power which He needed from day to day, the same as any sinful man who lives by faith and prayer. "I can of mine own self do nothing," He said. "As the living Father hath sent me, and I live by the Father: so he that eateth me, even he shall live by me" (John 6:57). He took the same place of dependence that the humblest believer takes today and in all things lived a life of self renunciation.

At last the climax came in the supreme trial of the judgment hall and the cruel cross. When He became obedient unto death, a death of shame and unparalleled humiliations, insults and agonies completed His life sacrifices for the salvation of His people. What words can ever describe, what tongue can ever tell the weight, the sharpness, the agony of that cruel cross, the fierceness of His fight with the powers of darkness and the depths of woe when even His Father's face was averted and He bore for us the hell that sin deserved.

After His resurrection, He still bore the marks of the cross. The few glimpses that we find of the risen Christ are all marked by the same touches of gentleness, self abnegation and remembered suffering. The very evidences that He gave them that He was the same Jesus were the marks of the spear and the nails; and in His manifestations to them, especially in that memorable scene at Emmaus, we see the same gentle, unobtrusive Christ, walking with them by the way unrecognized and then quietly vanishing our of their sight when at last they knew him.

And even on the throne to which He has now ascended, the same cross marks still remain amid the glories of the heavenly world. John beheld Him as "a limb as it had been slain." The Christ of heaven still bears the old marks of the cross as His highest glory and His everlasting memorial. Such are the marks of the Lord Jesus, and all who claim to be His followers and His ministers may well imitate them. The men who claim to be His apostles and ambassadors, and who come to us with the sound of trumpets, the bluster of earthly pageants and the pompous and egotistical boastings of pride and vainglory, are false prophets and wretched counterfeits of the Christ of Calvary and can deceive only the blind and ignorant dupes who know nothing of the real Christ.

These were the marks of the Master, and they will be worn by His servants, too.

The Cross Marks of the Christian

"The servant is not greater than his lord" (John 13:16). The tests of the Master must be applied to His followers. We may not preach a crucified Savior without being also crucified men and women. It is not enough to wear an ornamental cross as a pretty decoration. The cross that Paul speaks about was burned into his very flesh, was branded into his being; and only the Holy Ghost can burn the true cross into our innermost life.

We are saved by identification with Christ in His death. We are justified because we have already died with Him and have thus been made free from sin. God does not whitewash people when He saves them. He has really visited their sins upon their great Substitute, the Lord Jesus Christ, and every believer was counted as in Him when He died; and so His death is our death and it puts us in the same position before the law of the supreme Judge as if we had already been executed and punished for our own guilty, as if the judgment for us was already past. Therefore, it is true of every believer, "He that heareth my word, and believeth on hem that sent me, hath everlasting life, and shall not come into condemnation; but is passed from death unto life" (John 5:24). The cross, therefore, is the very standpoint of the believer's salvation, and we shall never cease to echo the song of heaven. "Worthy is the Lamb that was slain to receive ... honor, and glory, and blessing" (Rev. 5:12).

We are sanctified by dying with Christ to sin. When He hung on Calvary, He not only made a settlement for our acts of sin, but He bore with Him on that cross our sinful self; and by faith we reckon ourselves as actually crucified with Him there to the whole life of sin. It is our privilege, therefore, to identify ourselves with Christ in His death so fully that we may lay over our sinful nature upon Him and utterly die to it, and then receive from Him a life all new, divine and pure. Henceforth we may say, "I live; yet not I, but Christ liveth in me" (Gal. 2:20). Sanctification is not the cleansing of the old life, but the crucifying of that life and substituting for it the very life of Christ Himself, the Holy and Perfect One.

We must keep sanctified by dead reckoning. And dead reckoning is just the reckoning of ourselves as "dead indeed unto sin, but alive unto God through Jesus Christ" (Rom. 6:11). This is not merely a feeling or experience, but a counting upon Him as life and drawing from Him as breath from the air around us.

Our spiritual life is perfected by the constant recognition of the cross and by our unceasing application of it to all our life and being. We must live by the cross and must pass from death to death and life to life by constant fellowship with His sufferings and conformity unto His death, until at last we shall "attain unto the resurrection of the dead" (Phil. 3:11).

Now this principle of death and resurrection underlies all nature as well as the Bible. The autumn leaves with their rich crimson are just a parable of nature's dying to make way for the resurrection of the coming spring. Pick up an acorn in the forest, and in its heart, as you break the shell, you will find a crimson hairline as the cross mark of its hidden life. When it bursts through the ground in the spring, the first opening leaf is red, the color of the cross, and when the leaf dies and falls in autumn it wraps itself in the same crimson hue.

But all this is but a stepping stone of the life that follows. Look at the structure and growth of a flower. First, the calyx or flower cup tightly clasps the enfolding petals, refusing to let go. But gradually these fingers relax, these folds unclasp, and the petals burst open in all their fragrance and beauty. But still the calyx holds them tightly as if it would never let go, but hour by hour, as the flower life advances, those petals have to be relinquished from the grasp, and in a little while the blossom floats away on the summer winds and seems to perish. "The flower fadeth," the beauty of nature dies. But observe that after death comes a richer life. Behind the flower you will notice a seed pod. It also is held for a time by the grasp of another cup. But as the seeds ripen, even they must let go this grasp, and gradually the seed pod relaxes and at length bursts open and the seeds are scattered and sink into the ground and die. But from the buried seed comes forth a new resurrection of plants and trees and flowers and fruits. The whole process is one of dying and living, one life giving place to a higher, and all moving steadily on to the reproduction of the plant and the stage of fruit bearing.

So marked is this principle in the natural world that botanists tell us that when a flower gives too much attention to the blossom and develops into a double flower, which is the most beautiful form of the bloom, it becomes barren and fruitless. Nature puts its ban upon self life even in a flower. It must die and pass away if it would bear much fruit. A beautiful double petunia is no good; but a single-petalled blossom has in it the life of another generation. And so our spiritual life must pass down to deeper deaths and on and up to the higher experiences of life, or we shall lose even what we have. We cannot cling to the sweetest spiritual experiences, the fondest object of our highest joy, without ceasing to grow and ceasing to bear that fruit which is the very nature of our salvation.

The Principle of Death in Our Deeper Life

We must learn not only to give up our wrongs, but even our rights. It is little that we should turn from sin; if we are to follow Christ and His consecration, we must turn from the things that are not sinful and learn the great lesson of self renunciation even in rightful things. The everlasting ideal is He who though in the form of God, thought it not a thing to be eagerly grasped that He should be equal with God, but emptied Himself and become obedient unto death, even the death of the cross. There are many things which are not wrong for you to keep and to hold as your own, but in keeping them, He would lose and you would lose much more.

We have the cross mark upon our affections and friendships. Thus Abraham gave us his Isaac, and received him back with a new touch of love as God's Isaac. We shall find that most of the lives that counted much for God had somewhere in them a great renunciation, where the dearest idol was laid upon Moriah's altar and from that hour there was new fruit and power.

Our prayers must often have the mark of the cross upon them. We ask and we receive the promise and assurance of the answer; and then we must often see that answer apparently buried and forgotten, and long after come forth, to our amazement and surprise, multiplied with blessings that have grown out of the very delay and seeming denial.

So the life of our body which we may claim from Him must be marked with the cross. It is only after the strength of nature fails us that the strength of God can come in. And even then the answer is sometimes not given until we have first surrendered it to Him and have been willing to give up even life itself and have learned to seek the Blesser rather than the blessing. Then often God reveals Himself to us as a Healer, as He could not do until we were wholly abandoned to His will.

Our religious experiences must have the mark of the cross upon them. We must not cling even to our peace and joy and spiritual comfort. Sometimes, the flower must fade that the fruit may be more abundant, and that we may learn to walk by faith and not by sight.

Our service for God often must be buried before it can bring forth much fruit. And so God sometimes calls us to a work and makes it appear to fail in its early stages, until we cry in discouragement, "I have labored in vain, I have spent my strength for naught." Then it comes forth Phoenix like from the flames, and blossoms and buds until it fills the face of the world with fruit. So God writes the mark of the cross on everything, until by and by, the very grave, may be the passport to a better resurrection and death will be swallowed up in victory. In fact, we believe that the universe itself has yet to pass through its dissolution and come forth in the glory of a final resurrection so that the marks of the Lord Jesus may, as last, be written upon the very earth and heaven, and so that the universe to its furthest bounds may re-echo the great redemption song: "Worthy is the Lamb that was slain."

Beloved, have you the marks of the Lord Jesus? These sacrifices to which He sometimes calls us are just great investments that He is asking us to make and that He will refund to us with accumulated interest in the age to come.

Good Richard Cecil once asked his little daughter, as she sat upon his knee, with a cluster of pretty glass beads around her neck, if she truly loved him, and if she loved him enough to take those beads and fling them into the fire. She looked in his face with wonder and grief; she could hardly believe that he meant such sacrifice. But his steady gaze convinced her that he was in earnest, and with trembling, reluctant steps she tottered to the grate, and clinging to them with reluctant fingers, at last dropped them into the fire, and then flinging herself into his arms, she sobbed herself to stillness in the bewilderment and perplexity of her renunciation. He let her learn her lesson fully, but a few days later, on her birthday, she found upon her dressing case a little package, and on opening it she found inside a cluster of real pearls strung upon a necklace and bearing her name with her father's love. She had scarcely time to grasp the beautiful present as she flew to his presence and throwing herself in his arms, she said, "Oh, Papa, I am so sorry that I did not understand."

Some day, beloved, in His arms, you will understand. He does not always explain it now. He lets the cross have all its sharpness. He lets the weary years go by; but oh, some day we will understand and be so glad that we were permitted to bear with Him and for Him the "brand marks of the Lord Jesus."

Chapter 4.
THE UPLIFT OF THE CROSS

"And I, if I be lifted up from the earth, will draw
all men unto me" (John 12:32).

A story is told of a medieval saint who asked his attendants to lift him from his death bed and place him on a cross. As he lay there and breathed out his life, he kept repeating with glowing eye and shining face the simple words, "It lifts me up, it lifts me up."

These words suggest the uplifting power of the cross of Jesus Christ. That which naturally suggests only suffering, ignominy and defeat has become the noblest sign of all that is lofty, heroic and glorious in the story of redemption and the experience of the Christian.

The Uplift of the Cross in the Experience of the Lord Jesus Christ Himself

Speaking of it He said, "I, if I be lifted up from the earth." To Him it brought no sense of degradation or failure, but only a sense of glory and honor and victory. As He spoke of it to His disciples in advance it was always only as a stepping stone to the resurrection which was to follow. On the Mount of Transfiguration His heavenly visitors conversed of nothing else, but they spoke of it as "his decease which he should accomplish at Jerusalem," and the word decease expresses not so much the idea of death as of departure. It was but the beginning of a glorious ascension which was to lift Him up to higher honors and loftier ministries through the ages to come. The Apostle Paul, speaking of the cross, can only express himself in terms of the loftiest exultation, "God forbid that I should glory, save in the cross of our Lord Jesus Christ." In the visions of the Apocalypse we find it occupying the place of highest honor in the heavenly world. It is the continual theme of the songs, both of the angels and the ransomed, and the highest distinction of Him who shares the Father's throne is the mark of the cross. He is described as the "Lamb that was slain."

The cross of Jesus Christ has exalted Christ Himself by giving to the universe a manifestation not only of the wisdom and love of God nowhere else found, but especially a manifestation of the self-sacrificing love of Christ Himself transcending all other revelations of His character and glory. In human history there is something higher than wealth, power, or brilliant gifts of intellect. Grecian history commemorates the heroes of Thermopylae above all the other records of their country. Rome gloried in the legend of Horatius far more than in the pomp and pageantry of Augustus and Hadrian. The fame of Lincoln and McKinley has been heightened by the tragic story of their martyrdom, And the annals of Christian biography are rich in the record of heroic sacrifice. But there is no heroism like the story of Calvary, and there is no glory which shall ever be laid at the feet of the Lamb of God to be compared with the crimson of the cross and the crown of thorns.

But the cross has brought to the Lord Jesus Christ a yet higher recompense in the approval of His Father and the love of His people. What human imagination can conceive the rapture of that hour, when at last He rested on His Father's bosom, after the anguish of the garden and the crucifixion, and the awful descent among the dead. Speaking of the Father's recompense the inspired apostle says, "Wherefore God also hath highly exalted him, and given him a name which is above every name" (Phil. 2:9). Almost as sweet to His heart is the devotion of His people and the love and gratitude of those for whom He died. How much a brave man will often dare for the object of his affection, and there is no reward so sweet to him as the thanks of some one dear to his heart whom he has been permitted to help or save. When we think of the myriads whom Jesus Christ has rescued from sin and despair, we can form some conception of the meaning of that promise, "She shall see of the travail of his soul, and shall be satisfied" (Isa. 53:11). As we think of the beautiful lives that we have known, the Christians we have met, the saints we have seen pass through the gates with robes made white in the blood of the Lamb, doubtless we have often felt that for such it would not be too much even for us to die. This was "the joy that was set before him" for which H "endured the cross, despising the shame, and is set down at the right hand of the throne of God" (Heb. 12:2). The day is coming which will make up for all His shame and sorrow, when He shall present to Himself His glorious bride, "not having spot, or wrinkle, or any such thing," and He "shall be satisfied."

The cross has brought to Christ a glorious and everlasting kingdom. The throne which the Father hath prepared for Him as our Mediatorial King is a far more glorious throne than that of Deity. The kingdom which the coming ages is to bring is the recompense which He has won through the work of redemption; and the scepter, which He is to wield over the millennial world and the new heavens and earth, is one which He could never have possessed but for the sharpness of the cross and the humiliation of Bethlehem and Calvary. Therefore, it is indeed true the cross has lifted up the Con of man as well as all who follow Him in that pathway of suffering and glory.

The Uplift of the Cross in the Believer's Life

It lifts us up from hell to heaven, from the curse of the broken law to the acceptance of God and the justification, forgiveness and salvation which place us on a plane of loftier righteousness than even if we had never sinned.

It lifts us up from sin to righteousness, from the degradation and defilement of our natural condition to the image of Christ and the righteousness of God. "Unto him that loved us, and washed us from our sins in his own blood" is the tribute which every saint has brought to the cross of Jesus Christ. Not only does it save, it also sanctifies. But it sanctifies in a way which lifts us higher than any holiness that Adam ever knew. It sanctifies by the process of crucifixion and resurrection. It puts not only our past sins, but our sinful nature on the cross with Jesus Christ, so that we pass out in our own sinfulness and are reckoned dead, and then in Christ Jesus we are resurrected and filled with His nature and spirit, so that we become partakers of His holiness and stand in the same place as Christ Himself in spotless holiness and blamelessness before the throne of God.

The cross lifts us above our sickness and infirmity and makes us partakers of the resurrection life and strength of the Lord Jesus even in our mortal frame, for "Himself took our infirmities, and bare our sicknesses" and "with his stripes we are healed." This is but the beginning of a physical immortality which is yet to transform us into the likeness of His glorified body and the possession of physical attributes and qualities infinitely grander than the race of Adam could ever have known, but for the work of redemption.

The cross lifts us up above the world's ambitions and sordid interests and makes us the citizens of heaven. This was the supreme reason why Paul gloried in the cross. "Whereby," he says, "the world is crucified unto me, and I unto the world." By the cross of Christ we are the same as if we had died as citizens of this world, and had been sent back to it from heaven as divine messengers and missionaries in the very same sense as Christ Himself was sent. Its pleasures and pursuits, therefore, have no right to control us. We are not of it any more than He was of it, and we are in it as men who walk with our feet on earth and our hearts and heads in heaven.

It lifts us up above the power of Satan and makes us conquerors in the conflict with the powers of darkness. "They overcame him by the blood of the Lamb" (Rev. 12:11). The cross was Satan's Waterloo. Not only was he beaten there, but he was captured and hung up on the cross as a scarecrow to show the children of God that the devil is a defeated foe and that we need no longer fear him or even fight him in our own name and strength, but we may hand him over to the Captain of our salvation who has conquered him for us and will conquer him in us when we fully trust Him. "Having spoiled principalities and power, he made a show of them openly, triumphing over them in it" (the cross) (Col. 2:15).

The cross lifts us above the fear of death and gives to us the right to the resurrection and the life immortal. Indeed, it is our privilege to regard death as already behind us. Wit Him we have died on the cross and for us death never can be the same again. The form of death may come, but all that has death in it has already passed upon Him, and for us it is but a transition to the life beyond. "If a man keep my saying," He has told us, "he shall never see death" (John 8:51). All he shall see is the presence of the Lord encompassing him and hiding from him all other consciousness and every fear and every foe. From the standpoint of the cross we are not now looking into the grave but into the heavens "from whence also we look for the Savior, the Lord Jesus Christ: who shall change our vile body, that it may be fashioned like unto his glorious body" (Phil. 3:20,21).

The cross lifts us above the natural to the supernatural, from the human to the divine, from the Adamic race to the family of God where we are joint heirs with Jesus Christ and sons of God. Henceforth we live not according to the limitations of human nature, but "according to the working of his mighty power, which he wrought in Christ, when he raised him from the dead, and set him at his own right hand in the heavenly places, far above all principality, and power, and might, and dominion, and every name that is named, not only in this world, but also in that which is to come" (Eph. 1:20-22).

The cross lifts us up from law to grace, from trying to trusting, from having to, to loving to, from our deadly doing to His finished work, from Christian endeavor to divine achievement and victorious all sufficiency. Henceforth it is not what we are to do, but what we are to receive and let Him work in us "to will and to do of his good pleasure."

The cross lifts us up from the life of repression and depression to the life of inspiration, liberty, spontaneity and fullness. Henceforth we are not everlastingly dying, but we have died and are alive forevermore. The cross has taken us across the dark abyss of death and planted us forever on the shores of life for "Christ...hath abolished death, and hath brought life and immortality to light through the gospel" (2 Tim. 1:10).

The cross lifts us up from a life of selfishness to a life of sacrifice and love. Its message is "the love of Christ constraineth us; because we thus judge, that if one died for all, then were all dead; and that he died for all, that they which live should not henceforth live unto themselves, but unto him which died for them, and rose again" (2 Cor. 5:14,15). No spirit that truly touches the cross can ever henceforth live for self alone. The law of the cross is the law of sacrifice. There is a school of religious teachers who hold and teach that the one meaning of the cross is simply a pattern of divine love given to us for our imitation. According to this view Christ died to lift men from ignoble selfishness to heroic sacrifice and holy service. They see no place for the doctrine of substitution and atonement for sin, but see only a splendid object lesson of benevolence and sacrifice. It must be said that oftentimes the lives of the men and women who hold this lower view of the cross are by no means inconsistent with their teaching and that they have given many beautiful examples of the loveliest virtues and the loftiest benevolence. Surely while we believe in the loftier conception of the cross of Jesus we should not leave out the lower, and our lives should show a still higher conformity to the Gospel we preach and be no less noble, self-denying and beneficent than the lives of men and women who have no such inspiration as comes to us from the Source of our redemption. Perhaps it may be said for them, that believing as they do not so much in grace as in gracious works on their own part, they make more strenuous efforts to live their religion, but surely love and gratitude should win from us a nobler response than mere self-righteousness from others. While we accept His grace and praise Him for His precious blood, oh, let us not forget to follow in His blood marked steps, and to live as well as sing,

> "Cross of Christ lead onward
> in this holy war:
> In Thy name we conquer
> now and ever more."

The Believer's Attitude toward the Cross

In conclusion, what is our attitude toward the cross of Christ? Near the cross? No, that will never do. At the cross? No, that is not yet near enough. On the cross? That is our true place. Our sins on the cross? No, our very selves upon the cross. But we must not linger on the cross forever. There is another stage. In the fifteenth chapter of First Corinthians, the apostle declared, "Christ died for our sins according to the Scriptures; and ... was buried." Too often we forget this part. This is not on the cross, but beneath the cross and beyond the cross. Like Him we are to pass from the cross to the grave. Burial with Him in baptism is the Christian symbol of this glorious fact that the cross of Christ has finished for us the question of our death with Him and has brought us to the place of resurrection and life forevermore. Is that our place? Are we reckoning ourselves dead indeed unto sin, but alive unto God through Jesus Christ our Lord?

Finally, let us not forget to take up our cross and follow Him, and inject the spirit of the cross, which is the spirit of sacrifice, of service and self forgetting love, into everything we think and say and do. "He died for all, that they which live should not henceforth live unto themselves, but unto him that died for them, and rose again."

Chapter 5.
ENEMIES OF THE CROSS

"They are the enemies of the cross of Christ" (Phil. 3:18).

"They crucify to themselves the Son of God afresh" (Heb. 6:6)

Once more we stand facing the cross of Jesus Christ, that wondrous cross which is at once the measure of the love of heaven and the sin of man. For as the cross represents the supreme act and evidence of the love of God, even so our attitude toward it represents for us the greatest blessing or the greatest sin. It is still true, as of old, "on either side one, and Jesus in the midst." That central cross divides the world into the saved and the lost, the heirs of glory and the children of wrath.

Something like this must have been in the mind of the author of the epistle to the Hebrews when he penned that dismal sentence, 'They crucify to themselves the Son of God afresh, and put him to an open shame." All that he meant by that awful word of warning may be difficult to define, yet it is wise to trace those steps that may lead some day to that dreadful place where the very cross that was meant to save, can only become "the savor of death unto death."

It is possible to be among the enemies of the cross of Christ long before we have reached that final state and "crucify the Son of God afresh and put him to an open shame."

We may take the wrong side of the cross of Christ by ignoring or depreciating the doctrine of the cross. The very foundation of Christianity is the Gospel of the cross. Take that away and we have nothing left but a scheme of philosophy and morals. But alas, in the craze for novelty, religious leaders are growing weary of the old story and they invent a new doctrine of the cross. They tell us that Jesus Christ died not to atone for the sins of men or to bear our guilt and stand beneath the judgment of God as our Substitute and Sacrifice for sin, but simply that

He might inspire other men to live a similar life of sacrifice for their fellows. The atonement, according to these wild weavers of the spider's webs of the New Theology, is simply learning to imitate the self sacrifice of the Lord Jesus and, like Him, give our lives for our fellowmen. Is it to much to say that such a caricature of Calvary and Christianity "crucifies the Son of God afresh, and puts him to an open shame"?

We may also take the wrong side of the cross by believing false doctrine respecting the cross and the precious blood. The Roman Catholic sacrifice of the Mass is a fearful misrepresentation of the cross of Christ. In that man-made ceremonial the Lord Jesus is represented as really offered again in actual sacrifice every time the worshipper receives the sacrament. It is literally crucifying Hem afresh. In distinction from this, how emphatic is the teaching of the Epistle to the Hebrews, that "once in the end of the world," or better, "once for all hath he appeared to put away sin by the sacrifice of himself" (Heb. 9:6).

We may be enemies of the cross by neglecting to give due emphasis and importance to the doctrine of the cross and the blood of Christ. This charge holds against much of the preaching today. As the expression goes, all roads lead to Rome, so all truths point to Calvary and there is probably no Gospel message in which the cross of Christ should not find some place. And yet, in answer to a challenge from a brother minister, the writer once searched through volume after volume of published sermons of one of the greatest preachers of modern times in a vain endeavor to find one single mention of the atoning blood.

We may also be enemies of the cross by accepting the Gospel and yet doubting the efficacy of the blood of Christ for our salvation and our sins. After you have laid your sins upon that cross with you crucified Savior, you have no business ever to touch them again. You honor the blood of Christ by simply and fully believing that the Lamb of God taketh away the sins of the world and your sins also. When you go back and dig up your buried bones, you are really crucifying Christ afresh and it is no wonder that your soul is poisoned and your spiritual health destroyed by the resurrection of you buried sins. You are really crucifying Christ afresh when you put back on Him the sins which have once been confessed and cleansed by His precious blood. Therefore, doubting is a dangerous and almost fatal sin. We are made partakers of Christ if we hold the beginning of our confidence steadfast unto the end (Heb.3:14).

We may be on the wrong side of the cross by failing to claim and receive the full purchase of His blood and the full meaning and value of the cross. That blood was too sacred and costly for us to waste, and we have no right to let one drop of it be shed in vain. Not only did He die that our sins might be forgiven, but that our souls might be cleansed and sanctified. "By one offering he hath perfected forever them that are sanctified" (Heb. 10:14). "The blood of Jesus Christ his Son cleanseth us from all sin" (1 John 1:7). If, therefore, we fail to enter into our full inheritance of Grace and holiness, we are dishonoring the cross and suffering Him to die in vain.

That cross embraces our healing, also. "Surely he hath borne our griefs (sicknesses), and carried our sorrows ... and with his stripes we are healed" (Isa. 53:4,5). When we fail to claim our physical redemption through Christ's atonement, we dishonor His cross to that extend; and when we take our full redemption for soul and body in His name and through the purchase of His blood, we honor the Son of God and exalt the glory of the cross before both earth and heaven. And by that precious blood and that mighty cross, He has purchased for us all our redemption rights and all our inheritance of spiritual blessing. By virtue of it we have access to God in prayer and may ask according to the full measure of the value of the precious blood. Are we entering into this full inheritance, or are we coming short of anything which He died to purchase for us?

We may also be enemies by cherishing an unforgiving spirit toward those whom God has forgiven and for whom Christ died. Do you realize that when you harbor a spirit of resentment against your brother and dwell bitterly upon his faults and sins, that those very sins have already been borne by his Redeemer and yours upon the cross, and that God is saying to you, "Who shall lay anything to the charge of God's elect? It is God that justifieth. Who is he that condemneth? It is Christ who died" (Rom. 8:33.34). You are really crucifying Christ afresh by taking your brother's sins off that cross and putting them back on Him again. How dare you thus dishonor and insult the blood to which you owe your own salvation?

By claiming salvation through the blood of Christ and yet continuing in sin, we also prove ourselves to be enemies of the cross. If Christ has borne your sins, you have no right to lay them upon Him again by continuing in the same course from which He saved you at such tremendous cost. All willful sin is a crucifying of Christ afresh and a denying of the blood that bought you. The little child expressed the true spirit of the cross when she said, "Yes, I have laid my sins on Jesus, but God helping me, I do not want to lay any more on Him." "Shall we continue in sin, that grace may abound? God forbid. How shall we, that are dead to sin, live any longer therein?" (Rom. 6:1,2). Do you expect the Lamb of God to come back and be crucified again for the sins you are presumptuously allowing? There is infinite room in the mercy of God and the blood of Christ for our frailties and our shortcomings, but the soul that persistently and willfully continues in any known course of evil is insulting the name of Jesus and is running close to the tremendous warning of this solemn text.

By giving place to the devil and failing to treat him as a conquered foe, we are enemies of Christ's cross. The testimony of the Holy Ghost in the New Testament to the cross of Jesus is that by the cross Satan has been disarmed and now we may meet him as a conquered foe. "Having spoiled principalities and powers, he made a show of them openly, triumphing over them in it (his cross)" (Col. 2:15). Satan's weapons have been hung up in derision on the cross of Calvary and Satan himself has been put on exhibition there, like the brazen serpent of old, as a mere empty, fangless thing. He is as powerless to harm as that metal figure hung up in the wilderness of Sinai, as a parody and mockery of his boasted power. Beloved, are you thus treating your spiritual enemy in the light of the cross of Calvary, or are you letting the mighty victory of the Captain of your salvation go for naught?

By shunning the crosses that God permits us to share with Jesus we show that we are enemies of the cross. For His cross means our cross too, the fellowship of His sufferings and the partnership of His burdens. If we believe He bore our cross, we shall be lad to share His and "rejoice, inasmuch as (we) are partakers of Christ's sufferings; that, when his glory shall be revealed, (we) may be glad also with exceeding joy" (1 Peter 4:13). It will make an infinite difference in the trials of life if we will learn to accept them from the hands of Jesus as tokens of His confidence and love and of our fellowship with Him in His burdens. And when we rebel at our hard fortune, shun our cross and seek for a life of self-indulgence, we are really crucifying the Son of God afresh. While He has borne all that is necessary for our salvation, He has left behind some suffering for each of His disciples and if we refuse to take our share, we virtually declare that we are willing to crucify Him afresh and to make Him bear a second cross instead of us.

Finally, we are enemies of the cross when we fail to give the Gospel and lift up the cross to all our fellowmen. For there is for our blessed Lord a greater anguish than even that bitter cross; namely, the sorrow of dying in vain for some of those precious souls who have never yet heard the story of His love. His part was to bear their cross, but our part is to tell them the story of His love and bring them to share the joy of His salvation. It is thus that He shall "see of the travail of his soul, and shall be satisfied," and if we are denying Him this satisfaction, we are laying upon His heart a far heavier burden than they laid in that tragic day eighteen hundred years ago, when they compelled Him to bear His cross and then pierced His hands and feet and brow and side with the cruel nails and thorns and spear.

Beloved, this vision was the sublime joy that gave Him strength to endure the cross and despise the shame, even the vision that came to Him just as He was marching down that valley of the shadow of death, that vision that led Him to cry, "Now is the Son of man glorified," and "I, if I be lifted up from the earth, will draw all men unto me." Oh, are you and I holding back any part of that joy from the Master's heart? Are we selfishly hoarding this great salvation, and absorbed in the cares and ambitions of earth, scarcely lifting a hand or sacrificing a single indulgence to send the Gospel to those perishing millions who are like fields white to the harvest and whom God's providence has placed within our reach by the most extraordinary opportunity that any age or generation ever saw? God save us from the guilt and danger by this awful neglect, of crucifying the Son of God afresh and being found enemies of the cross of Christ.

> Under and Eastern sky,
> Amid a rabble cry,
> A Man went forth to die
> For me.
>
> Thorn-crowned His Blessed head,
> Blood-stained His weary tread,
> Cross laden He was led
> To me.
>
> Pierced were His hands and feet,
> Three hours upon Him beat
> Fierce rays of noontide heat
> For me.

Thus wert Thou made all mine;
Lord, make me wholly Thine,
Grant grace and strength divine
For me.

In thought and word and deed
Thy will to do; O lead
My soul, e'en though it bleed,
To Thee.

It goes without saying that these are the enemies of the cross of Christ who reject the Lord Jesus and permit Him, as far as they are concerned, to die in vain. The awfulness of that sin is one of the lurid messages of the Epistle to the Hebrews: "How shall we escape," the writer asks, "if we neglect so great salvation?" In another place he speaks of the sinner who, turning away from the Lord Jesus, has "trodden under foot the Son of God, and hath counted the blood of the covenant ..., and unholy thing, and hath done despite unto the Spirit of grace."

We have read of a man rushing madly to suicide over the body of a loving wife who vainly sought to hold him back and who shrank beneath his violence as he rushed to his destruction over her bleeding body. Oh, sinner, if you reject the Son of God and if you dare face eternity without having definitely accepted the Lord Jesus, you are plunging in over the bleeding body of the Son of God and you are staining you willful feet with His precious blood. No other sin can damn your soul. "He that believeth not is condemned already, because he hath not believed in the name of the only begotten Son of God" (John 3:18). Still it is true that that central cross divides the world. "On either side one, and Jesus in the midst." Oh, dear friend, be sure you are not on the wrong side of the cross.

> Two souls went forth from the cross that day,
> Both dying by Jesus' side.
> On either side with the Lord between,
> But apart how far and wide?

Cross of Christ

For one went out into endless night,
Heaven open before his eyes,
And one went in with the Son of God
Through the gates of Paradise.

Two souls will go from this place today,
Both children of guilt and sin,
But one has said "no" to the Son of God,
The other has let Him in.

And bright as the light of love and heaven,
Redeemed one, thy path shall be.
But the gloom and the doom of endless night,
Poor lost one await for thee.

Chapter 6.
THE CROSS AND THE WORLD

"If the household be too little for the lamb, let him and his neighbor next unto his house take it according to the number of the souls" (Ex. 12:4).

The Paschal lamb was God's special type of Jesus Christ, "the Lamb of God which taketh away the sin of the world." The lamb selected for the Hebrew passover was kept apart until the fourth day so that all might have an opportunity of inspecting his perfect blamelessness; and then it was slain and its blood sprinkled upon the door posts, and the flesh eaten by the household. So Jesus Christ, the Lamb of God, was set apart and manifested to all the people for three and a half years, that all might see that He was "holy, harmless, undefiled, separate from sinners." Then in the fourth year He too was slain for the sins of men, and His life became the Living Bread of all the household of faith.

Jesus, The Lamb of God

God's most precious gift to us lost and sinful men was the Lamb of God. As we realize the curse of sin -- and each of us has sometimes felt the dreadfulness of a sense of guilt and condemnation -- and then look upon the sprinkled blood and hear God say, "When I see the blood, I will pass over you," we must feel that among all precious things there is nothing like "the precious blood of Christ, as of a lamb without blemish and without spot" (1 Pet. 1:19). And as we realize our weakness and step out on our pilgrim path through the desert of life, it is even more precious to feed upon His very life and echo back His own gracious word, "My flesh is meat indeed, and my blood is drink indeed" (John 6:55). The old redemption song may have lost its charm for an age of higher criticism and self-sufficient humanitarianism, but for us the sweetest note in earth and heaven shall ever be

> Dear, dying Lamb, Thy precious blood
> Shall never lose its power,
> Till all the ransomed Church of God,
> Be saved to sin no more.

It was one of the provisions of the Passover Law that no man could eat his passover alone. It was a fellowship and family sacrifice. Together the household sat down and looked up at the door post dripping with the sprinkled blood, with a sense of infinite safety, and then together partook of the flesh of the lamb. So the sacrifice of Jesus Christ can never be an object of selfishness or a monopoly of the few. Men can monopolize many earthly honors and treasures, but the blood of Jesus Christ belongs to all our sinful race.

No doubt the household suggests the family. From the beginning God has included the home circle in the covenant of redemption. He recognizes the tender and sacred ties that bind us to our loved ones, and the promise is to us and to our children, "Believe on the Lord Jesus Christ, and thou shalt be saved, and they house" (Acts 16:31). One of the sweetest joys we have is the joy of praying for the salvation of our homes and thanking God for children in the household of faith. And one of the saddest shadows that has rested upon our hearts has been to think of the blighted homes and lost lambs of the heathen world where the Gospel has never been known. If ever you have had to part at the graveside with a beloved child, saved perhaps from great sin in answer to your prayers through the precious blood of Jesus Christ, I am sure your heart has gone up to heaven with a thrill of joy and thankfulness even greater than for you own salvation, and you have blessed His holy name for the arms that could reach out where yours could not have reached and could rescue from the gulf of sin and hell and carry through suffering and death that life which was dearer than you own. Thank God for the Lamb that is sufficient for our households as well as ourselves.

But the household has a wider meaning. It takes in the whole household of faith and the whole family of God. The blood of Jesus Christ has redeemed His church and is the bond that binds it into a greater family. The apostle, speaking of the relation of the church to the redemption of Christ, uses this language: "The church of God, which he hath purchased with his own blood" (Acts 20:28). And again we read, "Christ also loved the church, and gave himself for it; that he might sanctify and cleanse it with the washing of water by the word, that he might present it to himself a glorious church, not having spot, or wrinkle, or any such thing" (Eph. 5:25-27). In this sense the Lamb is for the whole household of faith, and we together share the redemption and a grateful song, "unto him that loved us, and washed us from our sins in his own blood, and hath made us kings and priests unto God and his Father; to him be glory and dominion forever and ever" (Rev. 1:6).

But there is a wider circle than this. In this ancient appointment of the passover, God seemed to have been looking down the ages and to have anticipated the selfishness and bigotry of His earthly people, Israel, and of the spiritual church which should succeed to her privileges. The striking language of verse four, "If the household be too little for the lamb," was evidently meant to remind Israel that while the Lamb of God primarily came to be their Redeemer, His message of grace was not limited to them, but He was also to be "a light to lighten the Gentiles" as well as "the glory of (his) people Israel." The household of Israel was too little for the Lamb of God. Even if they had accepted Him as their Messiah, they would have been led out in a larger ministry to the Gentile world for which He had also died. For us too there is the same significant hint that God will not permit us to monopolize His grace or keep His blood bought salvation for ourselves alone. Christ is too much for what we call Christendom, and He bids us share His precious blood and His victorious life with our neighbor and our race.

The largeness of the Lamb of God, the scope of the Gospel of Jesus Christ, the boundless length and breadth of divine love, the universality of the message of salvation, the right of every sinful man to hear and accept the mercy of God, this is the glorious thought that this ancient text suggests. The Bible is full of this glorious theme. "God so loved the world, that he gave his only begotten Son, that whosoever believeth in him should not perish, but have everlasting life" (John 3:16). The mercy of heaven is big enough to take in all our sinful race. The blood of Christ is rich enough to cover the guilt of every child of Adam. The Gospel is broad enough to take in whosoever will. The life of Jesus Christ is full enough to save and sanctify and keep all the myriads of our race, if they will but accept it. The heaven that He has provided is vast enough for all earth's lost generations. And the Divine plan is grand enough to take in every kindred and tribe and tongue, all earth's countless inhabitants. There may be limitations in the receiving of God's grace on our part through the ignorance, willfulness, or indifference of sinful men, but there is no limitation to the sufficiency of Christ's redemption and the universal and all embracing fullness of the Gospel of salvation.

Sharing the Lamb

What does all this mean for us as redeemed men and women? Surely this, that we have no right to claim the purchase of the Savior's blood for ourselves alone, and that we are guilty of selfishness, dishonesty and base ingratitude if we can be content to be saved without having done everything in our power to give to our fellowmen an equal opportunity of eternal life. Have we understood this? Have we lived it? Is it the spirit and purpose of our whole conduct, or are we guilty of the crime of hoarding the Gospel and keeping to ourselves that great salvation which was committed to us as a sacred trust?

But who is the neighbor with whom we are to share God's Lamb? He is spoken of here as the one that is over against us, the one that is in closest contact with us. Surely, that means that God brings people into touch with us in order that we may be stewards of His grace to them. The people in your family, the servant in your household, your fellow travelers, the partners of your social and business life -- these are among the neighbors to whom you owe a spiritual responsibility. Have you met it according to your utmost ability and can you truly say, "I am pure from the blood of all men"?

But that is the narrowest circle. What about that larger world of lost men and women that God has also brought into touch with His church? Is there not a responsibility which a modern writer has well called "the white man's burden," but which means far more than Kipling ever dreamt? How marvelously God has brought over against us as Christian nations the peoples of heathen lands as our great wards. Look at the millions of Indian tribes scattered over this western hemisphere, still in paganism and many of them in barbarism. Surely, they are over against us in the most providential way. We have taken their country from them. We have driven them from their heritage. What have we given them in return?

Look at the two hundred millions of Africa. God has placed in our country eight or ten millions of their children as hostages for this mighty race. God has given Christian nations a mighty trusteeship by virtue of their colonial possessions, their commercial interests and their social connections and ties in that great continent. Look at the millions of the West Indies and the Philippines. Surely God has brought them over against us in His providence and created for us an inexorable responsibility, not only to give them the citizenship of earth, but of heaven also. Look at the Hindu people. Great Britain was in the providence of God the guardian of their liberties, and her Christian people should surely be the stewards of God's richer blessings of life and salvation to these benighted and yet most gifted people. And what shall we say of China? It confronts us on the shore of the great Pacific Ocean as our nearest and mightiest neighbor. Its people have come to us hostages for their nation. Its commerce is attracting our enterprise. Surely, its awful spiritual need and immense possibilities for God and humanity constitute a responsibility and a call which no language can adequately express. These are our neighbors in the most providential, practical and present tense way. We have given them our literature. We have given them our commerce. We have given them our civilization. We have taught them to surpass us in the arts of peace and war. Have we given them the Lamb of God, the Gospel of Christ. the chief heritage of blessing that has come to us, the opportunity of eternal life through Jesus Christ, our Lord? Oh, what splendid disciples these mighty nations offer for new triumphs of the glorious Gospel of Jesus Christ! What it has done for us may be duplicated and multiplied a thousand times among these teeming millions. Our household is too small a theater for all the purposes which God has intended through these new communities and nations.

There came a time in the history of apostolic missions when God pushed out His servants into the continent of Europe, because it was to be the theater for the coming centuries of the world's greatest events. So in later centuries God has still further pushed on the course of empire. Think of the immense issues that have followed the discovery of America and the opening up of this continent to modern civilization. But if God could accomplish so much with a hundred million in the land in a single century, how much more can He accomplish through the Gospel with the millions in the vaster continent of Asia, who are just awaking to all the possibilities of life, progress and intellectual and spiritual power. It was the Reformation and the light of spiritual life that gave to modern Europe, and later to America, its intellectual and political revival. And it is the Gospel that will kindle the Orient and lift the intellects of China, India and Japan to a plane much higher than ours, as ours is higher than the life of the dark ages of medieval Europe. A morning is dawning, a day is breaking over earth, a time of great and glorious things of which we dimly dream. Let us rise to the might purpose of God, to the larger meaning of our times and to the glorious trust of setting free these mighty forces, by the salvation of Jesus Christ, until it shall reach the magnificent ideal of the thought of God and the divine plan of this lost age of time.

How shall we share our Lamb with our neighbor? First, let us recognize that God has saved us that we may save others. We are stewards, trustees of the Gospel.

Next, let us use every practical opportunity to bring Christ into the lives of the people over against us in our own homes, in our social relations, in our businesses, in all the opportunities of life.

Again, let us become possessed with the full realization of the extent of God's love to men and the purpose of His grace for the race. Let us dwell upon this till our hearts become stirred and enlarged by it, and we know and share the heart of God toward lost and perishing sinners everywhere.

Then also, let us make the work of missions in some definite way the supreme business of our lives. Let us recognize it as the great trust of the Christian church today. Let us in every possible way impress upon men and women this thought of the church's responsibility for the heather world. Let us circulate the light and educate the public opinion of our age along this line by conversation, by testimony, by literature, and by promotion in every way, every means by which God's people shall be brought to a profounder interest in this great work of our generation. Then let us identify ourselves with some definite plan of action. Let us give systematically. Let us be in touch with the work through its Boards, its missionaries, its literature, its plan. Let us count it our work and as much as in us lies do our best to strengthen and extend it. And above all else let it be the supreme object of our prayers. Prayer will set our own hearts on fire with missionary enthusiasm. And then prayer will kindle the same flame in other hearts and will bring actual forces and influences to work in every part of the world. It will lead men and women to give themselves to it. It will bring means from the most unexpected sources. It will send down the power of God upon the missionary field and lead to revivals, conversions, open doors and harvests of blessings in every land.

And finally, let us embrace such definite opportunities as God shall give to us for a direct personal work in this great cause. Some of us will give our children, some of us will give ourselves, and some of us, if we cannot go, will become responsible for those who can and thus in person or by substitute will have an actual part in telling the story of salvation and spreading the Gospel to the uttermost part of the earth.

Chapter 7.
VOICES OF THE RESURRECTION

"According to the working of his mighty power, which he wrought in Christ, when he raised him from the dead" (Eph. 1:19-20).

The first message of the resurrection is that Christ is the Son of God and Christianity is Divine. He was "Declared to be the Son of God with power ... by the resurrection from the dead." The one test which He always offered in proof of His lofty claims was that He should die and rise again. His sign was the sign of the prophet Jonah, or as He put it at another time in another figure, "Destroy this temple, and in three days I will raise it up." So well did His enemies understand this challenge that they took every precaution to guard His tomb and prevent any possible stratagem on the part of His disciples to steal Him away. There was an ample guard, a great stone at the mouth of the tomb with the seal of Rome upon it, which it was treason for any man to break. But in spite of all, that Easter morning saw the sepulcher empty, the stone rolled away and the Lord of life again among His disciples. And "after his passion by many infallible proofs, (he was) seen of them." For forty days He repeated the evidence of His resurrection on various occasions and to different witnesses, until even Thomas, the most incredulous of all, was compelled to confess, "My Lord and my God." Still later Saul of Tarsus, the bitter enemy of Christianity, beheld in a vision the actual form of the risen Christ, and added his testimony and the testimony of his life of sacrifice and suffer to the witnesses of the resurrection. So complete is the proof of this transcendent event that we have seen a gifted lawyer completely convinced after a life of skepticism by simply following the line of evidence which Horace Bushnell has laid out in his volume, Nature and the Supernatural. And this gentleman has afterwards frankly admitted that the proof of

Christ's resurrection, by the ordinary rules of evidence, is sufficient to bring conviction to any unprejudiced judge or jury.

Dear friends, if you have ever been troubled, or if you have friends who are troubled with skeptical questionings about the Bible and Christianity, let all the other issues go; drop the questions of Moses, Isaiah and Jonah, and settle the whole issue upon this supreme question, Did Jesus of Nazareth really die, and did He really rise again? And if you are fair and candid, you will be compelled to conclude, or to bring conviction to your doubting friend, that these are indeed "infallible proofs" and that the whole fabric of Christianity rests upon one supreme foundation, one rock of ages, "For if Christ be not risen, then is our preaching vain, and your faith is also vain ... But now is Christ risen from the dead, and become the first fruits of them that slept" (1 Cor. 15:14, 20).

The second voice of the resurrection is that the sacrifice of Calvary is accepted, the atonement is complete and the great redemption is accomplished. That great Sufferer went down to the grave a prisoner of the law which man had broken, bearing the penalty of the whole guilt of the human race. Had He remained immured in the tomb, it would have been apparent that the debt was not discharged and the price was not sufficient, that He had sunk beneath His heroic but futile effort and had tried in vain to save our ruined race. But when we see Him come forth on the resurrection morning, with the approval of His Father, the presence of the angels of glory, and the portents of nature in the rending earthquake and the opening tombs around, and afterwards ascend in supernatural power to the right hand of God and send down the Holy Ghost as the seal of His complete acceptance and ours, we know that His great task has been completed, that He has finished transgression and made an end of sin, and that

> The great redemption is complete
> And Satan's power o'erthrown.

When the high priest of old on the great Day of Atonement passed in behind the curtains of the Tabernacle to bear the sins of the people and make reconciliation by blood and incense in the Holy of Holies, the people outside, in solemn suspense, waited for the tinkling of the bells that hung from the skirts of his priestly garments, that they might be assured that the lightnings of divine judgment had not stricken him down for their sins, but that his offering was accepted and their guilt was covered by the sprinkled blood. And when as last he came forth through the parting curtains and raised his hands to pronounce the Levitical benediction upon their heads they raised a great shout and fell upon their faces, for they knew that his offering was accepted, that his atonement sufficed, and that for one year more the presence of Jehovah should lead them, and the light of His countenance continue to rest upon them.

It is in direct allusion to this type that the apostle said, "God, having raised up his Son Jesus, sent him to bless you, in turning away every one of you from his iniquities." The same thought lies back of Paul's triumphant challenge, "Who is he that condemneth? It is Christ that died, yea rather, that is risen again, who is even at the right hand of God, who also maketh intercession for us."

The third message is that the resurrection of Jesus Christ assures us of our justification. "(He) was delivered for our offenses, and was raised again for our justification." The salvation of Jesus Christ is not a mere pardon doled out to a criminal, not a probation offered so long as we stand on our good behavior; but it is a complete justification, a divine decree of righteousness that puts us in the same position as if we had ourselves been already executed for our crimes and sins. and brought back again from the dead to live a second life free from all liability for our former transgressions as distinctly as if we had ceased to be the former personality. This is the force of the apostle's strong statement in the epistle to the Romans, "He that is dead is freed from sin."

And the margin is still stronger, "Is justified from sin." The second Adam hung on Calvary that day with all His spiritual children embodied in His own suffering frame, and His death was their death and His resurrection was also theirs. All that we need, therefore, is to be identified with Him in that death and resurrection. How shall we effect this? Must we somehow penetrate the secrets of the skies and see if your names are written in His book of life and if we belong to that mysterious seed who share the death and resurrection and righteousness of the second Adam? Nay, so marvelous is the free and universal offer of the Gospel that each of us can determine for himself his identification with Christ. Just as Ruth, when she learned that she had a legal right to the great Levirate Law that gave her a claim upon her kinsman redeemer, modestly, yet boldly, presented herself at his feet and pressed that claim until it was recognized and honored; so each of us may write our own names in the book of life and say

> When Jesus rose to life divine,
> I, too, was there.
> His resurrection life is mine,
> And as the branches and the vine,
> His fullness I may share.

Fourth, the resurrection of Jesus Christ is the efficient cause of our sanctification. I cannot better express this great truth than by quoting the following paragraphs from an old and little known volume that is worthy of permanent and wide circulation, Marshall's Gospel Mystery of Sanctification.

"The end of Christ's incarnation, death and resurrection was to prepare and form a holy nature and frame for us in Himself, to be communicated to us by union and fellowship with Him; and not to enable us to produce in ourselves the first original of such a holy nature by our own endeavors.

"1. By His incarnation there was a man created in a new holy frame, after the holiness of the first Adam's frame had been marred and abolished for the first transgression; and this new frame was far more excellent than even the first Adam's was, because man was really joined to God by a close, inseparable union of the divine and human nature in one person -- Christ; so that these natures had communion each with the other in their actings, and Christ was able to act in His human nature by power proper to the divine nature, wherein He was one God with the Father.

"Why was it that Christ set up the fallen nature of man in such a wonderful nature of holiness in bringing it to live and act by communion with God living and acting in it? One great end was, that He might communicate this excellent frame to His seed that should by His Spirit be born of Him and be in Him as the last Adam, the quickening Spirit; that as we have borne the image of the earthly so we might bear the image of the heavenly (1 Cor. 15:45, 49), in holiness here and in glory hereafter. Thus He was born Emmanuel, God with us; because the fullness of the Godhead with all holiness did first dwell in Him bodily, even in His human nature, that we might be filled with that fullness in Him (Matt. 1:23; Col. 2:9, 10). Thus He came down from heaven as living bread, that, as He liveth by the Father, so those that eat Him may live by Him (John 6:51, 57), by the same life of God in them which was first in Him.

"2. By His death He freed Himself from the guilt of our sins imputed to Him, and from all that innocent weakness of human nature which He had borne for a time for our sakes. And, by freeing Himself, He prepared a freedom for us from our whole nature condition; which is both weak as He was, and also polluted with our guilt and sinful corruption. Thus the corrupt nature state which is called in Scripture the 'old man,' was crucified together with Christ, that the body of sin might be destroyed. And it is destroyed in us, not by any wounds which we ourselves can give it, but by our partaking of that freedom from it, and death unto it, that is already wrought our for us by the death of Christ;

as is signified by our baptism, wherein we are buried in Christ, by the application of His death to us (Rom. 6:2,3,4,10,11).

"'God sending his own Son in the likeness of sinful flesh, and for sin' (or, 'by a sacrifice for sin,' as in the margin) 'condemned sin in the flesh; that the righteousness of the law might be fulfilled in us, who walk not after the flesh, but after the Spirit' (Rom. 8:3,4).

"Let these Scriptures be well observed, and they will sufficiently evidence that Christ died, not that we might be able to form a holy nature in ourselves, but that we might receive one ready prepared and formed in Christ for us, by union and fellowship with Him.

"3. By His resurrection He took possession of spiritual life for us, as now fully procured for us, and made to be our right and property by the merit of His death, and therefore we are said to be quickened together with Christ. His resurrection was our resurrection to the life of holiness, as Adam's fall was our fall into spiritual death. And we are not ourselves the first makers and formers of our new holy nature, any more than of our original corruption, but both are formed ready for us to partake of them. And by union with Christ, we partake of that spiritual life that He took possession of for us at His resurrection, and thereby we are enabled to bring forth the fruits of it; as the Scripture showeth by the similitude of a marriage union, Romans 7:4: We are married in Him that is raised from the dead, that we might bring forth fruit unto God."

The fifth message that the resurrection of Jesus Christ is the source of that higher physical life which faith may claim in the experience of divine healing. While this blessed experience is founded on the death of Christ, it is much more closely connected with His risen life. The Man who rose on Easter morning was a physical man; the body that Thomas touched was a material organism brimming with life and energy not only sufficient for Himself but for all who touch Him and live in vital touch with

Him. He belongs to us as our living Head, and as He lived upon His Father so we may live by Him. Referring to His own physical life at a crisis time, the Apostle Paul says: "We should not trust in ourselves, but in God which raiseth the dead." And again he says: "The life also of Jesus (is) made manifest in our body." And yet again: "We are members of his body, of his flesh, and of his bone." This is indeed a sacred mystery which few appear to comprehend or realize, but which is the true source and fountain of physical energy, health and strength to those who have dared to claim all the fullness of this complete redemption. It is an open secret which all may share, but into which we can only come by the great law of the fitness of things, and by coming so close to the Master that we can say with the beloved apostle: "That ... which we have heard, which we have seen with our eyes, which we have looked upon, and our hands have handled, of the Word of life; for the life was manifested, and we have seen it, and bear witness, and show unto you that eternal life, which was with the Father, and was manifested unto us" (1 John 1:1, 2).

The sixth voice is that the resurrection of Christ Jesus is the type and guarantee of our resurrection. It is impossible for us to explain or understand the physiological difference between the resurrection body of our Lord and that mortal frame that was nailed to Calvary's cross three days before. That it was the same body substantially the Scriptures have left no doubt; but that there were infinite differences is also as clear. It had been refined and glorified in some ineffable way beyond all that even the most advanced science has taught us of the possibilities of matter. It could come forth from the tomb, passing through the great stone which closed the sepulcher before the stone was rolled away. It could rise without an effort and by the sheer force of will from earth to heaven in spite of the laws of gravitation. It could pass through closed doors and become visible and invisible at will. Something faintly approximating such higher forms of matter has been illustrated by the discoveries of science in connection with radium. At one time the atom was considered the smallest particle of matter, and an atom is so small that three hundred millions of them could lie side by side and form a row less than a yard long. But radium has opened the way for the discovery that a single atom contains smaller particles known as electrons, and that these are intensely active and are ever moving about each other as the planets around the sun, and flashing out at times a swift radiation into space at the tremendous velocity of a hundred thousand miles a second. And yet in its primal form radium is just pitch blend or uranium, a mass of dull brown matter scarcely distinguishable from the dust of the ground. If you think of the lower form, and then of the higher, so mighty in its material energy that a flash-light from it could go round the globe four times in a second, and a few ounces of it would be sufficient to completely annihilate by explosion the greatest city in the world in a moment of time, you will get some conception of the possibilities of matter. Apply all this to these bodies of clay which we are now carrying about with us with their burdens of infirmities and their fetters of disease; and then think of the time when transfigured, glorified, and conformed to the body of His glory, we shall reach our splendid and eternal destiny, We shall sweep from star to star as thought sweeps swiftly now; we shall shine forth like the sun, and we shall share the omnipotence of Him who created the universe, and who tells us that "when he shall appear, we shall be like him." These are the prospects and hopes which the resurrection of Jesus Christ has guaranteed.

    Not only so, but that resurrection has established a precedent for the whole universe of God, and before the great plan shall have been accomplished the mark of the cross and the glory of the resurrection will be stamped upon the whole creation, for the day is coming when He that sitteth upon the throne shall say: "Behold, I make all things new," and earth and heaven shall have their baptism of death and resurrection.

A seventh message is that the resurrection of Christ as its crowning glory gives us back Christ Himself. For a brief moment of eclipse the Sun of Righteousness went out in the darkness of the grave, but with the Easter morning came a sunrise that shall nevermore decline. That glorious morning gave us back the crucified Jesus as our living and everlasting Friend, to be with us in a sense and in a fullness not possible had He continued to live as the Christ of Galilee. Then His presence was limited to a single spot and to a little group of friends. Now He says to us without restriction or limitation: "Lo, I am with you all the days, even unto the end of the age." His resurrection was the stepping stone to His ascension and to His high priesthood before the throne where He ever lives to make intercession for us, and it is leading on to the greater glory of His second as King of kings and Lord of all the ages.

Finally, the resurrection of Christ established a precedent for the highest things that faith and prayer can claim. Our text gives this mighty measure where the apostle prays that their eyes may be illuminated to "Know .. the exceeding greatness of his power to usward who believe, according to the working of his mighty power, which he wrought in Christ, when he raised him from the dead." After the resurrection, nothing is too hard for God. After the rolling away of that stone, no barrier need ever stand in your way again. After the victory of the Conqueror of death, no foe need ever dismay you. Oh, let us ask and believe and expect according to the mighty power which He wrought in Christ when He raised Him from the dead.

And now, in conclusion, there are several great and might words which seem to stand out in raised letters over the gateway of the Easter morning. The first is life. It is the voice of the Spring; it is the voice of the resurrection. It is the key word to our great salvation -- life. Have we received God's mighty gift --eternal life?

Another phrase is springing life, that life which is given to the beautiful season of Spring; that life which makes the Christian life not an effort by an impulse, not a stagnant pool but a glorious artesian well.

Another is fullness of life. All about us in nature are scattered in profusion the prodigal and redundant gifts of the Spring. Oh, let us realize that He who gave the sun its light, the trees their foliage, and the landscape its myriad beauties that no human eyes shall ever fully trace, is able to do much more for the children of His grace. Let us enter into the fullness of His resurrection.

Another phrase is newness of life. Rejuvenescence, the scientists call it. And that is what we need in our spiritual experience, the freshness that will make us like Aaron's rod, ever budding, blossoming and bearing abundant fruit.

Another is gladness, joyfulness. This is above all the spirit of the Spring. This is above all the spirit of the Spring. This is the spirit of the resurrection morning. All Hail! is the message of the Risen One. Fear not! is His reassuring word. Oh, let us emulate the songs of the birds, the sunshine of the sky, the blossoms of the Spring, the shining faces of the angels who came to herald the resurrection!

Another is victory. That triumph assures all other victories, and bids us go forth with the shout, "Thanks be unto God, which always causeth us to triumph in Christ."

One other word let us not forget. The Spring is the season of planting and the resurrection calls us to the true Springtime of a fruitful and unselfish life.

> O let us sow "beside all waters,"
> Plant blessings and blessings will spring;
> So truth and truth will grow.
> Nor ever forget what a wonderful thing

A. B. SIMPSON

Chapter 8.
SEEKING THE LIVING AMONG THE DEAD

"Why seek ye the living among the dead?" (Luke 24:5).

A Dead Christ

These women were looking for a dead Christ and of course they could not find Him, for He was living. How often since have men sought for Christ where He could not be found! How sad is the long vigil of Israel's sons and daughters for the Messiah that does not come and never will come as they are looking for Him! Some day they will behold Him as the Living One and weep and wonder because so long they vainly sought Him in a false ideal among the dead hopes of their earthly national ambitions. So also Romish superstition paints the Christ with all the hideous and ghastly accompaniments of the crown of thorns, the pallid brow of death and the cerements of the tomb. There is no such Christ; "He is not here, but is risen." The crucifix is not the true symbol of redemption. That is the cross with the suffering Christ upon it; that is past and gone forever. Rather, the cross shining in the halo of the glory beyond and the crown above is the true symbol of Christianity.

Thorwaldsen, the great Norwegian sculptor, has cut in marble a group known as "The Cross and the Vine," in which the outlines of the cross are covered and almost lost in the luxuriant foliage and hanging clusters of a splendid vine that grows from the foot of the cross. The vine represents the living Christ and the fruits of His resurrection and life, obliterating almost the figure of the cross from whose roots all these blessings spring.

To many a Christian, Jesus is still but a dead Christ or at least an historic Christ, but not a living and present reality. The meaning of Easter is that Jesus is alive and is the Living Head of Christianity and the personal and intimate Friend of every true disciple, to whom He becomes revealed as his indwelling life and the source of all his strength and victory.

Dear reader, do you know Him as the Living One? If you do not, Easter comes to you in vain with the sad cry of Mary: "They have taken away my Lord, and I know not where they have laid him."

You will observe in the story of the walk to Emmaus that Jesus Christ was not recognized by the two disciples until they received Him into their house and sat down to eat and drink with Him. It was then that He was manifested to them and "they know him; and he vanished out of their sight." While He merely walked with them by the way, they did not know Him, but when they took Him into the intimacy of their heart and home, then He was revealed to them as the Living One who had died upon the cross and had risen from the dead. And so, as you open the door of your heart and take Him as your guest and as your life, you too will so know Him; the supreme epoch of every Christian life will have come in your experience, the great transition from the earthly to the heavenly, from the human to the divine, from the struggles and failures of man's finite strength to the infinite possibilities of God's best.

A Dead Christianity

The question of our text may be addressed to those who are following a dead Christianity, for a dead Christ brings a dead Christianity. Coleridge's dream of the Ancient Mariner, in which a phantom ship floats upon the silent ocean with a dead man at the helm, a dead man on the bridge and dead men standing at their posts as if frozen by one fatal breath into ice or marble, is only too real a picture of many a church with a dead man in the pulpit and dead men in the pews and the entire ritual that of a solemn funeral. The tasks and fasts and penances and ceremonial rites which constitute the religion of many people are but the cerements of the dead, the grave clothes which the Master threw away that morning when He rose. This is not Christianity. The true religion of Jesus robes itself in garments of love and liberty and joy and goes forth to live for others and to bless the world.

It is remarkable that no mention is made of the Lord's apparel after His resurrection. We read of His seamless robe left behind Him when they nailed Him to the cross, and of the linen which they wrapped about Him at His burial and which they found, after His resurrection, neatly folded and laid away in the tomb; but nothing is said about His raiment as He appeared again and again to them. It is not probably true that the robes He wore were part of His very flesh, a living drapery that grew as naturally as the flowers of Spring and the tints of the rainbow our of the glorified life that was springing within Him? These will be no doubt the garments our resurrection bodies will take on as part of our very organism, the beauty and glory of our inner life, and, like the sunlit clouds of heaven, will change every moment with new attractions and splendors. So true Christianity does not need to be dressed in the cowl of the monk and the vestments of the choir and the elaborate ceremonial of Ritualism and Romanism. Its appropriate dress is the garment of praise, the mantle of love and the girdle of service as it goes forth in the glory of resurrection life and heavenly love to represent the Master in this world of sin and sorrow, and stands like the ancient vision of Solomon, bright "as the morning, fair as the moon, clear as the sun, and terrible as an army with banners." God give us this true Christian adorning and heavenly vestments compared with which our Easter fashions are but as "filthy rags."

Dead Souls

The question of our text might be asked of those who are seeking for spiritual life among the dry bones of our fallen human nature. Oh, ye that are trying to improve yourselves, to reform your lives, to build up your characters and to cultivate the fruits and grace of higher ethics and calling this religion, "Why seek ye the living among the dead?" Human nature is dead and beyond the power of self-improvement. God has simply provided for its burial and its resurrection life through the risen Christ. That is the meaning of this Easter day: the sentence of death has passed upon all man's best endeavors and the only hope of our fallen race is the new birth and the resurrection life through Jesus Christ. It is interesting to trace through the Scriptures the manifest truth that the first generation has always been a failure, and that it is the second birth that triumphs and remains. The first Adam fell, the second Adam achieved the destiny of humanity. The first Eden was lost forever, but the new heavens and the new earth shall bring back paradise restored. Eve's first son cruelly disappointed her; the second born and the third became the seed of promise. The old world passed out in the flood and the new world emerged under the arch of the rainbow on Mt. Ararat as a type of the great resurrection which Christ was to bring. Abraham's first born, Ishmael, had to be cast out and in Isaac, his second born, his seed was called. Esau, the elder, gave place to Jacob, the younger; David, the younger son of Jesse, was exalted above all his brethren as the Lord's anointed. In their journey to the Land of Promise, Israel's first generation failed; the second generation. consisting of their little children, was chosen to enter in while the bones of their fathers were buried in the sands of the desert.

 Even nature itself teaches us that a transformation must take place before the crawling worm can emerge from the chrysalis and become a soaring butterfly, and the seed has to die and rot in the ground and from its bosom comes forth the new germ that will bud and blossom and fill the earth with fruit. The tree that has but a natural birth must be grafted and cut down and wedded to a new branch before it can bear the best fruit. All nature is a parable of this mystery of mysteries. If we look at the lives of some of the typical characters of the Bible, we shall see the same principle running through them. Jacob had to pass through the narrow gates of his great conflict at Peniel in order to come forth a new man with a new name, Israel, a prince with God. Job had to find out that all his natural goodness was insufficient and, in the keen light of God's revealing, cry, "I abhor myself, and repent in dust and ashes," before there came to him a new life and righteousness and blessing. Isaiah had to see himself as all unclean and then receive the cleansing coal of fire which sent him forth empowered for his great prophetic ministry. Simon Peter had to fall so far that he broke his own proud neck in the fall and then came forth from the wreck and the shame with a new and divine strength which enabled him to die at last with downward head on his Master's cross. Paul had to find our that all his righteousness was as dross and had to be clothed in the righteousness of Christ alone and make this his watchword: "I am crucified with Christ: nevertheless I live; yet not I, but Christ liveth in me." This is the meaning of Easter. Have you entered into it and come forth with that death born life?

A Dead Humanity

The question of our text might be asked of the people that are teaching in our day the sufficiency of earthly culture, education, fine art humanitarianism to lift the race to its true plane and educate it out of its depravity and degeneracy. The world needs no sadder commentary on this stupendous folly than the late messages of poor Herbert Spencer to the world before he died, telling men of the best light that had come to him from the researches of eighty years and then adding that the outlook for him, as he faced the great crisis of life, was dark and depressing indeed.

The world has tried it many times. Culture can never do more for humanity than it did for ancient Egypt, Greece and Babylonia or for modern Italy in the brightest hour of art. But alas,

alas, these were the darkest hours in the records of human crime! "Why seek ye the living among the dead?" Humanity is like the dry bones of Ezekiel's vision, a moral cemetery, and nothing can lift it but the Omnipotent touch of a divine resurrection.

A Lifeless World

The question of our text might be addressed to the people that are looking for happiness in this doomed world and trying to find their true life among the dead ashes of earthly pleasure. God says of such a person, "He feedeth on ashes." Ashes are just the wreckage of organic matter that has been consumed and the substance burned our of it. The world has nothing to give you but ashes. The world's heart has gone out since God has gone out, and righteousness is lost. Will love make earth a heaven? Read the records of modern divorce. Will fame last forever? Look at the overturning of all the tables of human ambition. Is wealth an antidote for every human ill? Look at the story of the colossal fortunes of our day and the disappointment, the oppression, the countless calamities that follow in their train. The story has not only been told, but lived ten thousand times, and to the end of the chapter the conclusion will still be the same. Expressed in the language of human philosophy and experience, it is found in the last words of one of earth's most successful men, "I have been everything and everything is nothing." Expressed in the language of the Bible and the testimony of the prince of earthly pleasure, power and even wisdom, it is "Vanity of vanities, all is vanity and vexation of spirit."

Oh, turn from the ash heaps of this desert of spiritual desolation and in yonder garden by the open grave learn the secret of a joy that will never fade. "Whosoever drinketh of the water that I shall give him shall never thirst; but the water that I shall give him shall never thirst; but the water that I shall give him shall never thirst; but the water that I shall give him shall be in him a well of water springing up into everlasting life" (John 4:14).

A. B. SIMPSON

Dead Hopes

The question of our text speaks to the souls that are sitting in despair amid the dead hopes of their failures and disappointments. Rise up, despairing ones, bury your past in yonder grave, begin anew with Easter's dawning and know that the resurrection means for every discouraged man that God has established a great bankrupt court, where all the debts and losses of the past can be consigned to eternal oblivion and you can start anew with a heart as fresh and a hope as bright as if your life had this moment dropped from heaven and you were not and never would be again the same man as he who wrought the sin, the shame, the failure and the wreck that lies behind you. Leave it at the cross and rise up and take the fortune that He has purchased for you and is waiting to give you as the gift of His free and sovereign grace.

Someone tells of an old man that was riding through a country district when he was accosted by a native who asked him for a ride. He soon began to talk to the man and found that he was not saved. The native asked him after a while what his business was in those parts. He said,

"I represent a very large estate that has just been divided by the will of the testator and some of the heirs live around here, and I am looking for them. Their family name begins with the letter 'S,' and they are a very large family." Immediately the man became greatly interested.

"Why," he said, "I know some of them; they are the Smith's, are they not?"

"No," said the man, as he looked him earnestly in the face. "Their name is 'Sinner,' and I think you are one of them, and I have come to bring you a fortune."

Dear friend, that is the meaning of this bright Easter morning. The Friend who loved you before you were born, has paid all your debts, has discharged your liabilities, has blotted out your past, and He brings you an inheritance of love and hope and everlasting joy which you may freely have by accepting His grace and giving yourself to Him in loving return.

Our Holy Dead

Finally, the angels bear this message to some who are living among the tombs of their earthly bereavements and thinking of their loved ones as dead. They are not hear; "Why seek ye the living among the dead?" The pathetic story is told of two little children who, after the death of their mother, were digging a hole in the garden with their feeble hands. When asked why, they explained that they were digging a way to heaven to find mother. Someone had told them, when they saw her body lowered into the dark, cold ground, that she had gone to heaven, and they thought that heaven was somewhere in the ground. Alas, how many hearts are buried there. This is the very opposite of what God has intended. He has taken your loved ones to lift your hearts to that heavenly home where they are risen and rejoicing now, and to help us to realize that world which is the true goal of all our hopes and the only changeless home where parted friends shall meet again. "Why seek ye the living among the dead?" Arise and live with Him in the things above.

And so we might apply at greater length this searching question to all the things that we are vainly searching for below the skies. Lift up your eyes, lift up your hearts, look forward and remember that "the times of restitution of all things" are to come not hear but by and by when Jesus comes. Even much that we have prayed for, believed for and spiritually attained in part only, is waiting for us yonder. Then shall come back to us all we have sacrificed and surrendered hear. And this universe itself shall complete the mystery of the resurrection by passing through the ordeal of the last conflagration and shall come forth with the same mark of resurrection upon it that God is putting upon each of us now. Then, indeed, it shall be true that He that sits upon the throne shall say, "Behold, I make all things new."

Dear friend, are you living in this new world and for this coming age? There are two races crossing the narrow path of time. One is the Adam race, the other is the Christ race; one is the earthly race, the other is the heavenly people; one is doomed to remain among the dead, the other is pressing on to immortality and glory. "As is the earthy, such are they also that are earthy: and as is the heavenly, such are they also that are heavenly. And as we have borne the image of the earthy, we shall also bear the image of the heavenly" (1 Cor. 15:48,49). Beloved, come from among the dead and live forevermore.

Chapter 9.
THE POWER OF THE RESURRECTION

> "To whom also he showed himself alive after his passion by many infallible proofs, being seen of them forty days, and speaking of the things pertaining to the kingdom of God" (Acts 1:3).

Our Lord's earthly life may be divided into three sections: before His passion, during His passion, and the forty day interval between His resurrection and ascension.

Like the afterglow in an Oriental sky still shining long after the sun has disappeared, or like the Indian summer with its soft light and lingering sunshine, these days seem to have about them a mystic glory half way between the earthly and the heavenly. His feet still touched the earth, but His head was in the heavens.

The story of those days is but partly told, but we know enough to afford us seven distinct messages from the departing Master.

The Reality and Significance of the Resurrection

Strange it is that this should need to be demonstrated to Christian disciples, but it is the church of Christ that today is beginning to discredit the physical reality of the Lord's resurrection. Therefore, God had made it a demonstrable fact supported by "many infallible proofs." The Roman guards who were stationed around the tomb and whose silly lie about the stealing of His body was the very best proof that that body had gone; the angel messengers who repeatedly announced that He was risen indeed; His repeated appearings to His disciples and the testimony of Thomas in spite of his own skepticism --these form but a little part of the chain of evidence that so acute a mind as

Paul's considered unanswerable and that the profoundest judicial minds today have declared to be absolutely conclusive.

The nature of Christ's resurrection is as clear as the fact is certain. The picture given by the evangelists leaves no doubt of the absolute identity of the Christ of Easter with the Crucified of Calvary and the Man of Galilee. The very marks of the thorns and the spear were visible and tangible. So real was His humanity that they could handle Him and know by the evidence of their senses that He had actual flesh and bones and that He could eat the broiled fish they set before Him and distinguish the taste of the honeycomb as well. But so transcendently more mighty was His resurrection state than even His former physical life that His body could pass through the closed door and the stone that sealed the sepulcher without hindrance, and could rise and ascend to heaven in defiance of the law of gravitation without the faintest effort.

The significance of His resurrection is impossible to exaggerate. It is the fundamental proof of His Messiahship and of the truth of Christianity. It is the evidence of our justification. It is the source of our sanctification. It is the guarantee of our future resurrection. It is the pledge of all power that we can ever need in this present life, and is the pattern according to which faith may claim the "exceeding greatness of his power ... according to the working of his mighty power, which he wrought in Christ, when he raised him from the dead."

The Abiding Presence of Our Risen Lord

This is assured by His own announcement, every word of which is weighted with such force and suggestiveness, "Lo, I am with you always," or literally, "all the days, even unto the end of the world (age)." The importance of the announcement is attested by the first word, "Lo," which calls attention to its extraordinary significance. The identity of His presence with His life on earth is emphasized by the present tense of the verb, "I am with you." It was not a promise of some future visitation, but a presence that never should be withdrawn. And the beautiful translation, "all the days," makes that presence as perpetual and as new as the dawn of each succeeding day. He is present throughout all vicissitudes of life's changes and trials. The promise is not "all the years," but "all the days" -- every day and every sort of day: the cloudy days as well as the sunny ones; the days of trouble as well as the days of blessing; the lonely days, the days of weakness and even failure, "all the days, even unto the end of the age."

And as if this announcement were not sufficient, He illustrated it by several manifestations which seem to be prophetic of the way He might still be expected to show Himself to His earthly followers. How unspeakably precious is the picture of His walk to Emmaus with the two disciples! How simple, how natural, how almost playful was the way in which the Master dropped in upon them! How touching is the delicacy with which He acted as though He would have gone farther, and waited to be pressed to tarry in their home! How gladly He accepted the pressing invitation! How gloriously He manifested Himself in the breaking of the bread, and then how tactfully He vanished when the vision would have disturbed them from their simple life of faith if it had been further prolonged. So still He meets us along life's pathway. So still He sometimes unveils His glorious face. So still He quickly lets fall the curtain and leaves us to walk by faith and not by sight. How full of pathos is His message immediately after His resurrection: "Go, tell (My) disciples and Peter." So still He singles out the timid, the discouraged and the fallen. How full of comfort is that early morning visitation on the shore of the Galilean sea when the disciples had toiled all night and caught nothing, and the gray dawn found the Master there to supply their physical necessity and help them in their temporal distress, and then to lead them on to the higher lessons of suffering and service. It is in the light of these object lessons that we are ever to interpret that shining and everlasting promise, "Lo, I am with you all the days."

The Importance of His Word as the Vehicle of His Presence

It was as He talked with the disciples by the way and opened the Scriptures that their hearts first began to burn within them. He impressed upon them the prophetic word of which His sufferings and glory were the one continual burden. It is in His Word that we shall always find the Master near us. The warning of the beloved John concerning them that seduce us is that we are to continue in the Word which we have heard from the beginning. Spiritual manifestations are not always divine visitations. The test of every experience and of every spirit is the Word of Jesus Christ.

The Promise and the Presence of the Holy Ghost

How often this promise was repeated during the forty days. How imperatively they were bidden to tarry for His power. And yet the Lord began His ascension to anticipate the coming Pentecost, and as He breathed upon them, He commanded them to "receive ... the Holy Ghost." So still the Holy Spirit is a present fact and no believer need wait a single day for His coming, but the fullness of the Spirit is a larger promise and experience. As we wait for His infilling, there are heights and depths of power and blessing which are but as the pebbles on the shore compared with the mighty deep which lies beyond.

These after-Easter days should be for each of us days of the Holy Ghost, days of waiting for a deeper filling, a mightier baptism, a larger room for His incoming and a larger work for His outgoing through our lips and hands and feet and lives. Shall we take this blessed promise in its forcible, literal phrasing and prove it in both its meanings, "Behold, I send the promise of my Father upon you: but tarry ye ... until ye be endued with power from on high." The sending has already begun. The receiving is already in process. The ending is on its way. But the largeness of the blessing demands more than a passing moment, more than a formal prayer, more than a hurried meal at a quick lunch counter; it demands even days of waiting on the Lord, nights of intense communion, and all the days and all the years of our earthly lives to give sufficient room and time for us to take in the whole significance of that mighty promise "that ye might be filled with all the fulness of God."

The Call to Service: the Great Commission

The Master's parting messages justified no dream of selfish spiritual enjoyment, but called for the most strenuous service for the souls of men and the kingdom of God. Here are some flash lights upon the life of service as the Lord has outlined it: "Feed my lambs," "Feed my sheep," "Shepherd my feeble sheep." And again, "As my Father hath sent me, even so send I you." We are sent ones, we are apostles, we are ambassadors. We are not here because of our earthly citizenship. But because we have come, like our Lord, from heaven where our spirits were born to witness for Him on earth. And pre-eminent above all other ministries is the Great Commission for the evangelization of the heathen world. The command, "Go ye into all the world, and preach the gospel to every creature" requires a personal ministry from man to man and for every man beneath the sky. The command to begin "at Jerusalem" passes on to us the great trust for the chosen people. "Go ye ... and disciple all nations" raises the commission to a nobler plane and makes us ambassadors for the King of kings and trustees of the Gospel for every kindred and tribe and tongue. The command, "Ye shall be witnesses unto me both in Jerusalem, and in all Judea, and in Samaria, and unto the uttermost part of the earth" lifts the outlook beyond any section of humanity, any circle of selfish patriotism, any form of religious selfishness, and makes the work of evangelization the one supreme ministry of the church of Christ and the one paramount responsibility of every disciple of the Lord Jesus Christ. You certainly have not come into close touch with the risen Christ or caught the spirit of those last momentous days on earth if you are still inactive, indifferent or even neutral in this mighty enterprise which is the emergency work of our times and which is the one great business for which God has called and blessed us.

The Meaning of the Ascension

At length the forty days were ended, and in the simple story we are told that He led them out as far as Bethany and lifted up His hands and blessed them. "and it came to pass, while he blessed them, he was parted from them, and carried up into heaven." It is sweet to remember that the last attitude of the Lord Jesus on earth was that of stretching out His pierced hands in loving benediction. As He rose higher and higher in silent majesty, their last remembrance of Him would be that shining face and those outstretched and gracious hands.

It was necessary that He should pass from the earthly scene and return to His native heaven. The disciples must know, the world must know, the ages to come must know that this little planet is not all of God's great universe. Away beyond the blue dome of heaven, beyond the circling horizon, beyond the rising and the setting sun, beyond the stars of light, beyond the last gasp of dying agony, the mouldering grave and the mourner's tear, there is another realm, there is a greater and a better world, there is a home above, there is a heavenly land, the home of God and the great metropolis of His mighty universe. And when He had passed through every stage of earthly experience from the cradle to the grave, He passed on and took His place at the right hand of God amid glorious angels and ransomed men. It was necessary that the children of God should realize through the ascension of their living Head that this old earth is not their home, but, like their Master's, their citizenship too is in heaven. The ascension of Jesus Christ shifts our center of gravity, our meridian of latitude and longitude, our pole star of hope and expectation from earth to heaven.

But Christ's ascension meant much more for Him and us. It meant a new and higher ministry for Him and us. It meant a new and higher ministry for Him. It meant His heavenly priesthood as our Representative and Intercessor before the throne, presenting our worthless names with acceptance to His Father, presenting our imperfect prayers with the incense of His merits and saving us by His life as He had already saved us by His death. It meant His glorious kingship as Head over all things for His body, the Church. There He sits enthroned above all principality and power and every name that is named, ruling and overruling, conquering and to conquer, King of kings and Lord of lords, completing His Church and preparing for His coming. Christ's ascension and ministry on high was just as necessary as His life on earth, His death on Calvary and His resurrection on Easter morning.

> Where high the heavenly temple stands,
> A house of God not made with hands,
> A great High Priest our nature wears,
> The Guardian of mankind appears.
>
> He who for men their surety stood,
> And poured on earth His precious blood,
> Pursues in heaven the mighty plan,
> The Savior and the Friend of man.

The Hope of His Coming

The Master Himself had passed from view and the last echoes of His voice in benediction had died away, when suddenly another voice fell upon their ears, the voice of two celestial angels. Up yonder a chariot cloud had received the ascending Lord, perhaps a cloud of innumerable angels, so high above the earth that their forms could not be distinguished and they appeared to mortal vision like a distant veil of mist. But for a moment the Savior lingered behind that cloud and sent from the heavenly retinue that had come to attend Him home two special messengers to bear His postscript to His loved disciples. And it was this. "This same Jesus, which is taken up from you into heaven, shall so come in like manner as ye have seen him go into heaven."

Having sailed once from New York harbor for an absence of many months, the writer well remembers that just as the boat was about to leave the harbor, a messenger came to take ashore the last greetings of the passengers. There was only time for just a word, but that word from most of us was "Back soon." And that sweet hope cheered through the long months of parting the waiting hearts at home. This was the Master's thought as He left the harbor on time, on that old spring noontide on the hillside of Bethany: I have left you for a little while, but I will see you again and your hearts shall rejoice. Beloved, that is the goal, that is the outlook, that is the perspective of faith and hope -- not the cross, not even the resurrection, not the work of missions, not even the blessed presence of the Master and the power of the Holy Ghost. All these only lead up to that transcendent and eternal hope,

> That one far-off divine event
> To which the whole creation moves.

Dear friend, is that the goal to which you are moving? Have you inscribed on every friendship, every investment, every undertaking, every work, every joy and every sorrow, "Unto the coming of the Lord"?

Chapter 10.
AFTER-EASTER-DAYS

"He showed himself alive after his passion by many infallible proofs, being seen of them forty days, and speaking of the things pertaining to the kingdom of God" (Acts 1:3).

Easter morning is the beginning of a unique and most tenderly interesting portion of our blessed Savior's life. It is the transition period between His earthly ministry and His heavenly exaltation. Like the Indian summer of the year, there is a tender veil of loveliness and mystery about it which links it with both worlds, and makes it a peculiarly appropriate pattern of a life hid with Christ in God, in which we may walk with Him all our days with our heads in heaven while our feet still tread the earth below. May the Holy Spirit vividly reveal to us such glimpses of this blessed life as will enable us to reproduce it in our own experience and to walk with Him with a new sense of His abiding presence and glorious reality!

A Living Christ

This glad resurrection morning dispels from the religion of Jesus all the shadows of the sepulcher and all the morbid atmosphere of sorrow, depression and death. The Christ of true Christianity is not a bleeding, thorn crowned Ecce Homo, but a glad and radiant face, bright as the spring tide morning and radiant with immortal life. "I am he that liveth, and was dead," is His message, and "Behold! I am alive for ever more." Oh, may this day impress upon our hearts the reality of a Risen and Living Christ, until He shall be more actual to us than any other personality and we shall know what it means to be not only "reconciled to God by the death of His Son" but "much more we shall be saved by his life"!

A. B. SIMPSON

A Victorious Christ

What a picture of easy and uttermost triumph is that resurrection scene! Satan had done his utmost; men had done their best to hold the Captive of the tomb. But without an effort the Mighty Sleeper calmly rose before the Easter dawn, deliberately laying off the grave clothes and wrapping up the napkin and putting all in place as naturally as any of us this morning arranged our toilet; and then through that colossal stone that closed His tomb, He passed without even rolling it aside or breaking the seal, and before the guards could know that He was risen, He was standing calmly in the garden, talking with Mary as though nothing had happened. The infinite facility with which He put His feet on every foe and rose above every obstacle is, perhaps, the most overwhelming impression we have received from all the incidents of His resurrection.

So, too, we see the same victorious power expressed in the attitude of the angel who followed Him, and with a single touch rolled away the stone from the sepulcher and coolly sat down upon it, and then looked in the faces of the keepers till they grew pale with terror and flew in horror and dismay without a struggle.

Such is our Risen Christ still, the Mighty Victor over all His foes and ours. Could we see Him now, we would behold Him sitting on His Father's throne, undismayed by all the powers of darkness, and "from henceforth expecting till his enemies be made his footstool." Oh, how it cheers our timid hearts to behold our glorious and victorious Captain, and to hear Him say of every adversary and every difficulty, "I have overcome for you." God help us to see the Captain as Joshua beheld Him, and before Him the walls of every Jericho will fall and the legions of every opposing force shall melt away!

How natural, how easy, how artless His manifestations were through those blessed forty days! How quietly He dropped down among them, unheralded, unassuming, unattended by angelic guards, and sometimes undistinguished from themselves in His simple presence! Look at Him as He meets with Mary in that first morning interview, standing like an ordinary stranger in the garden, speaking to her in easy conversation, "Woman, why weepest thou? whom seekest thou?" And then, when the moment for recognition comes, He speaks to her heart in the one artless word of personal and unutterable love which disarmed all her amazement and fear, and brought back all the old recollections and affections of her throbbing heart! See Him again on the way to Emmaus! How naturally He drops in upon the little company as they walk! How unaffectedly He talks with them! How easily He turns the conversation to heavenly themes, and yet how free from strain His every attitude and word! All they are conscious of, is a strange burning in their hearts and a kindling warmth of love. At length they constrain Him and He allows Himself to be pressed to enter in. He sits down by their table, He eats bread, as if He had been another disciple like themselves; and only then, as He vanishes quietly from their sight, do they realize that it is the Lord.

And yet again, on the shores of Tiberias, how exquisite is His approach! How natural His greeting; how easy the mighty miracle of the draught of fishes; how calm and unaffected are the meeting as they reach the shore and the simple breakfast in which He Himself takes part. How exquisite the interview with Simon Peter, the delicacy and tenderness of which no word can ever express! On, what a picture of that Blessed One who still lives to be our constant Visitor, our ceaseless Companion and Friend; Who meets us like Mary in our hours of sorrow; Who walks with us, as with them, often unrecognized at first; Who greets us in the cold, sad morning after our long hours of waiting and toil and failure with His marvelous deliverance and yet more gracious words of love and instruction. So near is He that not even our nearest friends can come so close! So simple is He that His messages come as the intuition of our own hearts; and yet He is the wonderful Counselor and the mighty God for all our perplexities and all our hard places. Blessed Christ of the Forty Days, oh, help us, with a faith more simple and a love more childlike to walk with Thee!

The Mighty Christ

It is hard for us to realize the Presence that comes with such gentle footsteps and undemonstrative simplicity; but back of that gentle form and those noiseless steps is the Omnipotence that could say, "All power is given unto me in heaven and in earth." All power is His in heaven. He is the Lamb in the midst of the Throne, that holds in His hand the seven seals and unrolls the scroll of destiny and providence for all worlds and beings and events. All the mighty acts of God recorded in the Old Testament were but manifestations of His power. All the mighty movements which began with His ascension are the workings of His hands. All the movements of Divine providence are subject to His command. All the mighty angels of heaven's myriad hosts are subject to His bidding. All the powers of hell tremble at His name! All the promises of God are fulfilled with His endorsement. All the laws of nature are subject to His mandates. And all power on earth is subordinate to His power. Not a wind can blow without His permission, not a disease can strike but as He allows, not a human hand can hurt us while He shields us with His presence. The circumstances of life, the enemies of our souls and the infirmities of our bodies are subject to His Word. The very thrones of earth are subordinate to His authority. He can make a Cyrus send back the tribes of Israel by a national decree. He can make a Constantine behold the flaming Cross upon the sky and become a follower of the Heavenly Standard. He can open nations and kingdoms to the Gospel, and so He bids us go forth and disciple all the nations because of His Almighty power in our behalf! Ho mighty was the power of the resurrection! It surmounted the power of death and the grave; it passed through the solid stone; it defied the stamp of the Roman government and the sentinels of the Roman army. It could pass through the closed doors without rending them asunder. It could bring the miraculous draught of fishes to the apostle's net with a single word of command. It could rise without an effort in the chariot of His ascension. It could anoint those weak and timid men with the power that shook the world and laid the foundations of the Church. Oh, that our eyes were but opened that we might behold "the riches of the glory of his inheritance in the saints," and "the exceeding greatness of his power to usward who believe, according to the working of his mighty power, which he wrought in Christ, when he raised him from the dead, and set him at his own right hand in the heavenly places, far above all principality, and power, and might, and dominion, and every name that is named, not only in this world, but also in that which is to come: and hath put all things under his feet, and gave him to be the head over all things to the church, which is his body" (Eph. 1:18-23). Why is it that we do not receive and realize more of this Almighty Christ? Alas! because we cannot understand or stand the fullness of His power. God is ready to work through us the triumphs of His omnipotence, but we must be fitted vessels, open to His touch and able to stand His power. The ordinance that has to bear a mighty charge of powder must be heavy enough to stand the charge without explosion. And so hearts that are to know the power of Him who is able to do exceedingly abundantly above all we ask or think, must be "strengthened with might by his Spirit in the inner man," so that "Christ may dwell in your hearts by faith." To think of what Christ is ready and willing to do in us and for us would frighten some of us into apoplexy, and actually to realize it would snap the frail thread of life itself. Christ's heart is bursting with resources that the world needs and that He is ready to use if only He could find vessels ready and willing to use them. Oh, that we had the courage to see the power which He is waiting to place at the service of all who are consecrated enough to use it for His glory and close enough to receive the heavenly baptism! He has for us the power of the Holy Spirit, the power of prayer, the power that will conquer circumstances and control all events for His will, and the power that will make us the trophies of His grace and the monuments of His indwelling presence and victory. We shall find this power as we go forth to use it according to His own commission, "Go ye therefore, and teach all nations." Nothing but a work as wide as the world can ever make room for the power which Christ is waiting to bestow.

A Loving Christ

How unavailing all His power would be if we were not sure that it is available for us, and that His heart as tenderly loves us as His mighty hand can help us. How tender and loving the Christ of the Forty Days! See Him in the garden as He speaks to Mary with tender sympathy: "Women, why weepest thou? whom seekest thou?" He asks, and then calls her by her name in tones which must have expressed more than words could tell. What mourner can doubt henceforth His sympathy and love? What heart can hesitate to accept His friendship which still speaks to each of us with as direct and personal a call, and gives to each a name of special and affectionate regard?

Or look again at Him as He meets with Thomas, the doubting one, the willful disciple that petulantly demanded that the Lord should meet him with an evidence that He had given to none other, and that no human heart had a right imperiously to claim. But how tenderly the Lord concedes even his demand, until Thomas is ashamed to accept it and, more amazed at his Lord's magnanimity and omniscience than the evidence of His wounds, he cries, "My Lord and my God." Who that is harassed with doubts and difficulties need fear again to bring them to His presence, Who with such condescending love is ready to meet them all, and to make our hearts know by the deeper evidence of His own great love and the revealing of Himself that He is indeed the Son of God?

And look at His interview with Simon Peter! What backslider need ever doubt again the Savior's forgiving love, or fear to come and know that he will be welcomed to a nearer place in His heart and a higher service in His kingdom if only he can say as Simon said, "Thou knowest all things; thou knowest that I love thee."

So tender, so forgiving, so full of love He comes to us, to dry our tears, to satisfy our doubts, to forgive our failures, to restore our souls, and then to use us for a higher service, just because we have learned through our own infirmities the depths of His great love. The secret of walking closely with Christ and working successfully for Him, is to fully realize that we are His beloved. Let us but feel that He has set His heart upon us, that He is watching us from those heavens with the same tender interest that He felt for Simon and Mary, that He is working out the mystery of our lives with the same solicitude and fondness, that He is following us day by day as any mother follows her babe in his first attempt to walk alone, that He has set His love upon us, and, in spite of ourselves, is working out for us His highest will and blessing, as far as we will let Him; and then nothing can discourage us. Our hearts will glow with responsive love. Our faith will spring to meet His mighty promises, and our sacrifices shall become the very luxuries of love for one so dear. This was the secret of John's spirit. "We have known and believed the love that God hath to us." And the heart that has fully learned this has found the secret of unbounded faith and enthusiastic service.

The Physical Christ

He that came forth from Joseph's tomb came forth in the flesh, with a material body and the same form that He had laid down in death and the grave. He made this most emphatic in His interview with His disciples after His resurrection. He wished them to be thoroughly assured that there was no illusion about His body. "Handle me, and see," was His emphatic word, "for a spirit hath not flesh and bones, as ye see me have."

Indeed, His spiritual consciousness had not died; it was only His body that tasted death, and it was His body therefore that was raised from death. The resurrection of Christ, then, is a physical fact, and the physical meaning of the resurrection must be of surpassing importance. It means no less than this, that He has come forth to be the physical life of His people now, and in a little while the Fountain of their immortality and the Head of their resurrection bodies.

What a source of strength and inspiration it is for us to know that our blessed Lord has still the same physical organization that we possess, and is willing and able to share with these mortal frames His infinite and quickening life! He is our living Bread, and as He lived by the Father, so we may live by Him, and not only is He the source of health and strength to our material life, but He cares for the wants of the body. Hungry and cold were the disciples from their fruitless fishing that Galilean morning; He saw their need and tenderly asked them, "Children, have ye any meat?" and then, filling their empty nets and spreading the table on the shore, He said, "Come and dine." So still He thinks of the poor and the struggling, the hungry and the helpless ones, and stands beside them in their need, ready and able, by a word, to provide immediate and abundant supply.

Are we today in any place of need? The Christ of the Forty Days is nearer than we think, able to be "touched with the feeling of our infirmities," and ready to give us the greatest help in time of need. Like the fishers of that Galilean sea, our empty nets can be filled at His bidding; the perplexed workman can be directed to the very thing to do; the wretched failure can be all corrected. There is no need that He cannot supply, no counsel that He is not able to give, no regions where His power does not penetrate, no disciple that He does not love to help in every time of need. Oh, let us trust Him more with all our circumstances and sorrows, and our utmost need will only prove the more infinite resources of His love and grace.

The Ever-Present Christ

The Christ of the Forty Days is not a transient vision that has passed away forever, but the Christ of all the ages. Standing at the close of those blessed days midway between earth and heaven, He said, "Lo! I am with you all the days, even unto the end of the world." That blessed present tense has bridged the past and the present, and has prolonged those heavenly days after the resurrection through all the days since then, It is not "I will be," as one who has to go away and come back again; but "I am," as a presence that is never to be withdrawn, He is unseen, it is true, but is as real as any friend is real in his absence as well as presence. For in the spiritual world distance and time are eliminated; just as the telescope can bring the distant object near the eye, and the telephone can present the voice that is hundreds of miles away to the listening and attentive ear, so there is a spiritual mechanism that can make Christ as immediate to the heart as though He were still visibly by our side. Had we but another sense, all heavenly beings and realities would be directly present to our perception.

The promise of this beautiful passage is not only fulfilled in the presence of Christ in the heart of the believer, which is a literal and glorious truth, but it is a presence with us. It is more than the spiritual consciousness of the Lord's indwelling. It is His direct personality and constant companionship with all our life and His omnipotent cooperation in all our needs. It is the presence of One who has all power in heaven and in earth, and whose presence means the defeat of every adversary, the solution of every difficulty, the supply of every need. Oh, it does seem, in these days, as though we could almost see Him moving in the midst of His people, here and there, in His mighty working, on the mission field with the lone worker in the midst of dangers and foes, in the busy streets of the crowded city, in the mingled incidents of business life, in the whirl and confusion of our intense life today, in every department of human society -- touching with His hands all the chords of influence and power, moving the wheels of Providence, and working out His purpose for His people and the redemption of the world. Oh, that we might see Him as Joshua saw the Captain when He entered Canaan and camped around Jericho; as Stephen saw Him when he faced the crowd of wolfish foes that thirsted for his blood; as Paul saw Him amid the tempests of the Adriatic and the lions of the Coliseum; as John saw Him in the midst of the Throne, holding in His hand the seven stars and walking in the midst of the seven golden candlesticks, and then standing before the Throne with all the seals of human destiny in His own right hand! Then, indeed, no trail could discourage us, no foe intimidate us, no fear dismay us, no work overwhelm us; for above every voice of peril or of hostile power, we would hear His gentle whisper, "Lo, I am with you all the days, even unto the end of the age."

The promise is better translated "all the days," rather than "always." He comes to you each day with a new blessing. Every morning, day by day, He walks with us, with a love that never tires and a blessing that never grows old. And He is with us "all the days"; it is a ceaseless abiding. There is no day so dark, so commonplace, so uninteresting, but you find Him there. Often, no doubt, He is unrecognized, as He was on the way to Emmaus, until you realize how your heart has been warmed, your love stirred and your Bible so strangely vivified that every promise seems to speak to you with heavenly reality and power. It was the Lord! God grant that His living presence may be made more and more real to us all henceforth, and whether we have the consciousness and evidence, as they had a few glorious times those forty days, or whether we go forth into the coming days, as they did most of their days, to walk by simple faith and in simple duty, let us know, at least, that the fact is true forevermore, that He is with us, a presence all unseen but real, and ready if we need Him any moment to manifest Himself for our relief.

There is a beautiful incident related of the mother of an English schoolboy whom, when he was a lad, she sent to a boarding school, some distance from her home, where the rules of the school only permitted her to visit once a fortnight. But this was more than her mother heart could stand, and so, all unknown to her boy or his teachers, she rented a little attic overlooking the school, and often, when he little dreamed, she would sit in that upper room with her eyes on her darling boy as he played in that yard below or studied in the schoolroom. He could not see her, nor did he dream that she was there, but had he cried or called her name or needed her for a moment, he was within her reach.

The is a little parable of the sleepless love and the ceaseless oversight which our savior exercises towards His beloved ones, for He has His eye upon us by day and by night; and although we do not see His face and hands and form as He moves through our pathway, dissipating our foes and clearing our way, yet He is there, ever there "all the days, even unto the end." Let us believe His promise, let us assume the reality of His presence, let us recognize Him as ever near, let us speak to Him as one ever by our side, and He shall ever answer us, either by the whispers of His love or by the workings of His hand.

Thus shall we never be alone, thus shall we never be defenseless, thus shall we never be defeated, thus need we never fear. And even should the lonely vale itself open to us, it shall be but the opening vista of a larger vision and a closer and nearer presence, as we find that neither "death, nor life, nor angels, nor principalities, nor powers, nor things present, nor things to come, nor height, nor depth, nor any other creature, shall be able to separate us from the love of God, which is in Christ Jesus our Lord" (Rom. 8:38, 39)

The Fourfold Gospel

By
REV. A. B. SIMPSON, D.D.

With an Introduction by
REV. FREDERIC H. SENFT, D.D.

A. B. SIMPSON

Introduction

The title of this little volume, "The Fourfold Gospel," has been a familiar phrase to thousands of God's children during the past forty years. Not that the truths contained in the statement were unknown before, but the grouping of them in this form was given to Dr. A. B. Simpson after he had happily experienced the fulness of the Gospel in his own life.

This does not mean that the blessings of the Gospel are limited exclusively to four-Christ our Saviour, Christ our Sanctifier, Christ our Healer, and Christ our Coming Lord. In one sense it is a manifold Gospel with countless blessings and ever deeper and richer experiences of God's grace and love. "But there are four messages in the Gospel," says the author, "which sum up in a very complete way the blessings which Christ has to offer us and which it is especially important that Christians should emphasize today." These constitute four great pillars in the temple of truth.

Note the order of these great truths. First things first-Christ our Saviour. Rightly, the first has to do with the soul, lost through sin and estrangement from God, but "made nigh by the blood of Christ." It is no small thing to be saved-justified, forgiven, born again. This foundation truth needs to be reiterated in these days, when sin is minimized or explained away, and the atonement of Jesus Christ is rejected by many. The same is true of Sanctification-a word and experience misunderstood and evaded by many believers. It marks a definite and distinct crisis in the history of a soul. The unfolding of these four phases of the Gospel will be made fascinatingly clear to the reader of this book. It is well worthy of thoughtful and prayerful study, and best of all of appropriating the full-orbed message-the all-sufficient Christ for spirit, soul, and body.

Dr. Simpson proved this in his own life; otherwise, his preaching would have been in vain, the Christian and Missionary Alliance would not have come into existence, and multiplied thousands of people the world around would have been deprived of the knowledge and experience of a complete Christ. Addressing an audience in London many years ago, Dr. Simpson related the following experiences which marked three great epochs in his life: "Some twenty-seven years ago, I foundered for ten months. in the waters of despondency, and I got out of them just by believing in Jesus as my Saviour. About twelve years ago I got into another deep experience of conviction, and I got out of that by believing in Jesus as my Sanctifier. After years of teaching and waiting on Him, the Lord Jesus Christ showed me four years ago that it was His blessed will to be my complete Saviour for body as well as soul."

This exposition of "The Four-Fold Gospel" has had a very large circulation in past years, and in this new and attractive form we are confident it will be in great demand. Nothing better, outside of the Bible, could be put in the hands of converts. One of our evangelists in the earlier years of the work used hundreds of them in that way with marked results.

The message is simple, Scriptural, and satisfying. The Church needs it as antidote to error and apostasy, a sure remedy for failure, an answer to the cry of hungry hearts, a source of health for the body and an inspiration to complete the witness and bring back the King.

FREDERIC H. SENFT.

Chapter 1.
CHRIST OUR SAVIOUR

> "And they cried with a loud voice, saying, salvation to our God which sitteth upon the throne, and unto the Lamb."
> Rev. vii. 10.

This is the cry of the ransomed around the throne when the universe is dissolving in wreck, and terror is filling the hearts of men. It is the first cry of the ransomed after they reach their home and have seen all that it means to be lost and to be saved, while the earth is reeling, and the elements are melting, and all things are quaking and trembling in the first approaches of the great catastrophe. They see behind them all the way through which the Lord has led them; down that long vista they behold the toils they have come through and the perils they have escaped, and they recognize how tenderly the grace of God has led them on and kept them safe. They see the robes and crowns that are prepared for them, and all the joy of the eternal future which is opening before them. They see all this, and then they behold Him whose hand has kept it all safely for them, and whose heart has chosen it for them. They look back upon all the past; they look forward into all the future; they look up into the face of Him to whom it was all due, and then they lift up their voices in one glad exultant cry, "Salvation to our God which sitteth upon the throne, and unto the Lamb." This is what salvation means; this is what they have believed for; this is what He died to give them. They have it all. They are saved, and the full realization of it has come home to their heart at last.

Let us look a little at what it means to be saved. It is not at all a little thing. We sometimes hear that certain Christians are *only* justified. It is a mighty thing to be justified. It is a glorious thing to be born again. Christ said it was greater to have one's name written in heaven than to be able to cast out devils. What does salvation mean?

The Fourfold Gospel

I. WHAT IT SAVES US FROM.

1. It takes away the guilt of sin. It frees us from all liability and punishment for past offences. Sin deserves punishment. Salvation takes this all away. Is it not glorious to be saved?

2. Salvation saves us from the wrath of God. God hates evil and must punish it somehow. The wrath of God is revealed from heaven against all unrighteousness of men. But from this salvation delivers us.

3. Salvation delivers us from the curse of the law. We can recall the terrors of its revealing, the lightnings and thunder that surrounded the mountain, and the terror of Israel before it was given at all. They could not bear that God should speak to them thus, and they entreated Moses, "Speak thou with us and we will hear; but let not God speak with us, lest we die." But if the giving of the law was terrible, more terrible was the breaking. It is perilous to break the law of the land. The most tender appeal of affection did not avail to save those condemned anarchists in Chicago recently. The 'hand of the law was on their throats, and to the gallows they must go. I remember the days when the assassin of President Lincoln was stalking through the land. The law would have searched the world to find him out. How terrible it must have been for him to feel that the eye of justice was looking for him, and sooner or later would surely find him! The circle narrowed and narrowed around him, till at last he was grasped in the cordon. So the cordon of law tightens around the sinner who is under its power. Salvation delivers us from this curse through Him who was made a curse for us.

4. It delivers us also from our evil conscience. There is always a shadow left on our hearts by sin, and a feeling of remorse. It is the black wing of the raven, and its hoarse voice is ever whispering of despair. The memory of past guilt will follow people so that after many years they tell of crimes commit-

ted, the punishment for which they escaped, but the burden never left their conscience. Sometimes it seemed to slumber for a while, and at last it sprang upon them like a lion. Salvation delivers from our evil conscience. It takes the shadow from the heart and the stinging memory of sin from the soul.

5. It delivers from an evil heart, which is the source of all the sin in the life. It is natural for men to sin even while they hate it. The tendency to evil is in every nature, chained to it like a body of death, so that when we would do good evil is present with us. It takes possession of the will and heart like a living death. It is offensive, it smells of the sepulchre, it is full of the poison of asps, it putrefies the whole moral being and bears it, too, down to death. Salvation frees us from its power and gives us a new nature.

6. It frees us from the fear of death. It takes away the sting of that last enemy, through fear of whom we would otherwise all our lifetime be subject to bondage. I remember when I was a child what a shock a funeral bell would give me. I could not bear to hear of some one being dead. The love of Christ has taken this all away. The death-bed of God's children is to them the portal of heaven.

7. Salvation delivers us from Satan's power and kingdom. God hath "delivered us from the power of darkness and translated us into the kingdom of His dear Son." We are saved from the ills and the serpent and the bonds of sin, and the devil is for us a conquered foe. Salvation delivers us from much sorrow and distress in life. It brings a glorious sunlight into the life and drives away those clouds of depression and gloom which overwhelm us.

8. Beyond all else, salvation delivers us from eternal death. We are not going down into outer darkness and the depths of woe. Christ has unlocked the fetters of the pit and saved us from endless death. We are delivered from that terrible ag-

ony which the kindest lips that ever spoke has called "the worm that dieth not and the fire that is not quenched."

These are some of the things that salvation has delivered us from. Is it not indeed glad tidings?

II. WHAT SALVATION BRINGS TO US.

It brings the forgiveness of all our sins and entirely removes them. They are blotted out as completely as though we had paid all that was due for them, and they can never appear against us again.

1. It brings us justification in the sight of God, so that we stand before Him as righteous beings. We are accepted as though we had done everything He had commanded, and had perfectly kept the law in every particular. With one stroke of the pen He erases the account that was against us; with another stroke He puts there all the righteousness of Christ. We must take both sides of this. The spotlessness of Jesus is put to your account as if it were your own. All His obedience to the Father is yours. All His patience and gentleness are yours. Every service that He has rendered to bless others is put to your account as if you had done it all. Every good thing you can discover in Him is yours, and every evil thing in you is His. That is salvation. Is it not wonderful?

2. It brings us into the favor and love of God, and secures us full acceptance in the person of Jesus. He loves us as He loves His only begotten Son. The moment we are presented in the arms of Christ, we are accepted in Him. Dr. Currie, a brilliant writer connected with the Methodist Episcopal Church, has left a beautiful incident in his own life. He was the editor of one of the best journals of his church, and in many ways he was closely connected with its work. He dreamed one night, a little before his recent death, that he died and went up to the gate of heaven. There he met an

angel and asked to be allowed to enter. The angel asked him who he was. He answered: "I am Dr. Currie, the editor of the *Quarterly Review* of the Methodist Episcopal Church." The angel answered: "I don't know you, I never heard of you before." Soon he met another angel and told 'him the same story, and received the same answer: "I don't know you." At last one of the angels said: "Let us go to the Judge and see if He will know you." He went before the throne and told the Judge about his life and the 'work he had done for the church, but received the answer from the Judge: "I don't know you at all." His heart was beginning to gather the blackness of despair, when suddenly there was One at his side with a crown of thorns upon His head, who said: "Father, I know him. I will answer for him." And instantly all the harps of heaven began to sing: "Worthy is the Lamb that was slain," and he was ushered into all the glory of the celestial world. Not all the preaching we have done, or all the service we have rendered will amount to anything there. We must be identified with the Man who wore the thorns; we must be accepted in the Beloved, and then the Father will love us even as He loves His Son. We shall stand with Him even as Christ does.

3. Salvation gives us a new heart. It brings to us regeneration of the soul. Every spark of life from the old polluted nature is worthless, and the divine nature is born in us as a part of our very being.

4. Salvation gives us grace to live day by day. A man may be pardoned and so get out of prison, and yet have no money to supply his needs. He is pardoned, yet he is starving. Salvation takes us out of prison, and provides for all our needs besides. It enables us to rejoice in the glory of God, which is "able to keep us from falling, and to present us faultless before the presence of His glory with exceeding joy."

5. It brings to us the help of the Holy Spirit, who is ever at our side as a gentle mother, helping our infirmities and bringing grace for every time of need.
6. It brings to us the care of God's providence, causing all things, to work together for our good. This is never true until we are saved; but when we are the children of God all things in earth and in heaven are on our side.
7. Salvation opens the way for all the blessings that follow it. It is the steppingstone to sanctification and healing, and the peace that passeth understanding. From this first gateway the prospect opens out boundlessly to all the good land we may go on to possess.
8. Salvation brings to us eternal life. It is, of course, only the beginning, but the heavenly, land has its portals open even here, and when we at last reach the throne and look out and see all the possibilities that yet lie before us, we shall sing with the ransomed, "Salvation to our God which sitteth upon the throne, and unto the Lamb."

III. THE PROCESS BY WHICH THESE BLESSINGS COME.

1. They come through the mercy and grace of God. "God so loved the world that He gave His only begotten Son, that whosoever believeth in Him should not perish, but have everlasting life."
2. Salvation comes to us by the righteousness of Jesus Christ. He perfectly fulfilled for us every requirement of the law. Had He faltered in one temptation we could not have been saved. Think of that when you are tempted to speak a hasty word, and you almost give way for a moment. Suppose Jesus had done so, we should have been lost forever. Every moment He held steadfastly in the path of obedience, and His perfect grace and obedience are the price of your salvation.

3. Salvation comes to us through the death of Christ. His obedience is not enough. He must die. His crucifixion is the atonement for our sins.

4. Salvation comes through the resurrection of Jesus Christ from the dead, which was God's seal of His accomplished work and the pledge of our pardon.

5. Salvation comes through the intercession of Jesus at the right hand of the Father. He is our Great High Priest there, where He ever liveth to make intercession for us, and thus keeps us in continual acceptance.

6. Salvation comes through the grace of the Holy Ghost. The Spirit of God is sent down, through the intercession of Christ, to carry out in our hearts and lives His work. He keeps our feet in the way, and He will never leave His work until He has put us forever into the bosom of Jesus.

7. Salvation comes to us by the Gospel. It is presented to us through this message, and our refusal to accept it, or our neglect to do so, fixes irrevocably, by our own act, our eternal condition. If we are saved, we become so by accepting the Gospel, which is, therefore, called "the Gospel of your salvation."

IV. THE STEPS BY WHICH IT IS RECEIVED.

1. Conviction of sin. We must first see our need and our danger before we can be saved. The Holy Ghost brings this to our heart and conscience. Until there is this knowledge of the need of Christ, He cannot of course be received; but when the heart is deeply impressed under a sense of sin, Christ is precious indeed.

2. There must be next an apprehension of Jesus as our Saviour. The soul must see Him as both able and willing to save. It will not do merely to feel and confess your guilt. What is needed is to get the eye on Jesus. So Christ says to every

seeking soul, "Look! Look! Look unto Me and be saved !" "Every one which *seeth* the Son, and believeth on Him, may have everlasting life."

3. Salvation comes by repentance. There must be a turning from sin. This does not consist in mere emotional feeling, necessarily, but it does mean to have the whole will and purpose of heart turned from sin to God.

4. Salvation comes by coming to Jesus. The soul must not only turn away from sin. That alone will not save it. Lot's wife turned away from Sodom-but she was not in Zoar. There must be a turning to Jesus as well as a turning from sin.

5. Salvation comes by accepting Jesus as a Saviour. This does not mean merely crying out to Him to save, but claiming Him as the Saviour, embracing the promises He has given, and so believing that He is your personal Redeemer.

6. Salvation comes by believing that Christ has accepted us, and counting Him faithful who has promised. This will bring the sweetness of assurance and peace, and as we believe the promise the Spirit will seal it to the heart and witness that we are the children of God.

7. Salvation comes by confessing Christ as the Saviour. This is a necessary step. It is like the ratification of a deed or the celebration of a marriage, and stamps and seals our act of committal.

8. Salvation involves our abiding in Jesus. Having taken it for granted, once for all, that you are saved, never do the work over again. "As ye have, therefore, received Christ Jesus the Lord, so walk ye in Him."

V. THINGS THE BIBLE SAYS ABOUT SALVATION.

1. It is called God's salvation. It was not invented by man. God alone is the author of it, and He is the only Saviour.

2. It is also called "your own salvation," because you yourself must appropriate it.
3. It is called "the common salvation," because it is free to all who will accept it.
4. It is called a "great salvation," because it is full and infinite in its provisions. It is large enough for all your needs.
5. Christ is called the "mighty to save," because no matter how weak or how wicked the sinner may be, He is able to save him to the uttermost.
6. It is called a near salvation. "Say not in thine heart, who shall ascend into heaven? (that is, to bring Christ down *from above:*) Or, who shall descend into the deep? (that is, to bring Christ again from the dead.) But what saith it? The Word is nigh thee, *even* in thy mouth and in thy heart: that is, the Word of Faith which we preach: That if thou shalt confess with thy mouth the Lord Jesus, and shalt believe in thine heart that God hath raised Him from the dead, thou shalt be saved." We do not have to get up into some exalted state to find Christ, nor down into some profound and terrible experience, but we can find Him everywhere we are. Salvation is at our door. We can take it as we find Him very near to us. No steps were allowed to God's ancient altar, for then some poor sinner might not be able to get up to it. Jesus is on the very plane where you are this moment. You can take His salvation here now. Take Him as you are, and lie will lead you into all the experiences you need.

VI. WHY IT IS CALLED THE GOSPEL OF GOOD NEWS.

1. Because of its value. It comes laden With blessings to him who receives it.
2. Because of its freedom. It may be taken without money and without price.

3. Because of its availableness. It is easy of access, being on the level of the worst sinner.
4. Because of its universality. Whosoever will may take it and live.
5. Because of the security of its blessings. They are given forevermore. "Verily, verily, I say unto you, he that heareth My Word, and believeth on Him that sent Me, hath everlasting life, and shall not perish."
6. Because of the eternity of its blessings. The sun will have burnt itself into ashes, the earth will have been destroyed by volcanic heat, the heavens will be changed When salvation has only begun. Then thousand times ten thousand years shall pass away, and we shall have only begun a little to understand what salvation means. Blessed be God for the Gospel of Christ's salvation.

VII. CONSIDERATIONS WHICH SHOULD URGE US TO TAKE AND GIVE OUT THIS SALVATION.

1. Because of the fact that every man's salvation is hinged upon his own choice and free will. It is an awful thing to have the power to take salvation and to throw it away. And yet it is left to our choice. We are not forced to take it. We must voluntarily choose it or reject it.
2. Because of the tremendous responsibility to which we are held accountable for the salvation of our soul. God has put it into our hands as a jewel of inestimable value, and He will hold us to a strict account for the way we treat this precious thing. If we destroy it, how fearful will be our doom when we meet the Judge of all the earth, and hear the stern question from His lips, "Where is thy soul?"
3. Because of the guilt which will rest upon us for neglecting and despising the precious blood of Christ, which was shed for our salvation. To neglect it is to throw it away. He has

provided a great salvation. If it is worth so much to man, if it has cost God so much to provide it, what can be thought of him who makes little of it? Jesus suffered intensely to bring it to us, and shall we stumble carelessly over it? Oh, let us be more concerned than we are, both for the salvation of our own souls and for those around us who are not saved.

4. Because the little word "now" is always linked with it. It must be taken now or never. The cycle of life is very narrow. We do not know how soon it will end. "Behold now is the day of salvation."

5. Because its issues are for eternity. The decisions there are not reversible. The soul cannot come back when once it has left the body, and have another chance to secure its salvation. When once the Master has risen up and shut the door, the soul will find it has been left out for ever. The cry will then be, "I have lost my chance; it is too late." God's Word holds out no second chance to any human soul.

6. Because if salvation is missed there will be no excuse for it. Not one thing has been left undone in presenting it to men. God's best thought and Christ's best love have been given to it. All has been done that could be done. Salvation has been brought down to man's level. It has been placed where he can reach it. God has provided all the resources, even the grace, repentance and faith, if man will take them. If you lack anything, God will put His arms around you and lift you up to Him, breathing His faith into you, and carrying you Himself until you are able to walk. Salvation is brought to every sinner. If the soul is lost it is because it has neglected and defied God's love.

I am glad to bring you this salvation, but eternity will be too short to tell it all. Take it and then go out and gather others in to share it. You will receive a glorious crown, but the best of it all will be that men will be saved.

The Fourfold Gospel

In this city there is a picture hung up in a parlor and expensively framed. It is a very simple picture. It has just one word on it. On a little bit of paper-a telegraph form-is the one word,

SAVED!

It was framed by the lady of that mansion, and is dearer to her than all her works of art. One day when the awful news came to her through the papers that the ship on which her husband had sailed was a perfect wreck, that little telegram came to her door and saved her from despair.

It came across the sea. It was the message of that rescued man by the electric wire, and it meant to two hearts all that life is worth.

Oh, let such a message go up to-day to yonder shore. The Holy Ghost will flash it hence while I am drawing the next breath. The angels will echo it over heaven, and there are dear friends there to whom it will mean as much as their own very heaven.

I have seen another short sentence in a picture, too.

It came from one who had been rescued from a ship where friends and family had all perished. Those dear little ones were in the slimy caves of the cruel sea. Those beloved faces had gone down forever, but he was saved, and from yonder shore he sent back this sad and weary message:

SAVED ALONE!

So I can imagine a selfish Christian entering yonder portals. They meet him at the gates, "Where are your dear ones?" "Where are your friends?" "Where is your crown?" "Alas, I am saved alone." God help you, reader, to so receive and give, that you shall save yourself and others also.

> "Must I go, and empty handed,
> Must I thus my Saviour meet,
> Not one soul with which to greet Him,
> Lay no trophy at His feet?"

Chapter 2.
CHRIST OUR SANCTIFIER

"And for their sakes I sanctify myself, that they also might be sanctified through the truth." John xvii. 19.

The marginal reading of the last clause is, "That they also might be truly sanctified." This seems to imply that there is something, which passes in the world for holiness, which is not true sanctification. There are counterfeit forms of Christian life, and also defective forms, which do not represent all that the fulness of Christ is able to do for us. Sanctification is the second step in the Four-fold Gospel.

1. WHAT IT IS NOT.

We will look first at what it is not. There are good elements and even holy elements in Christian character, which are not sanctification.

1. It is not regeneration. Sanctification is not conversion. It is a great and blessed thing to become a Christian. It is never a matter of small account. To be saved eternally is cause for eternal joy; but the soul must also enter into sanctification. They are not the same. Regeneration is the be-ginning. It is the germ of the seed, but it is not the summer fullness of the plant. The heart has not yet gained entire victory over the old elements of sin. It is sometimes overcome by them. Regeneration is like building a house and having the work done well. Sanctification is having the owner come and dwell in it and fill it with gladness, and life, and beauty. Many Christians are converted and stop there. They do not go on to the fullness of their life in Christ, and so are in danger of losing what they already possess. Germany brought in the grand truth of justification by faith through the teachings of Martin Luther, but he failed to go on to the deeper teachings of the Christian

life. What was the result? Germany to-day is cold and lifeless, and the very hot-bed of rationalism and all its attendant evils. How different it has been in England! The labors of men like Wesley, and Baxter, and Whitfield, who understood the mission of the Holy Spirit, have led the Christian life of England, and America, her offspring, into deeper and more permanent channels. You will find that the men and women who do not press on in their Christian experience to gain the fullness of their inheritance in Him, will often become cold and formal. The evil in their own heart will assert itself again and will be very likely to overcome them, and their work will bring confusion and disaster to the cause of Christ. If they escape the result, it will be as by fire. You have doubtless noticed young Christians who have seemed to be marvelously converted and filled with the love of God, but they have not entered into the deeper life of Christ, and in an evil hour they failed. They had gained a new heart, but they had neglected to get the deeper teaching and life which Christ has for all His children.

2. Sanctification is not morality, nor any attainments of character. There is very much that is lovely in human life which is not sanctification. A man cannot build up a good human character himself and then call it the work of God. It will not stand the strain that is sure to come upon it. Only the house that is founded upon the Rock of Ages will abide securely in the wrath of the elements.

3. Sanctification is not your own work; it is not a gradual attainment which you can grow into by your own efforts. If you should be able to build such a structure yourself, and add to it year after year until it was completed, would you not then stand off with a pardonable pride and look upon it as your own work? No, dear friends, you cannot grow into sanctification. You will grow after you are in it into a fuller, riper and more mature development of life in Christ, but you must take it at its commencement as a gift, not as a growth. It is an obtain-

ment, not an attainment. You cannot sanctify yourselves. The only thing to do is to give yourself wholly to God, a voluntary sacrifice. This is intensely important. It is but a light thing to do for Him. But He must do the work of cleansing and filling.

4. Sanctification is not the work of death. It is strange that any one should think there could be a sanctifying influence in the dying struggle. Yet many have lived in that delusion for years. They expect that the cold sweat of that last hour and the convulsive throbbing of the sinking heart will somehow place them in the arms of their Sanctifier. This comes in some degree from the old idea that their sin is seated in the body- the old Manichaen teaching that the flesh is unholy, and if we were once rid of the body, the fleshless tenant would be free from sin and would spring at once into boundless purity. There is no sin in these bones and flesh and ligaments. If you cast off your hand you have lost no sin. If both hands are gone you are as sinful as ever. If you cut off your head and yield up your life, sin would still remain in the soul. Sin is not in the body, it is in the heart, and the soul, and the will. Divest yourself of this body of clay, and the spirit will still be left, a hard, rebellious, sinful thing. Death will not sanctify it. It is a poor time to be converted. It will be a poorer time to be sanctified. I would not advise any one to put off their salvation to the dying hour, when the heart is oppressed and the brain clouded, and the mind has need of confidence and rest and a sense of victory to enable it to enter into His presence with fullness of joy. Nor is it a better time for the deeper work of the Holy Ghost. Sanctification should be entered into intelligently when the mind is clear. It is a deliberate act calling for the calm exercise of all the faculties working under the controlling influence of the Divine Spirit.

5. Sanctification is not self-perfection. We shall never become. so inherently good that there will be no possibility or temptation to sin. We shall never reach a place where we shall not need

each moment to abide in Him. The instant we feel able to live without Him, there comes up a separate life within us which is not a sanctified life. The reason the exalted spirits in heaven fell from their high estate was, perhaps, because they became conscious of their own beauty, and pride arose in their hearts. They looked at themselves, and became as gods unto themselves. The moment you or I become conscious that we are strong or pure, that instant the work of disintegration begins. It has made us independent of Him, and we have separated ourselves from the life of Christ. We must be simple, empty vessels, open channels for His life to flow through. Then Christ's perfection will be made over to us. And we shall grow ever less and less in ourselves, as He becomes more and more within us.

6. Sanctification is not a state of emotion. It is not an ecstasy or a sensation. It resides in the will and purpose of life. It is a practical conformity of life and conduct to the will and character of God. The will must choose God. The purpose of the heart must be to yield to Him, to please and obey Him. That is the important thing, to love, to choose and to do His holy will. You cannot have that spirit in you and fail to be happy. The spirit that craves mere sensational joy has yet an unholy self-life. It must get out of that form of self and into God before it can receive much from Him.

II. WHAT SANCTIFICATION IS.

Let us look at the positive side.

1. It is separation from sin. That is the root idea of the word. The sanctified Christian is separated from sin, from an evil world, even from his own self, and from anything that would be a separating cause between him and Christ in the new life. It does not mean that sin and Satan are to be destroyed. God does not yet bring the millennium, but He puts a line of demarcation between the sanctified soul and all that is unholy. The great trouble with Christians is they try to destroy evil.

They think if sin could be really decapitated and Satan slain they would be supremely happy. It is a surprise to many of them after conversion that God still lets the devil live. He has nowhere promised that He will kill Satan, but He has promised to put a broad, deep Jordan between the Christian and sin. The only thing to do with it is to repudiate it and let it alone. There is sin enough in the world to destroy us all, if we take it in. The air is full of it, as the air in some of our Western States is full of soot from the soft coal that is burned there. It will be so to the end of time, but God means you and me, beloved, to be separated from it in our spirit.

2. Sanctification means also dedication to God. That is the root idea of the word also. It is separation from sin and dedication unto God. A sanctified Christian is wholly yielded to God to please Him in every particular; his first thought always is, "Thy will be done"; his one desire that he may please God and do His holy will. This is the thought expressed by the word consecration. In the Old Testament all things which were set apart to God were called sanctified, even if there had been no sin in them before. The Tabernacle was sanctified; it had never sinned, but it was dedicated to God. In the same sense all the vessels of the Tabernacle were sanctified. They were set apart to a holy use. Dear friends, God expects something more of us than simply to be separated from sin. That is only negative goodness. He expects that we shall be wholly dedicated to Him, having it the supreme wish of our heart to love and honor and please Him. Are we fulfilling His expectations in this?

3. Sanctification includes conformity to the likeness of God. We are to be in His image, and stamped with the impress of Jesus Christ.

4. Sanctification means conformity also to the will as well as the likeness of God. A sanctified Christian is submissive and obedient. He desires the Divine will above everything else in life as kinder and wiser for him than anything else can

be. He is conscious that he misses something if he misses it. He knows it will promote his highest good far more than his own will, crying instinctively, "Thy will be done."

> "Thou sweet, beloved will of God,
> On thee I lay me down and rest,
> As babe upon its mother's breast."

5. Sanctification means love, supreme love to God and all mankind. This is the fulfilling of the law. It is the spring of all obedience, the fountain from which all right things flow. We cannot be conformed to the image of God without love, for God is Love. This is, perhaps, the strongest feature in a truly sanctified life. It clothes all the other virtues with softness and warmth. It takes the icy peaks of a cold and naked consecration and covers them with mosses and verdure. It sends bright sunlight into the heart, making everything warm and full of life, which would otherwise be cold and desolate. The savage was able to stand before his enemies and be cut to pieces with stoical firmness that disdained to cry, but his indifference was like some stony cliff. It was not the warm, tender love of the heart of Jesus, which made Him bow meekly to His painful death because it was His Father's will. It was the spontaneous, glad outflowing of His loving heart. Dear friends, if we are so filled with love to God, it will flow out to others, and we shall love our neighbors as we love ourselves.

III. THE SOURCE OF SANCTIFICATION.

The heart and soul of the whole matter is seeing that Jesus is Himself our sanctification. We must not look at it merely as some great mountain peak where He is standing and which we have to climb, but between us and it there are almost inaccessible cliffs to ascend before we can stand at His side. But Jesus Himself becomes our sanctification. "For their sakes I sanctify Myself, that they also may be truly sanctified." It seems as though He was a little afraid His followers would get to looking for sanctification apart from Himself, and knowing that it could never reach them except through Him, He said, "I sanctify Myself."

1. He has purchased it for us. It is part of the fruit of Calvary. By one offering He hath perfected forever them that are sanctified. "By the which will we are sanctified through the offering of the body of Jesus Christ once for all."

2. It does not come to us by our efforts, but it is made over to us as the purchase of His death upon the cross. It is ours by the purchase of Jesus just as much as forgiveness is. You have as much right to be holy and sanctified as you have to be saved. You can go to God and claim it as your inheritance as much as you can your pardon for sin. If you do not have it you are falling short of your redemption privileges.

3. Sanctification is to be received as one of the free gifts God desires to bestow upon us. If it is not a gift, then it is not a part of redemption. If it is a part of redemption, then it is as free as the blood of Jesus.

4. It comes through the personal indwelling of Jesus. He does not put righteousness into the heart simply, but He comes there personally Himself to live. Words are weak; they, indeed, are utterly inadequate to express this thought. When we arrive at complete despair of all other ways we learn this truth. And Jesus Christ Himself comes into the heart and lives His own life there, and so becomes the sanctification of the soul. This is the meaning of the text. It is to His people that Jesus sanctifies Himself, and any who try to live a sanctified life apart from Him are not truly sanctified. They must take Jesus in as their life to be truly sanctified. That is the personal sense of divine holiness. "But of Him are ye in Christ Jesus, who of God is made unto us wisdom, and righteousness, and sanctification, and redemption." Jesus is made unto us of God wisdom. He is the true philosophy, the eternal *Sophia,* far above the deepest philosophy, righteousness, sanctification and redemption. So

Jesus in our heart becomes our wisdom. He does not improve us, and make us something to be wondered at. But He just comes in us and lives as He did of old in His Galilean ministry.

When the tabernacle was finished the Holy Ghost came down and possessed it, and dwelt in a burning fire upon the ark of the covenant, between the cherubim. God lived there after it was dedicated to Him. So when we are dedicated to God, He comes to live in us and transfuses His life through all our being. He that came into Mary's breast, He that came down in power upon the disciples at Pentecost comes to you and me when we are fully dedicated to Him, as really as though we should see Him come fluttering down in visible form yonder upon our shoulder. He comes from yonder world to live within us as truly as though we were visibly dwelling under His shadow. God does come to dwell in the heart and live His holy life within us. In the 36th of Ezekiel we have this promise: "I will sprinkle clean water upon you." That is forgiveness; old sins are all blotted out. "A new heart also will I give you"; that is regeneration. "I will put My Spirit within you, and cause you to walk in My statutes, and ye shall keep My judgments and do them"; ah! that is something more than regeneration and forgiveness. It is the living God come to live in the new heart. It is the Holy Spirit dwelling in the heart of flesh that God has given, so that every movement, every thought, every intention, every desire of our whole being will be prompted by the springing life of God within. It is God manifest in the flesh again. This is the only true consummation of sanctification. Thus only can man enter completely into the life of holiness. As we are thus possessed by the Holy Spirit we are made par-takers of the Divine nature. It is a sacred thing for any man or woman to enter into this relation with God. It places the humblest and most unattractive creature upon the throne with Him. If we know that God is thus dwelling within us, we will bow before the majesty of that sacred presence. We will not dare to profane it by sin. There will be a hush upon our hearts, and we will walk with bowed heads and conscious of the jewel we carry within our hearts. Do you know what it is to have Christ thus sanctified to you, beloved? Do you know personally what it is to be wholly dedicated to Him, and to hear Him say to you, "For your sake I sanctify Myself that you may be truly sanctified"?

IV. HOW IT IS RECEIVED.

1. We must have a Divine revelation of our own need of sanctification before we will seek to obtain it. We must see for ourselves that we are not sanctified, and that we must be sanctified if we would be happy. The first thing God does often to bring us where we will see this, is to make us thoroughly ashamed of ourselves by letting us fall into mistakes and by bringing our frailties to our notice. In these humiliating self-revealings we are able to see where we are not righteous, and we are made to learn that we cannot keep our resolutions of amendment that we make in our own strength. God has let His dear children learn this lesson all through the ages, and learn it by repeated failures, and each of us must ever learn it for himself.

2. We must come to see Jesus as our Sanctifier. If with one breath we cry out, "O wretched man that I am! who shall deliver me from the body of this death?" with the next we must add, "I thank God through Jesus Christ, my Lord." We must see in Him that great Deliverer, and know that He is able to meet our every need and supply it.

3. We must make an entire surrender to Him in everything. We must give ourselves to Him thoroughly, definitely and unconditionally, and have it graven in the heart, as if it were written on the rocks, or painted on the sky. Cut it deeply in the annals of your recollection. Always remember that on that day and on that hour I gave myself fully to Christ and He became entirely mine.

4. We must believe that He receives the consecration we make. He is as earnest and as willing and as real about it as you are. Amid the hush of heaven He stoops to hear your vows, and He whispers when you have finished, "It is done. I will give to him of the fountain of the water of life freely. He that overcometh shall inherit all things."

Many people make a mistake about some of these steps. Some of them are clinging to a little of their old goodness and therefore meet with failures. Others stumble at the second step. They do not see that Jesus is their complete Sanctifier. And many cannot take the third step and make a complete surrender of everything to Him. Multitudes fail even when they have taken these steps in not being able to believe that Jesus receives them. Keep these four steps clear. "I am dead, my own life is surrendered and buried out of sight. Jesus is my Sanctifier and my all-in-all. I surrender everything into His hand for Him to do with as He thinks best. I believe He receives the dedication I make to Him. I believe He will be in me all I need in this life or in the world to come." I am certain, dear friends, when you have taken these four steps you can never be as you were before. Something has been done which can never be undone. You have become the Lord's. His presence has come into your heart; it may be like a little trickling spring upon the mountain side, but it will become great rivers of depth and power.

V. PRACTICAL STEPS

by which this life of sanctification is lived out day by day.

1. We are to live a life of implicit obedience to God, doing always what He bids and being henceforth wholly under His direction.
2. We are to be ever hearkening diligently to His voice. We will need to listen closely, for Jesus speaks softly.
3. In every time of conflict or temptation or testing, we are to draw near to God and give the matter over to Him. Instead

of the sweet and happy experiences you would naturally expect after such a consecration, the devil comes and tries to shake your confidence by some trial or temptation. Stand in Him and rejoice that He counts you worthy to receive such trials. If you fail, don't say it is no use to try further. The principle is right. Perhaps you tried to do the work yourself and so you failed. Stop and lay it all at His feet and start afresh, and learn to abide in Him from your very failure. Israel, after their defeat at Ai, were stronger for the next conflict. Try to live out the secret you have learned. In human art there is always stumbling at first. You can learn the principles of stenography in a very little while, a few hours perhaps, but it takes months of patient practice to become expert at it. At one of our Western meetings recently, a lady was taking verbatim reports of the addresses. She was sitting at a little table with an instrument they call a stenograph. By touching the keys of this instrument a little needle cut impressions on a paper ribbon, representing with perfect accuracy the words that were spoken. She was able to learn the principle in a few hours, but it took many more hours of quiet practice before she was so accustomed to it that she could do it easily. The moment we are consecrated to Jesus Christ we learn the secret that He is to be all-in-all to us. But when we try to practice this truth, we find that it takes time and patience to learn it thoroughly. We must learn to lean on Him. We must learn little by little how to take Him for every need. The principle is perfect. It will become absolutely unfailing in practice. Remember the secret is, "Without Me ye can do nothing." "I can do all things in Christ, who strengtheneth me."

Chapter 3.
CHRIST OUR HEALER

"Jesus Christ the same yesterday, to-day and forever."
Heb. xiii. 8.

1. WHAT DIVINE HEALING IS NOT.

We will look at its negative side first. Wherever good is to be found a counterfeit of it also will soon appear. Any valuable coin is always imitated, and the great forger has been at work on this also. It is particularly necessary with this precious truth to guard against error.

1. Divine healing is not medical healing.. It does not come to us through medicines, nor is it God's especial blessing on remedies and means. It is the direct power of the Almighty hand of God Himself. "HIMSELF took our infirmities," and He is able to carry them without man's help. We have nothing to say against the use of remedies so far as those are concerned who are not ready to trust their bodies fully to the Lord. For them it is well enough to use all the help that nature and science can give, and we cheerfully admit that their remedies have some value as far as they go. There is some power in man's attempts to stop the tides of evil that sweep over a suffering world. But there comes a point in all efforts when we have to say, "Thus far shalt thou go and no further." Yet no one ought rashly to give up these human helps until they have got a better one. Unless they have been led to trust Christ entirely for something higher and stronger than their natural life, they had better stick to natural remedies. They need to be sure that God's Word distinctly presents healing for disease, and does it as definitely as it does forgiveness of sin.

2. Divine healing is not metaphysical healing. It is not a system of rationalism, which is taking on so many forms in the world today, like the chameleon, assuming the hue of the surrounding foliage, according to the class of people it comes in contact with. What is commonly known as mind cure or Christian Science, is one of the most familiar forms of metaphysical healing. In Chicago they call it the Science of Life, but it is practically the same thing. It puts knowledge and intellect, or the mind of man in the place of God. It is not healing by remedies, but by mental force. It is a system of false philosophy and a skeptical theology; a philosophy that is absurd and misleading, and a theology which is atheistic and infidel. The basis of it is, that the material world is not real. What seem to be facts are simply ideas. This church is only a circular idea in my brain, and you chance to have the same idea in yours, and so we call it a church; but it is not, it is only an idea. As you sit there before me you are not there in tangible form, but I have an idea of you in my brain, as sitting there. I am not here either in any physical sense, but I, too, am an idea lodged in your mind. So the teachers of this error go on to say that there is no body. Disease, therefore, is not real because it has no basis to work on. If you accept this philosophy, the bottom will drop out of all disease. If the idea of sickness has gone from your mind, the trouble has gone. This is a frank, candid statement of the principles of this theory. It has captivated hundreds of thousands of people in this country and hundreds of thousands of dollars have been made out of it. It is the old philosophy of Hume revived again. The Bible is treated by these teachers in the same way as the body. It is a beautiful system of ideas, but they are only ideas. Genesis is a beautiful story of creation, but it is only an allegory. The New Testament contains a charming picture of Jesus Christ, but it, too, has no foundation in fact. It is the old errors that the Apostle John wrote strongly against.

"Every spirit that confesseth not that Jesus Christ is come in the flesh, is not of God; and this is that spirit of Antichrist, whereof ye have heard that it should come; and even now already is it in the world." This philosophy denies that Jesus Christ has come in the flesh. It denies the reality of Christ's body; therefore, it is anti-Christian in its teaching. This is *not* Divine healing. There is no fellowship between the two. It is one of the delusions of science, falsely so called. It would undermine Christianity. Some of us have despised it so much that perhaps we have not guarded others against it as we should. We have felt it was so silly there could be no harm in it; but we forget how silly human nature is. The apostle tells us the wise in this world are fools with God. "He taketh the wise in their own craftiness." How truly this has been fulfilled in the case of New England! That land of colleges, the seat of American intelligence and culture, has given birth to this monstrosity. It is the most fatal infidelity. It does away entirely with the atonement, for as there is no sin there can be no redemption. I would rather be sick all my life with every form of physical torment, than be healed by such a lie.

3. Divine healing is not magnetic healing. It is not a mysterious current which flows into one body from another. It is a serious question whether there is such a force in nature as animal magnetism, and whether what this seems to be, is not rather an influence to which one person's mind is subject from causes within itself. Whether this is so or not, the thought or claim of such an influence is repudiated by all who act as true ministers of Divine healing. Such a one is most anxious to keep his own personality out of the consciousness of the sufferer, and hold the eye of the invalid only on Christ, that he may take his healing from Him. There is nothing to be so much feared in this work as becoming the object of attention. It is heart to heart, and soul to soul contact with the living Christ, and with Him alone, that will accomplish the result.

4. Divine healing is not spiritualism. It cannot be denied that Satan has a certain power over the human body. Certainly he must have if he is able to possess it with disease. And, if he has power to inflict ill health upon the body, I see no reason why he should not, if he please, open the back door and get out and leave the body well. If Satan had power to bind a woman in Christ's time for eighteen years, he had power to unbind her just as quickly. If sickness was his work then, it must surely be the same now. If he can use some persons better if they are strong and well, he will do so. Other instruments he can use better in weakness and pain. We cannot but notice the strange persistency with which people of all ages have resorted to evil power, either to appease them or enlist their help. The custom is as old as the earliest races. We find it with the wild Indian in the forest, and the equally savage African. Particularly have these wild incantations been performed for the healing of sickness, and it is said that many of them have actually resulted in the removal of the disease. There can be no question that great multitudes of spiritualistic phenomena are real. They give positive evidence of the reality of evil spirits, and they are proofs of God's terrible forewarning, that in the last days the spirits of devils shall be upon the earth working miracles, so that, if possible, they shall deceive the very elect. God's true child will not be deluded by them. If you are deceived about this thing, look out! You may not be God's true child. I warn you as you value your true welfare, avoid this seductive snare. You will find in it some reality, but it is a dangerous power and it will submerge your Christian faith beneath its hideous waves.

5. Divine healing is not prayer cure. There are many Christians who greatly desire others to pray for them. If they can secure a certain quantity of prayer there will come a corresponding influence for good upon them, and if all the Christians in the

The Fourfold Gospel

world were to pray for them, they would expect to be healed. There is a general notion that there is a great deal of power in prayer which must have an effect if it can be concentrated. And if enough of it could be obtained, it would remove mountains and perhaps be able to break down God's stubborn will. This is practically what this view teaches. There is no power in prayer unless it is the prayer of God Himself. Unless you are in contact with Christ the living Healer, there is no healing. Christ's healing is by His own Divine touch. It is not prayer cure, but Christ-healing.

6. Divine healing is not faith cure. The term gives a wrong impression, and I am glad it has been discarded. There is danger of getting one's mind so concentrated on faith that it may come between the soul and God. You might as well expect your faith to heal you, as to attempt to drink from the handle of the chain pump with which you get fresh water, or to eat the tray upon which your dinner is brought. If you get to looking at your faith, you will lose the faith itself. It is God who heals always. The less we dwell on the prayers, the faith, or any of the means through which it comes, the more likely we will be to receive the blessing.

7. Divine healing is not will power. No person can grapple with his own helplessness and turn it over into strength. It is a principle of mechanics that no body can move itself. There must be some power outside of itself to do this. Archimedes said he would be able to pry up the world if he could get some power outside of it to operate on it; but he could not do it from the inside. If man is down, all the power in his own soul will not avail to lift him up. The trouble too often is in his will. He tries to take hold of himself and lift himself up. He must have some power outside of himself to lift him, or he will remain down. The will must be yielded up to Christ, and then He will work in us to will and do of His good plea-

sure. Then the first thought will be-how easy, how delightfully simple it is to receive the power from Him which we need. It is only touching God's hand and receiving strength from His life.

8. Divine healing is not defiance of God's will. It is not saying, "I will have this blessing whether He wills it or not." It is seeing that in having it we have His highest purpose for us. We will not trust for physical healing till we know it is God's will for us, then we can say, "I will it, because He wills it."

9. Neither is it physical immortality, but it is fullness of life until the life work is done, and then receiving our complete resurrection life at the coming of Christ.

10. Divine healing is not a mercenary medical profession that men adopt as they would adopt a trade or profession in order to make something out of it. If you find the mercenary idea appearing in it for a moment, discountenance and repudiate it. All the gifts of God are as free as the blood of Calvary.

II. WHAT DIVINE HEALING IS.

1. It is the supernatural Divine power of God infused into human bodies, renewing their strength and replacing the weakness of suffering human frames by the life and power of God. It is a touch of the Divine omnipotence, and nothing short of it. It is the same power that raised Jairus' daughter from the dead or converted your soul. Is it strange that God should show such power? More power is required to regenerate a lost soul than to raise the dead. God could shiver the sepulchre and bring out the forms of those who have laid there for years with less expenditure of power than it costs Him to redeem one soul, and keep His saints steadfast unto the end.

2. It is founded, not on the reasoning of man, or the testimony of those who have been healed, but on the Word of God alone.

All the testimony that could be gathered from the whole universe would not establish the truth of such a doctrine, if it is not to be found in the Scriptures. All the deductions of the human intellect are worthless if they are not rooted there. This truth rests on God's eternal Word, or it is merely human.

3. It ever recognizes the will of God, and bows to that in profound submission. A Christian who is looking for Divine healing will wait till he knows the will of God, and having learned that, he will claim it without wavering. If a sufferer is convinced that the work God gave him to do is done, and that now he is called home, then he should acquiesce in that will and lie down in those blessed arms and rest. If that conviction has come to any of you, dear friends, I would not dare to shake you out of it, if you have been led into it by God. My only thought would be to sweetly smooth your last pillow, and let you depart in peace. If, however, you think your work is not done, if you have not clear light from God that this is so, if there is a true and submissive desire in your heart to live and finish your course with joy, then He who said nearly two thousand years ago, "Ought not this woman to be loosed from this infirmity?" is the same to-day as He was then. He is saying to you in the midst of your weakness, "Ought you not to be made well?" Surely that should be enough.

It may be, however, that your sickness has been allowed to come as a discipline. You may have been holding back part of the full testimony or service Christ has called you to. I am afraid, then, you cannot be healed till that difficulty is made right. You may be in some wrong and crooked attitude. He probably will not restore you till that is adjusted. He may have called you to some service and you are holding back. There will not be healing for the body till you have yielded at this point. There are hundreds of meanings in the sicknesses that are allowed to come upon God's dear children, and He will show you what His voice is for you. "For God speaketh once, yea twice, yet man perceiveth it not. In a dream, in a vision of the night, when deep sleep falleth upon me in slumberings upon the bed, then He openeth the ears of men, and sealeth their instruction, that He may withdraw man from his purpose, and hide pride from man. He keepeth back his soul from the pit, and his life from perishing by the sword. He is chastened also with pain upon his bed, and the multitude of his bones with strong pain; so that his life abhoreth bread, and his soul dainty meat. His flesh is consumed away, that it cannot be seen; and his bones that were not seen, stick out. Yea, his soul draweth near unto the grave, and his life to the destroyers. If there be a messenger with him, and interpreter, one among a thousand, to show unto man his uprightness, then he is gracious unto him, and saith, 'Deliver him from going down to the pit: I have found a ransom. His flesh shall be fresher than a child's; he shall return to the days of his youth." That is the meaning of many of God's chastenings. There is much that He would say to men through His dealings with their bodies, and it is necessary to get their full meaning into the soul before Divine healing can be received, and kept after it has been received. It is not a cast-iron patent that works inexorably in one way always; it requires a walk that is very close with God. When the soul is thus walking in harmony and obedience to Him, the life of God can fully flow into the body. Thank God, we cannot have it and have the devil, too.

4. Divine healing is part of the redemption work of Jesus Christ. It is one of the things He came to bring. Its foundation stone is the cross of Calvary. "He redeemeth thy life from destruction." "Deliver him from going down to death, I have found a ransom." Surely that healing comes from Himself alone.

"By His stripes we are healed." That is the redemption work of Christ. You have a right to it, beloved, for His body bore all the liability of your body on the cross. Take it and love Him better, because it came from His stripes. I love to think of that word as being in the singular number, stripe. That is the Greek meaning. His body was so beaten that it was all one stripe. There was not an inch of His flesh but was lacerated for us. There is not a fibre of your body but Christ has suffered there to redeem it.

5. Divine healing comes to us through the life of Jesus Christ, who rose from the dead in His own body. He has gone up to heaven with His living body. You can see Him there this morning, with hands and feet of living flesh and bones, which you could handle. He could sit with you at the table and eat today as He did of old. He is no shadowy cloud-like form, but He has flesh and bones as we have. That is our Christ, a living physical Christ, and He is able and willing to share His physical life with you, by breathing into you His strength. We are healed by the life of Christ in our body. It is a tender union with Him; nearer than the bond of connubial oneness; so near that the very life of His veins is transfused into yours. That is Divine healing.

6. It is the work of the Holy Spirit, quickening the body. When Christ healed the sick while He was upon earth, it was not by the Deity that dwelt in His humanity. He said, "If I cast out devils by the Spirit of God, then the Kingdom of God is come unto you." Jesus healed by the Holy Ghost. "The Spirit of the Lord is upon me, because He hath anointed me to preach the Gospel to the poor, to heal the broken hearts." The Holy Ghost is the agent, then, by which this great power is wrought. Especially should we expect to see His working in these days, because they are the days of His own Dispensation, the days in which it has been prophesied that there

shall be signs and wonders. How did Samson receive his strength? When the Spirit of the Lord came upon him. Then he was able to hurl the temple into ruins and their god Dagon with it. The Spirit of God was in his flesh. So when this electric fire is running through our frame, it brings healing and strength to every fibre.

7. Divine healing comes by the grace of God, not through the work of man. It cannot be bought, neither can it be worked for. We cannot help God out in it. We must take it as a gift. It comes to us as pardon does, a free gift from Him.

8. It comes to us by faith. It is not the faith that heals. God heals, but faith receives it. We believe that God is healing before any evidence is given. It is to be believed as a present reality, and then ventured on. We are to act as if it were already true. God wants us to lean on Him, and trust Him, and then rejoice and praise Him for what He has given, with no doubt or fear.

9. Divine healing is in accordance with all he facts of Church history. From the time of Irenaeus down to the present century there have been repeated examples of it. It is a long array, and great multitudes of healed ones proclaim with one voice: "Jesus Christ, the same yesterday, and today, and forever." All down through the middle ages the pure Church believed this truth and taught it. The Waldenses held it as an article of their faith. The times of the early Reformers are full of it. The lives of Luther and Baxter, and Fox and Whitfield, and John Wesley, give clear and convincing testimony that they believed this truth. In later times the examples of it are numerous. Germany, Switzerland, Sweden, Norway, England and her colonies, and the mission fields of the world, have many witnesses to the healing power of Jesus. Our own land, and even our own city, are full of it. You have many witnesses to it here in your midst. You

know them, and how some of them have stood the test of publicity and of years. They are not obscure cases. Many of them are men and women who have stood in the very front of Christian work. There is every kind of character and intelligence and temperament and disposition among them. There are children among them, as well as old men. Some of them have had lofty intellects, but they have been transformed into simple children. There are all classes of disease among them-from the terrible cancer to the most disordered of nervous organisms. And He has healed them all.

10. Divine healing is one of the signs of the age. It is the forerunner of Christ's coming. It is God's answer to the infidelity of today. Man may try to reason it down with the force of his intellect. God meets it with this unanswerable proof of His power.

III. HOW IS JESUS OUR HEALER.

1. Because He has bought healing for us with His stripes. It is a part of His purchased redemption on Calvary. "Surely, He hath borne our sicknesses and carried our pains."

2. Because it is in His risen life in us. We have healing not only from Jesus, but in Jesus. It is in His living body, and we receive it as we abide in Him and keep it only as we abide in Him.

3. Because He enables us to take it by becoming our power to believe. He gives the faith to trust Him if we will receive it. We have not to climb the heights to find Him, but He comes down to our helplessness and becomes our trust as well as our healing. A Chinaman was once telling the difference between Christ and Confucius and Buddha. He said: "I was down in a deep pit, half sunk in the mire and was crying for some one to help me out. As I looked up I saw a venerable, grey-haired man looking down at me. His countenance bore

the marks of his pure and holy spirit. 'My son,' he said, 'this is a dreadful place.' 'Yes,' I said, 'I fell into it. Can't you help me out?' 'My son,' he said, 'I am Confucius. If you had read my books and followed what they taught, you never would have been here.' 'Yes, father,' I said, 'but can't you help me out?' As I looked up he was gone. Soon I saw another form approaching, and another man bent over me, this time with closed eyes and folded arms. He seemed to be looking into some far-off, distant place. 'My son,' he said, 'just close your eyes and fold your arms and forget all about yourself. Get into a state of perfect rest. Don't think about anything that could disturb. Get so still that nothing can move you. Then, my child, you will be in such delicious rest as I am. 'Yes, father,' I answered, 'I'll do that when I am above ground. Can't you help me out?' But Buddha, too, was gone. I was just beginning to sink into despair when I saw another figure above me, different from the others. He was very simple, and looked just like the rest of us, but there were the marks of suffering in His face. I cried out to Him: 'Oh, Father, can you help me?' 'My child,' He said, 'what is the matter?' Before I could answer Him, He was down in the mire by my side; He folded His arms about me and lifted me up, and then He fed and rested me. When I was well, He did not say, 'Now, don't do that again,' but He said, 'We will walk on together now;' and we have been walking together until this day."

That's what Jesus Christ will do for you, beloved! He comes down to you where you are. He becomes your trust within you, and then you go on together until the resurrection light and glory of the coming age bursts in upon you. May God help us all to receive Him thus fully for His own name's sake! Amen.

Chapter 4.
CHRIST OUR COMING LORD

"I will give him the morning star." Rev. ii. 28.

The Second Coming of the Lord Jesus Christ is a distinct and important part of the Apostolic Gospel. "I declare unto you the Gospel," Paul says to the Corinthians, and then begins to tell them of the Resurrection and the Second Advent. It is, indeed, good news to all who love Him and mourn the sins and sorrows of a ruined world.

It is the glorious culmination of all other parts of the Gospel. We have spoken of the Gospel of SALVATION, but Peter says our salvation is "ready to be revealed in the last time." Then only, when we stand amid the wreck of time and secure upon the Rock of Ages,

> "Then, Lord, shall we fully know,
> Not till then, how much we owe."

We have spoken of SANCTIFICATION, but John says: "When He shall appear, we shall be like Him, and every man that hath this hope in him purifieth himself, even as He is pure." And we have spoken of DIVINE HEALING, but Paul says: "God hath given us the 'EARNEST' of the resurrection in our bodies now," and Divine healing is but the first-springing life of which the resurrection will be the full fruition.

So that the truth and hope of the Lord's coming is linked with all truth and life, and is the Church's great and blessed hope. In the very beginning of human history God placed this great hope before His children. In the hour when man fell from Paradise, God erected in that fallen Eden in the majestic figures of THE CHERUBIM, the prophecy and symbol of man's future glory. The faces of the lion, the ox, the man, and the eagle, were the types of royalty, the strength, the wisdom, and the lofty elevation to which redeemed man was to rise in Jesus. These figures run through all the dispensations. They are God's portrait of His redeemed child after redemption's work is done. God sets before Himself and before man His sublime ideal for his future, and He will never rest till it is fulfilled. It is, therefore, well that besides the Gospel for the present, we should understand, and live under the power of THE GOSPEL OF THE FUTURE and the blessed and purifying hope of Christ's glorious coming.

I. WHAT WE MEAN BY CHRIST'S COMING.

1. We do not mean His coming to the individual Christian's heart. He does thus come most truly and graciously, and this is the blessed mystery of which we have already spoken in connection with our sanctification. It is "Christ in you, the hope of glory." But this is not His second coming. Some persons are ready to say, with a great show of spirituality, I have the millennium in my heart, and the Lord in my heart; let those who have not, speculate about a material coming. Well, Paul had the Lord in his heart, and a millennium as near to the third heaven as these persons will probably claim; and John was about as near his Redeemer's heart as any of us can ever expect to get on earth; but they did speak and write in terms like this: "Then we which are alive, and remain unto the coming of the Lord, shall be caught up in the clouds to meet the Lord in the air." "We "We know that when He shall appear, we shall appear with Him in glory." "Behold, He cometh with clouds, and every eye shall see Him. Even so, come, Lord Jesus."

   Indeed, the more we know Jesus spiritually, the more will we long for His personal and eternal presence in the fuller and more glorious sense which His personal advent will bring.

2. We do not mean His coming at death. It is doubtful whether He does really come for us at death. Lazarus is represented as borne by angels into Abraham's bosom; and Stephen at

his glorious departing saw Jesus in heaven on the right hand of God, rising, it is true, to receive and honor His faithful servants, but not coming for him personally. The contrasts between death and the Lord's coming are very marked. We are not told to watch for death, but are delivered from its fear, but we are to watch for the Lord's coming. Death is an enemy; His coming a welcome visitation of our dearest friend. Death is a bitter bereavement to the heart; the Lord's coming is the very consolation of the bereaved, and the antidote of death. If death and the Lord's coming were identical, then the apostle would have said to the Thessalonian believers: "I would not have you ignorant concerning them that are asleep, that ye sorrow not as those that have no hope, for the Lord has come for them, and will soon in like manner come for you in death, and you shall be sweetly united in death once more." Does he say that? No! But he does say: "The Lord shall DESCEND FROM HEAVEN *** and THE DEAD IN CHRIST SHALL RISE first, and then we that are alive shall be caught up together with them, to meet the Lord in the air, and so we shall be ever with the Lord." It is not death he points them to, but that which is to overcome death, and of which he says in writing to the Corinthians: "Then shall be brought to pass the saying that is written, 'Death is swallowed up in victory.'" If the Lord's coming is to swallow up death in victory, it is very certain that it cannot be the same thing, or it would swallow up itself.

3. We do not mean the spiritual coming of Christ through the spread of the Gospel and the progress of Christianity. This is nowhere recognized in the Bible as the personal coming of Christ. "Behold, He cometh with clouds, and EVERY EYE SHALL SEE HIM, and they also which pierced Him, and ALL KINDREDS OF THE EARTH SHALL WAIL BECAUSE OF HIM." Now, that is not the way they do when they receive

the Gospel. They rejoice. But now they are startled and discouraged. And they cry, as represented in another place, to the rocks and the mountains to fall upon them and hide them from the wrath of the Lamb. So, also, the angels, speaking of this event to the eleven disciples, say: "This same Jesus SHALL SO COME IN LIKE MANNER AS YE HAVE SEEN HIM GO INTO HEAVEN." This cannot be the publication of the Gospel, but must be HIS PERSONAL, VISIBLE, AND GLORIOUS APPEARING. The Gospel is to be widely diffused; His truth is to prevail; His cause is to triumph, but He is coming personally, and He is infinitely more than even His truth and cause.

II. WHAT DO WE MEAN BY THE MILLENNIUM?

Some persons have stated that the doctrine of the millennium is a modern invention, and that the word itself is not found in the Bible.

The word millennium is not English, but is the Greek word for a *thousand years*. It is used repeatedly in the twentieth chapter of Revelation to denote the period during which Christ shall reign with His saints on the earth after the first resurrection. It is a time of victory, joy and glory. Seven especial facts are recorded concerning it here:

1. The resurrection and re-union of the saints.
2. Their reward and reign.
3. The complete exclusion of Satan from the earth.
4. The personal and continual presence of Jesus with them on earth.
5. The suppression of all enemies and the universal reign of righteousness.
6. The duration of a thousand years.
7. The immediately succeeding revolt of Satan and sinful man, and the final judgment of the wicked.

The Fourfold Gospel

If there was no other reference in the Bible to this time of blessing, these elements alone would be sufficient to constitute a state and time of exalted glory and happiness. Much more do they suffice to identify it as the golden age of which former prophets wrote and spake, when righteousness, truth and peace shall "cover the earth as the waters cover the sea."

III. THE ORDER OF THESE TWO EVENTS.

This is the next question to be settled, and upon it hang most of the issues of the question. Is the coming of Christ to precede or follow this millennial period?

1. The most obvious reason for believing that it precedes it, is found in the very passage just referred to where these events are both described. There can be no question that here the coming of the Lord precedes and introduces the millennium. His coming is minutely depicted in the whole procession from heaven to earth. Then follows the conquest and punishment of His earthly foes, the binding of Satan, the resurrection of the saints, the reign of the risen ones and the thousand years. The only way it is attempted to set this aside is to represent it as figurative and spiritual. Dean Alford's strong sense and honesty is the best answer to this. If this be so, he declares, then adieu to all definiteness and certainty in the Scriptures. If this be not a literal coming, resurrection, and millennium, then we do not know what our Bibles mean about anything.

2. The next argument for Christ's premillennial coming is the emphatic use of the word, "WATCH," in connection with it. Many times are we told to watch for it. Now if it is to be preceded by a spiritual millennium, the Lord would have told us to watch for this. How could the early Church watch for His coming, how can even we if we know that it is to be preceded by a clear thousand years? The very word watch

means immanency, and it is not immanent, if ten whole centuries must intervene. If it be objected that as a matter of fact Christ's coming did not occur during more than ten centuries, this does not alter its immanency. An event may be liable to occur at any moment for years, and yet be long retarded. That is quite different from its being understood as not to occur until the later period. Although God knew just the moment when His Son should appear, yet He wanted His Church to be always expecting it-at even, or at midnight, or at the cock crowing, or in the morning. The announcement of a fixed previous millennium would have been fatal to this design, and the Church would have gone to work to make her own millennium without Him. This is just what the Romish Church did, when Pope Hildebrand announced in the tenth century that the millennium had begun, and that Christ was already present through His vicar. And some Protestant teachers have the assumption to tell us today that this century of progress is the first age of the millennium.

3. The next proof of a premillennial coming is found in the picture Christ gives us of the condition of things as they were to be down to the close of the Christian age, and up to the very hour of His coming.

Just glance at a few bold touches in the picture.

Some seed fell by the wayside and the fowls of the air devoured them; some fell on stony places and perished; some were choked by thorns, and some fell on good ground and bore fruit.

But soon the enemy sowed the tares, and both grow together till the harvest.

The Church, externally, grows up into luxuriant strength like the mustard plant, but internally is full of leaven. The true and pure are like the hid treasure and the pearl, so hard to find. The net gathers of every kind and only the angels can separate the evil at the last.

As the ages roll on, there looms up the picture, not of a millennium, but a "Falling away first." "Wickedness shall abound and the love of many shall wax cold." "Many shall depart from the faith, giving heed to doctrines of devils." "In the last days perilous times shall come." There shall be plenty of church members, "having a form of godliness"; but these shall be the very enemies of the Cross of Christ, "denying the power thereof." A holy, happy world will not be waiting to welcome its King, but "as a snare shall He come unto all that dwell on the earth." "When they shall say, 'Peace and safety, then sudden destruction.'" And when it bursts upon them, it shall find them "as it was in the days of Noah and of Lot"; and the Master even asks, "When the Son of man cometh, shall He find faith on the earth?"

This is God's picture of the future of earth until Christ's coming. It does not look much like a previous millennium.

No, nor does the story of eighteen centuries move towards a spiritual millennium. New York with half the proportion of church goers and nearly double the ratio of drunkards, has not grown any nearer to it in two hundred years; London, with three million souls who never enter a church; Berlin, with one minister to fifty thousand people; these three capitals of the three great Protestant nations of earth hold out no signal of its coming. And what shall we say of wicked Paris, and rotten Constantinople, and idolatrous India, and conservative China, and savage Africa? When is there coming to them as much millennial light as we have? When will the Christian nations begin to move toward their golden age? Oh, if this be the best God has for us, then prophecy is an exaggeration and the Bible a poetic dream. Thank God, He is coming and His Kingdom shall transcend our brightest hope, and His own most glowing picture.

IV. OBJECTIONS.

The strongest objections that are made to this doctrine are:
1. It dishonors the work of the Holy Ghost, as if He were in-

competent to fulfill His administration, and were represented as having failed in His great mission to convert the world, and some other means had had to be provided. In reply it is enough to say that the Holy Ghost has not undertaken to convert the world, but to call out of it the Church of Christ and prepare a people for His name, and when this is done, and all who will accept Jesus as a Saviour have been called, converted and fully trained, the time for the next stage will have come, and Jesus will come to reign and restore His ancient people for their privileges and opportunities. The work of the Holy Ghost will not cease then, for He shall abide with us for ever, and the ages to come shall afford unbounded and more glorious scope for His grace and power.

2. It is objected that such a doctrine discourages Christian missions, and saps the foundations of the Church's most glorious hopes and prospects. On the contrary, it opens a prospect of far grander glory to the Church at her Lord's appearing, and bids her go forth, rapt with the desire to hasten it, to prepare the world for His appearing; for as an incentive to this work, He Himself has told her that when the message of salvation has been proclaimed to all the world, then shall the end come. The fact is that a large majority of the missionaries now in foreign lands believe and rejoice in the blessed hope of the Lord's coming, are animated by it to labor for the world's evangelization, and cheered by the blessed thought that their task is not to convert the whole human race, but to evangelize the nations, and give every man a chance to be saved if he will; and they would, indeed, be distracted and dismayed at the prospect they behold, did they feel that the world must wait until the present agencies have wrought out its full salvation, while meanwhile three times its entire population every century is swept into eternity unsaved. The coming of Christ is not going to suspend mission work. It

will bring the most glorious and complete system of evangelization earth has ever seen. And under its benignant influence the heathen shall all be brought to Jesus; all nations shall be blessed in Him, and all people shall call Him blessed. The most ardent friends of lost humanity must long the most for this, the world's best hope.

3. It is objected that this doctrine leads to fanaticism. Anything may be abused, but in the sober and Scriptural faith of this doctrine there is nothing fitted to minister to rashness, presumption or folly. Let us very carefully avoid all attempts to prophesy ourselves, or be wise above that which is written; but let us not be intimidated by the devil's howl, from the fullness of God's truth and testimony. This truth will make us a peculiar people. It will take away the charm of the world, and separate us from it. It will make us very unlike many selfish and comfortable Christians, and will set our soul on fire to serve God and save men. And if that be fanaticism, then welcome such fanaticism.

4. It is objected that it is gross and material, tending to promote earthly and carnal hopes in the heart and the Church, like the earthly ideas and ambitions of the primitive apostles which the Master rebuked, and taught them rather to look for a spiritual kingdom and a heavenly home. That was the extreme then, may not the opposite be now? Is not the true need the spiritual first, afterward the material, the resurrection life of the soul first, then the resurrection of the body? We do not hold nor teach any gross or material idea of the material idea of the millennial age. The bodies of the saints will be spiritual, and like His own. But if He was pleased to take such a body into the heavenly world and make it the center and crown of creation, is it anything but an affectation to try to be more spiritual than our Lord? Nay, it is all spiritual, and the true purpose and end of redemption is that "our whole spirit

and soul and body be preserved blameless unto the coming of our Lord Jesus Christ," and "the whole *earth* be filled with His glory."

V. THE SIGNS OF HIS COMING.

While the day and the hour shall be unrevealed, yet His children "are not in darkness that that day should overtake them as a thief." "None," as the end approaches, "none of the wicked shall understand, but the wise shall understand."

There is a distinct order revealed. He will first come for His own waiting ones, and they, with the holy dead, shall be caught up to meet Him in the air. The wicked world shall be left behind; a formal church and a multitude of nations shall live on and scarcely miss the little flock that has just been caught away. Then will begin a series of judgments and warnings, ending at last in the descent of Christ in power and glory, the revelation of His righteous judgment against His open enemies, and the beginning of His personal reign. There will thus be two appearings of Jesus Christ-the one to His own, the other, later, to the entire world; the first as a Bridegroom, the second as a King and Judge. The signs of the one do not therefore apply to the other. The first of these appearings is not so sharply defined as the other. It is more immanent and uncertain, and may come at any hour.

Many of the most important signs of the Lord's coming have already been fulfilled. For example:

1. The political changes and developments of Daniel's great visions have apparently all occurred. The great empires have come and gone, and the minor kingdoms which were to succeed them are now covering the regions which once they swayed.

2. The predicted "Falling away," has long ago begun, and the man of sin has sat in God's temple already the full time of the prophetic cycle, and the process has begun which is to "con-

sume and destroy unto the end." The Papacy has fulfilled almost all the lineaments of its marvelous portrait.

3. The Mohammedan power has waxed and waned, and the waters of this great spiritual Euphrates are being dried up every day to prepare the way of God's kingly people.

4. The Jewish signs have not been less remarkable. Jacob is turning his face again to Bethel, and Jerusalem is preparing to put on her beautiful garments again. Her sons are slowly gathering, while jealous nations are hastening the exodus, and fulfilling unconsciously the voice of prophecy.

5. The intellectual signs are not less marked. Knowledge is indeed increased, and many run to and fro, while human philosophy talks of evolution and declares that all things continue as they were, and nature is immutable and only material.

6. The moral signs are even more marked than Daniel's picture. "The wicked shall do wickedly," was never more true than today. Portentous forms of wickedness startle the moral sense every day, and invention is as ripe in evil as it is in material art.

7. The religious signs are growing more vivid. Lukewarmness and worldliness in the Church, intense longings after holiness on the part of the few, and a mighty missionary movement are the features of the age, and the signs of prophecy, that point to the day of the Son of Man.

8. And finally, an earnest, a growing and a world-wide expectation of His coming on the part of all those who love His appearing, is as profound today as it was in Judea, and even the Gentile world in the age preceding His advent at Bethlehem. The morning star is in the East. "The children of the day" have seen it. The cry has gone forth, "The night is far spent, the day is at hand"; and soon the Sun will fill the sky and cover the earth with millennial glory.

VI. THE BLESSINGS OF HIS COMING.

1. I. It will bring us Jesus Himself. This is the best of its blessings. Like all the other sections of this Gospel, this, too, is the Gospel of Himself. Not the robes and the royal crowns, not the resurrection bodies or reunited friends will be the chief joy, but

   «Thou art coming, we shall see Thee,
   And be like Thee on that day."

2. It will bring us our friends. "Them who sleep in Jesus will God bring with Him." They shall be alive, they shall be recognized, they shall be gloriously beautiful, they shall be ours forever. Not only the old ones, but such new ones, the good of all the ages, the men and women we have longed to know. What a family!

   «Ten thousand times ten thousand,
   In shining garments bright,
   The armies of the ransomed
   Throng up the steps of light;

   O then, what rapturous greetings
   On Canaan's happy shore,
   What knitting severed friendships up,
   Where partings are no more."

3. It will bring us perfect spirits, restored to His image, glorious in His likeness, free from fault, defect, or imperfection, removed above temptation, incapable of falling, and overflowing with unutterable blessedness. We shall wear His perfect image; we shall know as we are known; we shall be as holy as He is holy; we shall possess His strength and beauty and perfect love. The universe will gaze upon us, and next to the glory of the Lamb will be the beauty of the bride.

4. We shall have perfect bodies; we shall possess His perfect resurrection life; we shall forget even what a pain was like;

we shall spring into boundless strength; our hearts shall thrill with the fullness of immortal life, and space and distance be annihilated. The laws of gravitation will hold us no more. The streets of the New Jerusalem vertically and horizontally, the length and breadth, and the height thereof are equal. Our bodies shall be the perfect instruments of our exalted spirits, the exact reflection of His glorious body.

5. It will give us the sweetest and highest service. It will be no idle, selfish ecstasy, but will bring a perfect partnership in His kingdom and administration. We shall, perhaps, be permitted to fulfill the ideals of our highest earthly experiences, and finish the work we have longed and tried to do-with boundless resources, infinite capabilities, unlimited scope and time, and His own presence and omnipotent help. The blessed work will be to serve Him, to bless others, and to raise earth and humanity to happiness, righteousness and Paradise restored.

6. It will banish Satan. It will bind and chain the foe and fiend, whose hate and power have held the world in ages of darkness and misery. Oh, to be free from his presence for even a day! to feel that we need no longer watch with ceaseless vigilance against him! to walk upon a world without a devil! Lord, hasten that glorious day!

7. And it will bring such blessings to others, to the race, to the world. It will stop the awful tragedy of sin and suffering; it will sheathe the sword, emancipate the captive, close the prison and the hospital, bind the devil and his henchman, Death; beautify and glorify the face of the earth; evangelize and convert the perishing nations, and shed light and gladness on this dark scene of woe and wickedness.

> There shall he no more crying,
> There shall be no more pain.
> There shall be no more dying,
> There shall be no more stain.

Hearts that by death were riven,
Meet in eternal love;
Lives on the altar given
Rise to their crowns above.

Satan shall tempt us never,
Sin shall o'ercome no more,
Joy shall abide forever,
Sorrow and grief be o'er.

Jesus shall be our glory,
Jesus our heaven shall be;
Jesus shall be our story,
Jesus who died for me.

Hasten, sweet morn of gladness,
Hasten, dear Lord, we pray;
Finish this night of sadness,
Hasten the heavenly day.

Jesus is coming surely,
Jesus is coming soon;
O let us walk so purely,
O let us keep our crown.

Jesus, our watch we are keeping,
Longing for Thee to come;
Then shall be ended our night of weeping,
Then we shall reach our home.

VII. THE LESSONS IT LEAVES.

1. Let us be ready. "The marriage of the Lamb is come and His wife hath made herself ready, and to her it was GRANTED that she should be arrayed in fine raiment, clean and white." Thank God that the robes are *given*. Let us have them on. WHITE ROBES. When the Bride is dressed, the wedding must be near. So let us hasten His coming.

2. Let us be watching. "Behold, I come as a thief: blessed is he that watcheth and *keepeth his garments*, lest he walk naked and they see his shame." Let us not put off the wedding robe for an hour. Let us remember His words. "When these things begin to come to pass, then lift up your heads and bend YOURSELVES BACK (Dr. Young), for your redemption draweth nigh." Keep your faces turned heavenwards until your whole being shall curve heavenwards, like a dear, old colored saint we know, whose body, when she speaks and prays, describes a circle bending towards the sky.

3. Be faithful. It is to bring the reward of faithful servants. Let us "look to it that we lose none of the things which we have wrought, but may receive a full reward." "Hold fast that thou hast that no man take thy crown."

   In the ancient Church there was a noble band of forty faithful soldiers in one of the Roman legions who were condemned to die for their faith in Jesus. They were all exposed on the centre of a frozen lake, to perish on the ice, but allowed the choice of recanting from their faith at any moment during the fatal night by walking to the shore and reporting to the officer on duty.

   As the night wore on the sentinel on shore saw a cloud of angels hovering over the place where the martyrs stood, and as one by one they dropped, they placed a crown upon the martyr's brow and bore him up to the skies, while all the air rang with the song, "Forty Martyrs and Forty Crowns." At last they had all gone but one, and his crown still hung in the sky above and no one seemed to claim it. Suddenly the sentinel heard a step, and lo! one of the forty was at his side. He had fled. The sentinel looked at him as he took down his name, and then said: "Fool, had you seen what I have seen this night you would not have lost your crown. But it shall not be lost. Take my place, and I will gladly take yours;" and forth he marched to death and glory, while again the silent choir took up the chorus, "Forty Martyrs and Forty Crowns. Thou hast been faithful unto death and thou shalt receive a crown of life."

God help us to hear that chorus when He shall come!

4. Be diligent. There is much to do. You. can "hasten the coming of the day of God." The world is to be forewarned. The Church is to be prepared. Arouse thee, O Christian. Give Him every power, every faculty, every dollar, every moment. Send the Gospel abroad. Go yourself if you can. If you cannot, send your substitute. And may this last decade of the nineteenth century mean for you and for this world, as nothing ever meant before, a time of preparation for the coming of our Lord and Saviour Jesus Christ!

Chapter 5.
THE WALK WITH GOD

"He that saith he abideth in Him, ought himself so to walk even as He walked." I. John ii. 6.

The life naturally leads to the walk. The term describes the course of life, the conduct, the practical side of our Christian life. The reference to the walk of our Lord Jesus Christ recalls His character and life. The character of Jesus stands out as the divinest monument of the Bible and the Gospels.

Even men who do not believe in Him as we do have been compelled to acknowledge the grandeur and loftiness of His incomparable life. Here are some of the testimonies that the world's illustrious thinkers have borne to Jesus of Nazareth. Renan says "The Christ of the Gospels is the most beautiful Incarnation of God. His beauty is eternal; His reign shall never end." Goethe says "There shines from the Gospels a sublimity through the person of Christ which only the divine could manifest." Rosseau writes "Was He no more than man? What sweetness! What purity in His ways! What tender grace in His teaching! What loftiness in His maxims! What wisdom in His words! What delicacy in His touch! What an empire in the hearts of His followers! Where is the man, where is the sage that could suffer and die without weakness or display? So grand, so inimitable is His character that the inventors of such a story would be more wonderful than the character which they portrayed." Carlyle says "Jesus Christ is the divinest Symbol. Higher than this human thought can never go." Napoleon said "I am a man, I understand men. These were all men. Jesus Christ was more than man. Our empire is built on force, His on love, and it will last when ours has passed away."

But if Jesus Christ thus appears at a distance to the minds that can only admire Him, how much more must He be to those who know Him as a personal Friend and who see Him in the light of love, for

> The love of Jesus, what it is,
> None but His loved ones know.

The character and life of Christ have a completeness of detail which no other Bible biography possesses. The story has been written out by many witnesses, and the portrait is reproduced in all its lineaments and features. He has traversed every stage of life from the cradle to the grave, and represented humanity in every condition and circumstance of temptation, trial and need, so that His example is equally suited to childhood, youth or manhood, to the humble and the poor, in life's lowliest path, or to the sovereign that sways the widest scepter, for He is at once the lowly Nazarene and the Lord of Lords. He has felt the throb of every human affection. He has felt the pang of every human sorrow. He is the Son of Man in the largest, broadest sense. Nay, His humanity is so complete that He represents the softer traits of womanhood as well as the virility and strength of manhood, and even the simplicity of a little child, so that there is no place in the experiences of life where we may not look back at this Pattern Life for light and help as we bring it into touch with our need and ask, "What would Jesus do?"

God has sent forth the life of Christ as our Example and commanded us to imitate and reproduce Him in our lives. This is not an ideal picture to study as we would some paragon of art. It is a life to be lived and it is adapted to all the needs of our present existence. It is a plain life for a common people to copy, a type of humanity that we can take with us into the kitchen and the family room, into the workshop and the place of business, into the field where the farmer toils, and the orchard where the gardener prunes, and the place where the tempter assails, and even the lot where want and poverty press us with their burdens and their cares. This Christ is the Christ of every man who will receive

Him as a Brother and follow Him as an Example and a Master. "I have given you an example," He says, "that ye should do as I have done." He expects us to be like Him. Are we copying Him and being made conformable unto His image? There is but one Pattern. For ages God "sought for a man and found none." At last humanity produced a perfect type and since then God has been occupied in making other men according to this Pattern. He is the one original. When Judson came to America the religious papers were comparing him to Paul and the early apostles, and Judson wrote expressing his grief and displeasure and saying, "I do not want to be like them. There is but One to copy, Jesus Himself. I want to plant my feet in His footprints and measure their shortcomings by His and His alone. He is the only Copy. I want to be like Him." So let us seek to walk even as He walked.

The secret of a Christ-like life lies partly in the deep longing for it. We grow like the ideals that we admire. We reach unconsciously at last the things we aspire to. Ask God to give you a high conception of the character of Christ and an intense desire to be like Him and you will never rest until you reach your ideal. Let us look at this Ideal.

I. THE MOTIVE OF HIS LIFE.

The key to any character is to be found in its supreme motive, the great end which it is pursuing, the object for which it is living. You cannot understand conduct by merely looking at facts. You want to grasp the intent that lies back of these facts and incidents, and the supreme reason that controls these actions. When a great crime has been committed the object of the detective is to establish a reason for it, then everything else can be made plain. The great object for which we are living will determine everything else, and explain many things which otherwise might seem inexplicable. When the ploughman starts out to make a straight furrow he needs two stakes. The nearer stake is not enough. He must keep it in line with the farther one, the stake at the remotest end of the ridge, and as he keeps the two in line his course is straight. It is the final goal which determines our immediate actions and if that is high enough, and strong enough, it will attract us like a heavenly magnet from all lesser and lower things, and hold us irresistibly to our heavenly pathway. The supreme motive of Christ's life was devotion to the will and glory of God. "Wist ye not that I must be about My Father's business?" This was the deep conviction even upon the heart of the child (Luke ii. 49). "My meat is to do the will of Him that sent Me" (John iv. 34). "I seek not Mine own will but the will of the Father that sent Me" (John v. 30). "I came down from heaven not to do Mine own will but the will of Him that sent Me" (John vi. 38). This was the purpose of His maturer life. "I have glorified Thee on the earth. I have finished the work thou gavest Me to do." This was His joyful cry as He finished His course and handed back His commission to the Father who sent Him. Is this the supreme object of our life, and are we pressing on to it through good report and evil report, caring only for one thing to please our Master, and have His approval at the last.

II. THE PRINCIPAL OF HIS LIFE.

Every life can be summed up in some controlling principle. With some it is selfishness in the various forms of avarice, ambition or pleasure. With others it is devotion to some favorite pursuit of art or literature or invention and discovery. With Jesus Christ the one principle of His life was love, and the law that He has left for us is the same simple and comprehensive law of love, including every form of duty in the one new commandment "A new commandment I give unto you that ye love one another as I have loved you" (John xiii. 34; xv. 12). This is not the Old Testament law of love with self in the center, "Thou shalt love thy neighbor as thyself." But this is a new commandment with Christ in the center "that ye love one another as I have loved you." Love for His Father, love for His own, love for the sinful, love

The Fourfold Gospel

for His enemies, this covered the whole life of Jesus Christ and this will comprehend the length and breadth of the life of His followers. This will simplify every question, solve every problem and sweeten every duty into a delight and make our life as His was an embodiment of that beautiful ideal which the Holy Spirit has left us in the thirteenth chapter of First Corinthians. "Love suffereth long and is kind. Love envieth not. Love vaunteth not itself, is not puffed up, doth not behave itself unseemly, seeketh not her own, is not provoked, thinketh no evil, rejoiceth not in iniquity but rejoiceth in the truth, beareth all things, believeth all things, hopeth all things, endureth all things."

III. THE RULE AND STANDARD OF HIS LIFE.

Every life must have a standard by which it is regulated, and so Christ's life was molded by the Holy Scriptures. "These are the words that I spake unto you while I was yet with you that all things must be fulfilled which were written in the law of Moses, and in the prophets, and in the Psalms concerning Me" (Luke xxiv. 44). It was necessary that Christ's life should fulfill the Scriptures and He could not die upon the cross until He had first lived out every word that had been written concerning Him. It is just as necessary that our lives should fulfill the Scriptures and we have no right to let a single promise or command in this holy Book be a dead letter so far as we are concerned. God wants us while we live to prove in our own experience all things that have been written in this Book, and to bind the Bible in a new and living edition in the flesh and blood of our own lives.

IV. THE SOURCE OF HIS LIFE.

Whence did He derive the strength for this supernatural and perfect example? Was it through His own inherent and essential deity? Or did He suspend during the days of His humiliation His own self-contained rights and powers, and live among us simply as a man, dependent for His support upon the same sources of strength that we enjoy? It would seem so. Listen to His own confession (John v. 19, 30; vi. 57). "The Son can do nothing of Himself but what He seeth the Father do. I can of Mine own self do nothing. As I hear I judge. As the living Father hath sent Me and I live by the Father, so he that eateth Me even he shall live by Me." This seems to make it very plain that our Lord derived His daily strength from the same source as we may receive ours, by communion with God, by a life of dependence, faith and prayer, and by receiving and being ever filled with the presence and power of the Holy Spirit. Would we therefore walk even as He walked let us receive the Holy Ghost as He did at His baptism. Let us constantly depend upon Him, and be filled with His presence. Let us live a life of unceasing prayer. Let us draw our strength each moment from Him as He did from the Father. Let our life for both soul and body be sustained by the inbreathing of His so that it shall be true of us "In Him we live and move and have our being." This was the Master's life and this may be ours. What an inspiration it is for us to know that He humbled Himself to the same place of dependence to which we stand, and that He will exalt us through His grace to the same victories which He won.

V. THE ACTIVITIES OF HIS LIFE.

The life of Jesus Christ was a positive one. It was not all absorbed in self-contemplation and self-culture, but it went out in thoughtful benevolence to the world around Him. His brief biography as given by Peter is one of practical and holy activity. "He went about doing good." In His short life of three and a half years He travelled on foot over every portion of Galilee, Samaria and Judea, incessantly preaching, teaching and working with arduous toil. He was constantly thronged by the multitudes so that Luke tells us "there was not time so much as to eat." Once at the close of a busy day He was so weary that He fell asleep on the little ship amid the raging storm. Leaving His busy toil for a season of rest still the multitudes pressed upon Him, and He could not be silent. After a Sabbath of incessant labor at Capernaum we find Him next morning rising a great while before day, that He might steal from His slumbers the time to pray. His life was one of ceaseless service, and even still on His ascension throne He is continually employed in ministries of active love. So He has said to us that we must copy Him. No consecrated Christian can be an idler or a drone. "As My Father hath sent Me even so send I you." We are here as missionaries, every one of us with a commission, and a trust just as definite as the men we send to heathen lands. Let us find our work, and, like Him, "whatsoever our hand findeth to do, do it with our might."

VI. SEPARATION.

The true measure of a man's worth is not always the number of his friends, but sometimes the number of his foes. Every man who lives in advance of his age is sure to be misunderstood and opposed, and often persecuted and sacrificed. The Lord Himself has said "Woe unto you when all men speak well of you. Marvel not if the world hate you. If ye were of the world the world would love his own." Like Him, therefore, we must expect often to be unpopular, often to stand alone, even to be maligned, perhaps to be bitterly and falsely assailed and driven "without the camp" even of the religious world. Two things, however, let us not forget. First let us not be afraid to be unpopular, and secondly let us never be soured or embittered by it, but stand sweetly and triumphantly in the confidence of right, and our Master's approval.

VII. THE SUFFERING LIFE.

No character is mature, no life has reached its coronation, until it has passed through fire. And so the supreme test of Christ's example was suffering, and in all His sufferings He has as the apostle Peter expressed it, "Left us an example that we should follow His steps" (I.Pet. ii. 21). He suffered from the temptations of Satan for "He was in all points tempted like as we are, yet without sin," and in this He has called us to follow Him in suffering and victory, for "in that He hath suffered being tempted He is able also to succor them that are tempted." He suffered from the wrongs of men, and in this He has left us an example of patience, gentleness and forgiveness, for "When He was reviled, reviled not again; when He suffered He threatened not, but committed Himself to Him that judgeth righteously." Never was He more glorious than in the hour of shame. Never was He more unselfish than in the moment when His own sorrows were crushing His heart. Never was He more victorious than when He bowed His head on the bitter cross and died for sinful men. He is the crowned Sufferer of humanity, and He calls us to suffer with Him in sweetness, submission and triumphant faith and love.

VIII. THE FINER TOUCHES OF HOLY CHARACTER.

The perfection of character is to be found in the finer touches of temper and quality which easily escape the careless observer. It is in these that the character of Christ stands inimitably supreme. One of the finest portraits of His spirit is given by Paul in the third chapter of Philippians as he tells us of His humility which might have grasped at His divine rights, but voluntarily surrendered them, emptied Himself and gladly stooped to the lowest place (Phil. ii. 5-8). His unselfishness in dealing with the weak and the selfish is finely expressed in (Rom. xv. 1, 3, 7). "For even Christ pleased not Himself, but as it is written the reproaches of them that reproached thee fell on Me." His gentleness and lowliness is finely expressed in His own words, "Learn of Me who am meek and lowly in heart." The highest element of character is self-sacrifice, and here the Master stands forever in the front of all sacrifice and heroism. "If any man will come after Me let him deny himself, and take up his cross and follow Me. He that will be chief among you let him be the servant of all, for even the Son of Man came not to be ministered unto but to minister and to give His life a ransom for many." Here we are taught what it means to walk even as He walked. It is the surrendered life. It is the life of self-sacrifice. So the apostle has finely expressed it in (Ephesians v. 2) "Walk in love as Christ also has loved us, and given Himself for an offering and a sacrifice unto God for a sweet smelling savor." This is love, self-sacrifice, and this is to God as sweet as the fragrance of the gardens of Paradise. There was something in the spirit of Jesus, and there ought to be something in every consecrated life, which can only be expressed by the term sweetness. It is with reference to this that the apostle says in II. Cor. ii. 15, "We are unto God a sweet savor of Christ in them that believe, and in them that perish." God give to us this heavenly sweetness that breathes from the heart of our indwelling Saviour.

The refinement of Jesus Christ is one of the most striking traits of His lovely character. Untrained in the schools of human culture, He was notwithstanding as every Christian ought to be, a perfect gentleman. His thoughtful consideration of others is often manifest in the incidental circumstances of His life. For example, when Simon Peter was distressed about the tribute money at Capernaum, and was hesitating to speak to the Master about it, the Lord "prevented him," i.e., anticipated his very thought, and sent him down to the lake to catch the fish with the coin in his mouth, and then added with fine tact "That take, and pay for Me and thee," assuming the responsibility of the debt first for Himself to save Peter's sensitiveness. Still finer was His high courtesy toward the poor sinning woman whom the Pharisees had dragged before Him. Stoopinig down He evaded her glance lest she should be humiliated before them, and as though He heard them not He finally thrust a dart of holy sarcasm into their consciences which sent them swiftly like hounds from His presence and only when they were gone did He look up in that trembling woman s face, and gently say. "Neither do I condemn thee, go and sin no more." So let us reflect the gentleness and courtesy of Christ and not only by our lives, but our "Manner of love" commend our Christianity and adorn the doctrine of God our Saviour in all things.

There is one thing more in the spirit of the Master which He would have us copy, and that is the spirit of gladness. While the Lord Jesus was never hilarious or unrestrained in the expression of His joy, yet He was uniformly cheerful, bright and glad, and the heart in which He dwells should likewise be expressed in the shining face, the springing step, and the life of overflowing gladness. There is nothing more needed in a sad and sinful world than joyous Christians. There was nothing more touching in the Master's life than the fact that when His own heart was ready to break with the anticipation of the garden and the cross He was saying to them "Let not your heart be troubled. Let My joy remain in you and your joy be full." God help us to copy the gladness of Jesus, never to droop our colors in the dust, never to hang our harps upon the willows, never to lose our heavenly blessing or fail to "rejoice evermore."

IX. BUT WE MUST HASTEN TO NOTICE FINALLY SOME OF THE POSITIVE ELEMENTS OF FORCEFULNESS AND POWER IN THE LIFE OF JESUS.

It is possible to be sweet and good and yet to be weak and unwise. This was not the character of Jesus. Never was gentleness more childlike, never was manhood more mighty and majestic. In every element of His character, in every action of His life we see the strongest virility and we recognize continually that the Son of man was indeed a man in every sense of the word.

Intellectually His mind was clear and masterful and there is nothing finer in the story of His life than the calm, victorious way in which He answered and drove from His presence the keen-witted lawyers and scribes who hounded Him with their questions and who were successively humiliated and silenced before the jeering crowd until until they were glad to escape from His presence, and after that no man durst ask Him any more questions.

So majestic and impressive was His eloquence that the officers that were sent to arrest Him forgot all about their commission as they stood listening to His wonderful words, and went back to their angry masters to exclaim: "Never man spake like this Man." There was about Him a dignity which sometimes rose to such a height that we read on one occasion as He set His face steadfastly to go to Jerusalem, "As they beheld Him they were amazed, and as they followed they were afraid." In the darkest hour of His agony He reached such a height of holy dignity that even Pilate gazed with admiration and pointing to Him even amid all the symbols of shame and suffering, he cried: "Behold the Man." Even in His death He was a Conqueror, and in His resurrection and ascension He arose sublime above all the powers of death and hell.

In conclusion, How shall we walk like Him?

1. We must receive Him to walk in us for He hath said, "I will dwell in them and walk in them."
2. We must study His life until the story is burned into our consciousness and impressed upon our heart.
3. We must constantly look upon the picture and apply it to every detail of our own conduct and so "beholding as in a glass the glory of the Lord, we shall be changed into the same image from glory to glory even as by the Spirit of the Lord."
4. Do not be discouraged when you meet with failure in yourself. Do not be afraid to look in the glass and see your own defects in contrast with His blameless life. It will incite you to higher things. Self-judgment is the very secret of progress and higher attainment.
5. Finally, let us ask the Holy Spirit whose work it is to make Jesus real to us to unveil the vision and imprint the copy upon our hearts and lives, and so shall we be "changed into the same image from glory to glory even as by the Spirit of the Lord."

Chapter 6.
KEPT

"For I know whom I have believed and am persuaded that He is able to keep that which I have committed unto him against that day." II. Tim. i. 12.

"Kept by the power of God unto salvation." I. Peter i. 5.

The more precious any treasure is, the more important is it that it be guarded and kept. The figure of our first text is that of a bank deposit and literally reads, "He is able to keep my deposits against that day." When great deposits of gold are being conveyed to the vaults of some rich bank, whole squadrons of police stand guard, and the most powerful locks, bolts, bars, and walls and the most ceaseless and sleepless vigilance of watchmen and detectives are employed to guard them. Sometimes the figure is used in a military sense. The second text is of this kind and literally should be translated, "Who are garrisoned by the power of God through faith unto salvation." What vast expenditures and mighty armaments and armies are employed to garrison the great strategic points that guard the gates of nations, such as Port Arthur, Gibraltar, Quebec, and other citadels. Sometimes the figure is used of the shepherd and his flock, "He will gather Israel and keep him as a shepherd doth his flock."

But whatever figure or phrase may be employed, the one great thought that God would convey to the hearts of His tried and suffering people is, that they are safe in His keeping, and that He is able to guard that which we have committed unto Him against that day. Let us look at some of His gracious promises to keep His people.

1. He will keep us wherever we may go or be. Listen to the first promise of our Divine Keeper as it was addressed to Jacob in the hour of his loneliness and fear, "Behold, I am with thee and will keep thee in all places whither thou goest; for I will

not leave thee until I have done all that which I have spoken to thee of." How He kept that word to Jacob! How many the various places where providence cast his lot! The land of Laban, the cities of the Shechemites, the land of Goshen,-everywhere his covenant God guarded and kept him. He was not an attractive figure, he was not deserving of any special consideration. He was the "worm Jacob," but God loved him in his infinite grace, and kept him, disciplined him, taught him, and prepared him to be the head of Israel's tribes, and the day came when he could say, "The God that fed and led me all my life long, the angel that kept me from all evil."

Some of you may be in strange places, lonely places, hard places, dangerous places; but if you have taken Jacob's God as your covenant God, you can rest without a fear in that ancient word, "Behold, I am with thee and will keep thee in all places whithersoever thou goest; for I will not leave thee until I have done that which I have spoken to thee of."

«To me remains nor place nor time,
My country is in every clime,
I can be calm and free from care
On any shore, since God is there.

"Could I be cast where Thou art not,
That were, indeed, a dreadful lot,
But regions none remote I call,
Secure of finding God in all."

2. He will keep us as the apple of His eye. "Keep me as the apple of the eye" (Ps. Xvii. 8). This is a beautiful figure founded upon the sensitiveness of the eyeball to the approach of any intruding cinder or particle of dust. Instinctively the eyelid closes before the object can enter. There is no time to think, for the action is intuitive and involuntary. The idea is that we are as near to God as our eyeball is to us, and as much a part of the body of Christ as if it were really the crystalline lens

of His very eyes, and that He is as sensitive to the approach of anything that could harm us as you would be to the intrusion of a floating mote or grain of dust to your sensitive eye before you can even think or pray.

«God is the refuge of His saints,
When storms of sharp distress invade,
Ere we can utter our complaint.
Behold Him present with His aid."

3. *He will keep us in His pavilion.* "Thou shalt hide them in the secret of Thy presence from the pride of man: Thou shalt keep them secretly in a pavilion from the strife of tongues" (Ps. xxxi. 20). It does not take Him long to erect that pavilion in the most solitary place and hide His children safely within its curtains. The story is told of a Scottish assembly of faithful worshippers in one of the glens of the fatherland in the clays when the cruel Claverhouse was hunting for the blood of the saints. Suddenly the cry was made from the sentinel watching on a neighboring cliff that soldiers were coming, and the little company had been discovered. Escape was impossible, and they just knelt down and prayed, claiming this precious psalm, "Thou shalt hide them in Thy pavilion." Immediately there began to gather among the hills a thick Scotch mist, and everything was enveloped as in a curtain. Their enemies were baffled, and they quietly and securely escaped through the familiar pathways of the mountains. God had hidden them securely in His pavilion. We may not have the same bloody foe as the Scottish Covenanters, but the strife of tongues is here with sharper swords and more cruel hate. Oh, how often we find the psalmist calling out against the envenomed words of men, "What shall be given unto thee? Or what shall be done unto thee, thou false tongue? Sharp arrows of the mighty, with coals of juniper" (Ps. cxx. 3, 4). But He can shield us even from these and give us a blessing for every bitter blast from human calumny. "Let him curse,"

said David when they tried to quiet old Shimei, who was abusing the king in the hour of his sorrow; "it may be the Lord will requite me good for his cursing this day." Wherefore let them that suffer from the strife of tongues "commit themselves to Him in well doing as unto a faithful Creator."

He will keep us in perfect peace. "Thou wilt keep him in perfect peace, whose mind is stayed on Thee, because he trusteth in Thee" (Isa. xxvi. 3). Literally this reads, "Peace, peace." It is the double peace *with* God and *of* God. It is the Old Testament original of the Apostle's still more beautiful promise in the fourth chapter of Philippians, "Be careful for nothing; but in everything by prayer and supplication with thanksgiving let your requests be made known unto God. And the peace of God, which passeth all understanding, shall keep your hearts and minds through Christ Jesus." In both verses it is the same peace which is referred to, that deep, divine rest which Christ puts into the heart where He comes to dwell. It is the peace of God, and it passeth all understanding. It is not the result of reasoning or sight; it is not because things have changed, and we can see the deliverance coming. It comes when all is dark and strange, and we have nothing but His bare word. The Assyrian was at the gates of Jerusalem, and there seemed no possible escape when the voice of the prophet said, "Be strong and of a good courage, fear not, neither be dismayed; for they that be with you be more than they that be with him. With us is the Lord our God to help us, and to fight our battles." And then it is added, "The people rested themselves." The Assyrian was still there, and the danger was just as imminent, but there came upon them an unreasoning and supernatural confidence, for God had undertaken their defense. We know the sequel. How easy it was for Jehovah by the touch of a single angel's hand to lay those mighty hosts silent in the dust! So God's peace comes not by sight, but by faith. Its conditions are, "Thou wilt keep him in perfect peace whose mind is stayed on thee, because he trusted in thee."

Someone tells of two competing paintings of peace for which a great prize was offered. One was a beautiful and tranquil scene, a woodland valley with a gentle streamlet softly winding through grassy banks. There were warbling birds, and happy, playing children with the flocks lying down in green pastures, and earth and heaven were at rest. The other, and the picture that won the prize, was a raging sea, flinging high its billows and its foam around a naked rock, with a ship in the distance, driving before the hurricane with every sail furled, and the seabirds whirling through the leaden clouds in wild confusion-anything but peace. But far up in a cleft of that naked rock, above the surf and sheltered from the storm, there was a dove's nest with the mother quietly spreading her soft wings above her young in perfect peace.

When is the time to trust?

Is it when all is calm?
When waves the victor's palm
And life is one great psalm
Of peace and rest?

No! But the time to trust
Is when the waves beat high,
And storm clouds sweep the sky,
And faith can only cry,
Lord help and save.

The beautiful figure of the text in Philippians is that of a garrison, the peace of God which garrisons the heart and mind. The need of the garrison here is not because of outside, but inside foes. Nothing can harm us from the outside if we are kept in God's perfect peace. Notice also that there are two sections of this citadel that have to be garrisoned and guarded. One is the heart, the seat of doubts, and fears, and cares. The other is the mind where our thoughts become the sources of unrest, and we wonder, and worry, and look forward and back, and look everywhere, but to God. The peace of God can quiet all our thinking and hold us in stillness and sweetly say to us,

> Cease your thinking, troubled Christian,
> What avail your anxious cares?
> God is ever thinking for you;
> Jesus ev'ry burden bears.
>
> Casting all your care upon Him,
> Sink into His blessed will
> While He folds you to His bosom,
> Sweetly whisp'ring, "Peace, be still."

4. *He will keep us by His power.* This is the meaning of our second text, "Garrisoned by the power of God through faith unto salvation." It is a very fine passage. The apostle has just told us that the inheritance is kept for us up yonder. Now he tells us we are kept for the inheritance. The inheritance is reserved for you, and you are preserved for the inheritance. But while the figure of the garrison is the same as in Philippians, yet it is a different garrison. There it was peace, now it is power. The garrison of peace is to preserve the city from internal foes; the garrison of power is to protect it from its outward enemies. The one garrison polices the streets; the other mans the walls. And it adds to the force of the figure to note that the word *power* here in the Greek is *dynamite*. The garrison is armed with heavenly artillery. When first the English troops under Lord Kitchener met the vast armies of the Mahdi, the conquering leader of the fanatical hordes of the Soudan, who outnumbered them ten to one, they protected their camp by modern artillery while the Africans came against them with the old-fashioned muskets and rifles. A hundred thousand strong, that vast array hurled itself upon the little company of English soldiers and marched to the assault with flying

banners, galloping horses, and splendid enthusiasm. The historian graphically tells how quietly and confidently the English waited the onset, for they knew that they had power in their midst before which those legions could not for a moment stand. Suddenly the Maxim guns began their terrific rattle and like a hailstorm from the heavens a rain of bullets and shells was poured upon that black host, and they melted like snow before a summer sun. It was dynamite against mere human courage. God has garrisoned us with heavenly dynamite, the power of the Holy Ghost, and, like the English soldiers, we must have confidence in it, for we are kept by the dynamite of God through faith. We must count upon His mighty strength and ever go forth with the battle cry, "Thanks be unto God that always leadeth us in triumph."

5. He is able to keep us in the world and from the evil. This was the Master's prayer for His disciples. In John xvii. 15, we read, "I pray not that thou shouldest take them out of the world, but that thou shouldest keep them from the evil." Here is a double keeping. Kept from death and sickness and anything that could take us out of the world, and yet kept from the evil of the world and especially the evil one. This is a portentous phrase in the original, *tou ponero,* the Evil One. This is no abstract evil, but a great personal Devil, the adversary "who walketh about like a roaring lion, seeking whom he may devour." But the Lord's power and the Lord's keeping stand between us and his devouring jaws. He is a conquered foe, and we are to treat him as such and to go forth against him with the prestige of a victor in the name of his Conqueror, the Lord Jesus Christ. Sometimes he assails us by his wiles and sometimes by his fiery darts, but with the shield of faith we shall be able to stand against and quench them both. We must not be too frightened of the devil. Some people get so afraid of him that they almost fear to let the Lord have right away in His own meetings. The

dread of fanaticism, it is to be feared, has kept a good many well meaning people from the baptism of the Holy Spirit. Let us boldly come and take all God has for us and trust Him to keep the counterfeit away, for if we ask bread, He is not going to give us a stone, and if we ask fish and really want what He wants, He will not let us have a serpent. In the name of Jesus and through His precious blood, we shall be safe and kept from the evil one.

6. *He is able to keep us from stumbling.* Jude says, "Now unto him that is able to keep us from falling, and to present you faultless before the presence of His glory with exceeding joy." The English translation is inadequate. The word *falling* means *stumbling.* Of course, He is able to keep us from being lost, and too many Christians are content to just get through, if it be by the skin of their teeth. That is a poor, ignoble ambition. He is able to keep you even from stumbling and to present you faultless before the presence of His glory with exceeding joy. If He is able to keep you for one second, He can keep you for thirty-three million seconds, which means one whole year, and as much longer as you keep trusting Him moment by moment. Will you rise to a higher ambition and take Him to keep you even from slipping, and tripping, and stumbling?

7. *He is able to keep you from the touch of the adversary.* There is a fine promise in the last chapter of I. John. "He that was begotten of God keepeth him, and that wicked one toucheth him not." This is a different reading from the ordinary version, but it is very blessed to say, the only begotten Son keepeth the saint that trusts Him and so keepeth him that that wicked one toucheth him not. It is the old familiar picture of the fly on one side of the window and the bird on the other. The bird dashes for its prey and thinks it has it. The fly shudders and thinks so too, but there is a dash, and a thud, and some flustered feathers, and a badly frightened bird, but the fly is still there, wondering how it all did not happen. But to you

and me the secret is all plain, there was something between which the bird did not see and the fly forgot. Thank God, when the devil makes his fiercest dives, there is something between. He has to get through Jesus Christ to get you; and if you only abide in simple confidence, the devil will get a good deal more hurt than you.

8. *He is able to keep His servants and ministers.* Listen. "I the Lord have called thee in righteousness, and will hold thine hand, and will keep thee, and give thee for a covenant of the people, for a light of the Gentiles "(Isa. xlii. 6). This blessed promise belongs primarily to the Lord Jesus, but secondarily to every other true servant of Jehovah who is abiding in Him and working for Him. God holds His ministers in His right hand and says, "Touch not mine anointed and do my prophets no harm." He is a very reckless man that lightly speaks or acts against any true servant of the Lord. Be careful how you criticize the Master's servants. Listen. "Who art thou that judgest another man's servant? To his own master he standeth or falleth, for God is able to make him stand." "Who art thou that judgest another?" If you are serving Christ with a true heart, my brother, be not afraid. He whom the Father beholds will hold thy right hand, and keep thee, and say to thee, "Fear not, I will give men for thee and people for thy life." "I will work and who shall let it?" God will keep thee and say to thee, "I have covered thee in the shadow of Mine hand that thou mayest plant the heavens, and lay the foundations of the earth and say to *Zion,* Thou art my people." A single soldier of the cross standing for Jesus and trusting in Him is mightier than legions of powerful foes. Trust Him though dangers and foes surround thee and friends may often be few, the heavens will fall and earth be dissolved before He can fail one of His trusting servants.

9. *He will keep His cause, His Church, His vineyard.* "Sing ye unto her, A vineyard of red wine. I the Lord do keep it; I will water

it every moment; lest any hurt it, I will keep it night and day." Isa. xxvii. 2-3. We sometimes seem to get the idea that we are the keepers of God's cause, and that he has forgotten all about it, and we have to shout and cry to get Him to help us look after His own property. Why, dear friends, the Lord is looking after you and the cause too. "I, the Lord, do keep it, lest any hurt it, I will keep it night and day." No doubt there are dangers, trials, adversaries, but there is one thing more, the Lord. And two little words are stronger than all the D's in the dictionary, whether they be difficulty, discouragement, division, declension, the devil, or the D.Ds.- and these two words are BUT GOD. There is a fine prophetic picture in the opening of Zechariah which was written to comfort people in troublous times. First the prophet saw four horns, coming from all directions, sharp, cruel, powerful horns, pushing and piercing everything before them. If he looked north, there was a horn there, and south, there was another there, and they were soon to meet and he would find himself between the two. If he looked east, there was a horn there, and west, there was another there, and they were meeting in his unprotected breast. Then the scene changed, and he looked and saw four carpenters coming in the same direction, and each of them had a lot of tools-a good stout ax, and a sharp saw, and no doubt a heavy maul- and soon could be heard the sound of blows of axes and the buzzing of saws, and lo, the horns had lost their points and were pounded to a jelly and were soft cushions that could not hurt anything. Beloved, God has a carpenter for every horn and if the work you are doing is His work, the gates of hell cannot prevail against it.

10. *He is able to keep everything that is committed to Him.* "I know whom I have believed, and am persuaded that he is able to keep that which I have committed unto him against that day" (II. Tim. 1:12). The great question for you and me is, how much have we really committed?

Walking in the Spirit

By
A. B. Simpson

A. B. SIMPSON

Chapter 1.
LIVING IN THE SPIRIT

"If we live in the Spirit, let us also walk in the Spirit."
Gal. 5: 25.

What is it to Live in the Spirit?

It is to be born of the Spirit. It is to have received a new spiritual life from above. "That which is born of the flesh is flesh, that which is born of the Spirit is Spirit. "Except a man be born of water and of the Spirit, he cannot enter into the Kingdom of God." "If any man be in Christ, he is a new creature; old things have passed away; behold, all things have become new." We may have the brightest intellectual life, the most unblemished moral character, and the most amiable qualities of disposition, and yet without the new life of the Holy Spirit in our heart, we can no more enter Heaven than the lovely canary that sings in our window can become a member of our family, or the gentle lamb that our children play with can sit down at our table, and share our domestic fellowship and enjoyment. It belongs to a different world, and nothing but a new nature and human heart could bring it into fellowship with our human life. The most exalted intellect, and the most attractive, natural disposition, reach no higher than the earthly. The Kingdom of Heaven consists of the family of God, those who have risen to an entirely different sphere, and received a nature as much above the intellectual and the moral as God is above an angel.

A modern writer has finely wrought out this wonderful thought of the difference between the various orders of life, even in the natural world. The little tuft of moss that grows upon the granite rock can look down from immeasurable heights upon the mass of stone on which it rests and say, "I am transcendently above you, for I have life, vegetable life, and you are an inorganic mass!" And yet, as we ascend one step, the smallest insect that crawls upon the majestic palm tree can look down upon the most beautiful production of the vegetable world and say, "I am transcendently above you, for I have animal life, and you have not even the consciousness of your own loveliness, or of the little creature that feeds upon your blossom!" Still higher we ascend, until we reach the world of mind; and the youngest child of the most illiterate peasant can say to the mightiest creations of the animal world, to the majestic lion, king of the forest; the soaring eagle of the skies; the many-tinted bird of Paradise, or the noble steed that bears his master, like the whirlwind, over the desert, "I am your lord, for I possess intellectual life, and you have neither soul nor reason, and must perish with your expiring breath, and become like the clods beneath your feet, but I shall live forever. But there is still another step beyond all this. There is a spiritual world which is as much higher than the intellectual as that is above the physical; and the humblest and most uncultured Christian, who has just learned to pray, and say, "Our Father, who art in Heaven" from the depths of a regenerate heart, is as much above the loftiest genius of the world of mind as he is above the material creation at his feet.

This is the meaning of Christianity; it is the breath of a new nature; it is the translation of the soul into a higher universe and a loftier scale of being, even introducing it into the family of God Himself and making it a part of the Divine nature. This is indeed a stupendous mystery, and a bestowment whose glory may well fill our hearts with everlasting wonder, as we cry with the adoring apostle, "Behold what manner of love the Father hath bestowed upon us, that we should be called the sons of God!"

Not by adoption merely are we thus admitted to the Father's house, but by actual birth; from the very bosom of the Holy Ghost, as from a heavenly mother, has our new spirit been born; just as literally as Jesus Christ Himself was born of the eternal Spirit in the bosom of Mary. So it might be said of every newborn soul:

"The Holy Ghost shall come upon thee, and the power of the Highest shall overshadow thee; therefore, that holy thing which shall be born of thee shall be called the Son of God." Beloved, do we thus live in the Spirit? This is everlasting life.

2. To live in the Spirit is also to be baptized of the Holy Ghost, and have the Spirit as a Divine person living in us. There is something higher than the new birth, namely, the entering in of the Comforter, in His personal fullness and glory, to dwell in the consecrated heart and abide there for ever. Jesus was born of the Spirit in Bethlehem, but He was baptized of the Spirit thirty years later on the banks of the Jordan; and this made all the difference which we trace between His quiet years at Nazareth and His public ministry in Galilee and Judea. From that time there were two persons united in the ministry of Jesus of Nazareth. The Holy Ghost, as a Divine person, was united with the person of Jesus Christ, and was the source of His power and the inspiration of His teaching; and He constantly represented Himself as speaking the words and doing the works which the Spirit in Him prompted.

And so there is in the believer's life a similar experience, when the soul truly converted to God yields itself wholly to His control and becomes the living temple of the Almighty Spirit, who henceforth dwells in us, and walks in us, giving us not only a new nature, which we receive in regeneration, but a Divine Guest, a Presence to dwell in that new nature as its controlling guide and Almighty strength.

Then is fulfilled the double promise of Ezekiel: "A new heart will I give unto you and a new spirit will I put within you, and I will put my Spirit within you and will cause you to walk in my statutes, and ye shall keep my judgments and do them." Henceforth, we live in the Spirit in a higher sense than even before our conversion. Our life is not only spiritual but divine. Henceforth, it is not we who live, but Christ who liveth in us, and we draw from Him, through the Holy Ghost, every moment, life, and health, and joy, and peace. It is not living through the Spirit, but living in the Spirit. He is the very element of our new existence; before us, behind us, above us, beneath us, within us, beyond us, we are buried in Him, lost in Him, encompassed by Him as by the air we breathe. This is the yet higher mystery of the new life, greater than the new birth. This is the secret which Paul declares was hid for ages and generations, but now made manifest to His saints. "Christ in you the hope of glory."

It is, indeed, an epoch in the soul's existence as wonderful in its measure as when the Son of God became incarnate on earth, when the Holy One crosses the threshold of the heart, and makes the spirit his personal residence, sits down upon the throne of the human will and assumes the government and control of all our being and destiny. Henceforth, we may indeed walk with holy veneration and exalted hope, exultant in joy and triumph as wondering angels declare, "Behold the tabernacle of God is with men, He will dwell with them and they shall be His people; God Himself shall be with them and shall be their God."

Beloved, have you claimed this high privilege, and received this heavenly Guest into the golden casket of your regenerated souls? Have you received the invaluable jewel of the Living One Himself, as the treasure in the earthen vessel and the glory in the midst?

3. To live in the Spirit is to be sanctified by the Spirit; to receive the Spirit of holiness and thus be delivered from the power of sin. They, who thus receive the Holy Ghost can say, "The spirit of life in Christ Jesus hath made me free from the law of sin and death." This is divine holiness; it is the entrance into a sinful heart of a new life which excludes the old and takes its place. It is not the cleansing of the flesh or the improving of the life of self; but it is the imparting to us of a new life which is in itself essentially pure and cannot sin, even the holy life of God.

In our childhood many of us have roamed through the native woods and seen some old fallen forest tree rotting where it lay. Through the decaying wood the earthworms and insects burrow, and perhaps the adder has built its nest and raised its poisonous brood, so that we have feared to sit down on the old, putrefying mass, and have thought of it as a type of corruption and decay. That mass of putrefaction may well represent the ruin of our sinful nature. But have we not sometimes seen a little shoot of unsullied whiteness in the early spring growing up through the rotten wood, and rising out of the mass of corruption as undefiled as the sunny wing of a dove, or the gentle hand of a babe, beautiful and pure, and unstained even by the touch of the corrupting element around it, until it has grown into a tree and covered itself with luxurious green, and our hands have often plucked from its branches the luscious berries of the summer woods? It was life in the midst of death, purity amid corruption, having no connection whatever with the soil in which it grew and incapable of mixture with its defilement.

Precisely so is the life of holiness in the soul. Like that stainless shoot, it grew from a Divine root, and has nothing in common with our own sinful nature. It is of heavenly origin, and it grows up within us in its own Divine purity and fruitfulness, until it ripens into all the rich fruition of a consecrated and heavenly life, and yet at every stage we feel that it is in no sense our own life, but the indwelling presence and purity of God Himself.

Beloved, have we received this sanctifying Spirit and learned this heavenly secret of holy living? And in all the exquisite rest and conscious purity and overcoming power of His presence, have we learned to live in the Spirit?

4. To live in the Spirit is to receive the quickening life of the Holy Ghost in our physical being, and to find in Him the source of constant stimulus and strength for all the faculties of our mind, and all the functions of our body; "For if the Spirit of Him

that raised up Jesus from the dead dwell in us, He that raised up Christ from the dead shall also quicken our mortal bodies by His Spirit, that dwelleth in us." The subtle principle of life itself came originally, no doubt, from His inbreathing at man's creation, and why should it be thought anything incredible that He should still breathe upon our flesh the quickening life of the ascended Son of God? Are we not members of His body, and His flesh, and His bones, and does He not speak of a distinct sense in which our body is the temple of the Holy Ghost? Indeed it was the Holy Ghost, who, during Christ's ministry, always gave efficiency to His healing word, and who, through the apostles, continued to perform the same works of supernatural power. He is still the same infinite and inexhaustible life, and the bodies of His consecrated people are the subjects of His Divine influence, and His sustaining love and care.

Have we learned, beloved, the secret of His strength, and like Samson of old, do we know what it is to be moved by the Spirit until the earthen vessel becomes mighty through God to do and endure where earthly strength must fail? They, who thus "wait upon the Lord, shall renew their strength; mount up with wings as eagles; run, and not be weary, walk, and not faint."

Chapter 2.
WALKING IN THE SPIRIT

I. What is it to Walk in the Spirit?

Generally, it may be said, it is to maintain the habit of dependence upon the Holy Ghost for our entire life; spirit, soul and body. We know what it is at times to enjoy His conscious presence. We live in the Spirit, we have felt the touch of His quickening life, now let us walk in the Spirit. Let us abide in this fellowship. Let us lean continually upon His strength, and drink unceasingly from His life, a babe from its mother's breast. But more particularly.

1. To walk in the Spirit is to recognize the Spirit as present and abiding in us. How often, after we have asked His presence, we treat Him as if He had deceived us, and cry to Him as if He were afar off! Let us recognize Him as having come, and address Him as a present and indwelling friend. He will always meet our recognition, and speak to us as the ancient presence, not from the mount, or the pillar of fire, but from the tabernacle, and from the holy of holies in our inmost heart.

2. It means to trust Him and count upon Him in the emergencies of life, to regard Him as one who has undertaken our cause and expects to be called upon in every time of need, and will unfailingly be found faithful and all-sufficient in every crisis. The very name Paraclete means one that we can always call upon and find at our side. We must trust the Holy Spirit, and expect Him to respond to our need as implicitly as we expect the air to answer the opening of our lungs, and the sunrise to meet us in the morning. And yet how many treat the Holy Spirit as if He were a capricious and most unreliable friend! How may of our prayers are despairing groans or scolding reflections on His love and faithfulness!

It was for this that Moses lost the Promised Land; instead of quietly speaking to the rock and expecting its waters to flow forth to meet his call, he struck it with hasty and unbelieving violence and spake as one who did not fully trust the love and faithfulness of God. There is no need that we should strike the rock, or cry, like Baal's priests to the distant heavens for help. Let us gently and implicitly claim the love that is always in advance even of our prayer. Let us speak in the whisper of childlike trust to that bosom which is ever ready to pour its fullness into our empty hearts, and lo! the waters will gush forth, and the desert of our sorrows, doubts, and fears will blossom as the rose.

3. We must consult the Holy Spirit if we would walk in the Spirit. We shall often find that the things that seem most easy will fail and disappoint us when we rely upon their apparent probability and the mere promise of outward circumstances, and we shall also find where we commit our way unto Him, and acknowledge Him in all our ways, that He will so direct our paths that the things which seemed most difficult and improbable, will become the easiest and the most successful. He would teach us thus to trust in Him with all our heart, and lean not unto our own understanding; in all our ways to acknowledge Him and He will direct our steps.

The chief condition of His Almighty power is that we shall first have His omniscient wisdom. He is given to us as our wonderful Counselor and also as our Mighty God. And I have never taken Him as my Counselor and obeyed His guidance without finding that He followed it up as the Mighty One with His omnipotent working. The reason we do not more frequently find His power is because we try to turn it into the channels of our own wisdom instead of getting His mind, working in His will, and even knowing that we must have His effectual working. How blessed that the wonderful Counselor is always a child, and that His guidance offered to each of us is as simple, as accessible as the hand of a little child.

So let us walk in the Spirit, trusting His guiding hand, and committing all our ways to His wisdom and love.

4. If we would walk in the Spirit we must obey Him when He does speak, and we must remember that the first part of obedience is to hearken. It is not enough to say we have done all we knew. We ought to know, and we may know, for He has said that we shall know His voice, and if we do not it must be that we are to blame, or else God is responsible for our mistake. But this cannot be.

If we will be still and suppress our own impulses and clamorous desires, and will meet Him with a heart surrendered to His will and guidance, we shall know His way. "The meek will He guide in judgment, and the meek will He teach His way." The soul that walks in the Spirit will therefore be a hearkening spirit, watching daily at His doors, and longing to know His very commandments; and when we understand His voice we will implicitly obey it. The minding of the Spirit is life and peace. The very condition of His continual presence is obedience. "The Holy Spirit whom God hath given to them that obey Him." The secret of every cloud that has fallen upon the soul will probably be found in some neglected voice of our Monitor. He is waiting and has been waiting for us at that point where we have refused to follow, and when we step in His will we shall find Him there.

5. Walking in the Spirit implies that we shall keep step with the Holy Ghost, and that our obedience shall be so prompt that we shall never find ourselves a step behind Him, and following Him at a distance, from which we may find it hard to recover.

On our great railroads there are certain trains which run upon the highest possible schedule of time. The itinerary is so arranged that there is no margin allowed on which to overtake lost time, so that, should the train be late, it is scarcely possible to overtake the interval lost. God has drawn the plan of our life on such a scale that there are no minutes left blank, and if we lose one, the next has no margin to afford for its recovery. All that we can crowd into the future will be needed for the future itself, and therefore if we lose a step there is danger that we shall continue to be a step behind, and it will require the same exertion to keep up even a step behind as it would to walk abreast of God every moment.

Yonder mill-race needs just as much water to run at low as at high tide. The very same quantity of water, if kept up to the level of the wheel, will run all the ponderous machinery as that which on a lower level only wastes itself in fretting wavelets among the rocks of the torrent bed. And so it is just as easy for our spiritual life to move at the maximum as at the minimum if we only start at the right level, and so guard the moments that we shall not lose our headway, or get behind God. The secret of this one blessing is instant obedience and walking by the moment with Him in the fullness of His blessed will. Let us not disappoint Him. Let us not come short of all the good pleasure of His goodness. His thought for us is always best; His commandments "for our good always;" His schedule of our life-journey planned by unerring wisdom and unutterable love.

He has given us a gentle, patient Guide, who is willing to go with us all the way, and come into the minutest steppings of our life. Let us take heed that we grieve Him not away nor miss aught of His gentle will. Let us be sensitive to His touch, responsive to His whisper, obedient to His commandments, and able ever to say "He hath not left me alone, for I did always those things which please Him."

II. Some of the Blessings of thus Walking in the Spirit.

1. It will secure us a complete and delightful deliverance from sin. The expulsive power of His presence will drive out the presence of evil. "If we walk in the Spirit we shall not fulfill the lusts of the flesh." Our life shall thus be transformed from a defensive warfare, in which we are always attacking evil, to a glorious consciousness of God only, which shall exclude the evil from our

thought as well as from our life. We shall not have to constantly clear the sunken rocks from our channel, but on the high and full torrent of the Divine life we shall rise far above every obstruction and move, as in Ezekiel's vision, in a river of life which shall be above the ankles, and above the loins, a river to swim in, carrying us by its own substantial fullness.

2. Such a walk will give a delightful serenity, tranquility, and steadfastness to our whole life. We shall not be at the bidding of impulses or circumstances, but shall move on in the majestic order of the Divine will, carried above the vicissitudes of failure and outward change, and fulfilling, like the stars in their courses, the full circle of His will for our life.

3. Such a walk will enable us to meet the providences of God as they come to us in victory, and to maintain the perfect harmony between our inward life and the outward leadings of His own. We have some beautiful examples of the transcendent importance of this walking in the Spirit, in connection with the conjunctures of circumstances on which so much often hangs. There never was a moment in human history on which more depended than that when the infant Christ was first brought into the Temple. What an honor and privilege it was to be there and catch the first glimpse of His blessed face, and even hold in the embrace of human arms the Gift of ages! Yet that was the honor of two aged pilgrims who were walking in the Spirit. Simeon and Anna, led of the Holy Ghost, came in at that very moment into the Temple. Led of God unerringly, and walking step by step with Him, they were enabled to meet Him in this glorious opportunity, and be the first heralds of His coming. No wonder the aged Simeon, as he took him in his arms, could ask no more on earth: "Lord, now lettest Thou Thy servant depart in peace, for mine eyes have seen Thy salvation."

Only less important was the crisis in the apostolic church when the gospel was to be preached for the first time to a new circle of disciples. The man chosen to carry the glad tidings to the

Samaritans and the Gentiles, and to be the pioneer of Christianity among all the myriad tribes of the heathen world in that great progression of which the churches of Christendom today form the outcome, was a humble disciple, whom God could trust to walk in the Spirit and obey the slightest intimation of His will. It was Philip, the humble deacon. Already he had been sent to Samaria to preach the gospel in that city, no doubt in obedience to a similar Divine message. But, in the very height of his successful work in that city, the command suddenly comes to him to leave his work and go down to the desert of the South.

To most persons it would have seemed a misleading, a mistake, a neglect of providential duty, a waste of precious time, and an arresting of the great work in Samaria. But Philip immediately obeyed, and at every step of his journey he waited for new directions, and in due time the path was made plain. The first fruits of the heathen world were waiting at that very moment for his direction; and there on the crossroads of life, at the fitting moment, the Spirit brought those two men together, and the words were spoken in that chariot by the way, which changed the destiny of a life, and the course of a Dispensation, which opened the gospel to the whole world, and sent that Ethiopian prince to his home, to be, in all probability, the founder of many of those mighty churches, which for the next four centuries made Northern Africa the most important seat of ancient Christianity.

Yet, when his work with the eunuch was accomplished, the command was as distinct, to leave his new convert in the hands of the Lord, and follow on at the unknown leading of the same blessed Spirit that had brought them together." "The Spirit caught away Philip," we are told, "and the eunuch saw him no more." These are but some instances of the blessedness of this heavenly walk. Shall we trust our unseen Guide, and as we step out into the mysterious and momentous future, shall we walk more humbly, simply, instantly, and obediently in the companionship of His guiding hand?

Chapter 3.
PERSON AND ATTRIBUTES OF THE HOLY GHOST

"God hath not given us the Spirit of fear, but of power, and of love, and of a sound mind." 2 Tim. 1: 7.

I. The Holy Spirit is a Person.

The Holy Ghost is a distinct individual, and not a vague influence, or a phase of Divine working.

Just as there are three judges on the bench, constituting the one court, three persons in the household, constituting the one family, so there are three distinct persons in the Godhead, yet forming together the one Deity, and more perfectly one in nature, volition, and action than it is possible for any created beings to harmonize.

The Holy Spirit is constantly spoken of in the Scriptures as possessing the attributes of a person. The personal pronoun is used to describe Him not it, but He; and the strongest and most distinctive of the Greek pronouns, that word 'autos,' which means 'himself,' and distinguishes personality, as no English term can, is often used of Him; as, for example, in 1 Cor. 12: 11, "That one and the self-same Spirit." Again, the attribute of will is ascribed to Him in the same passage, "as He will," and there is no stronger proof of personality than the power of choice. It is the most distinctive thing in any human being, and it is constantly attributed to the Holy Ghost.

Again, all the emotions proper to a person are ascribed to Him; He knows, loves, is grieved, is provoked, vexed, resisted, and, in short, is susceptible to all the feelings that are proper only for an intelligent person.

II. The Holy Spirit is a Divine Person.

This glorious Being is no less than God. He receives the divine names. Peter tells Ananias that in lying unto the Holy Ghost he has not lied unto men but unto God. Christ declares that in casting out devils by the Holy Ghost, He does it by the finger of God. He possesses Divine attributes; He is omniscient; "The Spirit searcheth all things;" omnipresent; "Whither shall I go from Thy Spirit, or hide from Thy Presence;" omnipotent; for Christ declares that, "The things that are impossible with men," namely, the salvation of the human soul, "are possible with God," and it is the Holy Ghost that converts the soul, therefore, He must have the omnipotence of God.

He is called the Holy Spirit, and holiness is a Divine attribute. Again, He performs the works of God; He was a partaker in the work of creation; the Spirit of light, order, beauty and life. He accomplishes the regeneration and sanctification of the soul which are divine works; He effected the incarnation and resurrection of the Son of God, and He will participate in the final resurrection of the saints of God from the tomb, at the Lord's coming.

Such works could be performed by no man, and they stamp Him as Divine. And, finally, He receives Divine worship; His name is associated with the Father and the Son in apostolic benediction, the formula of baptism, and the worship of the heavenly host. And John opens the Apocalypse with an ascription of praise, which links Him with the Father, and would be blasphemy if it were not Divine.

III. The Personal Attributes of the Holy Ghost.

Three of these only we shall mention. The three named in our text. "He is the Spirit of power, and of love, and of a sound mind."

1. His power. He is Almighty. Within the sphere of His special office and operations there is nothing He cannot do; there

is no case too hard for His working, no soul too lost for Him to save, too hard for Him to soften, too vile for Him to sanctify, too weak for His use. He is the Spirit of creation. Look abroad upon the springing forces of nature, throbbing in the springtide of life and glory; how quietly, majestically and resistlessly nature is moving on to the resurrection of the year, to the fullness and glory of the summer and the harvest; how abundant and redundant the exuberant life and power we behold on every hand, covering the forest and the field with a wealth of luxuriance of flowers, and foliage, and fruitfulness, beyond the actual needs of earth's inhabitants; scattering with tropical bounty the gifts of God, as though His strength and love were so full He knew not how to find vent for all its overflow.

Why should He be less full, less bountiful, less Almighty in the realm of grace? Nay, larger and nobler still is His promise here. "I will pour water upon him that is thirsty, and floods upon the dry ground," is His blessed promise.

There is no stint to His resources. Let us enter into His omnipotence, and go forth knowing the might of our God, and claiming the full plentitude of His power and grace.

But mightier still is the power displayed in the resurrection of Jesus Christ. When the apostle would lift our conception up to an adequate realization of the hope of our calling and the riches of the glory of our inheritance, and the exceeding greatness of God's power to usward who believe, he points us to that transcendent miracle, the resurrection of Jesus Christ. He sees Him, without an effort, bursting the bonds of death, snapping asunder the sealed tomb, rising up above all the power of death and the natural law of mortality, above the laws of the material world, and passing through the closed door, and rising above the solid earth, as He triumphantly ascends above all might and dominion, far above all principality and power, higher and higher, till He is above the earth, above the sky, above the heavens, above every name that is named, not only in this world, but that which is to come. And then He sees us seated by His side, and raised up by the same Holy Spirit to share in all the fullness of Christ's ascension, glory and power. This is the measure of the power of grace; let us claim it in all its majestic fullness, and bring it down to lift up our life and the souls around us, to the heights of grace and glory.

2. Let us think of His love; it is greater than His power; all the terms in which He is described are notes of tenderness and expressions of gentleness, loveliness and grace. "I beseech you," says the apostle, "by the love of the Spirit." What love it was for Jesus Christ to live for thirty years and more in this uncongenial world, but oh! not less the love of the blessed Holy Ghost; He has lived for eighteen hundred years in this scene of sin, and this land of enemies.

How gentle the love of Jesus in coming so near to sinful men, but the Holy Ghost has come still nearer, but He enters our very hearts, and dwells in the inmost bosom of lost and worthless men. How marvelous the grace of Christ that endured the shame and spitting, the rejection and crucifixion of the Judgment Hall and the cross, but not less the gentleness which has pleaded for ages with wicked men, and borne all their resistance, rebellion and rejection, and yet waited through a whole lifetime to win the faintest response from their faith or love.

How much He has borne from each of us; how gently and patiently He has suffered our slights, endured our ignorance, stupidity, gross, and direct disobedience!

How close He is willing to come to the heart; how unreserved and condescending His intimacy and affection; how dear we are to His affection! None but His loved ones know how exquisite and intimate the communion which we may enjoy under His feathers and wings, and on the bosom of His love; telling Him all our sorrow and care, finding Him responsive to every whisper and breathing of our heart, and ever near, by day or by night, our blessed Paraclete, and ever present One, ready to help in every time of need.

He asks more of our trust and love: Oh! let Him not ask in vain. Let us know, and prove, and fully appreciate the love of the Spirit.

3. He is the Spirit of wisdom.

Not only can He give us wisdom, but with a wisdom greater than all that we may see, He is guiding, teaching, overruling all our life. Let us trust His wisdom, love, and power, and as we read these succeeding pages, yield ourselves with a glad " yes" to His every call, and know the full blessing of "Walking in the Spirit."

Chapter 4.
OFFICES AND RELATIONS OF THE HOLY GHOST

I. The Holy Spirit in Relation to the Godhead.

This Divine person has a special place in the Trinity, and in the Divine economy.

With respect to the Father, He is spoken of as proceeding from Him; the same term is also used of His relation to the Son; He has been called the executive of the Godhead.

Many figures have been used; although all such figures must ever be unsatisfactory to illustrate the relation of the Divine persons. Perhaps the most successful is that which compares them to the various forms of light; primeval light, representing the Father; solar light, that is, light centered in an actual sun, representing the Son, and atmospheric light, that is, the light reflected and refracted, and turned into vision and illumination in the atmosphere and the world around us, the Holy Ghost, who brings to us the Divine Presence, and practically applies to us the benefits of God's revelation and grace.

His relation to the second person of the Godhead is very clearly revealed; it was He who ministered in His incarnation, and through whom He became the Son of Man as well as the Son of God. It was He who personally united Himself with the person of Christ, and became the power of all His miracles and teachings. It was He through whom "He offered Himself without spot to God." It was He through whom He arose from the dead. And after His resurrection it was by the Holy Ghost that He gave commandment to His apostles of all things concerning the kingdom of heaven. Again, it was in His own person that He received and shed forth the same Spirit of Pentecost upon His disciples, so that Jesus is ever identified with the Holy Ghost in all His work and ministry.

Nor is there any reason to suppose that He will be sent from the world in the millennial kingdom, but will be an actual and joyful witness of the blessed fruits of His own gracious working, as well as the Savior's suffering and death.

II. The revelation of the Holy Spirit to the world and the sinner.

"Whom the world cannot receive" is Christ's own explanation of his relation to the unsaved, "because it seeth Him not, neither knoweth Him." The Holy Ghost cannot dwell in an unconverted soul. On man's flesh the anointing oil could not be poured of old, nor can it still.

At the same time, He can and does work in the hearts of the unconverted, producing conviction and conversion, and leading them to a saving union with the person of Christ. This is His own special work; the sinful soul is dead in trespasses and sins, and it is His to quicken it, to convict of sin; and then of righteousness and judgment, and bring to the heart the revelation of Jesus, and, as it accepts Him, the assurance of pardon, the peace of God, and all the quickened graces of the new life in Christ.

III. This relation to the believer.

Having led the soul to Christ, the Holy Spirit now becomes the personal Guide, Teacher, Sanctifier and Comforter of the believer. His various ministries will be unfolded in the following chapters.

When the heart is fully surrendered to Him, He becomes its personal, permanent, indwelling Guest; bringing with Him the manifested presence of the Father and the Son, leading into all truth, guiding in all the will of God, supplying all the needed grace, unfolding the life of Jesus Christ in the believer's daily life, and developing all the fruits of the Spirit in their full variety and complete maturity.

He is the Spirit of light and revelation, of guidance, and of wisdom. He is the Spirit of holiness. He is the Spirit of peace, joy and comfort. He is the Spirit of love, gentleness, patience, meekness, and forbearance. He is the Spirit of prayer and intercession. He is the Spirit of power for service, and the source of all our gifts as well as graces. He is the Spirit of physical life and healing. He is the Spirit of faith and hope, enabling us to claim the promises of God, and revealing to us the glorious prospects of the future. Our whole spiritual life is nourished and cherished by His love and care; and all we are, and have, and may become, in our Christian life, is due to His personal indwelling, and His faithful love and infinite grace.

But in all His work in the believer's heart and life, He ever represents and reveals, not His own person or ours, but the Lord Jesus: He is the Spirit of Christ; "He shall testify of me; He shall glorify me," was the Master's own language; "for He shall take of the things that are mine, and shall show them unto you."

He reveals to us our personal union with Jesus and makes Christ actual to our consciousness. "At that day," that is when He comes, "ye shall know that I am in my Father, and ye in me, and I in you."

Like the telescope, which shows the observer, not its own beauty, but the heavenly orbs on which we gaze through its crystal lens, so the Holy Ghost becomes the invisible medium through whom we behold the face of Jesus, and are brought into the consciousness of His grace and fellowship.

Therefore, the soul is conscious of Christ, rather than the Spirit, even in the moment of His most blessed visitations. And yet we may be directly conscious of the Spirit also, and hold immediate fellowship with Him personally, receive the assurance of His love, and pour out into His heart our gratitude and affection.

IV. Relation to the Church.

Not only to the individual believer, but to the collective body of the people of God does the Holy Spirit specially come. It is He who constitutes the Church, and clothes her with the life and power of her Living Head. Until the day of Pentecost and the descent of the Spirit, the apostles were not permitted to go forth, and to speak and work for the Master.

The Holy Ghost is the very life and power of Christianity, and without Him the Church is like a ship without fire in her engine, or steam in her boiler; like an army of soldiers lying lifeless; like Ezekiel's vision in the plain; like a body without an animated soul.

The Church was never intended to be a natural and intellectual organization, but a supernatural instrumentality wholly dependent upon the direct power of God for all her efficiency, and therefore, needing to be ever separated from the arm of flesh and the strength of mere human agencies.

The Church in which the Holy Ghost abides is no mere sectarian fragment, but the whole body of believers united to Christ, the Living Head. "There is one body, even as ye are called in one hope of your calling, for by one Spirit are we all baptized into one body;" and though there be diversities of gifts, it is the same Spirit; differences of administrations, it is the same Lord; varieties of operations, it is the same God which worketh all in all. For to one is given, by the same Spirit, the word of wisdom; to another the word of knowledge, by the same Spirit; to another faith, by the same Spirit; to another the gift of healing, by the same Spirit; to another the working of miracles, to another prophecy, to another discerning of spirits, to another diverse kinds of tongues, to another the interpretation of tongues; but all these worketh that one and the self-same Spirit, dividing to every man severally as He will

For as the body is one and has many members, and all the members of that one body, being many, are one body; so also is Christ. For by one Spirit are we all baptized into one body, whether we be Jews or Gentiles, whether we be bond or free; and have been all made to drink into one Spirit. For the body is not one member, but many."

V. The Revelation of the Holy Spirit to the various Dispensations.

In all the dispensational periods of the past, the Holy Ghost has been present. Even in the antediluvian days, He strove with men. Under the Levitical economy He was present, qualifying the builders of the tabernacle for their work, anointing Moses, Aaron, and Joshua for their ministry, inspiring the ancient prophets for their messages, and enabling the individual believers of the Old Testament to know, believe, and obey God in the measure of their spiritual life.

But until after Christ's ascension the Holy Spirit was not personally resident as He is now. His influences were exercised upon the hearts of men, but His presence was not localized, as it has been since the day of Pentecost, in the body of Christ, the Church. Just as Queen Victoria exercises her influence over her Canadian provinces, but does not reside there, so the Holy Spirit was present in the world potentially, but not personally, as now.

Since the beginning of the Christian dispensation, however, he has resided on earth, and not in heaven, and is here locally, as the Lord Jesus was during His earthly life. The transcendent preeminence which a New Testament saint enjoys is, that his soul and body become the living and actual temple of the Holy Ghost.

This is the time of His special working; in an age when we may look for His unlimited operations, and toward the close of which we should anticipate the mightiest triumphs of His grace and power, as He shall usher in the next, namely, the millennial age, with the personal presence of Christ once more on earth, as in the days of His flesh.

But, even then, the Holy Ghost will not be absent. He will ever reside in the believer and the Church.

The question has been argued whether the Holy Spirit will be present on earth during the tribulation days, after the saints have been translated to be with the Lord in the air. We cannot doubt that He will still remain on earth, for how else could the Jewish remnant, who shall follow the Lamb, be converted, sustained and saved; also the Gentile remnant, who during those awful days shall turn to the Lord, including perhaps many of the members of a cold church who were not ready for the Master's coming at the time of His appearing?

We, therefore, cannot agree with the view of some; that when the saints are caught up to meet the Lord, the Holy Spirit shall be taken away from earth. We believe He has chosen this dark abode of sin and sorrow as the scene of His ceaseless, and ultimately triumphant labors, and that He shall yet rejoice over it as a restored and renovated realm, shining in all the loveliness, sinlessness and blessedness of His accomplished restoration.

Chapter 5.
EMBLEMS AND ASPECTS OF THE HOLY SPIRIT

"The Seven Spirits which are before His Throne."
Rev. 1: 4.

This expression denotes the fullness of the Holy Spirit. The number seven is expressive of divine completeness, and the benediction of the seven spirits is equivalent to the ascription of Paul in the first chapter of Ephesians: "Blessed be the God and Father of our Lord Jesus Christ, who hath blessed us with all spiritual blessings in heavenly places in Christ Jesus."

In keeping with this seven-fold expression of the Spirit's fullness, is the fact that we have seven special emblems of the Holy Spirit given us in the Scriptures, each fitted to emphasize some special phase of His character and work. As the Holy Ghost has no personal and incarnate form like Christ, He has clothed Himself in the robes of symbol, and thus becomes to us more real and vivid in the figures of human speech and earthly imagery.

I. The Dove

1. The earliest symbol of the Holy Spirit is the dove. Not in express terms is this figure introduced in the Old Testament, but the allusion in the opening verses of Genesis is sufficiently clear to be recognized. "The Spirit of God moved upon the deep;" literally this is translated, "The Spirit of God fluttered or brooded upon the face of the deep." It is the picture of the mother-bird spreading her wing over the stormy elements, and incubating, as it were, her brood through the dark night of chaos.

It is the same typical figure that we meet again as the emblem of peace and gentleness, and the herald of the morning of the new world in the dark and stormy night of the deluge. It is the same blessed person, who, on the banks of the Jordan, descended in visible form like a dove, and abode upon the Lord Jesus, the herald of peace and love to a sinful world, and the emblem of the Spirit of Christ's ministry. As the dove, the Holy Ghost is the Spirit of peace, the Giver of rest.

This is also a figure of motherhood, which is constantly associated with the picture of the blessed Paraclete. In the Divine Trinity there is found the substance of all relationships, and that which is expressed in human motherhood must always have been in the bosom of God.

Of this the Holy Ghost is the personal expression. From that material breast our new life is born; by that gentle Spirit our spiritual childhood is nurtured, comforted, educated, developed, and matured. "As one who his mother comforteth," so doth the Comforter love and cheer our sorrowing hearts. As the brooding dove, so does this blessed One hide us beneath the wings of God, and cover us with the feathers of the divine sympathy and tenderness.

It is almost difficult to use the masculine form in speaking of this blessed person, so womanlike is the sweetness and softness of His touch.

> His is that gentle voice we hear,
> Soft as the breath of even,
> That stills each doubt, and calms each tear,
> And speaks to us of heaven.

II. Air is the next symbol of the Spirit.

This also appears in the opening chapter of Genesis. "The Lord God breathed into his nostrils the breath of life, and man became a living soul." And this we know was the Holy Spirit, for, we are told, "The inspiration of the Almighty giveth life." "Thou sendest forth thy Spirit, they are created."

The same figure is used by the prophet Ezekiel in describing the resurrection of the dry bones. It was the Spirit that came from the four winds and breathed upon the slain, and they lived.

Our Lord has used this figure in two very striking connections. The first is in relation to the regeneration of a soul. "The wind bloweth where it listeth, and thou hearest the sound thereof, but canst not tell whither it cometh nor whither it goeth, so is every one that is born of the Spirit."

It is like the voiceless wind, known not by visible perception, but by its effects.

Again he uses it in connection with the personal imparting of the Holy Ghost to His own disciples. "He breathed on them and said, receive ye the Holy Ghost."

In keeping with this figure the Hebrew and Greek word is the same as that used for the wind, or the breath. The Holy Ghost is the breath of God. This emblem expresses at once the gentleness and the strength of the Holy Ghost. His coming may be as quiet as the evening zephyr, or mighty as the tempest's power. When He descended on Pentecost, there was a sound as of a mighty rushing wind; when He came afterwards to the assembled disciples, the place was shaken where they were assembled; when He answered the prayer of Paul and Silas the prison rocked to its foundation, and the bolts and bars were loosed.

But above all the manifestations of His tremendous power the most blessed is His quickening breath. This figure especially expresses the idea of life, the Spirit that breathes the new life in conversion, that imparts the very life of Christ to the soul, and quickens the mortal body into His resurrection power.

III. The water.

This emblem runs through the whole typology of the Old Testament, and the figurative language of the New.

This was the significance of the stream that flowed from Horeb's riven rock, and the diverse washings of the Levitical system. It was of this that Jesus spoke when He said, "He that believeth on me, out of him shall flow rivers of living water." It was of this that the prophet said, "I will pour water upon the thirsty, and floods upon the dry ground, and they shall spring up as among the grass, as willows by the water courses." This is the rain that comes upon the new-mown grass, and the dew which revives the earth. It is the fulness of the Holy Spirit in His cleansing, refreshing, and comforting influences. This is He who comes to us in the washing of regeneration, and the renewing of the Holy Ghost which He sheds upon us abundantly. This is He who sends the times of refreshing from the presence of the Lord. This is He who baptizes us in the ocean of divine light and love, and fills us with all the fullness of God.

IV. The Oil.

The oil is another Old Testament figure of the Holy Ghost, appearing in all the anointings of the priesthood and tabernacle, and reappearing in the very name of Christ, which means the anointed One. It was of this that He said, "the Spirit of the Lord is upon me; for He hath anointed me to preach the gospel. to the poor; He hath sent me to bind up the broken-hearted, to preach deliverance to the captives, the opening of the eyes to them that are blind, to preach the acceptable year of the Lord."

This figure describes the Holy Ghost as the figure of light, consecration, and healing.

In the ancient ritual, the head, hands, and feet of the cleansed leper and the consecrated priest were touched with oil as a symbol of their dedication to God. Thus Aaron was set apart, thus David was consecrated, and thus we are dedicated to Christ, and divinely qualified for service by the anointing of the Holy Ghost.

But the oil was also the figure of light in the vision of Zechariah. The temple is lighted by seven lamps that are fed by two living olive trees, teaching us that the Holy Ghost is the constant and living source of His people's life and light.

It is in this connection that John says, "But ye have an unction from the Holy One, and ye know all things. The anointing which ye have received of Him abideth in you, and ye need not that any man teach you; but as the same anointing teacheth you of all things, and is truth, and is no lie, and even as it hath taught you, ye shall abide in Him."

And so, also, the oil speaks of His healing touch. Oil and wine are used in the parable of the good Samaritan as figures of physical restoration.

And so the disciples anointed the sick and commissioned the elders to continue the same rite in the command, James 5: 14, as a token of the touch of the Holy Ghost upon the suffering form, and communicating to each the love of the Lord Jesus Christ.

Oil might also be used as a symbol of gladness. The Psalmist speaks of oil which makes our face to shine, and describes Jesus Christ as anointed with the oil of gladness above His fellows. Isaiah speaks of the oil of joy for mourning, and the garment of praise for the spirit of heaviness. The Holy Ghost anoints us with the spirit of joy, and He radiates the face with the reflected glory of the indwelling God.

Have we received the divine anointing as our light and healing, our joy and consecration? The oil that fell on Aaron's head descended to the skirts of his garments; and from our Great High Priest the divine anointing descends to His lowliest member.

Let us consecrate our hands and feet, our head and heart to be touched and dedicated from this holy chrism, and go forth as the Lord's anointed.

V. The Fire.

The mightiest of human forces is the last figure implied to represent the Holy Spirit up to the time of His descent at Pentecost. It had appeared in the very beginning in the Shekinah which hovered at Eden's gate; the pillar of fire that led the camp of Israel, the descending flame that consumed the sacrifices in the tabernacle, the blaze of the burning bush in Horeb, the coals of fire in Isaiah's vision, the glowing symbols of Ezekiel's imagery, the figurative language of John the Baptist prophesying of

Him who should baptize with the Holy Ghost and with fire; and at length it was revealed in all its manifested meaning in the cloven tongues of Pentecost, and the fiery baptism of the assembled disciples.

It is the figure of destruction, reminding us of the Spirit which consumes not only the sin, but also the life of nature, and leaves the soul an empty vessel for the divine filling. It represents also, more emphatically than any other figure, the idea of cleansing; penetrating every fiber of our being, purifying with intrinsic power the inmost soul, and eliminating every particle of dross and evil.

This is also the figure of power, reminding us of the mightiest forces of human mechanics, electricity and steam, which are forms of fire, and the great dynamic center of our system, and the fiery sun which holds up the planets in their orbits by his power; so the Holy Ghost is the source of omnipotent power; impelling all the machinery of Christianity, moving all the forces of the soul, and enduing us with all we can ever know of power for service.

The fire is also the image of love; it is the force that melts, dissolves barriers, fuses hard substances, and welds the pieces into one.

And so the Holy Ghost is the Spirit of love, melting the stony heart, dissolving the prejudices of men, and uniting the people of God as one heart. It is His to give the glow of enthusiasm and the fire of holy zeal; it was He who clothed Elijah with his fervor, John with his love, Paul with his tremendous energy, Whitfield with his love of souls, and Fenelon, Rutherford and McCheyne with their seraphic piety.

Have we received the baptism of fire? It is the still unexhausted promise of the New Testament, waiting its mightiest manifestations just before the coming of the great and terrible day of the Lord.

VI. The Seal.

Another symbol has been added in the epistles, following with peculiar propriety the complexion of redemption, and the ratifying of the covenant by the death and resurrection of Jesus Christ, and the descent of the Holy Ghost.

It is the figure of the seal in the epistles of Paul. This figure is used respecting the work of the Holy Spirit upon the heart of the believer, "In whom after ye believed, ye were sealed with that Holy Spirit of promise."

And so again He says, "Grieve not the Holy Spirit by whom ye were sealed unto the day of redemption." The covenant completed, the will made effectual; it is fitting that the seal should be added. And this the Holy Spirit becomes, putting upon the heart the distinct stamp of Christ, touching and making divine things real and tangible as the impression upon the seal and the wax. This figure represents the idea of certainty and reality in connection with the work of the Spirit. There is such an experience in the Holy Ghost. It is not enough that we merely believe the truth, we may also know it and experience it. "We have known and believed," John says, "the love that God hath to us," and so the Holy Ghost becomes to us the witness to our consciousness of the reality of Divine things; enabling us to say, "I know Him whom I have believed;" "We know that He abideth in us by the Spirit that He hath given to us;" "We know that we have eternal life;" "We know that we have the petitions that we desired of Him."

It is very important that we do not reverse the order of this experience; it does not come before faith, but after it. "After ye believed, ye were sealed with the Holy Spirit of promise." We should not rest short of this blessed reality, and if we yield ourselves unto God in the surrender of consecration, and the simplicity of trust, we shall receive the touch of His blessed hand, and the stamp of His own personal presence, and the very image of His blessed face impressed upon our hearts, and be able to say,

"He who hath sealed us and anointed us is God, who hath also established us, and given us the earnest of the Spirit in our hearts.

This leads us to the last symbol of the Spirit, namely:

VII. The Earnest.

This also is added in the epistles along with the seal, and after the descent of the Holy Ghost at Pentecost. These two last symbols seem especially appropriate as added ones, in view of their special significance with respect to the finished redemption of Christ, and His approaching advent. All the other aspects of the Spirit's work have been expressed by former emblems, but there is still one more, namely, the prophetic. "He shall show you things to come;" so Christ promised regarding the Comforter. He was to be the foretaste of all the yet unrevealed and unrealized hopes of the glorious future, and one more term was needed to express this; this is afforded in the word 'earnest.'

An earnest in ancient legal customs was a handful of soil bestowed upon the purchaser of a piece of real estate, containing a portion of the very ground that he had bought, as a solemn pledge of the whole estate which was to be delivered in due time. It was not a handful of soil from any estate, but it was from the very ground that he had bought, and it guaranteed the identity, certainty, and completeness of the transfer in due time.

In this sense the Holy Spirit is to show a sample and pledge of our future inheritance. All that we are to be and to enjoy He brings us now in foretaste and in limited measure, as a pledge that it shall be all delivered in the fullness of time, in all its completeness.

The term is used in a two-fold connection in the epistles; first, of our spiritual inheritance, which the Holy Ghost foreshadows in our hearts by the experience of His sanctifying, comforting, and quickening life; giving us the measure in which we are able to receive amid the limitations of our mortal life, a real foretaste of the felicities and glories of heaven.

But there is a second sense in which He is also an earnest, namely: in our mortal bodies, into which he brings the physical life of Christ as an earnest and foretaste of the physical resurrection. Thus we have the firstfruits of the Spirit as the pledge that we shall yet have the full redemption of the body. "He that hath wrought us for this self-same thing," that is, for the future resurrection, "is God, who hath also given us the earnest of the Spirit."

Have we received this blessed token, and do we have in our measure all its meaning, in anticipation of the things which "eye hath not seen, ear hath not heard, and it hath not entered into the heart of man what God hath prepared for them that love Him," but of which it is added, "God hath revealed them unto us by His Spirit, for the Spirit searcheth all things, yea, the deep things of God?"

Can we claim the benediction of the seven Spirits which are before the throne, and say with the apostle, "Blessed be God, even the Father of our Lord Jesus Christ, who hath blessed us with all the blessings of the Spirit in heavenly places in Christ Jesus?"

A. B. SIMPSON

Chapter 6.
THE SPIRIT OF LIGHT

> "Now we have received not the spirit of the world, but the Spirit which is of God; that we may know the things that are freely given to us of God." 1Cor. 2: 12.

The first aspect in which the Holy Spirit is revealed to us is as the Illuminator and Guide of our life. Even in the story of creation the first result of His brooding over the face of the deep is the command, "Let there be light." He is the Creator of the human mind and the Source of all the true light of reason and natural religion in the world; and He is the true Source of spiritual light. One of His special emblems is the oil and the seven-fold lamp of the temple.

I. He Gives the Light of Truth.

He has inspired the Holy Scriptures, the revelation of God's will, and the invaluable light that shines upon the heart of man, the pathway of the unseen world. The Bible is a standard of spiritual truth, and in all His teachings and leadings, the Holy Ghost never contradicts His own word. They who are more fully led of the Spirit will always most reverence the authority of the Scriptures, and walk in the most perfect conformity with their principles and precepts.

But it is not enough to have the letter of the word, He who gave it must also interpret it and make it Spirit and life. It is His to unfold to the heart the power and reality of the written word and to bring it to our remembrance in the opportune moment as the lamp of guidance, or the sword of defense in the hour of temptation. "He will bring all things to your remembrance whatsoever I have said unto you." This is the blessed ministry of the personal Holy Spirit, and they who thus walk with Him shall find the Bible an ever new volume and the very light of life.

A prominent member of the House of Representatives, speaking the other day about the inestimable value of the National Library of Congress, was asked how it was possible for a busy member, without much study and labor, to know how to use it effectually, and to be able always to find the right volume or page where a given subject was discussed: "O," he replied, "that is made perfectly easy for us by our invaluable librarian who knows every book and subject, and all we have to do is to send a little page from our desk in the House with a note to him requesting the best authority on any subject we require, and he immediately comes back with the right book and the leaves turned down at the very spot where we need the information." Blessed be God, we have a Divine Librarian who understands the Bible better than we ever can, and who has come to be our Monitor and Guide, not only into its meaning, but also into its practical application to every need of life. "And if we walk in the Spirit He will guide us into all truth, and bring all things to our remembrance whatsoever Christ hath said unto us."

II. The Light of Revelation.

It is not enough to have a good light, we must also have the organs of vision or it is of no use; and we must have them in perfect condition. Now, the Holy Spirit comes to be to us sight as well as light; and as we walk in Him we shall be enabled to know the will of God as revealed in the Scriptures by a true spiritual apprehension, and from the very standpoint of God's own mind and thought.

In the chapter from which our text is taken the apostle uses a very fine analogy:

"No man," he says, "knoweth the things of a man except a spirit of a man which is in him; even so, knoweth no man the things of God except the Spirit of God is in us." You might sit down and talk to your little dog about the latest book, and explain to him in the clearest manner its wonderful teachings, and he would not understand a word; not from any defect in the truth, but because he had not the mind of a man to understand the things of a man; and so you might sit down and talk to the natural intellect about spiritual truth, even the brightest human intellect, and they would not comprehend it because it belonged to a higher sphere.

The only way by which that dog could understand you would be for you to impart to him a human mind, and the only way that man can understand the things of God is for God to impart to him the divine mind; therefore, the apostle says, "The natural man receiveth not the things of the Spirit, for they are foolishness unto Him; neither can he know them for they are spiritually discerned; but we have the mind of Christ."

This is the special work of the Holy Ghost, to give to us a new spiritual vision and organ of apprehension; so that the soul directly perceives divine things and realities. Perhaps the first effect of this divine illumination is that the things of God become intensely real, and stand out with vividness and distinctness, like figures cut in relief on the wall. The person of Christ, the light of His countenance, the distinct sweetness of His Spirit, the "peace that passeth all understanding," the joy of the Lord, the heavenly world, all become to the heart more actual and intensely vivid than the things we see with our outward eyes, and touch with our human hands; so that we can say of Christ with the apostle, "That which we have seen with our eyes, which we have looked upon, and our hands have handled of the Word of Life." This is the true meaning of this whole chapter. It is not a description of heavenly glories which we are going to see by-and-by, but of present revelations which the natural eye hath not seen, the material ear hath not heard, and the human heart hath not conceived: but which "God hath revealed to us by His Spirit; for the Spirit searcheth all things, yea, the deep things of God."

In the first chapter of Ephesians, the apostle Paul has given us a sublime view of the effect of this inward illumination upon the heart. "I cease not," he says, "to make mention of you in my prayers, that the God of our Lord Jesus Christ, the Father of glory, may give unto you the Spirit of wisdom and revelation in the knowledge of Him." "The eyes of your heart being enlightened that ye may know what is the hope of His calling, and what the riches of the glory of His inheritance in the saints."

"And what is the exceeding greatness of His power to us-ward who believe, according to the working of His mighty power."

"Which He wrought in Christ, when He raised Him from the dead, and set Him at His own right hand in the heavenly places,"

"Far above all principality, and power, and might and dominion, and every name that is named, not only in this world, but also in that which is to come;"

"Which is His body, the fullness of Him that filleth all in all."

"And hath raised us up together, and made us sit together in heavenly places in Jesus Christ;"

"That in the ages to come He might show the exceeding riches of His grace, in His kindness toward us through Christ Jesus."

Here we find it is not the eyes of our intellect, but the eyes of the heart that are to be illuminated, and when so quickened by the Spirit of revelation in the knowledge of Him, we shall understand what is the hope of our calling, and glorious privileges and prospects which we are to inherit in Christ.

The riches of the glory of His inheritance are not only for us, but even in us now. We shall be stirred with a realization of the exceeding greatness of His power toward us and for us. We shall rise to an adequate conception of the mighty things that we may dare to claim of Him; especially shall we see the full meaning of Christ's resurrection and ascension. We shall see Him lifted up, not only above the grave and the burden of our guilt and sin, but far above all beings, all forces of natural law, all might and dominion, and every name that is named, up to the very throne of God where all things are under His feet. Not only so, but we shall see ourselves lifted above our sins, and fears, and sorrows, and enemies, and difficulties, and imperfections, until we, too, are sitting with Him far above all principality, might and dominion, in the heavenly places in Christ Jesus, as safe and triumphant as if we were already in heaven and had been there for ten thousand years.

Oh! such a view takes the sting out of life and stimulates to higher aspirations and victories, conflicts and service. But we must first perceive our inheritance before we can claim it, and as we look out upon all the fullness of His promise and provision we arise and walk through the land in all the length and breadth of it and make it our own. Under this divine light the promise of God grows strangely real, and the heart swells with faith and confidence. Doctrines which in the abstract we could not understand become simple and living realities. The profound truth of the Trinity changes into the personal and sweet fellowship of the Father, the Son, and the Holy Ghost. The doctrine of sanctification ceases to perplex and discourage, and becomes a simple experience of union with Jesus and abiding in Him. The mightiest supernatural works of Christ even in our bodies cease to be strange and incredible. The doctrine of His personal coming becomes a bright and personal expectation, and the whole world of spiritual things is more real to us in our own consciousness.

Sometimes the vision opens upon our own hearts and we are permitted to see their failures, imperfections, and needs; but under the light of God this is never discouraging because there always comes with it the revelation of Him who is the supply of every need and the provision for every defect in sin. Satan's pictures of our sins are terrible and always depressing; but the light of heaven reveals our errors only to heal them, and brings such sweetness and rest that we can only thank Him for making greater room for His all-sufficiency.

Sometimes, too, the curtain is lifted upon the heavenly world, and some souls whom God can trust are permitted, like Paul, to be brought so near that they behold what it were unlawful for a man to utter, and know not whether they are in the body or out of the body. Let no one covet such experiences, for they bring with them many a thorn in the flesh, lest we be exalted above measure. And above all let us not seek, with morbid curiosity, to intrude into things which belong not to our simple sphere of humble duty, but rather seek the light that is practical and useful.

And yet, if God gives the higher visions at times, and even lifts the veil of things to come for humble and holy souls who dwell hard by the gates of heaven, let us not wonder or question; and let them use such glimpses of glory as the mariner uses the burst of sunlight that sometimes pierces through the skies that have been clouded for weeks, and sails, by the observations of that hour, through all the coming days of cloud and storm.

III. The Light of Guidance.

The Holy Spirit is promised to us as our personal Guide in the path of life. "As many as are led of the Spirit they are sons of God." Some persons are so zealous for the word of God that they deny any direct guidance of the Spirit apart from the Word, but if we truly believe the Word itself we will be forced to accept its distinct statements, that the personal presence of God is given to the humble and obedient disciple for the needed direction in every step of life. "I will instruct thee in the way that thou shalt go; I will guide thee with mine eye." The Lord shall guide thee continually: "When He putteth forth His own sheep He goeth before them and they know His voice." "In all thy ways acknowledge Him and He shall direct thy paths."

We find the apostle Paul constantly recognizing the personal direction of the Holy Spirit even in matters where there was no distinct direction in the Word. The whole course of Paul's missionary journeys was ordered by the personal direction of the Lord. Being sent forth, we are told, by the Holy Ghost, he and Barnabas sailed unto Cyprus. A little later the same Spirit restrained them from preaching in Bithynia and Asia, and led them from Troas to Philippi to begin their European ministry. Still later, we are told that he purposed in the Spirit to go to Jerusalem and Rome, and none of the perils of the way could afterward turn him aside from that which had come to him as the voice of God. No life was ever more practical, sensible, and scriptural than Paul's, and yet none more constantly recognized the supernatural direction of the Holy Ghost. The methods of divine guidance are various.

1. The Spirit guides us by the Scriptures, by their general principles and teachings, and by bringing to us special passages from the Word, either through the law of mental suggestion, and impressing them upon our heart, or by various ways fitted to emphasize a passage as a divine message to our hearts.

2. He also directs us by His own direct voice when necessary; and yet we must not expect the special and remarkable intimations of the Holy Ghost at all times, or when we have sufficient light from other sources. There is danger of fanaticism here. We have no right to ask God to give us a special revelation of His will where either the light of our own common sense or the teaching of Scripture have already made the matter sufficiently plain. For example: It would be foolishness to expect the Lord to show us by a direct message whether we ought to get up in the morning, to take our proper food, to attend to our daily business, to keep the Sabbath, or to perform the ordinary acts of kindness, courtesy and necessity; to pay our debts, to love our neighbor. All these things the Spirit has already told us, and it would be an impertinence to expect Him to come with a new revelation every time.

So, also, we cannot expect the Holy Spirit to reveal to us directly whether God will forgive us our sins, or sanctify our souls, because these things He has already explicitly promised us, and we can expect no added witness of the Spirit until we have first believed and acted upon His Word; then the Spirit will follow this by a confirming voice and a sweet inward assurance of the fulfillment of His promise. Many persons expect the Spirit to come to them with the assurance of forgiveness and salvation before they have even believed the promises that He has already spoken.

So also, we may add in regard to prayer for physical healing. When we are living in accordance to His Word it does not require a special revelation of the will of God, but that we should believe the revelation already made in the Scriptures, in His promises of healing through faith in Christ. But, where the matter is one on which the Scriptures have not spoken distinctly, and the circumstances are so peculiar as to require direct and new light, He has distinctly promised that He will lead us in the right way wherein we shall not stumble. He has said, "If in anything we be otherwise minded, and our views and ideas be mistaken, He will reveal even this unto us."

3. The Holy Spirit guides us most frequently by intuitions of our sanctified judgment, and the conclusion of our minds, to which He leads us with the quiet assurance of acting in perfect freedom and naturalness, and yet of being influenced by the presence and suggestion of His own Spirit. Under such circumstances the mind and judgment are perfectly simple and natural. The thoughts come as our own, with delightful tranquility, and a certainty, and a sort of intuition that it is the right thing to do, and yet the secret consciousness that it is not our wisdom, but has been somehow reflected upon the soul by another. It is not so much the Spirit speaking to us as the Spirit speaking with us as part of our very consciousness, so that it is not two minds, but one.

The truly consecrated spirit may expect to be thus held and influenced by the Divine wisdom; and it will often find itself restrained from things by an inward reluctance, or repulsion, which it cannot fully explain, and led to other things by a strong and distinct inclination and sense of rightness and fitness which afterwards prove, by the result, to have been the directing presence of God. Of course, as we shall see immediately, there must be real consecration and holy vigilance in such a walk, to guard against our own impressions and inclinations in cases where they are not the intimations of the Spirit's will.

4. We are sometimes taught that we are guided by providences. A devout mind will, of course, always have regard to the external providences of God, and will be habitually watching to see His hand in everything that occurs; but it would be very dangerous to allow ourselves to be directed by outward events apart from the distinct leadings of God in our spirit and by His Word. Quite as frequently we shall find ourselves led to go in the face of circumstances as to follow the favoring gales of outward events. Most of the important events and accomplished purposes in the lives of God's servants, as recorded in the Scriptures, were in direct opposition to all the circumstances that were occurring around them. Take, for example, the life of David. From the very first time that he received the call of God to recognize himself as Israel's future king, everything in his life for nearly ten years seemed to conspire to forbid any such expectation.

Take again the life of Paul. We find him directly led by the Holy Spirit to cross the Hellespont and begin his ministry in Greece. But instead of being met by open doors and favoring circumstances, everything opposed, until at last he found himself scourged and bound, a helpless prisoner in a Roman dungeon. Had he been watching for the guidance of circumstances he would have concluded that he had made a mistake, and would have hastened to get away; but on the contrary, the more firmly believed that God had led him, and ere long the very circumstances were conquered and transformed by the victorious power of faith. So again, he was led to Jerusalem and Rome, but from that moment everything opposed him. All along the way the people of God even seemed to throw themselves across his path.

At Ephesus, they wanted him to remain to preach the gospel in the very place where a year before he had in vain tried to enter; but instead of recognizing this as a providence that ought to change his purpose he quietly deferred his work in Ephesus and pressed on to Jerusalem. Again and again on his way did the very prophets of the Lord warn him against visiting Jerusalem, and plead with him to abandon the dangerous purpose which would perhaps cost him his life; but he only replied "What mean ye to weep and to break mine heart? I am ready not only to be bound, but also to die at Jerusalem for the name of the Lord Jesus." Arriving at Jerusalem all that had been intimated comes to pass. Instead of being received by his countrymen, he is mobbed and well nigh killed, but he still presses on and the Lord meets him at night in his dungeon to assure him of His protection and direction.

Next, he is detained at Caesarea for two whole years languishing in a prison; but, instead of doubting his divine direction he presses steadily on, and uses the delay as an occasion of service for the Master. At length he has embarked for Rome; but even then the storm pursues him and the wild Euroclydon threatens to engulf him in the depths of the sea; but he falters not in his purpose, but rises majestically above the storm and carries even the lives of his fellow passengers, on the wings of his mighty faith, above disaster and destruction. Narrowly saved from shipwreck on the shores of Malta, a viper from the ashes springs upon his hand, and it seems as though earth and hell had determined to prevent his reaching Rome, but he only flings it off and suffers no harm, and so at length he marches up the Appian way more like a conqueror than a prisoner, thanking God and taking courage, as he realizes that not one word of all God's promise and direction has failed. Thus must we ever interpret the providences of God; instead of yielding to opposition, or following that which seems to favor us, press firmly on in the path of conviction and obedience, and our way shall be established, and our very difficulties become the occasions of our greatest triumphs.

Let us notice also some of the principles and conditions of divine guidance.

The first is a surrendered spirit. Before we can know His will we must always first yield our own. "The meek will He guide in judgment, and the meek will He teach His way."

Next, there must be a readiness to obey. He will not give us light unless we mean to follow it; to do so would only add to our condemnation. "If any man will do His will he shall know." "Then shall we know if we follow to know the Lord."

Secondly, we must trust His guidance; we must believe that He is with us and directing us. We must lean upon His arm with all our heart, and implicitly look up into His face and expect Him to be true to us. We must also have "our senses exercised by reason of use, to know the difference between good and evil." Sometimes our mistakes will become most instructive to us by showing us the places where we have erred, and save us from repeating the mistake afterwards with more serious consequences. We must learn to distinguish between mere impressions and the deeper convictions of the entire judgment under the light of the Spirit, and between the voice of the Shepherd and that of the spirit of error. This He will teach us, and teach us more and more perfectly through experience. We shall have to learn also to walk with Him when we cannot understand the way. His path is often a way that we have not known, and the answer to our prayer may seem to lead us directly contrary to our expectation and to the ultimate issue.

Once in my life I was led to ask the Lord for a special building as a residence, and received full assurance that it would be given; almost immediately afterwards it was sold to a person who insisted on occupying it himself, and refused under any circumstances to part with it. After much prayer I was led to consent, most unwillingly, to accept, instead of the house I had most desired, another owned by this very man. So distasteful was it to me that on the night I went to sign the lease I walked repeatedly past the door before I could bring myself to enter. At length, in simple obedience to the Holy Spirit, I did, but, to my surprise, the man met me and said that very afternoon he had been led to change his mind. While attending the funeral of an old friend a strange dread came over him about occupying the house that he had purchased and he had just decided to let me have it on terms more favorable than I could have expected had not God interposed. Thus, as I went forward in the path of simple obedience, by a way that I could not understand the true way opened up, and it was only blessing and delight. The most remarkable feature of it was that the house thus given became afterwards the place where all the work of the Lord, in which we are now engaged, began. God thus signally chose the place for His work, and put His seal upon it as a pattern of the providences which we should afterwards expect. So, still, "through fears, through clouds, through storms, He gently clears our way."

Let us trust His guiding hand, and follow the Lamb whithersoever He goeth.

IV. Light for Service.

"It is not ye that speak but the Spirit of your Father that speaketh in you." "I will give you a mouth and wisdom which all your adversaries shall not be able to gainsay nor resist." "If any man speak, let him speak as the oracles of God. If any man minister, let him do it as of the ability which God giveth, that God may be glorified through Jesus Christ." "Say not I am a child, for thou shalt go to all that I shall send thee, and whatsoever I command thee thou shalt speak." "And the Lord put forth His hand and touched my mouth; and the Lord said unto me, behold! I have put my words in thy mouth." "The Lord God hath given me the tongue of one that hath been instructed that I might know how to speak the Word in season to him that is weary." "He openeth my ear morning by morning to hear as one that is instructed." This was the secret of even Christ's ministry. "The Word that I speak is not mine, but the Father's which sent me." "As I hear I speak."

Before we can speak God's messages we must learn to listen. The opened ear comes before the opened mouth. It is very hard sometimes to die to our own thoughts and elaborate preparations for service, and to be free and open for God to use us as vessels meet for the Master's use. Sometimes He has to humble us by showing us the barrenness of all our best intellectual work, and then lead us to receive the living messages of His Holy Spirit. Sometimes we may think the message very unworthy and almost unsuitable, but God loves to take "the things that are not to bring to nought the things that are, that no flesh may glory in His presence."

A saintly spirit whom God has greatly used in personal messages, tells how once she was distinctly sent by the Lord on a certain train; but when she arrived at the station the train was crowded and the guard told her she could not go. Still she waited, having learned that a point-blank refusal is often the best evidence of God's working; but just as the train was about to leave, suddenly the guard came to her and hurried her into a carriage which had just been put on. There she found herself sitting beside a young gentleman, and immediately the thought came, "This is the service the Lord has sent me to do." After a little she introduced the subject of personal religion, but he haughtily replied, "My family object to my being talked to on such subjects." "My dear sir," she replied, "I had supposed that this was not a question for your family, but for yourself." "Then," he answered, still more stiffly, "I object to be talked to on such questions." It seemed as though the way of service was blocked, and yet the unerring Spirit had led her there.

Then the thought came that she should give him a tract, and that God would bless the silent messenger even after they had parted. But as she searched through all her pockets she found she had forgotten all her tracts. Suddenly, amid her movements, her valise fell on the floor, and all its contents were poured in disorder at their feet. With the instincts of a gentleman he helped her to pick up the wreck, when suddenly her eye fell upon a single tract that had fallen out with the other articles; but as she picked it up she felt, why, this will never do, for it was a tract especially addressed to a young man that had just been saved from shipwreck. But the same unerring Guide whispered to her to put it in his hands and ask him to read it.

He took it, having grown a little freer, through their better acquaintance, and as he read the title his face became deadly pale. Before he had read the second page the tears were pouring down his cheeks. "Madam," he cried, turning to her, "who told you about me?" "Why, no one," she answered, "what do you mean?" "Why," said he, "Some one must have told you; did you not know that only last week I was rescued from shipwreck?" It was the arrow of the Infinite One whose wisdom never fails, and the humble worker, waiting His bidding, had not been suffered to err. The message reached his heart, and ere they parted he was saved. This is the true secret of effectual service, and when He becomes to us the Wonderful Counselor, we shall always find Him also the Mighty God.

A. B. SIMPSON

Chapter 7.
THE SPIRIT OF HOLINESS

"Elect according to the foreknowledge of God the Father, through sanctification of the Spirit, unto obedience and sprinkling of the blood of Jesus Christ." 1 Peter 1: 2.

It would throw a flood of light on the perplexing doctrine of election if we would remember, when thinking of this subject, that we are elected by God, not unto salvation unconditionally and absolutely, but unto holiness. We are predestined to be conformed to the image of His Son. It is idle and unscriptural, therefore, to talk about being elected to salvation irrespective of our faith or obedience. We are elected to obedience and sprinkling of the blood of Christ, and are summoned, therefore, to make our calling and election sure, by pressing on into the fullness of the grace of Christ. This work of sanctification is especially the work of the Holy Spirit. Let us look carefully at the principles that lie at the foundation of it, and its connection with the person and work of the Holy Ghost.

1. The holiness to which we are called, and into which we are introduced by the Holy Spirit, is not the restoration of Adamic perfection, or the recovery of the nature we lost by the fall. It is a higher holiness, even the very nature of God Himself, and the indwelling of Jesus Christ, the second Adam, to whose perfect likeness we shall be restored through the work of redemption. We are predestined to be conformed to the image of His Son. This will determine all our subsequent conclusions in the consideration of this subject. Sanctification is not the perfection of human character, but the impartation of the divine nature, and the union of the human soul with the person of Christ, the new Head of redeemed humanity.

2. Our sanctification has been purchased for us through the redemption of Christ. By one offering He has perfected forever

all them that are sanctified. When He came He said, "Lo! I come to do thy will, O God; yea, thy law is in my heart, by which will we are sanctified through the offering of the body of Jesus Christ once for all."

Our sanctification, therefore, as well as our justification, was included in the finished work of Christ, and it is a free gift of His grace to every ransomed soul that accepts it, in accordance with His word and will. It is one of our redemption rights in Christ, and we may claim it by faith as freely as our forgiveness. "For He gave Himself for us that He might redeem us from all iniquity, and purify unto Himself a peculiar people, zealous of good works."

3. It is the office of the Holy Spirit to lead us into the full redemption of Jesus Christ, and therefore, into holiness. In pursuance of this heavenly calling, the Holy Spirit leads us first to see our need of sanctification. This He does by a two-fold revelation. First, He shows us the divine will for our sanctification, and the necessity for our becoming holy if we could please God. By nature and tradition many persons are prone to take a very different view of this subject, and to regard the experience of holiness as a sort of exceptional life for a few distinguished Christians, but not expected of all the disciples of Christ. But the awakened and startled mind discovers, in the light of Scripture and of the Holy Spirit, the falseness of this delusion, and the inflexible terms in which God's Word requires that all His people should be holy in heart and life. In the searching light of truth it trembles as it reads, "Without holiness no man shall see the Lord." "Into heaven there entereth nothing that defileth, nor worketh abomination, nor maketh a lie." "Blessed are they that wash their robes that they may have right to the Tree of Life and may enter in through the gates into the city." "He that walketh uprightly and worketh righteousness shall see the King in His beauty and behold the land that is very far off." "Who shall ascend unto the hill of the

Lord or stand in His holy place? He that hath clean hands and a pure heart." "Be ye holy even as I am holy; be ye therefore perfect even as your Father in heaven is perfect." "These things have I written unto you that ye sin not. He that abideth in Him sinneth not; he that sinneth hath not seen Him neither known Him."

At this point the soul is compelled to face a very solemn crisis; either it must accept the Word of God literally and implicitly, or it must turn it aside by human tradition, and explain away its most plain and emphatic teachings, and render it of no effect in any of its promises or commands, and so enter upon a course which must end in practical infidelity. The latter alternative is taken by many; they content themselves with saying such a standard is impossible, nobody has ever reached it, and God does not actually mean it or require it. The result is that henceforth the Word of God becomes uncertain to them in all its messages, a practical faith ceases to be possible. But the other alternative drives the soul, if honestly faced, to self-despair; it can find no such holiness in itself, and no power to produce it.

The first effect, it is true, generally is to stir up the awakened heart to attempt a better life and try to work out a holiness such as God requires. Resolutions, outward amendments, perhaps many inward exercises, self-examinations, purposes of righteousness, and holiness, are the result. But in a little while there is a certain issue of failure and disappointment; perhaps the man becomes a Pharisee and deludes himself into the idea that he is complying with the divine standard. But, if the Holy Ghost is doing His office work thoroughly, he will soon become disgusted with his own righteousness, and find his utter inability even to reach his own standard. Some crucial test will come which he cannot meet, some command which strikes at the roots of his natural inclinations and requires the sacrifice of his dearest idols, and the poor heart will break down, and the will will shrink or rebel.

This was the experience of the apostle Paul; for the time he thought that he had attained unto the righteousness of the law,

Walking in the Spirit

but when the commandment came, sin revived, and he died. The Lord said "Thou shalt not covet," and instantly his throbbing heart awoke with all the intensity of its natural life, to a thousand evil desires, all the stronger because they were forbidden, until in despair he cried out "I know that the law is spiritual, but I am carnal." "O wretched man that I am! who shall deliver me from the body of this death?" Ah! this is the very preparation for sanctification. He is just on the verge of deliverance. He has found at length his helplessness. He has got down to the bottom of the ladder of self-renunciation. It is to such a soul that the Master is saying, "Blessed are the poor in spirit, for theirs is the kingdom of heaven." "Blessed are they that hunger and thirst after righteousness, for they shall be filled."

So of old, God came to Job in the revelation of his own worthlessness until he cried, "I abhor myself." So He came to Isaiah, just before his cleansing, until the prophet smote upon his breast and cried, "Woe is me! for I am a man of unclean lips." Happy the heart that can see itself at its worst, without, on the one hand attempting to excuse its failure, or on the other, giving up in despair. For such a soul the Holy Spirit waits to bring the next stage of His blessed work of sanctification namely:

4. The revelation of Jesus Christ Himself as our sanctification. It is the purpose of God that the person of Jesus shall be to us the embodiment of all that there is in God and salvation. Therefore, sanctification is not a mere human experience or state, but is the reception of the person of Christ as the very substance of our spiritual life. For He "is made unto us of God, wisdom, righteousness, sanctification, redemption." It is not a wealthy friend advancing us the money to pay our debts, but it is the friend coming into our business and assuming it Himself, with all its burdens and liabilities, while we simply become subordinate and receive all our needs henceforth from Him. This was the glad cry which Paul sent back the moment he had reached

the depths of self-despair: "I thank God through Jesus Christ our Lord." It is the Holy Spirit's function to reveal Him. "He shall take of the things of Christ and show them to us."

And so in the light of His revealing we behold Christ, the perfect One, who walked in sinless perfection through the world in His incarnation, waiting to come and enter our hearts, and dwell in us, and walk in us, as the very substance of our new life, while we simply abide in Him, and walk in His very steppings. It is not merely imitating an example, but it is living in the very life of another. It is to have the very person of Christ possessing our being; the thoughts of Christ, the desires of Christ, the will of Christ, the faith of Christ, the purity of Christ, the love of Christ, the unselfishness of Christ, the single aim of Christ, the obedience of Christ, the humility of Christ, the submission of Christ, the meekness of Christ, the patience of Christ, the gentleness of Christ, the zeal of Christ, the works of Christ, manifest in our mortal flesh, so that we shall say, "I live, yet not I, but Christ liveth in me." When the Holy Spirit thus reveals Him to the heart we can surely say, as a saint once said after such a vision, "I have had such a sight of Christ that I never can be discouraged again."

5. But the Spirit not only reveals Christ, but He actually brings him to occupy and abide in the heart. It is not enough to see, we must receive Him and become personally united to Him through the Holy Ghost. In order to do this there must be, on our part, a complete surrender and self-renunciation, followed by a definite act of appropriating faith. By it we receive the Lord Jesus Christ, and become filled with the Holy Ghost. In both of these we are led and enabled by the Holy Spirit. Through His gracious influence we present our bodies a living sacrifice, yield ourselves unto God in unreserved consecration, hand over to Him the old life of self and sin to be slain and buried forever, and offer ourselves to His absolute ownership, possession, and disposition, uncondi-

tionally and irrevocably. The more definite and thorough this act of surrender, then the more complete and permanent will be the result. It is true that, at the best, it will be an imperfect consecration, and will need His merits to make it acceptable, but He will accept a sincere and single desire, and will add His own perfect consecration to our imperfect act, thus making it acceptable to the Father through His grace.

It is most blessed to know that in the very first act of a consecrated life we are not alone, but He Himself becomes our consecration, as He will afterwards become our obedience, and our strength step by step to the end. Having thus surrendered ourselves to Him for His sanctifying grace, we must next accept Him in His fullness that He does become to us henceforth all that we take Him for, and that we are now owned, accepted, possessed, cleansed and sanctified by His indwelling, and that He is saying to us, and, recording our glad amen, without reserve, to every word of it. "Now are ye clean through the word that I have spoken unto you." "The blood of Jesus Christ cleanseth us from all sin."

6. The Holy Spirit next seals this act of union by His own manifested presence, and He makes us know that we have the abiding of Jesus by the witness of His presence, and the baptism of His love and power. Before, however, we can expect to receive this, we must simply believe the promise of Christ, resting in the certainty of our acceptance and consecration, and begin to act by implicit faith in Him as already in our hearts. When we do so, the Holy Ghost will not withhold the conscious witness of our blessing a moment longer than is really necessary for the testing and establishing of our faith.

He will become to us a most blessed and personal reality, and it shall be true of us, as the Master Himself promised, after the Comforter has come, "at that day ye shall know that I am in the Father, and ye in me, and I in you." The soul will be filled with the delightful consciousness of the presence of God, sometimes as the Spirit of ineffable rest and holy serenity, sometimes as the Spirit of unutterable holiness, filling the heart as with the searching and consuming fire of divine purity. Sometimes the consciousness will be that of an intense hatred of sin, and a spirit of self-renunciation and holy vigilance. Sometimes it will be a spirit of love, an intense consciousness of the divine approval, and of God's delight in us and love to us, until the heart is melted with the sense of His tenderness. Sometimes it is a Spirit of unspeakable joy and rapture, continuing for days together, until the very tides of God's bosom seem to swell within the heart with unutterable glory. Sometimes it is a very quiet, simple consciousness, prompting one rather to walk by faith moment by moment, and abide in Christ in great simplicity for every instant's need; and there is no transcendent emotion, but simply a satisfying consciousness of Christ sufficient for our practical life. But in every case it is really satisfaction, and we know that the Lord has come to abide with us forever, and be our all-sufficiency, and our everlasting portion.

7. The Holy Spirit now begins to lead us in the steppings of a holy life. We find it is to be maintained by the moment. We have no crystalized and stereotyped condition of self-centered life, but we have Christ for the present moment, and must abide in Him by the moment. We must walk in the Spirit, and we shall not fulfill the lusts of the flesh. We must be filled with the Spirit, and we shall have no room for sin. It is now that we find the importance of walking in the Spirit, and maintaining steadfastly the habit of obedience and fellowship with Him as the essential condition of the life of holiness. One of the first and most important lessons is to hearken to His voice. The minding of the Spirit is life and peace, but the minding of the flesh is death. The Spirit is given, we are distinctly told, to them that obey Him; and the disobedient and inattentive heart will find His fellowship constantly lia-

ble to be interrupted and suspended. The life of holiness is not a mere abstract state, but a mosaic, made up of a thousand minute details of life and action.

A Christian lady, while thinking of the subject of sanctification, found herself suddenly absorbed in a sort of waking vision, in which she seemed to see a builder erecting an edifice of stone. First, she saw a deep excavation, and at the bottom of it a solid rock on which the house was to be planted. Across this rock was written the name of Christ, with the words, "Other foundation can no man lay than that which is laid, which is Jesus Christ." Then a derrick swung before her eyes and a stone was deposited in the rear of the building. It was a very plain looking block of granite, with no decorations whatever on its face, and as it was deposited, in an obscure portion of the wall was the word "Humility." Next, the derrick swung around to the front of the wall and planted another foundation stone on the principal corner, and the name of this was "Faith." The walls now rose rapidly; block after block of enduring granite was planted and cemented, and at length was fashioned into a magnificent arch surrounded by a beautiful cornerstone, the most lovely stone in all the building, and across it was written the name, "Love" Between these principal stones the interstices were filled up with innumerable small pieces of every size and shape, and these were variously named by the qualities of the Christian character, such as meekness, gentleness, temperance, forbearance, patience, considerateness, serenity, courtesy, cheerfulness, etc., and then the whole facade was spanned by one glowing word in golden letters, "Sanctification." The prejudices of a lifetime were at once removed, and she saw the loveliness of a holy life and character, and the true meaning of the word that she had so long misconceived and disliked.

This, then, is the Holy Spirit's work in the life, and holiness; it is much more than a mere blank sheet of spotless white; it is the living portrait wrought out upon that sheet in all the lineaments of holy loveliness, and all the positive qualities of a practical and beautiful Christian life. "The fruit of the Spirit is love, joy, peace, longsuffering, gentleness, meekness, temperance, and faith," and "whatsoever things are just, whatsoever things are true, whatsoever things are pure, whatsoever things are honest, whatsoever things are lovely, whatsoever things are of good report, if there be any virtue, and if there be any praise, think on these things."

These things the Holy Spirit comes to transcribe in our hearts and to reflect in our lives, and yet these qualities are not our own, in any sense in which we could claim them as the result of our own goodness, or rest in them as permanent, personal attributes. They are rather to be regarded as the grace of Christ, supplied to us from His own indwelling Spirit moment by moment. "And of His fullness have all we received, and grace for grace." This is the grace to produce in us all the varied graces of the Christian life. As Peter expresses it, "We are called to show forth the excellencies of Christ," rather than our own, "who hath called us out of darkness into His marvelous light." These are the bridal robes which are granted to the Lamb's wife, "that she should be arrayed in raiment clean and white." These are like Rebecca's ornaments and veil, which are not woven by her hands, but brought her by Eleazar from Isaac himself, and which, she had simply to put on and wear as his gifts.

So, the Holy Ghost, typified by Abraham's servant, brings to us the wedding robe, and supplies to us day by day the special garment that fits us for each new situation and emergency, and we simply put on the Lord Jesus and walk in Him as our all-sufficiency for every place of duty and trial. The Spirit is ever present to reveal Him to us in every new aspect of grace and fullness; and every new need or failure is but an invitation to take Him in greater fullness, and prove in a higher sense that He is indeed able to save unto the uttermost, and to keep unto the end. Not only does the Holy Spirit thus lead us into the positive graces of the Christian life, but He also keeps us perpetually cleansed from all the stains of spiritual defilement, and even from the effects of

Walking in the Spirit

temptation and evil suggestion. If sin should touch the heart but for a moment, He is there to reveal instantly the evil and in the same flash of light to present and apply a remedy. "And, if we walk in the light as He is in the light, the blood of Jesus Christ keeps cleansing us from all sin."

Thus the soul, like the pebble in the stream, lets in the perpetual cleansing of His life. Indeed, we may walk so close to Him that before the sin is even admitted, before the temptation has reached the citadel of the will and becomes our own act, it is repelled at the entrance, and does not become our sin. He has promised to keep us as the apple of His eye, and, even as the eyelash is so constructed in the delicate organism of the human body that the very approach of the smallest particle of dust causes it instantly to close and repel the intruding substance, so the gentle Holy Ghost instinctively guards the heart and conscience from willful sin. There is something, however, even in the presence of temptation, and the surrounding atmosphere of a sin-defiled world, that spreads a certain contagion around us, like the air in the infected hospital. And it is necessary, therefore, that even this should be constantly cleansed, even as the falling showers wash away the dust from the pavements and the trees, and purify the summer air. This the Holy Spirit is constantly doing, and diffusing through the sanctified heart the freshness and sweetness of the heavenly atmosphere.

We find, therefore, in the Old Testament types, a beautiful provision for the cleansing of the people, even from the touch of the dead, through the water of separation. (Numbers 19.) This beautiful ordinance was a type of the Holy Spirit applying to us the atonement of Christ, and cleansing us habitually from the very breath, and even the indirect contagion of surrounding evil. Even if our old, dead carnal nature touches us, or the atmosphere of sin is around us, we have constantly this water of separation, and the moment we are sprinkled with it every effect is removed and the spirit is quickened into freshness and sweetness, even as the waters that revive the famished earth, and cause the desert to blossom as the rose.

We must ever bear in mind, in tracing the Holy Spirit's work in the believer's heart, the distinction between purity of heart and maturity of character. From the moment that the soul is yielded to Christ in full surrender, and He is received as its divine and indwelling life, we have His purity, and the old, sinful self is reckoned dead, and in no sense recognized as our true self. There is a complete and eternal divorce, and the old heart is henceforth treated as if it were not, and Christ recognized as the true I, and, of course, a life that is essentially pure and divine. But, although wholly separated from the old, sinful life, is the new spirit yet in its infancy, and before it lie boundless stages of progress and development. The acorn is as complete in its parts as the oak of a thousand years, but not as fully developed. And so the soul which has just received Christ as its abiding life and sanctification, is as wholly sanctified, and as completely one with Him as Enoch or John is today, but not as mature. This is the meaning of Christian growth; we do not grow into holiness, we receive holiness in Christ as a complete, divine life; complete in all its parts from the beginning, and divine, as Christ is. But it is like the infant Christ on Mary's bosom, and it has to grow up into all the fullness of the stature of perfect manhood in Christ.

This is the work of the Holy Ghost, as the mother and the nurse, the teacher, educator, cherisher of our spiritual life, and it is in this connection that we must learn to walk in the Spirit, and rise with Him into "all the good pleasure of His goodness, and the work of faith with power," until we shall have reached the fullness of His own prayer for us. "Now the God of peace that brought again from the dead the Lord Jesus Christ, great Shepherd of the sheep, through the blood of the everlasting covenant, make you perfect in every good work to do His will, working in you that which is pleasing in His sight, through Jesus Christ; to whom be glory forever and ever. Amen."

Chapter 8.
THE SPIRIT OF LIFE

Romans 8.

What is life? The unsolved question of science and philosophy. What is it that makes the difference between that soaring bird with buoyant wing and burnished breast, as it mounts the air, and that little limp, broken thing that the hunter gathers up in his hand a moment later, as it has fallen before the cruel fire? What is the cause of this strange, terrible change? The galvanic battery can mimic some of the movements of life in muscle and limb, but when the current ceases the movement stops, and in a few hours the flesh has yielded to the power of corruption, and is dissolving into earth again.

What life does, we know, but what it is, science marks with a note of interrogation.

One of the most remarkable popular books of science, from a Christian standpoint, is Professor Drummond's "Natural Law in the Spiritual World," but perhaps the only thoroughly weak and unsatisfactory chapter in it is that in which he tries to define life and death.

Science is approaching slowly the true center which the Bible gave us so long ago. It is steadily reducing all vital force to one essential principle, perhaps electricity. The Bible has settled the question long ago in regard to Him who is the source of life: "This is the true God and eternal life." God is the fount of life, and Christ is the life of God for men, and His life is the true source of life for the souls and bodies of His children. This life He imparts to us through the Holy Spirit, who becomes to the soul that is united to Him, the medium and the channel of vital union and communion with Christ, our Living Head. It is thus that the Holy Spirit is the Spirit of life in Christ Jesus, because He imparts to us the life of Jesus. It is especially of His part, in connection with our physical life, that we are to speak at this time.

That He should be able to quicken our mortal bodies should not seem strange even upon the most general view of the subject. As we have already intimated, even physical science has been learning, in some measure, to recognize life, not so much as a matter of external organism and coarse material elements, as of vital force.

Half a century has changed radically the methods of treatment known to medical science, and led physicians to rely much more upon natural forces and resources, and more subtle and vital elements, to counteract the power of disease than formerly.

The influence of air and occupation, of surrounding circumstances and mental conditions, all these have far greater weight today than formerly, because health is recognized as the result of inward forces more than of outward agencies. These are distinct approximations toward the higher truth, that the source of our strength must be looked for in the direct power and contact of that spiritual personality in whom "we live, and move, and have our being."

This is the plain teaching of the Holy Scriptures from beginning to end, and we shall probably be surprised to find how much is taught in these sacred pages respecting the relation of the Holy Spirit to our physical life.

I. The Part of the Holy Spirit in Creation.

We know that the Divine Spirit is recognized in the Scriptures as the direct agent in the original creation, and the Spirit of life and order in the whole domain in nature and providence.

How strikingly all this is described in the majestic Psalm of nature, the one hundred and fourth: "Thou hidest Thy face, they are troubled; Thou takest away their breath, they die, and return to their dust. Thou sendest forth Thy Spirit, they are created; and Thou renewest the face of the earth."

This is, however, the power that formed the heavens with their orbs of light, that covers the woods and fields with their robes of many-tinted glory, that animates the teeming world of insect and animal life, that breathed into man the breath of life at the beginning, and still sustains his physical existence, and that has created all his mortal powers and endowments. Why should it be thought strange that He who made us should sustain us, restore us, and "quicken our mortal bodies by His Spirit that dwelleth in us?"

II. The Work of the Holy Spirit in the Body in the Old Testament.

We have a very remarkable pattern of physical life in one of the Old Testament biographies. It is the story of Samson, and it was directly intended as a lesson of the true nature and source of physical strength.

Samson's stupendous power was not due to physical organization at all, but only and directly to the power and presence of the Holy Spirit, for in the very beginning of his strength it is repeatedly added, that "the Spirit of the Lord began to move him, the Spirit of the Lord came upon him," etc. Judges 12: 25; 14: 6; 14: 19; and 16: 28.

When he was deserted by the Holy Spirit he was helpless in the hands of his enemies, but when he was filled with the superhuman power of God's Spirit he could carry away the gates of the city, or hurl the walls of Dagon's temple upon the assembled thousands of his enemies.

The lesson of his life is unmistakably foreshadowed in the great New Testament truth that our bodily life as well as our spiritual has its root and nourishment in God, and that, as we walk in separation from evil, and fellowship with Him, "He that raised up Jesus from the dead will also quicken our mortal bodies by the Spirit that dwelleth in us."

III. The Part of the Holy Spirit in the Personal Ministry of Christ.

It was He that wrought the supernatural works of the Lord Jesus on earth. Not one miracle did he perform until He received the baptism of the Holy Ghost. Then he said, "The Spirit of the Lord is upon me, for He hath sent me to heal the brokenhearted, to set at liberty them that are bruised;" and when his enemies attributed his miracles to the power of Satan, He distinctly declared that they were performed by the power of the Holy Ghost, and added, "If I by the Holy Ghost cast out devils, no doubt the kingdom of God has come unto you." And then he proceeded to charge them with the fatal sin against the Holy Ghost in thus attributing His works to Satan. See Matt. 12: 28.

If then, Christ cast out demons and wrought miracles by the power of the Holy Ghost, and it is the same Spirit who still abides in the church, and dwells in the hearts and bodies of believers, why should it be thought strange that the Almighty Spirit, who thus wrought in the Son of God, should work in our bodies the same works, and thus quicken them, as our text declares?

IV. The Part of the Holy Ghost in the Apostolic Ministry, and in the Permanent Enduement of the Church.

It was not until the Holy Spirit descended that the apostles were permitted to exercise their ministry in power, and all the mighty works that followed are distinctly attributed by Peter and the other apostles to His personal working. He quotes from the prophet Joel the distinct promise, "I will pour out in those days of my Spirit," and it is followed by the announcement that shall ensue, "And I will show wonders in the heavens above, and miracles in the earth beneath."

It was after the Holy Ghost descended again, a little later, until the place was shaken, that we read, "By the hands of the apostles were many signs and wonders wrought among the people." And it was to be through His continuance and supernatural presence that the divine gifts were to be manifested in the church to the end of the dispensation. 1 Cor. 12: 4. "There are diversities of gifts, but the same Spirit. To one there is given the word of wisdom; to another the word of knowledge by the same Spirit, to another faith by the same Spirit, to another the gifts of healing by the same Spirit, to another the working of miracles by the same Spirit, but all these worketh that one and the self-same Spirit, dividing to everyone severally as he will."

Thus we see that all the supernatural effects of Christianity are accomplished through the Holy Spirit. It is His very province to perpetuate in the Church the very works that Christ performed through Him on earth, the Church being simply the body of the ascended Savior, and the channel through which He is to work in the same divine manner; even as the Master said when promising His coming: "The works that I do shall he do also; and greater works than these he shall do, because I go to my Father."

Why then, should it seem strange that this blessed Spirit should do the very work He came to do, and still quicken our mortal bodies as He dwells within us?

V. The Special Ministry of the Holy Ghost for our Bodies.

In the sixth chapter of 1 Corinthians, the dignity and sacredness of the human body are very clearly presented as an argument against impurity in our social relations. "Know ye not," He asks, "that your bodies are the members of Christ?" verse 15; and then, verse 19, "What! know ye not that your body is the temple of the Holy Ghost?" Previously, in this epistle, He had spoken of the Spirit's ministry within us in a more spiritual sense -- chapter 3: 16, 17 -- but here He refers explicitly to His union with our physical life, and with the body of Jesus Christ as God's substitute for unholy physical connection. The body is for the Lord and the Lord for the body; and it is the ministry of the Holy Ghost thus to unite our body to our Lord's, and to inhabit it and hold it in sacredness and purity for Him.

Let us distinctly understand that it is of our physical life that these Scriptures speak, not our spiritual. That is also united to Christ. But surely with so much teaching regarding that portion of our being, we can afford to claim these specific references for that which was intended by them -- our consecrated physical life.

The only way in which the simple and conclusive effect of our text can be turned aside is by attempting to apply it to the future resurrection, as sometimes has been done. It is therefore well that we should carefully look at its connection, and establish its true application on sound exegetical grounds.

1. The general connection of the whole chapter makes this very plain. No less an authority than John Calvin has proved that this passage cannot refer to the future resurrection, because the apostle is speaking, in this place, of the present work of the Holy Ghost in the believer, and it is not until much later that he advances to the future hopes that await us at the Lord's coming, which he does enlarge upon after the eighteenth verse. The subject of the chapter is the blessed indwelling of the Holy Spirit in those who have yielded themselves wholly to Christ.

The first effect of His indwelling is given in the second verse; it is deliverance from indwelling sin through the indwelling of the Holy Ghost.

The second is the new habit of obedience to the Spirit, expressed so beautifully in the eighth chapter of Romans, fifth and sixth verses, by the expression, "The minding of the Spirit is life and peace." "They that after the Spirit do mind the things of the Spirit."

The third effect of the Spirit's indwelling is His quickening life for our bodies, and this is here described in the text.

In the previous verse the body is recognized as well as the soul, as yielded up to death, and so reckoned as good as dead,

Walking in the Spirit

that we do not henceforth depend upon its natural strength as sufficient; but in contrast with this the Holy Spirit becomes its new life and quickens our mortal body by the same power which raised Christ from the dead.

This follows later in the chapter, verses 14, 15.

The blessed leading of the Holy Ghost through the experience of Christian life, culminating at last in the realization of our future hope when we shall enter into the full redemption of the body at Christ's second coming, verse 23; but even of this full redemption of the body, we are told in the same verse, that we have even now the first fruits of the Spirit. That is, of course, the quickening influence which the Spirit exercises, even in the present life, in our mortal bodies, and which is the foretaste of the full resurrection.

Thus, the very order of the chapter prepares us to apply the text to a present experience. John Calvin, as we have already stated, does so, but instead of recognizing that present Spirit as divine healing, of which probably the good reformer never thought, He regards it as the consecrating of our bodies to the service and glory of God, a sense, of course, which the word quicken does not bear.

2. This leads us to inquire into the meaning of the word "quicken."

It would require a very strong inversion, and, we almost think, perversion of the word, to apply this term to the consecration of the body, for it literally means the reviving, stimulating, animating, invigorating of its strength.

The nearest parallel passage where it is employed is in this same epistle, a few chapters previously, where it is applied, chapter 4: 17, to the act which God performed in quickening the body of Abraham when he was past age, and also the vital organs of Sarah, his wife, so that Isaac was born contrary to nature.

In this case, neither Abraham nor Sarah were dead, but their vital system was exhausted, and it was simply quickened, revived and renewed.

Thus the word would not suggest the literal resurrection of the dead, but rather the reviving and restoring of strength when it is exhausted; precisely what is done when our failing health is renewed, and our infirmities are healed by the indwelling power of the Holy Spirit through the name of Jesus.

3. It will make this conclusion still more obvious if we remember that it is our mortal bodies that are here described, not our souls at all, but our physical organization.

This, therefore, is a direct operation of the Holy Spirit upon our vital functions, organs and health, and any other application is contrary to the simple and natural meaning of the passage.

4. That this is not the resurrection body is certain from the fact that it is called the mortal body. Now the mortal body means a dying body, and certainly that is not a dead body, and still more certainly, it is not a resurrected body, for the bodies of the saints, when raised from the dead at Christ's coming, shall not be mortal bodies, but immortal, nor "can they die any more," our Lord Himself has said.

5. The whole induction of proof is crowned by the clause "that dwelleth in us."

Now that must mean the present dwelling of the Holy Spirit in our present mortal bodies. It cannot mean our buried dust, for then the Spirit will not be dwelling in us. It is a process which is now going on through the present indwelling and inworking of the Holy Ghost.

We might add to these thoughts the impressive one suggested by the terms, "the Spirit of Him that raised up Jesus from the dead." This is the Spirit of a physical resurrection. The resurrection of Christ from the dead was a spiritual resurrection. His soul was not dead, it was His body that was raised from the tomb, and if it be the pattern of the Spirit's working in us in this connection, it must have reference to our body too.

We have not sufficiently realized the physical meaning of Christ's resurrection, or given due weight to the stupendous fact that He who came forth from that grave has become the physical head of our life, and that "we are members of His body, His flesh, and of His bones," and have a right to draw from His glorious frame the fullness of His life and strength, so far as these vessels of clay can hold it and use it for His service and glory.

Thus we see that the Holy Spirit has a direct ministry for our bodies, even as Christ's body has a direct relation to our physical being. Have we thus received Him? Do we thus know Him? And, ceasing to depend upon our natural strength, have we learned the blessed secret, "He giveth power to the faint; and to them that have no might He increaseth strength." "They that wait upon the Lord shall change their strength; they shall mount up with wings as eagles; they shall run and not be weary, they shall walk and not faint."

VI. The Relation of the Holy Spirit to the Future Resurrection.

This is the climax of the simple argument respecting the blessed working of the Holy Spirit in our bodies.

While he quickens our mortal bodies now, there is awaiting us a glorious and immortal tabernacle which shall be fashioned like unto the body of His glory.

Speaking of it, the apostle says, "For we know that if our earthly house of this tabernacle were dissolved, we have a building of God, an house not made with hands, eternal in the heavens. For in this we groan, earnestly desiring to be clothed upon with our house which is from heaven; if so be that being clothed we shall not be found naked. For we that are in this tabernacle do groan, being burdened; not for that we would be unclothed, but clothed upon, that mortality might be swallowed up of life." And then he adds, "Now He that hath wrought us for the self-same thing is God," that is for the physical resurrection. And then follows this most important sentence which should be perfectly weighed, "who also hath given unto us the earnest of the Spirit."

Anyone who knows the meaning of the word "earnest" need not have it demonstrated that it implies the first sample in actual kind of the flower and fruit which is afterwards to follow.

An earnest of the harvest is the first sheaf, the very same in kind as that which is to come. An earnest of the field produced, is a handful of the very soil which we have bought. And so, an earnest of the resurrection is a part of that resurrection life experienced now in our physical frame.

To say that the Holy Spirit in our hearts is the earnest, would be to contradict the very meaning of the terms, to make a thing of a different class, an earnest of something utterly diverse. The Spirit in our hearts now is an earnest of our spiritual exaltation yonder, the Spirit in our mortal bodies now is an earnest of the resurrection of the body then in physical immortality.

This is exactly what the apostle said in parallel passage, Rom. 8: 23, "We ourselves, which have the firstfruits of the Spirit, even we ourselves groan within ourselves, waiting for the adoption, to wit, the redemption of our body."

We have the firstfruits of the resurrection, and we are waiting for the full harvest, and the firstfruits are, verse 11, "If the Spirit of Him that raised up Jesus from the dead dwell in you, he that raised up Christ from the dead shall also quicken your mortal bodies by his Spirit that dwelleth in you."

We have all we can hold in the vessel of clay now; we shall then have all we can contain in the larger vessel of glory, when, thrilled with the rapturous touch of His life, we shall soar away from the fetters of the tomb and the restraints of our present frailties and limitations, into all the might and majesty of His own glorious life and power. Then, like Him, our flesh shall be "like fine brass, as if it burned in a furnace, our eyes like flames of fire," our bodies able to penetrate through material barriers, to rise beyond the clouds, to spurn the restraining forces of matter and nature, to possess immeasurable space, and share his own divine and mighty works; for we shall be like Him when we see Him as He is.

But this we may have even now in foretaste, as the Spirit quickens our mortal bodies, until we take hold of the glory of the resurrection.

In Conclusion.

How shall we walk in this Spirit of life?

1. We must have Him as the occupant of our heart; we must know Him by a deep and real spiritual experience. Everything in its own order; and the new order is, first, the spiritual and then the material.

Like Him who came from the innermost shrine of the tabernacle, moving outward to meet His people, so the Holy Ghost still comes from the holy place to the heart until He fills all the extremities of our physical being, so that divine healing has been called the overflow of the Holy Ghost from a heart that can hold no more, and pours its redundant fullness into every open channel of our physical life.

2. We must distinctly recognize the promise of His residence in our bodies, and claim Him in this specific way. Every new experience must first be apprehended and then appropriated; and so we must see them to be a redemption right, and then put forth our hand and take of the Tree of Life and eat and live forever.

3. We must receive the Holy Ghost as an abiding guest into our flesh as well as our heart.

The word dwell, translated, in this verse, is a very strong one. It is the Greek word 'oikeo,' and in the last clause the still stronger expression, 'enoikeo.' It means to dwell habitually; to dwell as we dwell at home, to be the welcome, constant guest, and find His residence not only with us, but, as the last term expresses, in the innermost depths of our being.

4. We must abide in Him by hearkening to His voice, obeying His will, using our strength for His service and glory, and constantly recognizing Him, and not mere natural strength, as the source of our life.

This habit can be cultivated; God may have to train us in it by cutting off the outward supplies and sources of physical power; He may let the natural life wither until it seems we must sink and die, and, as stated in the previous verse, if Christ be in us the body is dead because of sin, but then we must remember that the Spirit is life because of righteousness. And though, like Paul in 2 Cor. 4: 11, we seem to be almost delivered unto death for Jesus' sake, yet we must receive the life of Christ in our mortal flesh, and we shall find that it is still as true as it was in Paran's desert and Judah's wilderness, that "man must not live by bread alone, but by every word that proceedeth out of the mouth of God."

Chapter 9.
THE SPIRIT OF COMFORT

"Walking in the comfort of the Holy Ghost." Acts 9: 31.

Our English translators have given to the Greek work 'Paraclete,' which the Lord Jesus applied to the Holy Ghost, the translation of the Comforter. And while this term is not expressive of the complete sense of the original, yet it expresses very beautifully one of the most blessed characters and offices of the Holy Spirit.

I. He is the author of peace.

It is twofold peace, peace with God and the peace of God. We find many references to this twofold rest. "Come unto me all ye that labor and are heavy laden and I will give you rest." This is the rest which the troubled soul receives when it comes to Christ for pardon. But then there is a deeper rest: "Take my yoke upon you and learn of me who am meek and lowly in heart, and ye shall find rest unto your souls." This is experienced after the surrender of the will to God, and the discipline of the Spirit fully received. So again the prophet Isaiah announces, "Thou wilt keep him in perfect peace, whose mind is stayed on thee."

There is a deeper peace, so we find the risen Savior meeting the disciples in the upper room with the salutation, "Peace be unto you," as He shows them His hands and His side; but later, He breathes on them and adds a second benediction of peace as they receive the Holy Ghost. Peace with God is the effect of forgiveness, "Therefore being justified by faith, we have peace with God through our Lord Jesus Christ." This is the gift of the Holy Spirit as He seals upon the heart the assurance of God's pardoning work, and breathes the witness of acceptance. And yet this is dependent upon our believing and resting in the promise. We must cooperate with the Holy Spirit. He witnesses 'with' our spirit, not 'to' our spirit, that we are the children of God. "In whom also, after that ye believed, ye were sealed with that Holy Spirit of promise." "The God of hope fill you with all joy and peace in believing that ye may abound in hope by the power of the Holy Ghost." Thus we see that we must cooperate in believing.

The peace of God is a deeper experience; it comes from the indwelling of God Himself in the heart that has been surrendered wholly to Him, and it is nothing less than the very heart of Christ resting in our heart, possessing our Spirit, and imparting to us the very same peace which He manifested even in that awful hour when all others were filled with dismay, but He was calm and victorious, even in the prospect of the garden and the cross. It is the deep, tranquil, eternal rest of God, taking the place of the restless, troubled sea of our own thoughts, fears and agitations. It is the very peace of God, and it passeth all understanding, and keeps the heart and mind through Christ Jesus our Lord. It is the special gift of the Holy Ghost; nay, it is rather His own personal abiding, as the Dove of Rest, spreading His tranquil wings over the troubled sea of human strife and passion, and bringing His own everlasting rest.

Have we entered into His rest, and are we walking with Him in the secret place of the Most High? What gift is more necessary and delightful in this world of disquiet and change? What would the world not give for an opiate that could charm away its cares and fears, and lull its heart to such divine repose; and yet from the Paraclete of love, and the brooding wing of the holy Dove, men refuse the gift for which their hearts are breaking, and their lives are wearing out in the fret and friction of strife and sin. This is the true element of spiritual growth and power. "In quietness and confidence shall be your strength," is the mission of the very Comforter to bring. "Let us, therefore, fear lest a promise being left us of entering into His rest, any of you would seem to come short of it. Let us labor, therefore, to enter into this rest lest any of you should fail after the same example of unbelief."

II. The Spirit of Joy.

This is a deeper and fuller spring, but the source is the same, the bosom of the Comforter. The kingdom of God, we are told, is not meat and drink, but righteousness and peace, and joy in the Holy Ghost. This also is the joy of Christ Himself. It is the Spirit's business to take the things that are Christ's and reveal them to us. And so the Master has said, "These things have I said unto you, that my joy might remain in you, and that your joy might be full." "Hitherto have ye asked nothing in my name; ask and ye shall receive that your joy may be full." We have some conception of His joy. Even in the dark and dreadful hour when the powers of darkness were gathering about Him for the final struggle, and even His Father's face was about to be covered with the awful cloud of desertion and judgment, still he could rise superior to His surroundings and so forget His own troubles as to think only of His disciples and say to them, "Let not your heart be troubled."

Like the martyrs, afterwards, at the stake and amid the flames, who testified that so deep was their inward joy that they were unconscious of external agony, so He was transported above His anguish by the very joy of His Father's presence and love. It was this that enabled Him to endure, "for the joy set before Him He endured the cross, despising the shame." He saw not the deep, dark valley of humiliation, but the heights of resurrection-life and ascension-glory just beyond; and He was lifted above the consciousness of the present by the vision of hope, and the joy of the Lord. This is the joy He will give to us. It is nothing less than the fullness of His own heart throbbing in our breast and sharing with us His own immutable blessedness.

Therefore, this joy is wholly independent of surrounding circumstances of natural temperament. It is not a spirit of native cheerfulness, but it is a perennial fountain of divine gladness, springing up from sources that lie far below the soil of human nature. It is the same anointing of which the prophet said of Christ Himself, "Thy God hath anointed thee with the oil of gladness above thy fellows."

Now this divine joy is the privilege of all consecrated believers. We need it for victory in the trying places of life. "The joy of the Lord is your strength." Satan always takes special advantage of a depressed and discouraged heart. Victory must be won in the conflict by a spirit of gladness and praise. The hosts of God must march into the battle with songs of rejoicing. The world must see the light of heaven in our faces if it would believe in the reality of our religion.

Therefore, we find the Scriptures exhorting us to "rejoice in the Lord always, and in everything give thanks, for this is the will of God in Christ Jesus concerning us." But the secret of such a love must be a heart possessed and overflowing with the Holy Ghost. "The fruit of the Spirit is love, joy and peace." We cannot find these springs in the soil of time, they flow from the throne of God and of the Lamb. But a soul that dwells in the innermost shrine of the Master's presence will ever know it and reflect it. It can no more be concealed than the sunshine of heaven, and it will light up the humblest life and the most trying situation, just as the sun itself lights up the lowly cabin, and shines through the dark vault, if only it can find an opening where it may enter in. Are you walking in the light of the Lord and filled with His joy? And can we sing:

> God is the treasure of my soul,
> A source of lasting joy;
> A joy which want cannot impair
> Nor death itself destroy?

III. The Spirit of Comfort and Consolation.

It is especially in the hour of distress and trial that the Comforter becomes manifest in His peculiar ministry of consolation and love. It is then that the promise is fulfilled which applies more especially to this person of the Godhead as the very Mother of the soul. "As one whom his mother comforteth, so will I comfort you; and ye shall be comforted in Jerusalem."

1. Comfort implies the existence of trial; and the happiest life is not the one freest from affliction, but they who walk in the Spirit will always be found familiar with the paths of sorrow and the adverse circumstances of life. Nowhere are the followers of the Man of Sorrows promised exemption from the fellowship of His sufferings, but every element of blessing they possess carries with it an added source of trial. To them the world is less a home than to its own children, and their dearest friends are the readiest to misunderstand their lives and cross their wishes. To them comes the experience of temptation and spiritual conflict, as it does not come to the worldling and the sinner, and they have often cause to feel and know

"The path of sorrow and that path alone,
Leads to the land where sorrow is unknown.
No traveler ever reached that blessed abode,
Who found not thorns and briers in the road."

But all these are but occasions to prove the love and faithfulness of God. The storm cloud is but the background for the rainbow, and the falling tear but an occasion for the gentle hand of the Comforter to wipe it away.

2. The comfort is in proportion to the trial. There is a blessed equilibrium of joy and sorrow. As the sufferings of Christ abound in us, so our consolation also abounds in Christ. As far as the pendulum swings backward, so far it swings forward. Every trial is, therefore, a prophecy of blessing to the heart that walks with Jesus. A dear saint of God once remarked, near the close of life, "God has seemed all my life to be so sorry for the trials He gave me in the beginning, that He has been trying to make up for it ever since." This is a blessed compensation even here, and by-and-by we shall find that "our light affliction, which was but for

a moment, worketh for us a far more exceeding, even an eternal weight of glory."

3. Times of trial are, therefore, often our times of greatest joy. God's nightingales sing at midnight, and

> Sorrow touched by God grows bright
> With more than rapturous ray,
> As darkness shows us worlds of light
> We never saw by day.

It was when the apostles were turned out of Antioch by a mob of respectable men and honorable women, that the record was added, "The disciples were filled with joy and with the Holy Ghost." It was when the fig-tree refused to blossom, and the vines were stripped of their accustomed fruit, and nature was robed in a winding sheet of death, that Habakkuk's song rose to its highest notes of triumph, and he could say "Yet I will rejoice in the Lord, and glory in the God of my salvation." There is such a thing as "sorrowful yet always rejoicing;" a bitter sweet which draws its quintessence of joy from the very wormwood and the gall, and which knows not whether to weep or sing as it cries, with Pascal, in the one breath "joy upon joy, tears upon tears!"

Oh! it is a blessed testimony to the grace of God and the Spirit's abundant love, when we can rise above our circumstances and "count it all joy, even when we fall into diverse temptations," and "rejoice, inasmuch as we are partakers of the sufferings of Christ, because when His glory shall be revealed we shall be glad with exceeding joy."

4. If we would know the full comfort of the Holy Spirit we must cooperate with Him, and rejoice by simple faith, often when our circumstances are all forbidding, and even our very feelings give no response of sympathy or conscious joy. It is a great thing to learn to 'count it' all joy. Counting is not the language of poetry or sentiment, but of cold, unerring calculation. It adds up

the column thus: sorrow, temptation, difficulty, opposition, depression, desertion, danger, discouragement on every side, but at the bottom of the column God's presence, God's will, God's joy, God's promise, God's recompense. "Our light affliction, which is but for a moment, worketh for us a far more exceeding, even an eternal weight of glory." How much does the column amount to? Lo! the sum of all the addition is "ALL JOY," for "the sufferings of this present time are not worthy to be compared with the glory to be revealed."

That is the way to count your joy. Singly, a given circumstance may not seem joyful, but counted in with God, and His presence and promise, it makes a glorious sum in the arithmetic of faith. We can rejoice in the Lord as an act of will, and when we do, the Comforter will soon bring all our emotions into line, yea, and all our circumstances too. They who went into battle with songs of praise in front soon had songs of praise in the rear, and an abundant, visible cause of thanksgiving. Therefore, let us say with the apostle, "I do rejoice, yea, and I will rejoice."

5. The Holy Spirit's joys and consolations are administered to the heart in His infinite and sovereign wisdom, according to His purpose, for our spiritual training, and with reference to our spiritual state, or our immediate needs and prospects. Frequently, He sends His sweetest whispers as the reward of special obedience in some difficult and trying place. Not only at the judgment, but now also does the Master say, "Well done, good and faithful servant, enter into the joy of thy Lord." That joy is experienced here, and the good and faithful servant has the recompense of special service and obedience in the place of difficulty and testing.

Sometimes, again, the Spirit's comforts are sent to prepare us for some impending hour of trial, that when the storm bursts upon us we may remember the Master's love, and be cheered and sustained through the trying hour, even as the Holy Spirit came on Jordan's banks, and the Father's voice just before the forty days of dark, fierce temptation. Sometimes, again, the Spirit's love-tokens come just after some dark and terrible conflict, even as the angels appeared after Gethsemane to comfort our weary and suffering Lord. Sometimes, also, His comforts are withdrawn to keep us from leaning too strongly on sensible joys, and to discipline us in the life of simple faith, and teach us to trust when we cannot see the face of our Beloved, or hear the music of His voice.

6. But we must ever remember, in connection with our varied experiences, that even comfort and joy are not to be the aim and goal of our hearts, but rather that the principle of our Christian life is simple faith, and the purpose, faithful obedience and service to our Master.

> "Not enjoyment and not sorrow
> Is our destined end and way;
> But to act that each tomorrow
> Finds us farther than today."

The life that is naturally influenced by sunshine or shadow will be ephemeral, and change its hue like the chameleon, with the seasons and surroundings. Indeed, the very source of lasting joy is to ignore our own emotions and feelings and act uniformly on the twin principles of faith and duty. Many people are trying to get joyful emotions just as they would buy cut flowers in winter. They are bright and fragrant for a few hours, but they have no root, and they wither away with the sunset. Far better and wiser to plant the root in the fertile ground, to water it, and to wait for it, and in a little while the lasting blossoms will open their petals and breathe out their fragrance on the air. So the joy that springs from trust and permanent spiritual life is as abiding as its source.

Let us, therefore, learn to ignore the immediate impressions that lie upon the surface of our consciousness, and steadfastly walk in the fellowship and will of the Divine Spirit, and thus there shall grow in our hearts and lives the roots of happiness and all their blessed fruits of joy and consolation. Often, therefore, has God to withdraw, for a time, the conscious joy, that He may prove us and develop in us the faith that trusts Him, and loves Him for Himself, rather than for the sweetest of His gifts.

A dear friend once came to us complaining that her spiritual joy had all left her, and that her heart was like a stone. There seemed no disobedience in her life, and no defect in her faith, and we could only commit her to the Master for all the teaching she might need. A few days afterwards she came with radiant countenance to tell how it had all ended. "The darkness," she said, "continued until I told the Lord that if He wanted me to be willing to trust Him in the dark, and to bear this for Him, I would do so as long as He was pleased to continue it. The moment I had yielded my will and accepted His, the dawn of heaven burst upon my soul, and the light returned with more than its former gladness, and I knew that He had only been testing me to teach me to trust Him for His own dear sake, and to walk by faith and not by sight."

Thus, let us delight ourselves in the Lord, and He will give us the desires of our heart. Let us aim supremely to please and glorify Him, and we shall find that "to glorify God" is "to enjoy Him forever." Let us rise above even the joy of the Lord to the Lord Himself, and having Him, it shall be forever true of us, "I will see you again, and your heart shall rejoice, and your joy, no man taketh from you." "My joy shall remain in you and your joy shall be full." "Thy sun shall no more go down, nor thy moon withdraw its shining, for the Lord shall be thine everlasting light, and thy days of mourning shall be ended."

Chapter 10.
THE SPIRIT OF LOVE

"Walk in love." Eph. 5: 2.
"The fruit of the Spirit is love." Gal 5: 22.

The legend has come to us that when the apostle John was old, and waiting for His Master's call, he used to rise in the pulpit of the church in Ephesus each Lord's Day, as it came, and looking tenderly in the faces of the assembled people, simply say, "Little children, love one another," and sit down. And when the brethren asked him why he said nothing else, he simply answered, "There is nothing else to say; that is all there is, for, He that dwelleth in love dwelleth in God, and God in him."

Certainly, both Christ and His apostles have given to love, at least, the supreme, if not the exclusive place in the circle of Christian graces. It was the new commandment which Christ left with His disciples, and to which John exclusively refers in his epistle, when he says, His commandments are not grievous, and this is His commandment, that we should believe in the name of His Son Jesus Christ, and love one another, as He gave us commandment. Paul also declares, "Love is the fulfilling of the law;" therefore, he that loveth another hath fulfilled the law. And Christ Himself has declared that the whole law is fulfilled in one word, even in this: "Thou shalt love thy neighbor as thyself."

Someone has beautifully analyzed the fruit of the Spirit in Gal. 5: 22, and shown that all the graces there mentioned are but various forms of love itself. The apostle is not speaking of different fruits, but of one fruit, the fruit of the Spirit, and the various words that follow are but phrases and descriptions of the one fruit, which is love itself. Joy, which is first mentioned, is love on wings; peace, which follows, is love folding its wings, and nestling under the wings of God; longsuffering is love enduring; gentleness is love in society; goodness is love in activity, faith

Walking in the Spirit

is love confiding; meekness is love stooping; temperance is true self-love, and the proper regard for our own real interests, which is as much the duty of love, as regard for the interests of others. Thus we see that love is essential to our whole Christian character, and indeed is the complement and crown of all else.

In the catalogue of spiritual gifts described by Paul in 1 Corinthians, it is named as preeminent to all the gifts of power, and the more excellent way than any enduement even of miraculous working or transcendent wisdom, without which all else will make us but as "sounding brass and a tinkling cymbal."

In the investiture of holy character, described by the apostle in Colossians, after all the old habiliments have been laid aside and the new robes of sanctity been put on, over all the rest we are invited to put on love, which is "the perfect bond" that is the girdle which holds all the other garments in their place and keeps them from falling off. And so, a soul without love must lose even the chief advantage of all other gifts, and faith and service be rendered ineffectual for lack of love. Therefore, it is the chief ministry of the Holy Spirit to teach us this heavenly lesson. In doing this

1. We must learn from Him that love is not a natural quality, but a direct gift of divine grace. The very word for love is charity, or 'caritas,' and this is derived from the root 'charis,' grace. So that the primary idea conveyed by the Bible term for love is, that it is a gift and not a natural quality. There is much earthborn love, and it would be narrow and blind to ignore the human virtues which have adorned the annals of history. The exquisite instinct of maternal love, the tender affection of the husband and wife, the brother and friend, the many refinements and amiabilities of the human character, the devotion of the patriot to his country, and the philanthropist to his kind -- these are holy affections which we would not, and do not, need to ignore. But human love has its limitations.

The love which the Holy Ghost teaches is not confined to any class or condition, but, like the love of God Himself, is able to reach and embrace not only the stranger and the alien, but also the unworthy, the unlovely, the unloving, and even the most malignant enemy and the most uncongenial object. It is nothing less than the very heart of God Himself infused into our heart. It is the love of God Himself imparted to us through the Holy Ghost. We cannot wring it out of our selfish hearts, or work it up by any effort of our will; it must come down to us from the very heart of God, and be shed abroad by the Holy Ghost Himself. This delightful fact makes the exercise of love a possibility for even the coldest and hardest heart. If it is a gift of grace, then it is available for all, and we have but to realize our need, yield ourselves unreservedly to God, be willing to receive it and exercise it and then claim it, and go forth to fulfill it in His strength. And as it is a gift, it involves no merit on the part of the receiver, for it is not our love, but the grace of our Lord Jesus Christ, to whom must ever be all the glory.

2. The love of God must be founded, like every other spiritual grace, on the exercise of faith. The apostle John, who understood this subject better than any other, gives the simple philosophy of love in these words, "We love Him because He first loved us;" and "we have known and believed the love that God hath to us." We must believe without wavering in God's personal love to us before we can love Him in return. A single doubt in the heart respecting this will cloud the whole heavens. The spirit of implicit confidence in God will always lead to a spirit of filial love; and if we love Him that begetteth, we shall also love them that are begotten of Him.

Faith is, indeed, the channel of all spiritual blessings; hence the apostle Peter has said, "Add to your faith virtue, knowledge, temperance, and all the other graces." Hence, also, the apostles, when Christ was enjoining upon them the height and depth

Walking in the Spirit

to which the forgiveness of injuries should extend, exclaimed, "Lord, increase our faith." They did not say, increase our love, for they seemed to have learned that if they had the faith which they should possess, they would inevitably possess the love. This is true. The fountain of love will always spring to the same height as the head-waters of faith have reached.

3. In order to receive this heavenly gift, the soul must be wholly surrendered to Christ, and receive the Holy Spirit as an abiding presence to bring into the heart the life of Jesus Christ, and to write the law of love upon the heart according to the terms of the new covenant. "I will write my law upon their hearts," is the promise of this new covenant, and put it into their inward part." This law is nothing but love, for love is the substance of the law, and the Holy Spirit came on the day of Pentecost, the anniversary of the law, as the spirit of power and obedience.

We enter into this new covenant, therefore, when we receive the Holy Spirit as our personal life, and indwelling guide and strength. And He brings into our spirit the abiding presence of Jesus Christ, uniting us to His person in such an intimate and perfect manner that we receive His very life into our own, and love in His love, and live in His very being. In order to do this there must, of course, be a renunciation of our own life and will, and the complete consecration of ourselves to Him. Then we receive Christ to abide, and all our life henceforth is through the virtue of His abiding union with us. This is the true secret of divine love.

A distinguished French evangelist was converted to God by preaching on the text, "Thou shalt love the Lord thy God with all thy heart, and soul, and mind, and strength." And finding, as he preached, his own inability to meet the demands of love, he was forced to fall back, even while preaching, upon the Lord Jesus Christ to meet his helplessness, and publicly acknowledge to the people that there was one way alone through which he could have help to obey this supreme law, the grace of the Lord Jesus Christ. In short, the secret of love is the same as all other graces, "Not I, but Christ that liveth in me." And this is what He is waiting to do for every willing heart.

4. But it is in the exercise of love in our practical Christian life that our chief lessons in walking with the Spirit must be learned, as our heavenly Teacher leads us in detail through the blessed, yet often painful discipline of the school of experience, and grounds us not only in the principles, but in the most difficult practice of this heavenly grace. One of His most frequent leadings is to bring us into a situation where we are required to exercise a love which we do not ourselves possess. We are confronted with circumstances which sorely test our spirit. Perhaps somewhere unkindness is allowed to be done to us, or we are associated with persons most uncongenial and disagreeable to us, or we hear of some trial that is before an enemy and are strongly tempted to conclude that they deserve the affliction, and are only suffering the judgment which they have brought upon themselves, when, on the contrary, the Holy Spirit is simply teaching us not to judge them at all, or even think a thought of condemnation, but rather pray for them and get our victory of love.

And yet, it is not in us to do this; our selfishness or pride leaps to the front, passes its judgment, recoils from the uncongenial touch, is tempted to take pleasure in their calamity, and at the same time is intensely conscious of condemnation and humiliation because of this ignominious failure in the grace of love. It sees the divine standard, "Charity suffereth long and is kind," charity maketh no account of the evil, charity is not provoked, beareth all things, believeth all things, hopeth all things, endureth all things, and yet it feels its inability to meet it. There is a painful conflict, perhaps a struggle with self, and the stronger uprising of the old spirit of prejudice and malice; and then the cry, "Oh! wretched man that I am, who shall deliver me?"

It is just at this point that Christ is revealed to us as the source of victory and the spirit of love. And, as we look away from our hearts to Him, and cling to Him in our helplessness, we find His love sufficient, and the heart is sweetly rested and filled with His thoughts, His gentleness, His divine forbearance, His forgiveness, meekness and patience, and we are strengthened according to His glorious power into all patience and longsuffering with joyfulness."

It often seems very strange to those who have just yielded themselves to God that they should be immediately thrown into circumstances more trying than they have ever experienced, and every right thing they try to do seems harder than before; but this is just God's way of impressing the lesson upon us, showing to us our own need, and throwing us upon His power and grace. When we have learned the lesson, the difficulty is always removed or made easier. It is a great thing to recognize in our trials as they meet us, not so much obstacles that have come to overwhelm us, as teachers that have met us on our way to bring us deeper lessons and higher blessings.

Another way by which the Spirit teaches us the exercise of love is by showing us God's thoughts in regard to ourselves, teaching us, like Himself, to see persons, not so much in their present character or personal unworthiness, as in their relation to Christ, and especially in the light of what His grace is working in them, and going to finally develop in their future character. God Himself looks at us, not as we are, but as we are to Christ; and loves us, not for our sake, but for Christ's sake, and for His own sake, because of something in Himself which cannot help loving even the unlovely. And then, God always looks beyond our present to the future ideal, which His love has for us, and to which, it is bringing us. God sees us, not as we are today, but as we shall be by-and-by, when He has accomplished the purpose of His grace in us, and we shall shine forth as the sun in the kingdom of our Father. And if we would, like Him, thus look at others, not of ourselves, but in Christ, and not in the present, but in light of the glorious future, we should love them as He loves them, and be lifted above all that is trying into the victory of faith and love. If we truly believe in God's purpose of grace for us, we must likewise for them.

There is nothing more beautiful than this spirit in God Himself, which refuses to recognize the faults of His children. He said, "Surely, they are my people, children that will not lie;" He was not willing to see their faults and sins. It was the blindness of love; the blessed blindness which He would teach us also, and in which we shall find our sweetest victories, and lose most of our burdens.

There is a parable of a man who met a traveler on the road, dragged down almost to the earth by an unequal burden which he carried on his shoulders. He had two sacks upon his back; one hanging in front, the other behind. The one that hung before contained the bad deeds of his neighbors, and it was so full that his head was bowed almost to the ground, while the odor that came up from the offensive mass almost suffocated him. The sack which he carried behind contained their good deeds, but it seemed almost empty, and was not able to balance the overwhelming weight that hung before. While the man was trying to persuade him to reverse the load, another traveler came up behind, walking lightly, with head erect and shining face. He, too, had two sacks upon his back, but they did not seem to oppress him, but rather to rest him. The one in front contained the good deeds of his neighbors, and he seemed to never tire of contemplating the present burdens, which, he said, instead of weighing him down seemed always to draw him forward on his journey. When the gentleman asked him what he carried in the other sack that hung behind, he said, "O, that is where I keep the bad actions of my friends;" "but," said the other, "I don't see any there."

"Well," said the traveler, "I have made a little hole in the bottom of the bag, and when anything disagreeable occurs I just pitch it over my shoulder into the sack and it drops out at the bottom, and so I have nothing to hold me back, but everything to press me onward, and my journey is a very delightful and easy one."

The greatest blessing of love is the blessing that it brings to us. The heaviest curse of hate is the corrosion it leaves upon the heart. Every time a temptation comes to us to judge harshly of another, and take any pleasure in their calamity, and we pray for them instead, we have ourselves obtained a blessing far richer than theirs. Every time we linger on an injury, even in our thought, and harbor an ungracious spirit, we have eaten so much carrion, and have depleted our spiritual strength in proportion. Therefore, love is not only duty, but it is also life, and selfishness is self-destruction. Never was there a truer sentence spoken than this, "He that loveth his life shall lose it, but he that hateth his life shall keep it unto life eternal."

While it is true that the Holy Spirit will always give us the victory and grace of love, yet we have a more solemn part ourselves to perform; we must be willing to choose it, and this is often the very crisis of defeat. Pride and bitterness are not willing even to receive the love of God; some would rather have their revenge than their victory. They would not forgive even if they could, and the Lord lets them have their way, and their sin become its own avenger.

Often have we met even Christian hearts who have said, "I do not want to love some people; I shall not respect myself if I did; I take a real pleasure in disliking them." Sometimes have we been asked by a heart that has struggled long for this grace of love, "Why is it God does not give me love?" and we have looked into their face and asked, "Do you really want it? Do you really choose to love some persons, and would you be glad this moment to be able to treat them, with all your heart, with tenderness and sweetness?" and they have looked into their heart and honestly replied, "I believe I am not willing;" and in that moment they have felt that they did not really want this blessing, and therefore did not have it.

Are any of our readers in this state? Beloved, pause and remember with deep solemnity your earliest, simplest prayer, "Forgive us our trespasses as we forgive them that trespass against us." There are two unpardonable sins; one is the unbelief that rejects Christ, the other is the bitterness that refuses to love our brother. For He has said, who died for His enemies, "If ye forgive not, neither will your heavenly Father forgive you." It is vain to say we cannot love; He knows we cannot, but He is willing to give us the love if we are honestly willing to receive it, so that we are without excuse.

There are many lessons in the school of love into which we shall be led as we walk in the Spirit day by day. We shall find the love of God Himself shed abroad in our heart, and our own love to Him shall be kept alive and quickened as an ever-burning fire. It shall not always be emotion, but it shall ever be the purpose of obedience, which is the truest test of love, for He has said, "If ye love me keep my commandments." And we shall find it so utterly His love, rather than our own, that we need not watch it as a transient and uncertain feeling which we are always afraid of losing, but it will possess us as a divine principle, springing up when needed as a well of water whose fountains are in the very heart of Christ. It will be the love of Christ Himself to the Father living and working in our hearts.

So, also, will we find our natural affections intensified, and we shall love our friends more fervently than before, and yet more restfully, more purely, and more for His sake and glory, and less for their sakes and our own.

So, too, shall we find our Christian ties divinely quickened, and our love to the brethren, like the great tides of God's own heart. We shall understand the language of the Bible which speaks of our Christian fellowship and unity. Our hearts shall be knitted together in love, and we shall know what Paul meant when he spoke of the consolation in Christ, the fellowship of the Spirit, the bowels and mercies, the mutual love of Christ's disciples, until it shall be indeed true that the ties of spiritual relationship seem to be even more intense than any of the bonds of human affection.

Our love for souls shall also be thus divinely-imparted and sustained. Men and women will be laid upon our hearts until we shall long over them with an intensity of desire to which there is no parallel in human nature or experience, and it will be a luxury of joy to labor for them, minister with them, and suffer, for their sake. We shall be able to spend our lives in the very cesspools of iniquity, and not feel the hideous surroundings. Our mission rooms, crowded with poverty and sin, and the air fetid with foul breath, unclean attire, and moral pollution, shall seem to us like the gate of heaven. Joy will give radiance to our face, and wings to our feet, in the errands of ministering love. No task will seem trying, and no sinner unattractive, to one whose heart has been thus possessed with the Savior's heart of love.

Love will make that mother bear for her child humiliating drudgeries and excruciating agonies which no servile wages could bribe her to endure, and love for souls will give zest, freshness, and perpetual delight to all the ministry. "So I was had home to prison," wrote the quaint John Bunyan of the place that the love of God had made a paradise; and "I wrote because joy did make me write," was his explanation of the book that has charmed all generations. And such service for Christ, and such alone, will sustain us amid the toils and sacrifices, amid the fields of wretchedness and sin. This love the Holy Spirit alone can give, and this He will freely give to every consecrated heart that receives Him fully. This is just the spirit of His own ministry. For eighteen hundred years the Holy Spirit has dwelt in a hospital of moral leprosy and contagion, and nothing could have held Him in such scenes of sin and repulsion but love more strong than aught that mortals know of love. This earth has been His chosen home, and the heart of sinful men His willing abode; and He will shed abroad the same love in every heart that receives Him.

Beloved, shall we open all our being to His heavenly power, and enter into all the fullness of the love of God? This is the divine nature; this is the substance of heaven; this is the essence of all enduring holiness and happiness; and this the Holy Spirit longs to teach to every willing disciple. So let us receive Him, and walk in Him, and so "walk in love."

Chapter 11.
THE SPIRIT OF POWER

"Ye shall receive the power of the Holy Ghost coming upon you."
Acts 1: 5.

The world is discovering, even in the scientific field, that power is not to be measured by mere mechanical and material forces. There was a time when the strength of an army could be estimated by the numbers and the fighting qualities of its soldiers, but today a small battery of artillery could destroy an entire phalanx of Nebuchadnezzar's, Alexander's, or Caesar's army.

The walls of Babylon would not stand a month against the mines and missiles of modern military science. The hand of a baby was mightier than the massive rocks of Hell Gate. The power of a sunbeam is stronger than the momentum of an iceberg. A single jet of gas will move the mechanism of machinery, when wisely applied, and we are approximating to some knowledge of the great fundamental force of electricity, which will perhaps ultimately be proved to be the principal form of material force in the natural universe. Of course, we know that power belongeth to God, and that the Holy Spirit, the Executive of the Trinity, is the dispenser and agent of the divine power.

Hence our departing Lord said "Ye shall receive the power of the Holy Ghost coming upon you." He is the personal power, and as we receive Him we are empowered for all His will and work.

Let us first consider the nature of true spiritual power.

1. It is not intellectual force. There is force in the human mind. Man can move his fellow-man by eloquence and persuasion, and can overcome the forces of matter by his ingenuity and skill; but this is not the power that the Holy Spirit gives us for the work of Christ. Often it is a hindrance to His effectual working, and it is

not until our confidence in our own thoughts and reasonings has been renounced that He can "use the foolish things to confound them that are wise, and the weak things to confound them that are mighty, that no flesh should glory in His presence."

The power by which the orator sways his audience, producing deep emotion and enthusiasm, and is admired as the master of all hearts, is not the power of the Holy Ghost. The same effect may be produced by delightful music or splendid acting; and the tears of the sanctuary may be no holier than those of the opera or the theater. Even the most logical presentation of divine things, which delights the hearers and impresses the imagination and the understanding, may be utterly destitute of real spiritual power. Hence, some of the most splendid preachers of the Christian pulpit classics of the past two centuries preached almost without definite spiritual results in the known conversion of souls.

It is not the mere truth as truth that produces spiritual results, but it is the power of God accompanying it through the Holy Ghost.

2. It is not the power of organization or numbers.

Much of the power of Christianity today is the natural result of organized forces. Many a successful church owes its prosperity, in a great measure, to the business principles on which it is run, and its influence is made up largely of the social elements which constitute it, the numbers which attend it, or the effective machinery by which it is moved; but this may involve no spiritual power whatever.

It is not inconsistent with spiritual power; the Holy Ghost may work in the channels of order and systematic work, but all of this may exist in the most complete form and yet it be simply a religious club and ecclesiastical machinery.

A minister may build up his church just as a man builds up his business, and the ambition which accomplishes his splendid ideal may be of precisely the same kind as that which has founded and consummated the great financial enterprises of our age. There is a no more perfect organization in the world than Romanism. Its machinery is superb, but it knows nothing of spiritual power.

Hood has drawn the picture in the "Ancient Mariner" of a ship of death drifting across the ocean, and manned by lifeless forms of men; a dead man at the helm, a dead man in the rigging, a dead man on the bridge, a dead man on the deck, drifting in silence across the deep. Some one has represented a formal church as a ship of death, with all the forms of life, but without the life; a dead man in the pulpit, and dead souls in the pews, while the voice of heaven sadly complains, "Thou hast a name that thou livest, and art dead."

Some writers are very fond of quoting statistics of Christianity, and speaking of the four or five hundred million who today are under Christian governments, so called, and the more than three hundred million who are nominally Christians. If we were to deduct from these figures the numbers who belong to the Papal church, and then the members of national Protestant establishments, which do not even profess to admit members on the ground of conversion, there would be a frightful deduction, and a very small remnant who might even be claimed as genuine Christians. How many would be left who even would themselves admit that they knew nothing of the power of the Holy Spirit? Spiritual power may operate without any organized basis. Like the torrent, it is very apt to break through the banks and barriers and sweep over the church of God regardless of its forms and formalities.

In our own day God has been pleased to give it in the most eminent degree, to the men and women that are not even members of the formal circle of the ordained ministry, but have been chosen by God partly because they represented none of the elements which are usually connected with power. We can have this power under any circumstances, and the feeblest church, the most isolated worker, the least influential minister of Christ, may become an instrument of blessing to the whole church of God.

I. What is Spiritual Power?

1. It is the power which convicts of sin. It is the power that makes the hearers to see themselves as God sees them, and humbles them in the dust. It sends people home from the house of God not feeling better but worse; not always admiring the preacher, but often so tried that they perhaps resolve that they will never hear him again. But they know from their inmost soul that he is right and they are wrong. It is the power of conviction; the power that awakens the conscience and says to the soul, "Thou art the man;" it is the power of which the apostle speaks in connection with his own ministry, "by manifestation of the truth, commending ourselves to every man's conscience in the sight of God."

They that possess this power will not always be popular preachers, but they will always be effectual workers. Sometimes the hearer will almost think that they are personal, and that someone has disclosed to them his secret sins. Speaking of such a sermon, one of our most honored evangelists said that he felt so indignant with the preacher under whom he was converted that he waited for some time near the door for the purpose of giving him a trashing for daring to expose him in the way he had done, thinking that somebody had informed on him.

Let us covet this power. It is the very stamp and seal of the Holy Ghost on a faithful minister.

After some of Mr. Moody's evangelistic meetings, it is said that thousands and thousands of dollars have been returned anonymously, or otherwise, to the original owners. Men's consciences have been awakened; the power of God has arraigned them before the bar of justice.

2. It is the power that lifts up Christ and makes Him real to the apprehension of the hearer.

Some sermons leave upon the mind a vivid impression of the truth; others leave upon the mind the picture of the Savior. It is not so much an idea as a person. This is true preaching, and this is the Holy Spirit's most blessed and congenial ministry. He loves to draw in heavenly lines the face of Jesus, and make Him shine out over every page of the Bible, and every paragraph of the sermon as a face of beauty and a heart of love.

Let us cultivate this power, for this is what the struggling, hungry world wants, to know its Savior. "We would see Jesus" is still its cry; and the answer still is, "I, if I be lifted up from the earth, will draw all men unto me."

3. This power leads men to decision. It is not merely that they know something they did not know before, that they get new thoughts and conceptions of truth which they carry away to remember and reflect upon, nor even that they feel the deepest and most stirring emotions of religious feeling, but the power of the Spirit always presses them to action, prompt, decisive, positive action.

This is the best test of power. It was the test of ancient eloquence; it was the glory of Demosthenes that while under the eloquence of other orators the multitudes hurrahed for the speaker; under his matchless tongue they forgot all about Demosthenes and shouted with one voice, "Let us go and fight Philip."

The power of the Holy Ghost leads men to decide for God, and to enlist against Satan, to give up habits of sin, and to make great and everlasting decisions.

The Lord grant us so to speak in His name, in demonstration of the Spirit and power, that the result shall be, as Paul himself expresses it on writing to the Thessalonians, "Our word came unto you not in word only, but in power, and ye turned from idols to serve the living and true God, and to wait for His Son from heaven, even Jesus, which saved us from the wrath to come."

II. The Elements and Sources of Power.

1. It is the power of Christ. It is His own personal working both in the worker and upon the hearers. "All power," He says, "is given unto me in heaven and on earth, and lo! I am with you always even unto the end of the age."

Power is not given unto us, but unto Him, and we are constantly to recognize His living and perpetual presence, and to count upon His direct working. If, therefore, we would have this power, we must be personally united to Him and have Him as an abiding presence. God does not want to glorify us and to show to the world our importance, but to glorify His Son Jesus Christ, and hold up His power and glory.

2. It is the power of the Holy Spirit.

He is the agent who reveals Christ, and manifests His mighty working; therefore, the power is directly connected with the Spirit personally, in the very promise of Christ respecting the Comforter. "When He is come He shall convict the world of sin, and of righteousness, and of judgment." It is not said that we shall convict, but that He shall convict, operating both in the worker and in the hearer's hearts.

So, again, in the promise of Christ just before His ascension, it is said, "Ye shall receive the power of the Holy Ghost coming upon you;" it is not power through the Holy Ghost, but it is the very power of the personal Holy Spirit.

In the account of 1 Cor. 12, of the gifts of the Spirit that were to remain in the New Testament church, all are directly connected with the personal working of the Holy Ghost, "To one is given faith, by the Spirit; to another the working of miracles;" but, lest in any case the power should be connected with the individual in any undue personal sense, it is added, "All these worketh that one and the self-same Spirit, dividing to every man severally as he will."

The history of the Christian church has no more striking feature or lesson than that connected with the phenomena of the Spirit of power. All that have been mightily used of God in the conversion of souls, and the building up of the kingdom of Christ, have recognized His personal baptism as the secret of their power. It was after He had come upon Peter at Pentecost that three thousand souls were converted by a very simple message. It was His fiery truth that made George Whitfield the power of God unto the salvation of innumerable thousands. It was He who fell upon Charles Finney and his audiences, and so filled the whole town, sometimes, where he ministered, with the Divine Presence, that the hands in the factories would fall down at their work and begin to plead for mercy. It is to the day when He fell upon an illiterate Sunday-school worker on the public streets, until he wept for holy joy, that Dwight Moody traces back all his unparalleled usefulness. And many a lowlier worker could tell of a similar story of weakness changed to might, and ignorance made into a channel of divine teaching and blessing through the power of the Holy Ghost in a consecrated heart and life.

Let us honor Him as the personal source of all spiritual power, and He will surely honor us. He holds the key to every human heart, He is the source of the highest thought and the truest feeling, and He has given to us our equipment for our holy ministry for Christ, and we may boldly claim His all-sufficient power and presence.

3. The power of truth.

When united to Christ and accompanied by the Holy Spirit, the gospel is the power of God unto salvation. Apart from the Spirit it is only "the letter that killeth," but accompanied by the Holy Ghost it is wonderfully and divinely adapted to convict of sin, to lead to Christ, and to establish the foundations of faith, hope, love, and holy character. It is not the way we present the gospel, but it is the pure and simple gospel itself which is the power of God, the fundamental elements of the gospel, especially the glorious truth that Christ has died for our sins, and brought in an everlasting righteousness and salvation by His resurrection and intercession.

It is simply wonderful how God uses the plain statement of the gospel oftentimes for the salvation of souls. The sermons of Peter and Paul in the Acts of the Apostles are destitute of either logic or rhetoric. They are simply statements of the great fact that Christ has died and risen to save men, and that by simply accepting this message we are saved. It does indeed seem foolish in its weakness, and yet again and again has God shown that it has the power to change the human heart as nothing else has. How stupendous its result at Pentecost when thousands were saved under the simple proclamation! How marvelous its fruits wherever Paul proclaimed it, not with wisdom of words, but purposely in great simplicity, lest it should be made of none effect!

The early missionaries in Greenland supposed that they must spend a long time in preliminary teaching, preparing the natives to understand the gospel; and so they taught them the principles of the Old Testament, the law of God, etc., but without spiritual fruit; but one day, when the missionary happened to read the story of the third of John, the old chief was overwhelmed with wonder and joy, and immediately spiritual fruit began, and he and many of his people gladly accepted the Savior of sinners.

One of the most remarkable results that we ever saw follow a single sermon, occurred through the preaching of a plain evangelist, especially on one occasion when his discourse was, humanly speaking, weaker than ever before, lacking animation and rhetorical effect, and consisting simply of a clear, plain, and rather a dry statement of the resurrection of Jesus Christ, as the ground of the sinner's hope. But the Holy Spirit used that simple truth to the conversion of a great number of people that night, many of whom remain until this day monuments of the grace of God.

There is in the gospel itself a divine potency that we may fully trust, when we present it in the power of the Spirit, to become God's instrument unto the salvation of all that believe. It has power to transform the whole eternal destiny of the soul, and to change its entire views of God and motives of life.

Let us be sure that we do not dilute its power by trying to mix with it our human reasonings, and let us be careful that we do not depend unduly upon the clearness or persuasiveness of our appeal but wholly upon the truth of the gospel itself, and the power of the Spirit that accompanies it.

4. The personal qualities which the Spirit produces in the instruments through whom He works. For, while the Spirit is the worker, He prepares the vessel through whom He works to be a fitting instrument for His service.

Let us look at some of the elements of power with which the Holy Spirit endues the consecrated heart.

1. Perhaps the most obvious quality in such a person would be earnestness; that intense fusing of all the capacities of the soul and being into one's work.

It is the secret of success even in human affairs, but it is preeminently the very element of power in Christian workers. It is a quality which the hearer instinctively discovers, and whose absence is fatal to effectiveness, notwithstanding all other gifts. Its essential root is sincerity and honesty of purpose. It was this which made the Master say, "My meat is to do the will of Him that sent me, and to finish His work." It was this which enabled Paul to exclaim, "If we be beside ourselves it is to God; for the love of Christ constraineth us." "My heart's desire and prayer to God for Israel is that they might be saved."

This was the secret of Whitfield's wonderful power; his whole soul was engrossed in his work. His one business was to preach the gospel and win souls. No sacrifice could appease him or deter him from his delightful task. It was an enthusiasm with him, and so it is with every earnest soul. This is the true meaning of the word enthusiasm, which literally signifies, God within us. Where the Holy Spirit possesses the heart there always is intense enthusiasm. The true minister should be both a burning and shining light, and the baptism of fire is always a baptism of intense earnestness.

2. Another element of spiritual power is holiness.

There is a certain atmosphere which a saintly soul carries with him which communicates itself to others, and is instinctively perceived even by the careless. There are men and women who awaken in all they come in contact with an irresistible respect, and even reverence. The spirit of godliness, like the nature of the rose, betrays itself in the look, the tone, the bearing, and awakens an unconscious response even in the hearts of ungodly men. The good man compels the homage of the bad, even when they hate and persecute him. The very look of the saintly MeCheyne often filled the hearts of his hearers with strange solemnity. The tones with which George Whitfield pronounced the simplest word sometimes made people weep. The godless Chesterfield declared, after a visit to Fenelon, that another day in his house would have made him a Christian in spite of himself. The very factory hands were sometimes smitten with conviction at their work as Charles Finney passed through the room. The influence of the Countess of Huntington was such, through her simple piety, that even her profligate king respected her, and said that He would be glad to go to heaven clinging to her skirts.

It is possible for us, like a spice-ship entering the harbor and filling the air with fragrance, so to bear about with us the atmosphere of heaven that it shall be true of us as it was of the apostles, "We are a sweet savor of Christ unto them that believe, and unto them that perish. To the one we are the savor of life unto life, and to the other of death unto death; and who is sufficient for these things?"

The Christian worker and divine messenger who comes to men fresh from communion with the skies, will have, like Moses, "some of the glory upon his brow, and the world will again take knowledge of him that he has been with Jesus." It was said of the good Mr. Aitkin, of England, the father of the well-known evangelist, that one always felt in his presence as though encompassed with the very presence of God. He seemed to carry Christ so about with him that people forgot the man in the overshadowing glory of the Master. This is the honor and the power which He will bestow upon every consecrated servant.

Let it be our high ambition thus to carry the seal of God upon our brow, and the witness of heaven in our every attitude, and look, and tone.

3. Faith is another element of spiritual power imparted by the Holy Ghost.

Our success will bear proportion to our expectation of results. The motto of the effective worker will be, "We believe, and therefore have we spoken."

A minister complained to Mr. Spurgeon that he thought that he must give up his ministry, and doubted if he had ever been called to it, giving as a reason that he had labored untiringly for four years, and had not seen a single fruit from his ministry. Mr. Spurgeon simply asked: "Have you always preached expecting conversions at each service?" He acknowledged that he had never thought of such a thing, but had eagerly desired them, and wondered that they did not come, "Why," said the good minister, "you did not expect them, and you did not receive them; God's condition of blessing is faith; and it is as necessary for our work as for our salvation."

This is, indeed, true; it is not in proportion to our desperate efforts that we should see the results; but to our simple trust in the power of God, to honor His own Word, and work by His own Spirit in the hearts of men. The most of the great revival movements have thus begun.

A. B. SIMPSON

A humble working man in the north of Ireland read the story of George Muller's life, and immediately thought, why cannot I have the same answer to prayer in the salvation of souls? He immediately began to pray for a great outpouring of the Holy Spirit upon his city and country; soon he was joined by another, and then another, and before long a flood of fire was sweeping over all the land, and hundreds of thousands of souls were mightily converted to God. It was thus that Mr. Finney always prepared for his work. We can read in his biography how he used to retire with a friend, sometimes into the woods, and spend hours on his knees until he felt the blessing was claimed and the power was coming, and then he would go forth about his work with the tranquil certainty that God was there and would be revealed in all His power and glory, and the result always was the mighty working of the Holy Ghost.

Not always is it the preacher who exercises the effectual faith; sometimes it is a silent and obscure heart whom no one shall know until the day when all things shall be revealed.

A celebrated preacher of the middle ages was always accompanied by a quiet and insignificant man, without whom he would never preach. The man never opened his lips in public, and seemed to be a useless appendage. He afterwards explained that while he preached his companion prayed, and that he attributed all the marvelous results of his messages to his believing intercessions. There is no Christian but can thus claim and exercise the very power of God even in the most silent capacity, and it will be found in the great day that God has not failed to credit the recompense to the real instrument through whom the divine working came. It will very likely be found in that day that the voice that spake from the pulpit had but a fractional share in the real work which the Holy Ghost accomplished, but that some humble saint was the real channel through whom the fire of God fell upon, convicted and converted souls.

But it is not only for the conversion of souls that God will give us His power, and faith to claim His working, but for everything connected with His cause, and our ministry shall touch every part of His work.

Faith is the true channel of effectiveness, simply because faith is merely the hand by which the forces of Omnipotence are brought to bear upon the work. The removing of obstacles, the influencing of human hearts and minds, the bringing together of workers, the obtaining of helpers, the supply of financial needs; all these are proper subjects for believing prayer, and proper lines for demonstrating the all-sufficiency of God. And if, instead of begging for help, and compromising the honor of Christ by despairing appeals to the church and the world, the people of God would more simply trust Him, they would be saved a thousand embarrassments, and His name would be constantly glorified in the manifestation of His all-sufficiency before an unbelieving world.

A few stupendous examples of God's faithfulness in answering the prayers of His people in the supply of money and men, such as have been afforded by the story of George Muller's Orphanage, the China Inland Mission, and similar works by faith, were not intended to be isolated instances, but to prove to the world that Christ is able always to meet His people's needs, and to be but samples of a principle which should be the rule of Christian work; that God in all things might be glorified through Jesus Christ, not only in the spiritual, but in the temporal and practical needs of His kingdom.

4. Love.

Still more necessary is the spirit of love as the very element and character of every true Christian worker. "Lovest thou me?" is the prime condition on which Christ's saints are to minister to His flock, and love for souls is the only bond that can win and hold them and can sustain our own heart amid the trials and discouragements of Christian work. Human love will make any task a delight. For the child of her affection the mother can toil and suffer without weariness, and count life itself a small sacrifice for her loved one.

And so the love of souls will inspire us and sustain us in the face of every discouragement and disagreeable surrounding, until the most loathsome and offensive scenes will be a delight to us, and the most coarse and degraded souls will be dear to our hearts as our beloved friends, and it shall become the passion of our life to win them for Christ.

A noble woman died lately in Indiana, who had a remarkable record of success in dealing with hardened women. She was the superintendent of a large institution for this class, and her influence over them was irresistible; it was the power of love. Often when met by stormy passion and wild, coarse, desperate wickedness, has she thrown her arms about some degraded woman, and by a kiss of unfeigned love and the hot tears of her tender compassion, melted the heart of stone. We must love people if we would do them good, but such love must be divine. Mere human sympathy does not go to the depths of their heart, but the love which is born of God and inbreathed of the Holy Ghost, always finds its way to every citadel of rebellion, and wins the soul for God.

At a railway station a brutal criminal was being conveyed to the penitentiary. Sitting on the benches with his keepers, he was awaiting the incoming train. A little girl sat watching him beside her father. Her heart was overwhelmed with the strange sight, and at length she stole up to him, unnoticed by her father, and looking earnestly in his face, she said, while the tears were in her eyes, "Poor man, I am so sorry for you" The shock aroused him for a moment to realize his condition; his eye flashed, his frame shook with passion, and he repelled her from his presence as though he had been insulted, and almost tried to strike her. She

Walking in the Spirit

cowered back to her father's knee, the tears still in her eyes, and still watched him; but in a little while she managed to slip away again from the arms of her father, who supposed she had been frightened effectually away from approaching him, and stealing up to him again she looked once more in his hideous face and said very slowly, "Poor man, Jesus Christ is so sorry for you." Instantly he seemed utterly changed and subdued. That name had power to overcome the demon in his heart; his wild defiance broke quite down and he began to weep like a child. Years after he often told the story himself, when a happy, useful Christian man, and he said it was that message that broke his heart, and never left him till he found the Savior. It was not the child's love merely, but the Savior's love in the child that won.

There is much danger of turning the gospel of Christ and the power of God into human sentiment. Mere compassion for people, and even a costly show of interest and sympathy, will not save them, but the love born of the Holy Ghost will go as deep as the height from which it springs; and if we walk in the Spirit we shall find Him ever breathing upon us in our work that love which will brood over souls with a divine motherhood, loving them even before we know them, praying for them in the Spirit before we have singled them out of our audience; and then when we meet them recognizing them with a thrill of joy as the souls that we have been bearing on our hearts as a burden of prayer.

This love will strangely endear to us the most repulsive beings and make the most dreadful scenes more delightful than the surroundings of culture and affection, and a life of luxury and indulgence. This is the passion that has drawn so many noble men and women to the wretched fields of sin, until their heavenly love has gathered, like the magnet to itself, the lost and wretched, and bound them forever to the heart of Christ. This is the sweetest, highest gift of the Holy Ghost; the most tender, irresistible element of spiritual power. This was the force that drew souls to Jesus.

A. B. SIMPSON

Chapter 12.
THE SPIRIT OF PRAYER

"Likewise the Spirit also helpeth our infirmities; for we know not what we should pray for as we ought; but the Spirit itself maketh intercession for us with groanings which cannot be uttered." Rom. 8: 26.

"Praying in the Holy Ghost." Jude, verse 20.

The mystery of prayer! There is nothing like it in the natural universe. A higher and a lower being in perfect communion. A familiar intercourse, yet both as widely distinct as the finite is from the infinite. More wonderful even than that we should be able to hold converse with the insect that crawls beneath our feet, or the bird that flutters on the branches at our window! Marvelous bond of prayer which can span the gulf between the Creator and the creature, the infinite God and the humblest and most illiterate child!

How has this been accomplished? The three Divine persons have all cooperated in opening the gates of prayer. The Father waits at the throne of grace as the hearer of prayer; the Son has come to reveal the Father, and has returned to be our Advocate in His presence. And the Holy Spirit has come still nearer, as the other Advocate in the heart, to teach us the heavenly secret of prayer, and send up our petitions in the true spirit to the hands of our heavenly Intercessor. It is to this ministry we are to speak now.

The very name given to the Holy Ghost, literally means the Advocate, and the chief business of the one Advocate is to prepare our cause in the office, and the other to plead it before the Judge. We have the whole Trinity in our behalf. The Holy Spirit prepares our case, the Lord Jesus presents it, and the Judge is our Father. What an infinite light, and what an unspeakable comfort this sheds on the subject of prayer!

Our need of this Advocate is referred to in our text very impressively: "We know not what to pray for as we ought." We are often ignorant of the subjects for which we ought to pray; and often, when we know our needs, we know not how rightly to present them. There is much expressed in these words. We are often deeply ignorant of our truest needs, and the things we wish most for are not the things we most require. Our minds are blinded by prejudice and passion; the things we would sometimes ask for we shall afterwards find would have been only an injury. Besides, we know not the future, and cannot, intelligently, anticipate the needs and dangers against which we should pray, while a thousand unseen elements of peril continually surround us and need a wiser forethought and insight than our own to guard against.

And often "we know not how to pray as we ought." Prayer is a high art, and must be divinely taught. We would not rashly send a crude and unprepared case before an earthly tribunal, and he is greatly mistaken who thinks that the thoughtless and random dashes of human impulse, or even sincere earthly desires, are all accepted as prayer. Many "receive not because they ask amiss." If we regard iniquity in our hearts the Lord will not hear us. We must ask in faith, nothing doubting. These and other qualities must be taught and impelled by the Holy Spirit. "We know not how to pray as we ought."

The right motive which seeks supremely the glory of God, the right spirit recognizing submissively and joyfully His sovereign will, the deep and sincere desire, the faith which dares to ask as largely as the measure of the Father's will and promise, the patience that tarries if it waits, knowing that it will surely come, and will not tarry too long, the obedience that steps out upon the promise all these elements of prayer are operations of the Holy Spirit, and we cannot too devoutly thank Him that He is willing thus to teach our ignorance and simplicity the heavenly secret of prayer. "The Spirit helpeth our infirmities, and maketh intercession within us, with groanings which cannot be uttered.

1. The Holy Spirit reveals to us our needs. This is always the first element in prayer, a painful consciousness of failure and necessity. The prophet's word to Jehoshaphat was, "Make the valley full of ditches," and then, the second, "The valley shall be full of water." The heart must be ploughed up into great channels of conscious need to hold the blessing when it comes; and this is often painful work, but, "Blessed are they which hunger and thirst after righteousness, for they shall be filled."

When the Spirit of grace and supplication is poured out upon Jerusalem, the effect is a deep and universal sorrow. "They shall look upon Him they have pierced, and they shall mourn as one that mourneth for an only son, and be in bitterness as one is in bitterness for a firstborn." The Spirit of prayer is the spirit of dependence, deep humility and conscious need.

2. The Holy Spirit next awakens in the soul holy desires for the blessings that God is about to give. Desire is an element in prayer. "Whatever things ye desire," our Lord says, "when ye pray believe that ye receive them." These deep, spiritual longings are like the rootlets by which the plant draws the nourishment from the soil; like the absorbing vessels of the human system, which take in and assimilate nourishment and food. The desires give intensity and force to our prayer, and enlarge the heart to receive the blessing when it comes. God, therefore, often keeps His children waiting for the visible answer to their petitions, in order that they may the more ardently desire the blessing, and be thus enabled to receive it more fully and appreciate it more gratefully when it comes.

When we were traveling in Italy we were often serenaded by parties of native musicians, whose sweet strains were sometimes very delightful. But we noticed that whenever we paid them their little gratuity they always stopped the music and they went away, and when we wished to listen longer to their sweetest strains, we waited before handing them their charity. So God loves to hear His people's holy desires and earnest prayers, and often prolongs the petition because He delights to hear us pray, and then gives us the larger blessing in proportion to our waiting. Often has your heart longed for some special blessing until it seemed that it would break for desire. You almost thought that you never should possess the holiness you so longed for. But now, as you look back, you see that this deep hunger was just the beginning of your blessing. It was the shadow side, the Holy Ghost awakening all the receptive capacities of your being, to absorb it when it came.

Once we saw a party of children sending up a balloon of tissue paper. First, the balloon was carefully constructed of the lightest fabric, and then suspended with light cords a few feet above the ground. Its little beacon light was attached, and then they began to prepare the force that was to be used for its ascension. It was nothing more than simply building a little fire below the open mouth of the balloon and allowing the heated air to ascend until it filled the entire space within. The moment this was done the little vessel swelled and reached out for its ascension, pulling hard at the restraining cords, and pressing upwards. When it was thoroughly filled with the heated air it was only necessary to cut the cords, and instantly it sailed away to the upper air. So it seems the warm breath of holy desire and earnest purpose in prayer, when inspired by the Holy Ghost, bears up our petitions to the throne of grace, and makes the difference between the mere words of formalism, and the "effectual working prayer of the righteous man which availeth much."

3. The Holy Spirit lays upon the heart wherein He dwells the special burden of prayer. We often read in the old prophetic Scriptures of the burden of the Lord. And so still the Lord lays His burden on His consecrated messengers. This is the meaning of the strong language of our text, "The Spirit maketh intercession within us with groanings which cannot be uttered." Some-

times this burden is inarticulate and unintelligible even to the supplicant himself. Perhaps some heavy shadow rests upon the soul, some deep depression, some crushing weight under which we can only groan. With it there may come the definite thought of some personal need, some apprehended evil that overhangs us, or some dear one who is brought to our spirit as somehow connected with this pressure. As we pray for this especial person or thing, light seems to open upon the heart, and an assurance of having met the will of God in our prayer; or sometimes the burden is not understood; and yet, as it presses heavily upon us and we hold it up to Him who does understand, we are conscious that our prayer is not in vain; but that He who knows its meaning and prompts its cry, is granting what He sees to be best under the circumstances for us or others, as the burden may apply.

We may never know in this world just what it meant, and yet, often we will find that some great trial has been averted, some impending danger turned aside, some difficulty overcome, some sufferer relieved, some soul saved.

It is not necessary that we should always know; indeed, perhaps we should never fully know what any of our prayers wholly mean; God's answer is always larger than our petition, and even when our prayer is most definite and intelligent there is a wide margin which only the Holy Ghost can interpret, and God will fill it up in His infinite wisdom and love. That is what is meant by the significant language of the text, "He that searcheth the heart knoweth what is the mind of the Spirit, for He maketh intercession for the saints according to the will of God." The Father is always searching our hearts and listening, not to our wild and often mistaken outcries, but to the mind of the Holy Spirit in us, whom He recognizes as our true guardian and monitor, and He grants us according to His petitions and not merely our words. But if we walk in the Spirit and are trained to know and obey His voice, we shall not send up the wild and vain outcries of our mistaken impulses, but shall echo His will and His prayer, and thus shall ever pray in accordance with the will of God.

The sensitive spirit grows very quick to discern God's voice. That which would naturally be considered as simple depression of spirits comes to be instantly recognized as a hint that God has something to say to us, or something to ask in us for ourselves or others. Often our physical sensations come to be quick, instinctive interpreters of some inward call; for when we do not quickly listen to God's voice He knocks more loudly, until the very body feels the pain and warns us that the Lord hath need of us. If we were but more watchful we would find that nothing comes to us at any moment of our lives which has not some divine significance, and which does not lead us in some way to communion or service. He who thus walks with God soon learns the luxury of having no personal burdens or troubles, but recognizing everything as service for God or for others.

This makes the ministry of prayer a very solemn responsibility, for, if we are not obedient to His voice, some interest must suffer, some part of His will be neglected, some part of His purpose frustrated, so far, at least, as our cooperation is concerned, and, perhaps, someone very dear to us will lose a blessing through our neglect or disobedience; or we ourselves find that we are not prepared for the conflict or trial against which He was providing by the very burden that we would not understand nor carry.

Thus it was with the disciples and the Master in the garden of Gethsemane. That was for Him the anticipation of the cross; and, as He met the burden in advance, He was prepared for the awful hours that followed, and went through them in victory, and thus redeemed the world. But the disciples could not watch with Him one hour; they neglected the call to prayer, and slept when they should have hearkened and prayed, and the result was that the morning found them unprepared, and the trial ended in shameful failure, and only His previous intercession for him saved Peter from entire wreck, and perhaps a fate desperate as that of Judas.

God has placed within our breast a monitor who is always looking forward to our needs and anticipating our situations; let us, therefore, be quick to hearken and obey His voice, as He calls us to the ministry of prayer, and in so doing we shall not only save ourselves, but also many a heart that perhaps is not able to pray for itself.

4. The Spirit brings to our hearts, in the ministry of prayer, the encouragement of God's Word, the promises of His grace, and the fulness of Christ to meet our need. It is He who gives us such conceptions of Christ as awaken in us confidence of blessing. He opens to our vision the infinite resources of the grace of God, and shows us all the rich provision of our Father's house. He unfolds to us the grounds of faith in the gospel, and teaches us to understand our redemption rights, our filial claims, and our high calling in Christ Jesus. He breathes in our heart the Spirit of sonship, and He inspires the faith which is the essential condition of effectual prayer. And so He leads us to present to the Father, in the name of the Lord Jesus, not only the right desires, but in the right spirit: "By one Spirit we have access unto the Father."

Thus He is in us the Spirit of faith, the Spirit of adoption, the Spirit of liberty in prayer, the Spirit of holy confidence and enlargement of heart, and the witnessing Spirit, who, when we pray in faith, seals upon our soul the divine assurance that our prayer is accepted before God, and that the answer will be surely given. We must first, however, believe God's promise in the exercise of simple faith, and, as we do, the Spirit witnesseth with our spirit and often fills the soul with joy and praise which anticipates the answer long before it is apparent. This is the highest triumph of prayer, to look within the veil, even before the curtains are parted, and know that our petition is granted; to hear the sound of the bells upon our High Priest's garment, even from the inmost chambers, and to rejoice in the anticipation of our blessing as fully as if we already saw its complete fulfillment.

Our Lord always requires this faith as the condition of answered prayer. "Whatsoever things ye desire, when ye pray, believe that ye receive them, and ye shall have them." "Let him ask in faith, nothing doubting. For he that wavereth is like a wave of the sea, driven with the wind and tossed. Let not that man think that he shall receive anything of the Lord." But this is the special work of the Holy Ghost. He is the Spirit of revelation and of faith, and as we pray in His fellowship, and according to His will, we shall be enabled through His grace to ask with humble and confident expectation of His blessing.

5. The Holy Spirit will also teach us when to cease from prayer, and turn our petition into thanksgiving, or go out in obedience to meet the answer as it waits before us, or comes to meet us. There is a place for silence as well as prayer, and when we truly believe, we shall cease to ask as we asked before, and henceforth our prayers shall simply be in the attitude of waiting for our answer, or holding up God's promise to him in the Spirit of praise and expectation.

This does not mean that we shall never think any more about that for which we asked, but we shall think no more of it in a doubtful manner; we shall think of it only with thanksgiving and restful expectation. We may often remind God of it, but it will always be in the spirit of trust and confidence. Therefore, the prophet speaks of those who are "the Lord's remembrancers," those that remind God of His promises and wait upon Him for His fulfillment of them. This is really a spirit of prayer, and yet it is not perhaps a spirit of petition so much as praise, which indeed is the true exhibition of the highest form of faith.

Sometimes, too, after our prayer, the Holy Spirit will have a subsequent ministry of obedience for us; there will be something for us perhaps to do in receiving the answer, and He will show us, interpreting to us God's providences as they meet us, and enabling us to meet them in a spirit of cooperation and vigilance.

He also will be present to support our faith in its tests and painful trials, and enable us to rejoice and praise God, often amid the seeming contradictions of His Providence. For faith is always tested, and "we have need of patience, that having done the will of God we might receive the promise."

Chapter 13.
COOPERATING WITH THE HOLY GHOST

"Receive ye the Holy Ghost." John 20: 22.

"Be filled with the Spirit." Eph. 5: 18.

While we recognize the sovereign power of the Holy Ghost, visiting the heart at His pleasure, and working according to His will upon the objects of His grace, yet God has ordained certain laws of operation and cooperation in connection with the application of redemption; and He Himself most delicately recognizes His own laws, and respects the freedom of the human will; not forcing His blessings upon unwilling hearts, but knocking at the door of our heart, waiting to be recognized and claimed, and then working in the soul as we heartily cooperate, hearken, and obey. There is, therefore, a very solemn and responsible part for every man in cooperating with, or resisting and hindering the Holy Spirit.

"The manifestation of the Spirit is given to every man to profit withal," that is to say, it rests with the man who receives the first movement of the Holy Spirit to determine how far he will embrace his opportunity, cooperate with his heavenly Friend, and enter into all the fullness of the good and perfect will of God.

Perhaps the pound, represented in the parable as given to every one of the servants, was meant to express that gift of the Spirit which every Christian receives, and the various uses which the servants made of this common enduement may represent the degrees with which the children of God double and use their spiritual advantages.

One improved his pound until it had become ten; another until it had increased five-fold, and another neglected it and hid it in the earth. So, three men receiving in the beginning of their experience an equal measure of spiritual things, may show in the end just as great a diversity in the use that they have made of the precious trust. By a diligent and vigilant obedience the one has grown to be a Paul, crowned with ransomed souls, and clothed with all the fullness of heavenly power. The other has become, perhaps, a proud Diotrephes, seeking chiefly his personal ambition and using the divine grace for his own advantage.

The Holy Spirit is especially sensitive to the reception He finds in the human heart; never intruding as an unwelcome guest, but gladly entering every open door, and following up every invitation with His faithful love and power. How are we to cooperate with Him, and how may we grieve and hinder Him?

1. We are commanded to receive the Holy Ghost.

This denotes an active and positive taking of His life and power into our hearts and lives. It is not a mere acquiescence in His coming, or passive assent unto His will, but an active appropriating and absorbing of His blessed person and influences into our whole person. It is one thing to have our dinner brought to us, and it is another thing to eat it, drink it, assimilate it, and be nourished by it.

It is thus that we are to receive the Holy Ghost, with an open, yielding, hungering, thirsting, believing, accepting and absorbing heart, even as the dry sand receives the rain, as the empty sponge receives the moisture, as the negative cloud receives the current from the positive, as the vacuum receives the air, and the babe drinks in the mother's life from her offered breast.

There are spiritual organs of reception as well as physical. There are vessels of heart-hunger and absorption which can be cultivated and exercised, and there are those who, "by reason of use," have their senses thus exercised to receive the grace of God.

Are we receiving the Holy Ghost? are we taking the water of life freely? are we putting forth our hand grasping the tree of life and eating of its fruit?

Let us remember that we are receiving a person, and that in order to do so we must recognize that person individually, and treat Him as we would a welcome guest.

Have we thus received the Holy Spirit as a person, invited Him into our hearts, believed that He really came, and then begun to treat Him as an actual person; to talk to Him, to commune with Him, to enjoy His fellowship, to call upon His help, and practically recognize Him as a present Guest.

Not only do we receive the Holy Spirit as a person, but having thus recognized Him we are to receive His influences as He imparts them, to be open to His touch, attentive to His voice, responsive to His love, and empty vessels for His constant use and filling.

2. We are to be filled with the Spirit.

While it is true that there is a definite moment when the Holy Spirit comes to reside in the heart, yet there are repeated experiences of His renewing, quickening, reviving, refreshing influences; these are called by the apostle, in Jude, "the renewings of the Holy Ghost," which He sheds on us abundantly, and by Peter, in the Acts of the Apostles, "the times of refreshing from the presence of the Lord." The expression, "baptized of the Spirit" may be applied perhaps to our first marked experience of this kind, and in this connection we are glad that the term 'baptism' means a very thorough and complete immersion in the ocean of His love and fullness. But it is not once that He is asked to manifest His love and power.

We read in the Acts of the Apostles that after the day of Pentecost there came another day when the disciples were assembled in a time of peril and trial in prayer before the Master for His interposition, and that when they had prayed, the place was shaken where they had assembled, and they were all filled with the Holy Ghost, and the mighty power of God was manifested afresh in their midst.

And so the Apostle says in Ephesians, "Be not drunk with wine, but be filled with the Spirit." The filling of the Spirit is here contrasted with the exciting influence of earthly stimulants, as if he had said, there is one draught of which you can never drink too much; you can safely be intoxicated with the Holy Ghost.

In the twelfth chapter of First Corinthians, Paul uses the same expression in connection with the figure of baptism: "By one Spirit have we all been baptized into one body, and been made to drink of that one Spirit." It is the figure of being submerged in the ocean, and then, when lost in the depths of the sea, opening our mouths and beginning to drink of its depth and fullness. We are plunged in the Holy Spirit until He becomes the element of our being, like the air in which we move, and then we open all the faculties of our being and drink from His inexhaustible supplies.

How great the capacity of the human soul to be filled with the life of God it is impossible to say. Surely, if the sun can fill a flower with its glorious light in all the many-tinted colors; surely, if the cloud can drink in his rays until they grow with all the tints of light, O, surely the human soul can absorb all there is in God and then give it forth in the reflected light of holiness. Surely, if the earth can drink in the rain, and then give it out in the plants, and fruits, and flowers of summer, the human heart can draw from God the elements of His very being, and turn them into all the fruits of holy living and useful deeds. Surely, if His own beloved Son could dwell in His bosom ages upon ages before an angel ever sang or a planet swept along its heavenly way, or an object of creation filled the plains of immensity, and found in His Father's heart the rapture of His joy, so that He could say, "I was daily His delight, rejoicing always before Him," O, surely, the human soul can fill all its little vessels and satisfy the measure of its capacities in His divine love and benignity.

Let us receive Him in all His fullness, let us be filled with the Spirit, let us drink of the ocean in which we have been baptized.

A Christian friend wrote the other day that his old neighbors had got up a report that he had turned out badly in his Christian life and taken to drinking. He replied, very happily, that it was true he had taken to drinking of late, but that if his old friends could only know what he was drinking then they would all join him, for he had found the fountain of living waters, and was drinking from the Holy Spirit and could say, "He that drinketh of this water shall never thirst again."

3. Let us trust the Holy Spirit.

We must believe in the Spirit as well as in the Son, and treat Him with confidence, expecting Him to meet us and bless us, and communicate unto Him all our needs, perplexities, and even our temptations and sins. He was the antitype of the water of Horeb's ancient rock, and it is as wrong today as it was for Moses to strike that rock in unbelieving violence, when God bids us simply to speak to it in gentleness and trust, and expect its waters to gush forth at our whispered call and satisfy out every need.

The Holy Spirit is sensitive to our distrust. Many persons cry for Him and pray to Him as though He were a distant and selfish tyrant, insensible to His children's cry. It is a mother heart to whom we speak, and one who is always within whispering distance of her little ones.

Let us nestle beneath her wings, let us walk in the light of her love, let us trust the Holy Ghost with implicit, childlike confidence, and always expect the answering voice and presence of the Comforter, and it shall be true, "Before they call I will answer, while they are yet speaking I will hear." The apostle asks the Galatians, "Received ye the Spirit by the works of the law, or by the hearing of faith?" and adds after, "we might receive the promise of the Spirit through faith."

This is the only way that we can receive a person -- by treating him with confidence, believing that he comes to us in sincerity, and opening the door to him at once, recognize him as a friend, and treat him as a welcome guest. So let us treat the Holy Spirit.

4. Let us obey the Spirit.

The first thing in obedience is to hearken. Especially is this necessary with the gentle Comforter. So gentle is this mother that her voice is not often loud, and may be missed by the inattentive ear; therefore, the beautiful expression is used by the apostle Paul in the 8th chapter of Romans, which reminds us of a mother's voice; "The minding of the Spirit is life and peace." We are to mind the Spirit, we are to pay attention to His counsels, commands, and slightest intimations. God never speaks an idle word, nor gives a lesson that we can afford to slight or forget. They who will listen will have much to listen to, but they who slight the voice of God need not wonder that they are often left in silence.

The Spirit's voice is "a still small voice." The heart in which He loves to dwell is a quiet one, where the voice of passion and the world's loud tumult is stilled, and His whisper is watched for with delight and attention.

But not only must we hearken; when we know we must obey. The voice of the Spirit is imperative; there can be no compromise, and there should be no delay. God will not excuse us from His commandments. His word is very deliberately spoken and for our good always, and when the command is given it cannot be recalled. Therefore, if we do not obey we must be involved in darkness, difficulty, and separation from Him. We may plunge on, but the Spirit waits at that point, on the crossroads of life, and we can make no progress until we return and obey Him. Many a bitter experience, many a tear of brokenhearted disappointment and failure have come from refusing to obey. Indeed, such disobedience must be fatal if persisted in. It was just there that Saul halted and lost his kingdom, through disobedience and willfulness in neglecting the voice of God. It was there that Israel found the fatal crisis of their history at Kadesh Barnea. It was there that, in the apostolic days, a nation was about to reap the same fatal error, and the apostle pleaded with his countrymen so solemnly and gently: "Today if ye will hear His voice harden not your hearts."

Happy the heart that promptly obeys the voice of God. The Spirit delights to lead such a soul. How beautifully we see this illustrated in the experience of Paul! At one period of his ministry he was in danger of pressing on in his work beyond the divine command, and so, we are told, he was forbidden of the Spirit to preach the Word in Asia, and essayed to go into Bithynia but the Spirit suffered him not. Happy for him that he obeyed both these restraints. Had he persisted in his way, and even succeeded in getting down to Ephesus, he would have found every door closed, and his visit would have been premature. Waiting on God's bidding and way a year longer, he was permitted to go afterwards and found the door wide open; and his next and perhaps most successful ministry was given to him at Ephesus, while in obedience, that which led him now into Europe. He was permitted to establish the Gospel in that mighty continent.

A little later, we see the very opposite lesson exemplified in his life. We are told that he purposed in Spirit to go to Jerusalem and Rome. This was a personal direction of the Holy Ghost to him, and in consequence he determined upon the greatest purpose of his life, to carry the gospel to his countrymen at Jerusalem, and then to establish Christianity in the capital of the world.

It was well that he proposed it in the Spirit, and that he was sure of God's command, for the difficulties that afterwards met him would have been insuperable on any human line.

First, the very servants of God met him all along the way, and even prophetic messengers warned him not to go to Jerusalem, but the brave apostle kept to his promise and pressed divinely on.

Next, the whole power of unbelieving Judaism arrayed itself against him, tried to mob him at Jerusalem, to assassinate him on the way to Caesarea, and then to condemn him before the tribunal of Felix, Festus and Agrippa, but still he pressed steadfastly on.

Next, the intriguing policy and imperial power of Rome itself confronted him, and held him two years a prisoner at Caesarea, but he never for a moment abandoned his purpose.

At length he was on his way to Rome, but then the very elements of nature and the powers of hell combined in one last effort to destroy him. The fierce Euroclydon of the Mediterranean wrecked his ship, and on Malta's shore the viper from the flames fastened upon his hand, but he still pressed on in indomitable might, in obedience to the Holy Ghost, and so he reached Rome and planted the standard of the cross before the palace of the Caesars, witnessed for Christ in the face of imprisonment and martyrdom, and at last looked down from heaven on the spectacle of Christianity the established religion of the whole Roman empire three hundred years later.

Thus let us obey the Holy Ghost, whether it be in silence or in activity, and we shall find that if He be to us our Wonderful Counselor, He shall certainly prove our mighty God.

5. Let us honor the Holy Ghost.

Less than any other person does He honor Himself. His constant business is to exalt Christ and hide behind His person. Therefore, the Father is pleased when we exalt and honor Him, and He Himself will especially use the instrument which gives Him the glory. "Honor the Holy Ghost and He will honor you," was the counsel of an aged Christian patriarch who had seen many a mighty awakening in the church of God.

It is indeed true and especially important in this material and rationalistic age, when even the ministers of Christ sometimes seem to wish to eliminate the supernatural from the Scriptures and the church, and find any other explanation than the power of God for His supernatural working.

The special dispensation of the Holy Ghost is drawing to its close. We may therefore expect that He will manifest His power in unusual methods and degrees as the age draws to its close.

Let us understand Him and be in sympathy with His divine thought, and ready to follow His wise and mighty leadership unto the last campaign of Christianity. Why should we ever be looking back to Pentecost? Why should we not expect His mightiest triumphs in the immediate future, and, as Joel has prophesied, "before the great and terrible day of the Lord."

Chapter 14.
HINDERING THE HOLY SPIRIT

"Grieve not the Holy Spirit of God." Eph. 4: 30.

"Ye do always resist the Holy Ghost." Acts 7: 51.

"Quench not the Spirit." 1 Thess. 5: 19.

It is very touching and solemn that while the Holy Ghost might, in the exercise of His omnipotence, coerce our will, and compel us to submit to His authority, yet He approaches us with the most deferential regard for our feelings and independence, even suffering us to resist and disobey Him, and bearing long with our willfulness and waywardness.

There are several terms used in the Scriptures to denote the manner in which we may sin against the Holy Spirit.

I. We May Quench the Spirit.

This has reference, perhaps, mainly to the hindrance we offer to His work in others, rather than to our resistance of His personal dealings with our own souls.

Among the various hindrances which we may offer to the Holy Spirit may be mentioned such as these:

1. We may refuse to obey His impulses in us when He bids us speak or act for Him. We may be conscious of a distinct impression of the Spirit of God bidding us to testify for Christ, and by disobedience, or timidity, or procrastination, we may quench His working, both in our own soul and in the heart of another.

2. We may suppress His voice in others, either by using our authority to restrain His messages, when He speaks through His servants or refusing to allow the liberty of testimony. Many hold the reins of ecclesiastical authority unduly, and thus lose the free and effectual working of the Holy Ghost in their churches and in their work.

Walking in the Spirit

There is a less direct way, however, of politely silencing Him by forcing Him out, and so filling the atmosphere with the spirit of stiffness, criticism, and a certain air of respectability and rigidness that He gently withdraws from the uncongenial scene, and refuses to thrust His messages upon unwilling hearts.

3. The Spirit may be grieved by the method of public worship in a congregation.

It may be either so stiff and formal that there is no room for His spontaneous working, or so full of worldly and unscriptural elements as to repel and offend Him from taking any part in a pompous ritual. An operatic choir and a ritualistic service will effectually quench all the fire of God's altar, and send the gentle dove to seek a simpler nest.

4. The Spirit may be quenched by the preacher, and his spirit and method.

His own manner may be so intellectual and self-conscious, and his own spirit so thoroughly cold and vain that the Holy Ghost is neither recognized nor known in his work. His sermons may be on themes in which the Spirit has no interest, for He only witnesses to the Holy Scriptures and the person of Christ, and wearily turns away from the discussion of philosophy, and the stale show of critical brilliancy over the questions of the day or the speculations of man's own vain reason.

Perhaps his address is so rigidly written down that the Holy Spirit could not find an opportunity for even a suggestion, if He so desired, and His promptings and leading so coolly set aside by a course of elaborate preparation which leaves no room for God.

5. The spirit of error in the teachings of the pulpit will always quench the Holy Spirit.

He is jealous for His own inspired Word and when vain man attempts to set it aside He looks on with indignation, and exposes such teachers to humiliation and failure.

The spirit of self-assertion and self-consciousness is always fatal to the free working of the Holy Ghost.

When a man stands up in the sacred desk to air his eloquence and call attention to his intellectual brilliancy, or to preach himself in any sense, he will always be deserted by the Holy Spirit. He uses the things "that are not to bring to naught the things that are." And before we can expect to become the instruments of His power, we must wholly cease from self and be lost in the person and glory of Jesus.

6. The spirit of pride, fashion and worldly display in the pews, is just as fatal as ambition in the pulpit.

Such an atmosphere seems to freeze out the spirit of devotion, and erect on the throne of the lowly Nazarene a goddess of carnal pride and pleasure, like the foul Venus that the Parisian mob set up in the Madeleine at Paris in the days of the revolution, as an object of worship. From such an atmosphere the Holy Ghost turns away grieved and disgusted.

7. The quickening and reviving influences of the Holy Ghost are often quenched in the very hour of promise by wrong methods in the work of Christ's church.

How often, on the eve of a real revival, the minds of the people have been led away by some public entertainment in connection with the house of God, or its after-fruits withered by a series of unholy fairs and secular bids for money, and the introduction of the broker and the cattle-vender into the cleansed temple of Jehovah, as in the days of Christ.

8. The spirit of criticism and controversy is fatal to the working of the Holy Ghost.

The gentle dove will not remain in an atmosphere of strife. If we would cherish His power we must possess His love, and frown down all wrangling gossip, evil speaking, malice, envy, and public controversy in the preaching of the Word.

Walking in the Spirit

Sometimes a single word of criticism after an impressive service will dispel all its blessed influence upon the heart of some interested hearer, and counteract the gracious work that would have resulted in the salvation of the soul.

A frivolous Christian woman returning one night from church with her unsaved husband, was laughing lightly at some of the mistakes and eccentricities of the speaker. Suddenly she felt his arm trembling; she looked in his face and his tears were falling. He gently turned to her, and said: "Pray for me; I have seen myself tonight as I never did before." She suddenly awoke with an awful shudder to realize that she had been frivolously wrecking his soul's salvation, and quenching the Holy Ghost.

And so, public controversy is as fatal to the Spirit's working as personal criticism.

It is when the children of God unite at the feet of Jesus, and together seek His blessing, that He comes in all the fullness of His life-power.

At the Council of Nice it is said that a great number of grievances were sent unto Constantine, the presiding officer. After the opening of the great Council, he ordered them to be gathered into the center of the large hall, and then a fire kindled under them, and as they went up in smoke and flame, the Spirit of God fell upon the assembled multitude, and they all felt that in the burning of their strifes and selfish grievances they had received the very baptism of the Holy Ghost.

The Spirit may be quenched in the hearts of our friends by unwise counsel, or ungodly influence.

The little child may be discouraged from seeking Christ by a worldly parent, or the ignorant assumption that it is too young to be a Christian, or too busy with its studies, or its social enjoyments, for such things.

The attractions of the world and claims and pressures of business, may be interposed in the way of some seeking heart, and we find in eternity that we put a stumbling-block in our friend's way, from which he fell into perdition.

Let us be very careful lest, in our willfulness and pride, we not only miss ourselves the inner chambers of the kingdom of heaven, but hinder those that would enter from going in.

Oh! if we would cherish the faintest breath of life in the rescued waif that has been snatched from a watery grave, if we could fan the expiring flame of life in a friend's bosom, let us be careful lest we quench the spark of everlasting life in a human soul, and stand at the last, responsible for the murder of immortal beings, and crimson with the blood of souls. "Quench not the Spirit."

II. We May Grieve the Spirit.

This is a very tender expression; it suggests His gentleness and patience; grieved rather than angry with His unfaithful and distrustful children.

1. We may grieve Him by our doubts and distrust of His love and promises. Thus Moses grieved Him when he struck the rock instead of gently speaking.

Many are afraid of the Holy Ghost and think Him a despot and a terror; shrinking even from His too close approach, as though He would consume us by His holiness. He wants us to love Him, and come near to Him as the gentle mother; to believe in His promises, to count Him faithful, and to treat Him as one who does come to us and dwell within us.

2. We grieve the Holy Spirit when we refuse to wholly yield ourselves to Him, and hold back from entire abandonment and surrender, or when, having so surrendered ourselves, we shrink back from His actual leading and refuse to meet the tests He brings, and lie upon the wheel in stillness while He molds the plaster in clay.

He is grieved at our willfulness and rebellion and resistance. He knows we are losing a blessing, and that we must again go

Walking in the Spirit

through the same discipline if we are to have our blessings from Him.

He sees in it the spirit of distrust and unbelief, and He feels wounded and slighted by our shrinking.

3. We grieve the Holy Spirit when we fail to enter into the fullness of His grace, and receive the Lord Jesus Christ as our complete Savior.

He has not written one word that we can afford to allow to become of none effect. It is an insult to His wisdom and love to treat the higher visions of His grace as if they were not binding upon our life.

They should fully honor Him, press forward into all His will, and feel they owe to Him as well as themselves that they should lose nothing of all that He has wrought, nor seem to come short of entering into His rest.

Oh, how many of His children are grieving Him as a mother would be grieved, if after having, at great cost and toil, provided bountifully for her children, they should refuse her bounty or despise her rich provision!

4. We grieve the Holy Spirit when we fail to hearken to His voice.

He is constantly calling upon us to listen, and He never speaks in vain, nor can we ever afford to miss the slightest whisper. When, therefore, we fail to hearken, and dash along with heedless impulsiveness, He is deeply grieved, and has to call in the loud and painful tones of trial and chastening.

How He bewails His ancient people for their refusing to listen to His living voice: "Oh, that my people had hearkened to my commandments, then had their peace been like a river, and their righteousness as the waves of the sea."

5. We grieve the Holy Spirit when, having heard, we presume to disobey His voice.

This is very serious, and full of terrible danger. It is an awful thing willfully to neglect or defy the distinct command of the Holy Ghost. We cannot do it without losing the sense of His presence, and being conscious that He has withdrawn the manifestation of His love, until we deeply and penitently recognize our sin, and step into the path of obedience where we separated from His companionship.

6. Nothing grieves the Holy Spirit more than a divided heart and the cherishing of any idols in our affections which separate our supreme love from Christ.

There is a remarkable passage in the book of James which declares that "the Spirit which dwelleth in us loveth us to jealousy" (marginal reading), and in the same connection it is added, "Ye adulterers and adulteresses, know ye not that the friendship of the world is enmity with God?" that is, a heart set upon earthly things is guilty of spiritual adultery, the Holy Ghost looks upon it with jealous love, grieved and insulted by the dishonor done to our divine husband by our unfaithful affections.

7. We grieve the Holy Spirit whenever we neglect, pervert, or dishonor the Holy Scriptures.

This is His word, and not one utterance or one jot shall fall to the ground. How we grieve Him when we explain its precious promises, and make of none effect its exact commands; and how He loves the heart that feeds upon the truth and honors the Bible in its least promise and command!

8. Especially do we grieve the Holy Ghost when we dishonor Jesus, or let anything separate us from Him, or cloud our conception of Him, and interrupt our devotion to Him.

He is jealous for the honor of Christ; therefore, whenever self, or any human being comes between us and Christ, whenever the glory of the Master is obscured by the glory of the servant, whenever even truth or work becomes more distinct than Christ

Himself, the Holy Ghost is grieved; and He is pleased when we exalt the Savior, and give Him all the glory.

9. The Holy Spirit is grieved when we ignore Him.

He longs after our love and trust.

10. The Holy Spirit is especially grieved by a spirit of bitterness toward any human being, and therefore the apostle says, "Let all bitterness, and wrath, and anger, and clamor, and evil speaking be put away from you with all malice. And grieve not the Holy Spirit of God, whereby we are sealed unto the day of redemption."

III. We May Resist the Holy Spirit.

This has special reference to the attitude of the unbeliever, with whom the Holy Ghost is striving with a view to convict him of sin and lead Him to the Savior.

1. The sinner resists the Holy Spirit when he tries to shake off religious impressions.

This may be done in many ways. Sometimes the soul, under the Spirit's striving, tries to quench its impressions in pleasure, excitement or business. Sometimes it treats them as nervous depression, low spirits or ill-health, and seeks a remedy in change of scene or thought; very often it resorts to light reading, worldly amusements, frivolous society, perhaps indulgence in sin, and the devil always has plenty of auxiliaries to suggest distracting thoughts, and help to dispel the sacred influences that God is gathering around the heart.

Very often it will become provoked and offended with some acts on the part of Christians, sometimes perhaps connected with the religious services, and will resolve to give up attending, or find some petty excuse for getting out of the way of the influences that are troubling its contentment. All these efforts to escape are but the stronger evidence of the Spirit's striving, and He patiently and lovingly continues to press the arrow still more keenly into the wounded heart, until it is laid prostrate at the feet of love.

2. The sinner resists the influences of the Holy Spirit in leading him to conviction of sin.

It is not enough to awaken concern in the soul, and even alarm -- there must be a distinct working of Scriptural conviction in order to secure lasting peace and sound conversion; and, therefore, the Holy Ghost has promised to convict the world of sin.

He does this by bringing before the conscience the memory of actual transgressions -- the recollection of any forgotten sins, the iniquities of youth and childhood, the secret sins known to God only, the aggravations of sin, the warnings and light against which it has been committed, the love that has been resisted, the threatenings of the divine law, the unchangeable holiness of the divine character, the tremendous sentence against all iniquity, the deep inward consciousness of guilt, the still more terrible sense of the wickedness of the sinner's heart, the hopeless depravity, the consciousness of willfulness and unbelief, and the dreadful fear of its hopelessness, the impossibility of its salvation.

Thus the Great Advocate sets in array our transgressions, until the heart seeks some escape from itself, and Satan is ready to suggest a thousand excuses, palliations and false hopes, through which the guilty spirit seeks to evade the force of its conviction.

It thinks of the faults of others, and plausible reasons that it is no worse than they; it eagerly seizes upon the inconsistencies of Christians, and tries to excuse itself by their failure; it recalls its own miserable attempts at goodness, and tries to find some comfort in its own righteousness; it seeks false refuge in the mercy of God, and eagerly tries to persuade itself that the picture of Christ's anger against sin, and the stories of judgment and perdition, are fictions of obsolete theology.

It says peace, peace, when there is no peace, and heals slightly its hurt, resisting with all its might the blessed Spirit, who wounds only that He may heal.

Happy they who fail in the foolish attempt, and in whose hearts the arrows of the King are so sharp and keen that the wound can never be stanched save by the blood of Calvary.

3. The sinner resists the work of the Holy Ghost in leading him to decision.

Even after he has been driven from his previous refuges, and has been awakened to his profound concern, and thoroughly convicted of his sin, and fully admits the claims of religion and the justness of his condemnation, he seeks another door of escape in procrastination.

He will surrender, he will resist no more, he will accept the Savior, but not now, he is not quite ready yet.

Perhaps he argues that he does not feel strongly enough, that he wants a deeper conviction, more light, a little more deliberate consideration, perhaps a little more time to alter his circumstances and change his life; but really what he is pleading for is a reprieve for his sinful heart, a little longer in the indulgence of his self-will, and disobedience to the gospel.

And his course is just as dangerous and just as truly a rejection of Christ as if he did it deliberately and directly; while at the same time it has the self-deceiving aspect of being a sort of yielding, at least a nominal consent, to all the pleadings of the Holy Ghost. He is resisting the Spirit, and his tomorrow often means, as the eyes of heaven read the words, NEVER.

4. The sinner resists the Holy Spirit in His gracious attempts to convict the soul of righteousness and lead it to believe on the Son of God.

The Spirit's object is not merely to produce concern, alarm, and even the profoundest repentance, but the blessed goal of all

His gracious movements is the trustful acceptance of Jesus, and the believing assurance of His forgiveness and salvation.

It is here that Satan and self-will fight their hardest battle. The soul will consent to live a better life, will be willing to weep and mourn, will do anything rather than accept the very gift of salvation and believe the naked word of God, that its sins are forgiven for His name's sake, and that it is accepted in Jesus Christ, as He is accepted.

How desperately it fights against this simple act, clothing its unbelief in the guise of humanity and modesty, and thinking it presumption to dare to make such a claim!

Many souls hold back at this point for months and years, and know not that in all their doubts and fears, their hard thoughts of themselves and of God, they are simply resisting the Holy Ghost, who is striving with them to lay their sins forever at the feet of Jesus, and go forth into His everlasting peace.

5. At this point the resisting soul is led by this great enemy to erect a whole line of false refuges, and run under their cover, instead of fleeing for refuge directly to the hope set before it in the gospel.

One of these refuges is outward reformation of life. The sinner will do better, will take the pledge, will turn over a new leaf, will make large promises and comfort his soul with the flattering unction that he is a changed man, while all the while he has the same evil heart, and it will produce the same fruits when the mere effort of will has spent itself.

Another refuge of lies is a religious profession. He will get confirmed or join the church and begin a life of formalism; perhaps give something to the cause of Christ, and even attempt some Christian work, but he is only a whitewashed Pharisee, and within the sepulcher are dead men's bones and all uncleanliness; and he will find before long, that his old heart has still the same loves and hates, yet he has effectually suppressed the voice of the Spirit.

He meets every fear and conviction with the consciousness of his religious profession, and he will even go to the gates of the judgment hall saying, "Have we not eaten and drunken in Thy presence! and Thou hast taught in our streets;" but He will profess unto them, "I never knew you."

Poor Ignorance, in Pilgrim's Progress, went up to the very gates of heaven with an easy conscience; every conviction had been stifled by his shallow professions and imagined works of self-righteousness; and so multitudes have escaped the pain of an evil conscience, and the Spirit's striving, to find it turn in the hour of judgment into the remorseful horror of eternal condemnation.

And so we might speak of almost countless other false refuges, all of which have the effect of quieting the troubled heart, but not saving the soul. They are like sandbags thrown up in the outworks of our souls, in which the arrows of the Lord are lost or muffled, but which are no protection from the armies of destruction.

6. It is possible for the soul to resist the Holy Ghost openly, directly, willfully, and presumptuously, until it drives Him from its door and commits the fatal sin of willfully rejecting the offered Savior in the full light of the Holy Spirit's revealing, and perhaps with the full consciousness that it is defiantly refusing God.

There is such a thing referred to in the Scriptures, "If ye refuse and rebel ye shall be destroyed;" "I called and ye refused." "If we sin willfully after that we have received the knowledge of the truth, there remaineth no more sacrifice for sins, but a certain fearful looking for of judgment and fiery indignation, which shall devour the adversaries. He that despised Moses' law died without mercy under two or three witnesses. Of how much sorer punishment, suppose ye, shall he be thought worthy who hath trodden under foot the Son of God, and hath counted the blood of the covenant, wherewith he was sanctified, an unholy thing, and hath done despite unto the Spirit of grace? For we know Him that hath said, Vengeance belongeth unto me, I will recompense, saith the Lord. And again, The Lord shall judge His people. It is a fearful thing to fall into the hands of the living God."

The blasphemy of the Pharisees against the Holy Ghost seems to have consisted in rejecting Jesus after they had sufficient light to know that He was the Son of God.

It was, therefore, not only the rejection of Jesus, but the deliberate rejection of the Holy Ghost and His witness to Jesus, when they knew it to be His witness.

Essentially, therefore, it is the same sin as any soul may now commit, when in the full light of God, and conscious that He has directly called it to accept the Savior, it defiantly refuses.

The effect of such an act may be, and perhaps usually is, the withdrawal of the Spirit from the soul until it is left, past feeling, to a hardened heart, and a doom on which the voice of divine appeal and the light of mercy will never fall again.

This is, perhaps, what is meant by the blasphemy against the Holy Ghost which never hath forgiveness.

Let no one think he has committed this sin if still in the heart there is a willingness to yield to God and accept the Savior.

If there is even a fear that any reader may have committed this sin, and a great longing that it may not be so, rejoice exceedingly, and yield this moment even to His faint touch of heavenly influence, lest it should be withdrawn, and the soul left under the sad sentence, "He is joined to his idols, let him alone." The good Payson once said to his young friend, who had spoken of a slight religious influence, and wondered if it was enough to act upon, "A little cord has dropped from heaven, so fine that you can scarcely feel it or perceive it; it just touches your shoulder for a moment; dear friend, grasp it quickly, for it fastens to the throne of God, and it is for you perhaps the last strand of saving mercy; grasp it and never let it go, and it will grow into a cable of strength that will anchor you to the skies and keep your precious soul unto everlasting life."

Oh! let us be fearful and careful lest we sin against the Holy Ghost by quenching the Spirit, by grieving the Holy One, by resisting our best Friend, or by blaspheming His mighty name.

A Larger Christian Life

By
A. B. Simpson

A. B. SIMPSON

Chapter 1.
THE POSSIBILITIES OF FAITH

"If thou canst believe, all things are possible to him that believeth."-Mark ix: 23.

These are bold and stupendous words. They open the treasure house of the Eternal King to sinful worms, and offer to the children of clay the privilege of God's own omnipotence and all the possibilities of His infinite resources. Side by side these two astounding declarations stand, *"All things are possible with God;" "All things are possible to him that believeth."*

I. Let us consider the possibilities of faith:

1. Salvation is possible to him that believeth. No matter how vile the sin, how many or how great the sins, how aggravated the guilt, how deep the corruption, how long the career of impenitence and crime, it is everywhere and forever true, "He that believeth on the Son hath everlasting life," "Believe on the Lord Jesus and thou shalt be saved." And thus alone can any soul be saved, for it is just as true forever, no matter what qualifications the soul may possess, whether the highest morality or the deepest depravity, "He that believeth not shall be damned." This blessed text opens the gates of Paradise and all the possibilities of grace to any and every sinner, and "whosoever will, may come, and take the Water of Life freely."

2. Sanctification is possible to him that believeth. "Inheritance among them that are sanctified by faith that is in me," is still the inscription over the gates of our full inheritance. "Purifying our hearts by faith "is still the Divine process of full salvation. Thus alone can the soul be sanctified. It is not a

work, but a gift of grace, and all grace must be by faith. It is not possible by painful struggling; it is not possible by penance and self-torture; it is not possible by sickness, suffering or self-crucifixion; it is not possible by moral suasion, careful training, correct teaching and perfect example; it is not possible even by the dark, cold waters of death itself. The soul that dies unsanctified shall be unsanctified forever. "He that is holy, let him be holy still: he that is filthy, let him be filthy still." But it is possible to him that believeth. It is the gift of Jesus Christ; it is the incoming and indwelling of Jesus Christ; it is the interior life and divine imparting of the Holy Ghost, and it must be by faith alone. And it is possible to any soul that will believe, no matter how unholy it has been, no matter how perverse it is; as mean perhaps and crooked as Jacob, as gross as David in his darkest sin, as self-confident as Simon Peter, as willful and self-righteous as Paul-it may be and shall be made as spotless as the Son of God, as holy as the holiness of Jesus Himself, who comes to dwell within, if we will only believe and receive.

3. Divine Healing is possible to him that believeth. "The prayer of faith shall save the sick," is still the Master's unaltered word for His suffering church. And this faith must be the faith of the receiver, for in the epistle it is said, "Let not him that wavereth think that he shall receive anything of the Lord." Still it is as true as when the Master touched the eyes of the blind men to whom He said it, "According to your faith be it unto you." It matters not how serious the disease, it may be as helpless as the cripple's who could not in any wise lift herself up; as chronic as the impotent man who lay for thirty and eight years helpless at the pool; as obscure and as despised a case as the poor blind men who begged by the wayside and whom the multitude thought unworthy of Christ's attention, or as the sinful woman of Syro-Phoenicia, whom even the

Saviour called a dog, and yet to her, as to others, the healing came when He could say, "Great is thy faith; be it unto thee even as thou wilt." It is not the faith which heals, it is the God that the faith touches; but there is no other way of touching God except by faith, and, therefore, if we would receive His Almighty touch, we must believe.

4. All power for service is possible to him that believeth. The gift of the Holy Ghost is received by faith. The power of the apostles was in proportion to their faith. Stephen "full of faith and power" could meet all the wisdom of Saul of Tarsus and the synagogue of the Cilicians. The simple story of Barnabas is that "he was a good man. and full of faith and the Holy Ghost, and much people were added unto the Lord." The secret of effective preaching is not logic, or rhetoric, or elocution, but to be able to say, "I believed and therefore have I spoken." The success of some evangelists and Christian workers is out of all proportion to their talent or capacity in any direction, but they have one gift which they faithfully exercise, and that is expecting God to give them souls; and, therefore, they are never disappointed. The church has yet to see in the present generation the full possibilities of faith in the work of the Lord. The examples of a Moody and a Harrison are but types of what is possible for the humblest worker who, with a single eye to the glory of God and simple fidelity to the gospel of Christ, will dare to expect the mightiest results. Both these examples, perhaps the most marked instances of wide fruitfulness in the present generation, are persons without great natural gifts or educational advantages, and, therefore, the more encouraging as incentives to the work of faith. Humble toiler in the vineyard of the Lord, will you go forth to all the possibilities of faith in your work for Him as you realize the strength of your weakness and the might of your God? for it is "not by might or by power but by my Spirit, saith the Lord of Hosts."

The day has come for God to reveal Himself through the very weakness of His instruments, and to prove once more that He has chosen the foolish things of the world to confound the wise, and the weak things to confound the things that are mighty.

5. All difficulties and dangers must give way before the omnipotence of faith. By faith the walls of Jericho fell down after they had been compassed seven days, and still the mightiest citadels of the adversary must give way before the steadfast and victorious march of faith. By faith Daniel stopped the mouths of lions, and was delivered, we are expressly told, because he believed in his God. It was not his uprightness of life, or courageous fidelity that saved him, but his confidence in Jehovah. Such faith has carried the intrepid Arnot through the jungles of Africa, and delivered the heroic Paton from the murderous fury of the savages of Tanna, and held back the stroke of death and the threatened disaster from many of us in the humbler experiences of our providential lives. Still the God of faith is as near, as mighty and as true as when He walked with the Hebrew children through the fire, and guarded the heroic Paul through all the perils of his changeful life. There is no difficulty too small for its exercise, and there is no crisis too terrible for its triumph. Shall we go forth with this shield and buckler, and prove all the possibilities of faith? Then, indeed, shall we carry a charmed life even through the very hosts of hell, and know that we are immortal till our work is done.

6. All the victories of prayer are possible to him that believeth. "Whatsoever ye shall ask in prayer, believing, shall ye receive." "When ye pray, believe that ye receive the things that ye ask, and ye shall have them." It is not the strength or the length of the prayer that prevails, but the simplicity of its confidence. It is the prayer of faith that claims the healing power

of the unchanging Saviour. It is the prayer of faith that reaches the soul that no human hand, perhaps, can approach, and sometimes brings from Heaven the answer before the echo of the petition has died away. Yonder in the city of Cleveland a brokenhearted wife is praying with an evangelist for her husband's soul. At that very hour an influence all unknown to himself is leading him into a prayer-meeting in Chicago at noon, and before that prayer is ended the choirs of Heaven are singing over a repentant soul, and the Holy Ghost is whispering to her heart that the work is accomplished, not less surely than when on the morrow the swift mail brings the glad tidings from his own hand. The prayer of faith has reared those enduring monuments on Ashley Down, where two thousand orphan children are fed every day by the hand of God alone, in answer to the humble, believing cry of a faithful minister. These are but patterns of what God has always been ready to do and hindered only by His people's unbelief. Beloved, these possibilities are open to each of us. We may not be called to public service, or qualified for instructive speech, or endowed with wealth and influence, but to each of us is given the power to touch the hand of omnipotence and minister at the golden altar of prevailing prayer. One censer only we must bring-the golden bowl of faith, and as we fill it with the burning coals of the Holy Spirit's fire, and the incense of the great High Priest, lo! there will be silence once again in Heaven, as God hushes the universe to listen, and then the living fire will be poured out upon the earth in the mighty forces of providence and grace by which the kingdom of our Lord is to be ushered in.

7. All peace and joy are possible to him that believeth. The apostle's prayer for the Romans is that the God of hope shall fill them with all joy and peace in believing. It is God's will and purpose that the unbelieving soul shall be an unhappy

soul, and that he shall be kept in perfect peace whose mind is stayed on God and trusting in Him. Would you then know the peace that passeth all understanding? Be careful for nothing, and steadfastly believe that the Lord is at hand, supreme above every circumstance, and causing all things to work together for good to them that love Him. Would you be happy in the darkest hour? Then trust in the Lord and stay yourself upon your God. Would you have the perennial overflowings of joy? Then learn to say, "Though now we see Him not, yet believing we rejoice with joy unspeakable and full of glory." The joy of mere paroxysmal emotion is like the cut flower of a brief winter's day, separated from the root and withering before another sun goes down. The joy of faith is the fruit and perpetual bloom that covers the living tree, or springs from the rooted plant in the watered garden.

«The men of faith have found
Glory begin below-
Celestial fruit on hostile ground
From faith and hope may grow."

8. The evangelization of the world is to be given to faith. The most successful missionary operations of to-day are sustained wholly through faith in God and the power of prayer. If China is to be evangelized in the present century it will be due to the faith of one humble missionary who has dared to attempt great things for God and to expect great things from Him. There is no field for faith so vast and so sublime as the mission field to-day, and there is no limit to the possibilities which faith may claim. Oh, that some of us may rise to the magnitude of this great opportunity and become workers together with God for the greatest achievement of all the Christian centuries.

9. The Lord's coming will, doubtless, be given at last to faith. There will be a generation who shall say, "Lo! this is our

God, we have waited for Him." As yet it is our blessed hope, but it will some day become more. And reading both upon earth and sky the tokens of His coming, His waiting bride shall hear the glad cry, "The marriage of the Lamb is come." To Simeon of old it was made known that he should see the Lord's Christ, and to some shall be given in the last times the Morning Star that shall precede the Millennial dawn. The Lord help us so to understand our times and the work the Master expects of us to prepare His coming, that we shall be permitted to share its glorious recompense of faith and even hasten that joyful day.

10. But beyond all that has been said this promise means that *all* things are possible to him that believeth. It is possible to have any or even many of the achievements specified and yet miss the all things of God's highest will. The meaning of this promise in its fullness is that faith may claim a complete life, a blessing from which nothing shall be lacking, a finished service, and a crown from which no jewel of recompense shall be found wanting. There are lives which are not wholly lost and yet are not saved to the uttermost. There are rainbows whose arch is broken, but there is a rainbow round about the throne whose perfect circle is the type of a completed record and an infinite reward. Many of us are coming short of all that God has had in His highest thought for us. When the king of Israel stood by the bedside of the dying prophet of the Lord, Elisha put his hand upon the hands of Joash and helped him shoot the arrows which were symbolic of faith and victory; but then the prophet required that the king should follow up this act of mutual faith by a more individual expression of the measure of his own expectation. Alas, like most of us, his faith evaporated long before its needed work was done. He smote thrice upon the ground and then he stayed. Too late for him to recover his lost blessing, the grieved and angry

prophet upbraided him for his negligence and narrowness of heart, and told him sorrowfully that his blessing should be limited according to the measure of his own little faith. Never shall I forget the solemnity with which God brought this passage to my soul in a crisis of my life, and asked how much I would take from Him and how little would satisfy my faith. Thank God He enabled me to say with a bursting heart, "Nothing less than all Thy highest thought and will, even the all things of faith's greatest possibilities." The Lord help us to look forward ever to the time when all these opportunities shall be passing from our grasp, and to live each day under the power of those holy aspirations whose true value we shall then be able to understand, and evermore to say with Him who cherished the same lofty ambition, "I count not my life dear unto myself that I may finish my course with joy." Beloved, are you missing anything out of your life, your one precious, narrow span of earthly opportunity, the pivot on which eternity revolves, the one eternal possibility that never will return again? God is waiting to give you all, and all things are possible to him that believeth.

II. The reasonableness of faith. Why should God make all things dependent upon our faith?

1. Because the ruin of the race began with the loss of faith, and its recovery must come through the exercise of faith. The poison Satan injected into the blood of Eve was a question of God's faithfulness, and the one prescription that the Gospel gives to unsaved sinners is, "Believe on the Lord Jesus Christ and thou shalt be saved."

2. Faith is the law of Christianity, the vital principle of the Gospel dispensation. The law of faith the apostle calls it in distinction from the law of works. The Lord Jesus expressed it in the simple formula which has become the standard of an-

swered prayers and every blessing that we receive through the name of Jesus. God is, therefore, bound to act according to our faith and also according to our unbelief.

3. Faith is the only way known to us by which we can accept a gift from God, and inasmuch as all the blessings of the Gospel are the gifts of grace, they must come to us through faith and in the measure of our faith, if they come at all.

4. Faith is necessary as a subjective influence to prepare our own hearts for the reception of God and His grace. How can the Father communicate His love to a timid, trembling heart? How can God come near to a frightened child? I have seen a little bird die of terror in my hand, when I intended it no harm but tried in vain to caress it and win its love. And so the individual heart without faith would die in the presence of God in absolute terror, and be unable to receive the overflowing love of the Father which it could not understand.

5. Faith is an actual, spiritual force. It is, no doubt, one of the attributes of God Himself. We find it exemplified in Jesus in all His miracles. He explains to His disciples that it was the very power by which He withered the fig tree, and the power by which they could overcome and dissolve the mightiest obstacles in their way. There is no doubt that while the soul is exercising through the power of God the faith that commands what God commands, that a mighty force is operating at that very moment upon the obstacle, a force as real as the currents of electricity or the power of dynamite. God has really put into our hands one of His own implements of omnipotence and permitted us to use it in the name of Jesus according to His will and for the establishment of His Kingdom.

6. The pre-eminent reason why God requires faith, is because faith is the only way through which God Himself can have absolute room to work, for faith is just that colorless and

simple attitude by which man ceases from his own works and enters into the work of God. It is the difference between the human and the divine, the natural and the supernatural. The reason therefore why faith is so mighty and indeed omnipotent is that it just makes way for the omnipotence of God. Therefore the two sentences are strangely and exactly parallel. "All things are possible with God." "All things are possible to him that believeth." The very same power is possessed by God and him that believeth, and the reason is that the latter is lost in, and wholly identified with, the former. How shall we illustrate the mighty distance between the earthly and the heavenly, the human and the divine, the finite and the infinite? Some one has said, take the strongest piece of artillery, load it to the muzzle with powder or dynamite, put in it the most perfect steel ball, be sure you have all the latest improvements in advance, then fire it, and your bullet will sweep through space at the rate of six hundred feet in a second. But in that second let God, with a single flash of light and without an effort or a sound, propel a ray from yonder sun or star or midnight lamp, and it will fly six hundred thousand miles. Six hundred feet, six hundred thousand miles! This is a feeble figure of the difference between the human and the divine. That ponderous gun with its slow but destructive power is a type of man's works. That gentle sunbeam and lightbeam with its silent, swift, beneficent minis-try is a type of God's infinite resources. This is the world into which faith introduces us. Surrendering its own insufficiency, it links itself with the all-sufficiency of God, and goes forth triumphantly exclaiming, "I can do all things through Christ who strengtheneth me," while approving Heaven echoes back, "All things are possible to him that believeth."

III. The possibility of faith.
"If thou canst, believe."

1. Of course we need scarcely say that faith is dependent upon obedience and rightness of heart and life. We cannot trust God in the face of willful sin, and even an unsanctified state is fatal to any high degree of faith, for the carnal heart is not the soil in which it can grow, but it is the fruit of the Spirit, and is hindered by the weeds of sin and willful indulgence. The reason that a great many Christians have so little faith is because they are living in the world and in themselves, and separated in so large a part of their life from God and holiness. When the Lick Observatory was built on the Pacific coast, it was necessary to go above the valleys and lowlands of the coast, where the fogs and mists hung heavily over the land, and select a site on the top of Mount Hamilton, above the fogs and vapors of the ground, and in clear, unobstructed view of the heavens. So faith requires for its heavenly vision, the highlands of holiness and separation, and the clear, pure sky of a consecrated life.

   Beloved, may you find in this the explanation of many of your doubts and fears, that your plane is too low, your heart is too mixed, and your life is too near this "present evil world."

2. Faith is hindered by the weak and unscriptural way in which so many excuse their unbelief and lightly think and speak of the sin of doubting God. If we would have strong faith we must recognize it as an imperative and sacred obligation, and steadfastly and firmly believe God, and refuse ever to doubt Him. Let us not say we cannot believe. It is true, we cannot of ourselves, but all that God also provides, and He has provided for us the power to believe if we will choose to do so. Let us then no more condone and palliate our doubts as harmless infirmities and sad misfortunes, but "take heed

lest there be in any of us an evil heart of unbelief in departing from the living God."

3. Faith is hindered by reliance upon human wisdom, whether our own or the wisdom of others. The devil's first bait to Eve was an offer of wisdom, and for this she sold her faith. "Ye shall be as gods," he said, "knowing good and evil," and from the hour she began to know she ceased to trust. It was the spies that lost the land of promise to Israel of old. It was their foolish proposition to search out the land, and find out by investigation whether God had told the truth or not, that led to the awful outbreak of unbelief that shut the doors of Canaan to a whole generation. It is very significant that the names of these spies are nearly all suggestive of human wisdom, greatness and fame. And so in the days of Christ, it was the bondage of the Jews to the traditions of the fathers and the opinions of men, that kept them back from receiving Him. "How can ye believe," He asked, "which receive honor from men, and seek not that which cometh from God only?" This, to-day, has much to do with the limitation of the church's faith. The Bible is measured by human criticism, and the promises of God are weighed in the balance of natural probability and human reason. Our own wisdom is just as dangerous if it take the place of God's simple word, and therefore, if we would "trust the Lord with all our heart," we must "lean not to our own understanding."

4. Self-sufficiency and dependence on our strength is also a hindrance to our faith.

    God, therefore, has to reduce us to helplessness before we can have much trust in Him. The hour of His mightiest interposition is usually the time of our greatest extremity.

    A secular weekly tells the story of a little fellow whose experience represents a good many older people. He had reached that epoch in a boy's life when he gets his first pants, and the uplift unsettled his spiritual equilibrium. Hitherto he had been a devout little Christian and usually joined his little sister every morning in asking the Lord's help and blessing for the day, but this morning, when he looked at his new pants, and felt himself a man, he stopped his little sister as she began to pray for him as usual, "Lord Jesus, take care of Freddie to-day, and keep him from harm," and like poor Simon Peter, in his own self-sufficiency, he cried out, "No, Jennie, don't say that; Freddie can take care of himself now." The little saint was shocked and frightened, but knew not what to do. And so the day began, but before noon they both climbed up into a cherry-tree, and while reaching out for the tempting fruit, Freddie went head foremost down into an angle between the tree and the fence, and with all his desperate struggles and his frightened sister's, he was utterly unable to extricate himself, and at last he looked up to Jennie with a look of mingled shame and intelligence and said, "Jennie, pray; Freddie can't take care of himself after all." Just then a strong man was coming along the road, and the answer to their prayer quickly came as the sturdy arms in a few minutes had taken down the fence and Freddie was free, and went forth a lesson for life, to walk like Simon Peter, with downward head and humble trust in a strength and care more mighty than his own.

Truly this is the soil of faith! Wisely said Habakkuk, centuries ago, as he contrasted pride and confidence, "His soul which is lifted up is not upright in him; but the just shall live by faith."

Beloved, has God brought you to the end of your strength? Rejoice and be exceeding glad, for it is the beginning of His Omnipotence, if faith will but fall into His mighty arms and cry like those of old, "Lord, it is nothing with Thee to help by many or with those who have no power. Help us, Lord, for in Thy Name we go against this great multitude."

A Larger Christian Life

5. Faith is hindered by sight and sense, and our foolish dependence upon external evidences.

   The very evidence in which we must live and grow is the unseen, and therefore all outward things must be withdrawn before we can truly believe; and as we look not at the things which are seen but on the things which are not seen, they grow real, more real than the things of sense, and then God makes them real in actual accomplishment. But faith must first step out into the great unknown, and walk upon the water to go to Jesus, nay, walk upon the air; but where was something only void it will find the rock beneath, like the traveler in the Alps who had reached the end of the mountain path as it suddenly disappeared beneath a great mass of ice and snow and became a subterranean torrent, while the mountain rose sternly in front and the miles of desolation which he had traveled lay behind. What should he do? Suddenly his guide exclaimed, "Follow me!" and plunged into the descending torrent and then disappeared from his view under the great mountain which it tunnelled. It was an awful venture, but he must either follow or die, and plunging in, there was a sudden shock, and the whirl of waters and blackness of darkness, and then a burst of light, and he was lying on the banks of a quiet stream on the other side of the mountain, in the sweet valley below. The unseen way had led to life and light.

   So faith still walks in paths of mystery oft-times, but God will always make it plain. Is not this the hindrance to your faith, that you hesitate to believe before you venture upon the naked word of promise? Your faith alone is the substance of things hoped for, the evidence of things not seen. God help us to walk by faith and not by sight!

   Therefore God has to train us in the way of faith by difficulties, trials, and seeming refusals, until like the Syro-Phoenician woman, we simply trust on and refuse to be refused.

He is always waiting to recompense our trust by the glad words, "Great is thy faith! Be it unto thee even as thou wilt."

6. Finally, this faith is hindered most of all by what we call "our faith," and our fruitless struggles to work out a faith which after all is but a make-believe and a desperate trying to trust God, which must ever come short of His vast and glorious promises. The truth is that the only faith that is equal to the stupendous promises of God and the measureless needs of our life, is "the faith of God" Himself, the very trust which He will breathe into the heart which intelligently expects Him as its power to believe, as well as its power to love, obey, or perform any other exercise of the new life.

Blessed be His name! He has not given us a chain which reaches within a single link of our poor helpless heart, but that one last link is fatal to all the chain. Nay, the last link, the one that fastens on the human side, is as divine as the link that binds the chain of promise to His Throne of promise in the heavens. "Have the faith of God," is His great command. "I live by the faith of the Son of God," is the victorious testimony of one who had proved it true.

Beloved, in the light of this great provision, listen to the mighty promise now, and in His faith rise to claim, "If thou canst, believe. All things are possible to him that believeth," and cry, "Lord, I believe, nay, not I, but Thou! Help Thou my unbelief."

And now, beloved, this mighty engine of spiritual power is placed in our hands by Omnipotent love. Shall we claim, and by the help of God, rise to its utmost possibilities, and shall we from this hour turn it, like a heavenly weapon, upon the field of Christian life and conflict, and use it for all to which God has called us in the great conflicts of the age and for the Kingdom of our Lord and Saviour Jesus Christ? Our lot has fallen upon momentous times; the last decade of this stupendous century has just begun, and it finds the Church of God awaking to the greatest campaign of the Christian centuries, the evangelization of the world, with a view to the preparation for our Lord's immediate coming. What a glorious possibility! It is one of the possibilities of faith.

Last night as I sat at my open window, far into the night watches, from one of the cottages yonder, I heard the voice of prayer go forth all night long. It was a ceaseless and mighty cry that the mighty God would work with all His power and glory, and though the same words were oft repeated by the same voice, it never seemed to grow monotonous, for there was so much that language could not express in that prayer that it touched my heart with tenderness and solemnity, and seemed like a prophecy of that which I trust is to go forth from this mighty convocation and be caught up by all the world until it shall be answered by the voices of heaven above, proclaiming, "The kingdoms of this world have become the kingdom of our Lord and of His Christ. Allelnia! The Lord God Omnipotent reigneth." Oh, shall we take this engine of omnipotence, the prayer of faith, and turn it toward the heavens, and turn it upon the earth, and turn it against every foe, until we shall find it wholly true, "All things are possible to him that believeth?"

It has been proposed that we should form, this day, a Prayer Alliance, for the evangelization of the world during this present century, and the speedy coming of our Lord Jesus. Beloved, can there be a grander opportunity for the practical application of this great theme, and shall we not with one heart, join hands in believing prayer, around the world, until the happy day when we shall join hands once more around the Millennial Throne and praise Him for the glorious fulfillment?

A. B. SIMPSON

Chapter 2.
THE JOY OF THE LORD

"The joy of the Lord is your strength." Neh. viii:10.

There is no more pointed difference between Christianity and all other religions than the element of joyfulness.

The natural countenance of heathenism is gloomy, and often profoundly sad. The true expression of a consecrated face is radiance and gladness. True, this is not always realized as it ought to be, but when the Holy Spirit shines in the consecrated heart, the face will reflect its glory, and, like Stephen's, be often like the face of an angel. The reporter of a weekly paper once remarked as he described the services of one of our happy conventions, "one thing that characterized all the faces was their wondrous joyousness." Surely this ought to be ever true! Look at those two sisters, born of one mother, rocked in one cradle, educated in one school, yet parted now by a distance far greater than leagues can measure. The younger sister is rich, prosperous, admired by a wide circle of friends, loved by every member of her family, and indulged in every gratification that social position or ample wealth can procure. The other is poor; her life is a struggle with circumstances, her time is crowded with toil and care; her dearest friends often misunderstand her religious attitude, and rudely blame her for the very things which are the highest services and sacrifices of her love. And yet her face shines with a deep, transparent joy, compared with which the other is dull and tame. The daughter of wealth and prosperity has got so used to her surroundings that they are no more to her than the humble circumstances of the other are to her. External luxuries have palled her appetite long ago, and no deeper springs have opened in her empty heart. Look at her when circumstances change! She has no other resources. Bereavement and death find her without consolation, and when she loses earth she loses all she had, and the parting is the more terrible in proportion to the pleasure of the possession. But the other has an inner source of peace and happiness that external vicissitudes cannot affect. Her trials throw her more wholly upon that hidden source of joy, and when all else is overshadowed with darkness, you may often see her face, as it were the face of an angel, and when sobs and tears are heard on every side, around her dying couch, her voice is melodious with praise and her face is shining with the reflected glory of the everlasting day.

Why should it not be so? "God is Light and in Him is no darkness at all." The blessed God must be the source of blessedness. His Beloved Son, our Pattern and our Saviour, is the Prince of Peace, and the Royal Bridegroom, whom God "hath anointed with the oil of gladness above His fellows," and surely His salvation should be a glad salvation; His touch should bring joy and sunshine, and they who follow Him should be true to His own ideal of that happy company who "shall come to Zion with songs and everlasting joy; they shall obtain joy and gladness, and sorrow and sighing shall flee away." As we look over the earth we find that God has put beauty and gladness wherever He can. He has made us to be happy, and He has sent redemption to restore and consummate our joy, and so His great salvation is inseparably linked with a rejoicing spirit. True, it can stoop to sorrow; it will enter the saddest home and the darkest midnight, but it cannot dwell with gloom. It must banish sorrow as well as sin, and live in the light of joy.

And so we must give up trying to combine religion and melancholy, for Christ will have none but a happy people. Even old Judaism robed itself in bridal garments whenever it could and went forth with songs of rejoicing. Under the Mosaic law there was a constant succession of feasts, and the whole nation was required every little while to go on a great religious picnic to keep them from settling down into selfishness and melancholy. And in the closing festival of the sacred year they were required to spend an entire week in the most romantic and picturesque religious rejoicings, dwelling in rustic booths and uniting in festal services and sacred songs and ceremonies, which must have formed a grand and impressive spectacle of national rejoicing.

It was this Feast of Tabernacles that Nehemiah and the people were now observing, yet, like some of us, they had come with long faces, and thought it becoming to celebrate the occasion by a few appropriate tears, as they thought of the desolations of Zion which had just been removed and restored. But Nehemiah told them that it was no time for mourning, simply because it was a holy day, and holiness and tears did not go well together; that the sorrows were past, and therefore there was no cause for mourning any longer, but this was a day for gladness and praise, and the spirit of praise was necessary in order even to their own preparation and strength for the tasks in which they were engaged; "for the joy of the Lord," he declares, "is your strength."

1. This is true of us also, even in connection with the ordinary duties of daily life. How much one can do when the heart is light and free, and how long and heavy the easiest task when it is irksome! That mother can toil half the night, that father can sweat all the day, for the joy of knowing that it is for the child of his love. Listen to the words of the sailors as they heave their heavy loads into the hold of yonder vessel with their ringing chorus sometimes of two syllables; but if it is only Ho-Hay, they sing it and they sing it in unison, and the great packages seem like feathers in their hands. Look at the soldiers as they march over the long tramp of many miles! But the beat of the drum or the chorus of their battle songs lighten up all the toil of the way.

    Quaint old John Bunyan puts it happily when he tells us how he wrote the Pilgrim's Progress in his old Bedford dungeon. "So I was had home to prison," he goes on to say, "and I sat me down and wrote and wrote, because joy did make me write." The old dungeon with its stinted rays of light, its clumsy table, its wooden stool, its pallet of straw, was heaven to him because the joy of the pilgrim and the pilgrim's home and the pilgrim's story were bursting in his happy heart. Oh, how we need this joy amid the plod and the drudgery of the one hundred and forty-four hours of every week, in the factory, in the shop, over the counter, in the kitchen, at the desk, on the street, on the farm, and we may add, in what are often the harder places of public life, and the weary monotony of publicity, and the great heartless noisy world! But, thank God! circumstances will make little difference where the everlasting springs are bursting from the deep well of His joy in the heart.

>The joy of the Lord is our strength for life's burdens,
>And gives to each duty a heavenly zest;
>It will set to sweet music the task of the toiler;
>And soften the couch of the laborer's rest.

David has beautifully expressed this blending of common life with heavenly gladness in one of the Psalms, where he says, "Thy statutes have been my songs in the house of my pilgrimage." Statutes are just precepts of daily duty, and David enjoyed them by setting them to music and translating them to ceaseless praise. This, in a word, is the meaning of the one hundred and nineteenth Psalm. It is all about duty, and yet it is the most exquisitely constructed in the Hebrew Psalter. As it has been well said, it is duty set to music.

This is the way to make duty easy and acceptable to God. I have known a servant girl whose life was intolerable, and whose mistress was regarded as a petty tyrant, become so happy in the same home and with the same woman after she received the baptism of the Holy Spirit that she would not have exchanged her place for any other, and her mistress actually came to her to ask what had happened, and became an earnest inquirer through her beautiful transformation.

Beloved, let us take the joy of the Lord into the dark places and the hard places and the low places, and the dusty, grimy streets and lanes of life! Let us plant the flowers around the little cottage as well as the great mansion! Let us have the song of the birds along the wayside, and even in the night, as well as in the gilded cage of the drawing-room and in the broad sunshine of the day! Let us rejoice in the light evermore and go through the pathways of common life so filled with the Spirit that like men intoxicated with the wine of heaven, we shall be heard "speaking to ourselves in psalms and hymns and spiritual songs, singing with grace in our hearts to the Lord," and then it shall be true, "Whatsoever we do in word or deed," we shall "do all in the name of the Lord Jesus giving thanks unto God by Him."

2. The joy of the Lord is our strength for the trials of life. There are two ways of bearing a trial; the one is the spirit of stoical endurance, and the other through the counteracting forces of a holy and victorious joy. It was thus that Christ endured the cross for the joy that was set before Him, and then He could despise the shame and not even allow the smell of fire to remain upon His garments. We read in the first chapter of Colossians the prayer of the apostle for a company of saints who had already reached such a measure of holiness that they were made partakers of the inheritance of the saints in light; but there was something higher and better for them, namely, that they should be "strengthened according to His glorious power unto all patience and longsuffering with joyfulness." "Patience" to endure the trials that come from the hand of God, and "longsuffering" to endure those which come from men, and both to be endured with real joyfulness. In fact, there is nothing to endure when the heart is full of

joy. It lifts us wholly above the trial, and we do not realize that we are being afflicted or wronged. The blessedness of true self-sacrifice is in being so filled with God that we will not have any sacrifice. What luxury of grace it is thus to be lifted above all that could even try the heart! The rocks are not taken from the bottom of the stream, but the blessed tides rise so high that the ships sail far above them in the current of God's great joy. And so the apostle explains his self-sacrifices for the Philippians, "Though I be offered on the sacrifice and service of your faith, I joy and rejoice with you all."

The Hebrew Christians were congratulated that they had been enabled to take "joyfully the spoiling of their goods." This is not a very common experience. Some good women lose their sanctification over a set of smashed dishes by a careless servant, or the spilling of coffee over the new tablecloth or dress, or the spots on the little dresses of heedless children; and some men get very angry over the mistakes or failures of employees or servants that injure their business or lose large sums of money.

Sir Isaac Newton once lost all the calculations of twenty-five years by the burning of a lot of papers through the carelessness of a little dog, and the world remembers him with more admiration than for all his discoveries because he simply answered, "Poor thing! You little know the mischief you have done."

The joy of the Lord always counts on something better than we lose, and remembers that there is one above who is the great Recompenser and Restorer, and will give a thousand times more by-and-by for one victory of patience and love than all the world is worth to-day.

Yes, the joy of the Lord is our strength for life›s trials,
And lifts the crushed heart above sorrow and care,
Like the nightingale's song, it can sing in the darkness,
And rejoice when the fig tree is withered and bare.

3. The joy of the Lord is our strength for temptation. "Count it all joy," James says, "when ye fall into divers temptations." One reason for this is because it is the best way to meet them. The devil always gets the best of a melancholy soul. Despondency will always bring surrender. Satan is so little used to joy in his own home that a happy face always scares him away. Amalek got hold of the hindmost of Israel's camp, the discouraged ones who were dragging behind and fretting about the hot weather and the hard road they had to travel. Such people always find the way harder before they get through. The fiery serpents, which were the devil's scouts, stung the murmuring multitudes, and it was an upward look to the brazen serpent that healed them. Jehoshaphat's armies marched to battle and victory with shouts of faith and songs of praise, and so still the joy of the Lord is the best equipment for the great conflict. But the apostle also means, no doubt, that temptation is no cause for despondency, but rather a great opportunity of spiritual progress. It is the proving of our armor and an evident token that the devil sees something in us worth trying to steal, and we may be very sure where the army of the enemy is encamped there the army of the Lord is also near. "The trying of our faith worketh patience, and let patience have her perfect work." Let us go through all the discipline and learn all that it has to teach us, and "when we are tried we shall receive the crown of life which the Lord has promised to them that love Him."

Let us then go forth into the conflicts which await us without a fear or cloud, and when we cannot feel the joy, but "are in heaviness through manifold temptations," let us "count it all joy," and say, "I will rejoice in the Lord, and I will be joyful in my God."

The joy of the Lord is our strength for temptation,
And counts it the testing of patience and grace;
It marches to battle with shouts of salvation,
And rides o'er its foes in the chariots of praise.

4. The joy of the Lord is our strength for the body. "A merry heart doeth good like a medicine." This is the divine prescription for a weak body. And so on the other hand, despondency and depression of spirits are the cause of nervousness, head-ache, heart-break, and low physical vitality. A word of cheer and an impulse of hope and gladness will often break the power of disease.

I remember a dying man whom I visited in the earliest years of my ministry, who was given up by his physicians and pronounced in a dying condition, so that they gave up the case and expected his death during the night. But as I visited him, as I supposed, for the last time, and tenderly led him to the Saviour, and as he accepted the gospel and became filled with the peace of God and the joy of salvation, there came upon him such a baptism of glory and such an inspiration of the very rapture of heaven, that he kept us for hours beside his bed as he shouted and sung, what we all believed to be the beginning of the songs of heaven, and we bade him farewell long after midnight, fully expecting that our next meeting would be above. But so mighty was the uplift in that soul that his body, unconsciously to himself, threw off the power of disease, and the next morning he was convalescent, to the amazement of his physicians, and in a few days entirely well. I knew nothing, at that time, of Divine Healing, but simply witnessed with astonishment and delight, the Divine joy to heal disease. Many a time since have I seen the healing and the gladness of Jesus come together to the soul and body, and the night of weeping turned into a morning of joy. Many a time have I seen the darkly-clouded and diseased brain lighted up with the joy of the Lord, and saved from insanity by a baptism of holy gladness.

It is true there is a deeper cause and a diviner power than the mere natural influence of joy. Incurable disease can only yield to the actual touch of Divine omnipotence, but joy is the channel through which the healing waters flow, and the overflow of the life of Christ in both soul and body. If you would live above your physical conditions, if you would renew your strength continually and "mount up on wings as eagles, and run and not be weary, and walk and not faint," if you would carry in your veins the exhilaration and zest of unwearied youth and freshness, if you would know, even here, in all its fullness, the foretaste of the resurrection life in your body, if you would be armed against the devil's shafts of infirmity and pain, and throw off his arrows upon your body as the heated iron repels the water which will not lie upon it, then, beloved, "Rejoice in the Lord always, and again I say, Rejoice."

To return to our figure-the humblest housewife knows that water cannot rest upon a red-hot stove-cover, but leaps and dances over it in consternation, and flies off in explosions of helpless effervescence. So the devil will try in vain to pour cold water upon your life and work, and even your frame, if you keep ever in the white heat of heavenly joy.

5. The joy of the Lord is our strength for service and testimony. It makes all our work easy and delightful. It gives a perpetual spring in the hardest fields of Christian service. It goes with the city missionary and the all-night worker in the dives and slums, and takes away the natural shrinking from the degraded and unclean, the horror of filth and vermin, the fear of violent and wicked men and all the repulsiveness and hideousness of the surrounding scenes; and it makes the work, that naturally would be revolting, a perfect fasci-

nation, and enables the consecrated heart to say, "None of these things move me, neither count I my life dear unto me that I may finish my course with joy, and the ministry which I have received of the Lord Jesus to testify of the gospel of the grace of God."

Not only does it give a constraining motive to our service, but it also gives it a divine effectiveness and power. It illuminates the face with the light of heaven, and melts the heart with accents of tenderness and love. It gives our words a weight and winning power which men cannot gainsay. They know that we possess a secret to which they are strangers, and our gladness awakens their longing to share our joy. A shining face and radiant spirit are worth a ton of logic, rhetoric and elocution. A poor, crippled saint, standing up in a meeting and telling what God hath done for her soul, with a face divinely beautiful in all its homeliness, will bring more souls to Christ than the eloquence of a dozen college graduates without the joy of the Lord.

A scholarly minister once gave a course of lectures on the "Evidences of Christianity," for the special purpose of convincing and converting a wealthy and influential sceptic in his congregation. The gentleman attended his lectures and was converted, and a few days after the minister ventured to ask him which of the lectures it was that impressed him decisively. "The lectures!" answered the gentleman, "my dear sir, I don't even remember the subjects of your lectures, and I cannot say that they had any decisive influence upon my mind. I was converted by the testimony of a dear old colored woman who attended those services, and who, as she hobbled up the steps close to me, with her glad face, as bright. as heaven, used to say, 'My blessed Jesus! my blessed Jesus!' and turning to me would ask, 'Do you love my blessed Jesus?' and that, sir, was my evidence of Christianity."

Bless the Lord! we can all shine like that, "burning," as well as "shining" lights, and setting hearts aglow with the contagion of our joy. The world is looking for happiness, and if it find the secret in a genuine form, will try to get it. Charles Finney tells us how the good deacons used to ask him in prayer-meeting, when he attended it in his ungodly days, if he did not want them to pray for him. "No," he said, "I should be very sorry to have you pray for me. For, in the first place, if I were converted through your prayers I should be as miserable as you are; and in the next place, I do not believe that your prayers would have any power to bring about my conversion, and I suspect that you yourselves would be a good deal surprised if they had, for you have been praying in the same melancholy way ever since I came to this town, for a revival, and I can see by your tones and your faces that you have no idea that it is ever coming. When I am converted I want a religion that will make me happy, and a God who will do what I ask Him."

Beloved, the Lord save us from religious melancholia, and send us out to work for Him with shining faces, victorious accents and hearts overflowing with contagious joy. Then, like Stephen, we will be able to look into the faces of our enemies and confound them by our very countenances, and force the world to "take knowledge of us that we have been with Jesus."

«Let the joy of the Lord be the strength of our service,
As it speaks in our faces and accents of love,
As it wins the sad world to the fullness of Jesus,
And draws hungry hearts His salvation to prove."

II. The secret of this joy.

1. It springs from the assurance of salvation. It is the joy of salvation. Its happy song is,

«Blessed assurance, Jesus is mine,
Oh, what a rapture of glory Divine!
Heir of salvation, purchased of God,
Born of His Spirit, washed in His blood.

This is my story, this is my song,
Praising my Saviour all the day long."

If you would know it you must accept His promise with full assurance of faith, and rest upon His word without a wavering or a doubt.

2. It is the joy of the Holy Ghost. "The fruit of the Spirit is love, joy." It is not indigenous to earthly soil; it is a plant of heavenly birth. It belongs to the kingdom of God, which is "righteousness, and peace and joy in the Holy Ghost." To know it we must receive the baptism of the Pentecostal Spirit in full surrender and simple faith. It is the characteristic of all who receive this baptism that they know the joy of the Lord, and until we do receive this eternal fountain in our heart, all our attempts at joy are but surface wells ; they are waters often defiled and their bottom often dry. This is the great Artesian stream, the "well of water" Jesus gives "springing up unto everlasting life."

3. It is the joy of faith. "Now the God of hope fill you with all joy and peace in believing." There is indeed a deep delight when God has answered prayer, and the joy of fulfillment and possession overflows with thankfulness, but there is a more thrilling joy when the heart first commits itself to His naked promise, and standing on His simple word in the face of natural improbability, or even seeming impossibility, declares, "though the fig-tree shall not blossom nor fruit be in the vines, yet will I rejoice in the Lord and joy in the God of my salvation." If you are doubting God you need not wonder that your joy is intermittent. The witness of the Spirit always follows the act of trust. "Thou wilt keep him in perfect

peace whose mind is stayed on Thee, because he trusteth in Thee," but it is just as true, "Surely, if ye will not believe, ye shall not be established."

4. The joy of the Lord is sustained by His word and nourished by His "exceeding great and precious promises." "I rejoice in Thy Word," exclaims the Psalmist, "as one that findeth great spoil." Oh, the rich delight of beholding in the light of the Holy Spirit, the heavenly landscape of truth open before the spiritual vision, like some land of promise shining in the glory of the sunlight, the whole Bible seeming like the vision Moses saw from Pisgah's top! We have found great spoil, and it is all our own. "We have received the Spirit that we may know the things that are freely given us of God," and we can truly say like the same Psalmist again, "Thy testimonies are the joy and rejoicing of my heart." How sweet the voice in which the Spirit speaks the promises to the sorrowing heart and makes this precious word a living voice from our Beloved!

    Dear friends, do you know the joy that lies hidden in these neglected pages, the honey that you might drink from this garden of the Lord, these blossoms of truth and promise? Oh, take your Bibles as the living love-letters of His heart to you, and ask Him to speak it to you in joy and faith and spiritual illumination, as the sweet manna of your spirit's life and the honey out of the Rock of Ages!

5. It is the joy of prayer. Its element is the closet, and its source the Mercy-seat. No prayerless life can be a happy one. "They that wait upon the Lord shall mount up on wings as eagles." "Ask and ye shall receive, that your joy may be full."
    «This is the place where Jesus sheds
    The oil of gladness on our heads;
    The place than all besides more sweet,
    It is the blood-bought Mercy-seat."

6. It is the joy of meekness and love. "For the meek shall increase their joy in the Lord," and the loving spirit ever finds that "it is more blessed to give than to receive." Selfishness is misery, love is life and joy. The gentle, lowly, chastened spirit shall find all the flowers in bloom and the waters flowing in the valleys of humility. The unselfish heart shall never fail to prove the promise true, "If thou draw out thy soul to the hungry, and satisfy the afflicted soul, the Lord shall satisfy thy soul in drought, and thou shalt be like a watered garden and a spring of water whose waters fail not."

    Beloved, do you know the gladness which comes from yielding to the will of God, or bearing patiently the wrong, from being silent under the word of reproach, from returning good for evil, from the word that comforts the sorrowing heart, from the cup of cold water to another given, from the sacrifice of your own indulgence that the saving may be given to Him? Oh, then it is that all the bells of joy are heard softly ringing, and the Master whispers to the hearts that tremble with its gladness, "ye did it unto me."

7. It is the joy of service and especially of winning souls. All true work is a natural delight, but work for God in the true spirit and in the power of the Holy Ghost, is the very partnership of His joy, whose meat and drink it was to do the will of Him that sent Him and to finish His work. If you would have a life lifted above a thousand temptations and petty cares be busy for your Master, and let each moment see

    «Some work of love begun,
    Some deed of kindness done,
    Some wanderer sought and won,
    Something for thee."

    We cannot convey the Living Water to another heart without being watered ourselves on the way. There is no joy more exquisite than the joy of leading a soul to Christ. It is like the mother's strange, instinctive rapture over her newborn babe. The other day a precious friend passed through the gates a few moments after her babe was born, but in the hour of her agony her very first word was, "How is my babe?" It was the first thrill of that strange delight which is the very touch of the love which the Holy Ghost will give us for the souls He permits us to win for Christ. It is, indeed, a spiritual, motherhood, and it has all the joy and all the pain of a mother's love.

Beloved, do you know the ecstasy of feeling the new life of an immortal spirit sweeping through your very veins, as, kneeling by the side of one just born to die no more, you place it, as a newborn babe in the bosom of your Saviour? You may know this joy, and every Christian ought to know it a hundred-fold. It is the joy of angels, setting all the harps of heaven ringing, and surely it were strange if it were not the higher joy of ransomed saints.

8. It is the joy of the faithful servant. There is a sense even here, in which as often as we are true to God and faithful to the call of duty and opportunity, His Spirit gives us a present reward and a baptism of joy, and whispers to the faithful heart, "Well done, good and faithful servant! Enter thou into the joy of thy Lord."

9. It is the joy of hope. "We rejoice in hope of the glory of God." It is the reflected light of the coming Sunrise and the Millennial Day. Except the death and resurrection of Jesus and the baptism of the Holy Ghost, there is nothing that sheds within the heart a diviner gladness, and on the brow a holier light, than the blessed hope of the Lord's Coming. It is, indeed, "a light in the dark place," the very Morning Star that presages the Rising Sun. Then let us in this blessed hope "lift up our heads, for our redemption draweth nigh."

10. And finally, it is the joy of Christ Himself within us. "These things have I spoken unto you, that my joy might remain

in you and that your joy might be full." This is the deepest secret of spiritual joy; it is the indwelling Christ Himself rejoicing in the heart as He rejoiced on earth even in the darkest hour of His life, and as now, in heaven, He realizes the fulfillment of His own Messianic words in the sixteenth psalm: "Therefore my heart is glad and my glory rejoiceth; my flesh also shall rest in hope. For Thou wilt not leave my soul among the dead, nor suffer Thy Holy One to see corruption. Thou wilt show me the path of life; in Thy presence there is fullness of joy, and at Thy right hand are pleasures for evermore." In the fullness of joy He is reigning now, and its tides are swelling and rising to the same level in every heart in which He dwells.

Walking along the ocean beach hundreds of feet from the shore you may dig a little hole in the dry sand, and it will fill with water. Underneath the sand the waters flow and fill the pool to the level of their source. And so the life that is hid with Christ in God is in constant contact with the fountain of life, and though the world may not always see the overflow, yet the heart's depths are ever filling, and we only need to make room, and lo! the empty void, whether great or small, is full to the measure of the fullness of God. This, beloved, is why we beseech you to receive the indwelling Christ. He is the source of the River of the Water of Life that flows from the Throne of God and the Lamb, and those whose hearts are His temple can sing, no matter how the tempests rage and the fig-tree withers,

«God is the Treasure of my soul,
The source of lasting joy;
A joy which time cannot impair,
Nor death itself destroy."

Chapter 3.
FILLED WITH THE SPIRIT

"Be filled with the Spirit." Eph. v: 18.

"Ye are complete (filled) in Him." Col. ii: 10.

The emphatic word in both these verses "filled." It is the Greek *plaroo* which means to fill full, so full that there will be no room left empty. This is the thought which, with the assistance of the Holy Spirit, we desire to impress in this message. It does not mean to have a measure of the Holy Spirit, and to know a good deal of Christ, but to be wholly filled with, and possessed by, the Holy Ghost, and utterly lost in the life and fullness of Jesus. It is the completeness of the filling which constitutes the very essence of the perfect blessing. A fountain half full will never become a spring. A river half full will never become a water power. A heart half filled will never know "the peace which passeth all understanding" and the power which flows from the inmost being, as "rivers of living water."

I. THE NATURE OF THIS FILLING.

1. It is all connected with a living Person. We are not filled with an influence; we are not filled with a sensation; we are not filled with a set of ideas and truths ; we are not filled with a blessing, but we are filled with a Person. This is very strange and striking. It is wholly different from all other teaching. Human systems of philosophy and religion all deal mainly with intellectual truths, moral conditions or external acts. Greek philosophy was a system of ideas; Confucianism is a system of morals; Judaism is a system of laws and ceremonies; Christianity all centres in a living Person, and its very essence is the indwelling life of Christ Himself. He was not only its Head and Founder, but He is forever its living Heart and Substance, and the Holy Spirit is simply the agent and

channel through whom He enters, possesses and operates in the consecrated heart. This reduces Christian life to great simplicity. We do not require to get filled in a great many compartments, and with a great many different experiences, ideas, or influences, but, in the centre of our being to receive Him in His personal life and fullness, and then He flows into every part and lives out His own life in all the diversified experiences and activities of our manifold life.

In the one garden we plant the living seed, and water it from the same great fountain, and lo! it springs up spontaneously with all the varied beauty and fruitfulness of the lily and the rose, the foliage plant and the fruit tree, the clinging jessamine and the spreading vine. We have simply to turn on the fertilizing spring and nature's spontaneous life bursts forth in all its beautiful variety.

This, by a simple figure, is Christ's theory of a deeper life. Our being is the soil, He is the seed, His Holy Spirit is the Fountain of living Waters, and "the fruit of the Spirit is love, joy, peace, long-suffering, gentleness, goodness, faith, meekness, temperance."

Out in the great West lie millions of acres of barren land. They are a great possibility, but practically fruitless and waste. Beneath the soil of these Saharas lie undeveloped riches, all that is needed being one single element that would develop them into fruitfulness. That element is water. Let the mountain stream be turned into yonder valley, let the irrigating channels spread their network over all their vast fields, and lo! you behold a paradise, as lovely as the streets of Salt Lake City or some of the sweet villages and towns of California, with a luxuriance of beauty such as none of our eastern lands can show. The soil was empty and barren until it became filled with the seed and the springs, and then the transformation sprang up with spontaneous luxuriance. So the human heart is not self-constituted or self-sufficient; it is a bare and barren possibility. It may struggle its best to develop itself, but it will only develop, as those Western deserts the sage brush and stunted palm which cover them to-day. But give it two things. Drop into that soil the living Christ, and flood it with the water of the Spirit's fullness, and lo! it reaches the realization of its true idea, and the promise of His own simple parable is perfectly fulfilled, "He that abideth in me and I in him, the same bringeth forth much fruit; for apart from me ye can do nothing."

Shall we then realize, beloved, that God has made each of us, not a self-contained world of power and perfection, but simply a capacity to receive Him, a shell to hold His fullness, a soil to receive His Living Seed and fertilizing streams, and to produce, in union with Him, the fruits of grace? And shall we realize, on the other hand, that God has so constituted Christ and the Holy Spirit, who is just the Spirit of Christ, as perfectly to meet and satisfy the capacities and possibilities of our being; so that, while we are nothing without Him, His life and grace equally require us for their full development? Into His living Son God has poured all His fullness, so that "in Him dwelleth all the fullness of the Godhead bodily." The Holy Spirit has now become the great Reservoir and system of distributing pipes and channels through which His fullness flows into us, and there is nothing which God requires of a man, or which man can ever need in the varied exigencies of life but Christ possesses for us, and we may have an exact adjustment to our every need, by simply receiving Him. This is the meaning of that beautiful expression, "Of His fullness have all we received, even grace for grace. For the law was given by Moses, but grace and reality came by Jesus Christ." All other systems gave us merely the ideas of things or the commandments or laws which require them of us. But Christ brings the power to realize them and is Himself the reality and substance in our hearts and lives. He is the Great Typical Man. But He is more than a pattern or a type, exhibiting what we ought to be, and demanding our imitation. He is also the Living Head and Progenitor of the very life which He Himself exhibits, begetting it in each of us by a living impartation of His very being, and reproducing Himself in us by the very power of His own life, and then feeding and nourishing this life by the Holy Spirit out of His own being.

Christ's Person, therefore, is far more than a pattern. It is a power, a seed, a spring of Living Water, nay, the very substance and support of the life He requires of us.

2. This Person is the true fullness of every part of our life. The idea of filling implies universality and completeness in the range within which He fills us. We are not filled unless we are filled in every part. This is just what Christ proposes to do in our full salvation.

He fills all the requirements of our salvation, all the conditions involved in connection with our redemption, reconciliation, justification. He just takes the indictment against us and fills it in with His own precious atonement, and in His own blood writes, "Settled forever." He takes the broken law and the sad and humiliating record of our failures, omissions and transgressions, and fills it up with its own perfect righteousness and writes over all our record, "Christ is the end of the law for righteousness to every one that believeth," "Accepted in the Beloved;" "He was made sin for us who knew no sin that we might be made the righteousness of God in Him."

And so "we are complete in Him." "By one offering He hath perfected forever them that are sanctified," and we are as fully saved as if we had never sinned.

Now, beloved, the great thing is to realize right here that this is complete, and, at the very threshold, to begin to enter into the fullness of Christ by recognizing ourselves as fully justified and forever saved from all past sin and transgression through the complete redemption of Jesus Christ. The lack of fullness in our subsequent experience is largely due to doubts and limitations which we allow to enter here. Christ's work for our redemption was finished, and when we accept it, it is a complete and eternal salvation.

Again, Christ fills the deeper need of sanctification. He has provided for this in His atonement and in the resources of His grace. It is all wrapped up in Him, and must be received as a free and perfect gift through Him alone. "For of Him are ye in Christ Jesus who of God is made unto us sanctification." Is sanctification the death of the sinful self? Well, this has been crucified with Him already upon the Cross, and we have but to hand it over to Him in unreserved committal, and He will slay it and bury it forever in His grave. Is sanctification a new life of purity, righteousness, peace and joy in the Holy Ghost? Still more emphatically is it true that Christ Himself must be our life, our peace, our purity, and our full and overflowing joy?

Again, He is the fullness of our heart life. There is no place so sacred to us as our affections, no place so claimed by the great adversary of our souls, and so impossible to regulate by our own power and will. But Christ will give us His heart as well as His Spirit, and will love in us with the love which loves "the Lord our God with all our heart and soul and strength and mind," and which loves "one another even as He has loved us." Oh, how blessed that we have One who will really fill all the delicate and infinitely difficult and varied requirements of these sensibilities and affections, which carry with them such a world of possibility for our own or others' weal or woe.

Again, Christ will fill all the needs of our intellectual life. Our mental capacities will never know their full wealth of power and spiritual effectiveness until they become simply the vessels of His quickening life, and these brains of ours are laid at His feet simply as the censers which are to hold His holy fire. He will think in us, remember in us, judge in us, impart definiteness and clearness to our conceptions of truth, give us the tongue of fire, the illustration that both illuminates and melts, the accent and tone of persuasiveness and sympathy, the power of quick expression and utterance, and all the equipment necessary to make us workmen "that need not to be ashamed, rightly dividing the word of truth." Not of course without diligent and faithful attention to His wise and holy teaching, as He leads us in His work to see at once our own shortcomings and His full purpose for us. We must be taught of God, and teaching is sometimes very gradual, and even slow; but "He will guide us into all truth," and "perfect that which concerneth" our education and preparation for His work and will; and the mind that the Holy Spirit quickens and uses shall accomplish results for God which all the brilliancy of human genius and the scholarship of human learning can never approach.

Again, He will fill the needs of our body, for His body has been constituted, by the resurrection from the dead, a perpetual source of physical energy, sufficient for every member of His body the church, and adapted to every physical function and every test that comes in the pressure of human life, and the experience of a world where every step is beset with the elements of disease, suffering and physical danger. Christ is the true life of a redeemed body, and His Holy Spirit is able so to quicken these mortal bodies, as He dwells within us, that they shall receive a supernatural vigor directly derived from our exalted Head.

Again, Christ will fill all the situations of providence and all the needs that arise in our secular callings and the circumstances of our daily life. There is not one of them that may not be recognized as coming from Him, and meant to prove His all-sufficiency in some new direction. Oh, had we the faith to see God in everything as it meets us day by day, every chapter of life's history would be a new story of the romance of heavenly love in its magical power to transform darkness into light, difficulty into triumph, sorrow into joy, and the earthly into the heavenly; and Christ would be enabled to manifest Himself in His grace and power to innumerable witnesses, who never hear of Him from a pulpit, or read the story of His grace in anything else but human lives, in whom they could thus behold Him.

Again, Christ will fill our capacities for happiness. He is the fullness of our peace and joy. He is the true portion of the souls that He has made; and, wholly filled with Him, there is no room for either care or fear.

Finally, Christ will fill that fundamental need on which every other experience of His fullness depends, namely, the faith that receives Him. This too, is but the life of Christ within us, and our highest part in the life of faith is to so abandon even our highest and hardest efforts to trust God, and so boldly venture that we can receive the very faith of God and claim the "all things that are possible to him that believeth."

3. To be filled with Christ is not only to be filled with the Divine life in every part, but it is to be filled every moment. It is to take Him into the successive instants of our conscious existence and to abide in His fullness. For this is not a reservoir but a spring. It is a life which is continual, active and ever passing on with an outflow as necessary as its inflow, and if we do not perpetually draw the fresh supply from the living

fountain, we shall either grow stagnant or empty. It is, therefore, not so much a perpetual fullness as a perpetual filling.

It is true there are periodical experiences of spiritual elevation which are part of God's plan for our life in Christ, and are designed no doubt to lift us to a higher plane of abiding union with Him. There are the Pentecosts and second Pentecosts, the great freshets and flood-tides, all of which have their necessary place in the spiritual economy. But there is the continual receiving, breath by breath and moment by moment, between these long intervals and more marked experiences, which is even more needful to spiritual steadfastness and healthfulness. God would have us alive to all His approaches, and open to all the "precious things of heaven, the dew, and the deep that coucheth beneath, the precious fruits brought forth by the sun, the precious things put forth by the moon, the precious things of the earth and the fullness thereof." Such lives will find that there is no moment of existence, and no part of our being which may not be some minister of God and draw some blessing from Him.

II. THE EFFECTS OF THE DIVINE FILLING.

1. It is the secret of holiness. There is a measure of the Holy Spirit's life in every regenerate soul, but it is when every part of our being is filled with His love and possessed for His glory that we are wholly sanctified, and it is this divine fullness which excludes and keeps out the power of sin and self, even as it was the descending cloud upon the tabernacle which left no room for Moses within.

   Would you have continual purity of heart and thought and feeling, and entire conformity to the will of God? "Be filled with the Spirit;" "Of his fullness have we received, even grace for grace." Let the heavenly water flow into every channel of irrigation and by every garden bed and plant, until all the graces of our Christian life shall be replenished by His grace, and bloom like the garden of the Lord. Only abide in Him and have His abiding, and you shall bring forth all the fruit of the Spirit.

2. It is the secret of happiness. A heart half full is only full enough to make it conscious of its lack. It is when the cattle are filled that they lie down in the green pastures. "These things have I spoken unto you that my joy might remain in you and that your joy might be full."

3. It is the secret of power. The electric current can so fill a little wire that it will become a force to turn the great wheels of the factory, and the overflowing sluice of the village stream has power enough to run a score of factories all along the river banks, but it is simply because it is overflowing. Only full hearts accomplish effectual work for God. Only the overflow of our blessing blesses others.

III. THE CONDITIONS OF BEING FILLED.

1. He has promised to fill the hungry. "Blessed are they which do hunger and thirst after righteousness, for they shall be filled." Many who read these lines are no doubt longing for this experience and thinking with discouragement of how far short they come. Dear friend, this deep desire is the very beginning of the blessing you seek, and already the Holy Spirit is at work preparing your heart for the answer to your cry. No soul finds the fullness of Jesus so speedily as the one that is most deeply conscious of its failure and its needs. Thank God for that intense desire that will not let you rest short of His blessing.

An eastern caravan was overtaken once in the desert with the failure of the supply of water. The accustomed fountains were all dried, the oasis was a desert, and they halted an hour before sunset to find, after a day of scorching heat, that they were perishing for want of water. Vainly they explored the usual wells, for they were all dry. Dismay was upon all faces and despair in all hearts, when one of the ancient men approached the sheik and counselled him to unloose two beautiful harts that he was conveying home as a present to his bride, and let them scour the desert in search of water. Their tongues were protruding with thirst, and their bosoms heaving with distress. But as they were led out to the borders of the camp and then set free on the boundless plain, they lifted up their heads on high, and sniffed the air with distended nostrils, and then, with unerring instinct, with course as straight as an arrow, and speed as swift as the wind, they darted off across the desert. Swift horsemen followed close behind, and an hour or two later hastened back with the glad tidings that water had been found, and the camp moved with shouts of rejoicing to the happily discovered fountains.

So still there is a hart that can ever find the springs of living water. It is the heart that hungers and thirsts for God. Thank God, beloved, if you have this deep spiritual instinct in your soul! Follow it as it leads you to the Throne of grace, to wait, and cry, and receive, until you can say, "Satisfied with favor and full with the blessing of the Lord."

2. The empty are always filled. "He hath filled the hungry with good things, but the rich He hath sent empty away." "Blessed are the poor in spirit, for theirs is the kingdom of heaven." "Having nothing and yet possessing all things." This is the paradox of grace. We never can be filled until we have room for God. Every great blessing begins with a great sacrifice, a great severance, a great dispossessing. "He brought them out that He might bring them in." Abraham must let Lot have his choice before he can have his full inheritance. Isaac must be offered on Mount Moriah before God can make it the seat of His future temple. Moses must let go the

honors and prospects of his Egyptian princedom before he can receive his great commission, the lasting honor of his life work. The heart must be emptied of self and the world before it can be filled with Jesus and the Holy Ghost. Probably each of us is as full as we can hold, because the places God does not fill are crammed with something else and God finds no room. Are we willing to be emptied? "Make the valley full of ditches," is still the prophet's command, "and the valley shall be filled with water." Are we in the valley of humiliation, and have we opened in the valley the still deeper ditches of need and conscious insufficiency? In proportion as we can say, "I am not sufficient," we shall be able to add, "My sufficiency is of God." Have we not only emptied out the old pirate self-will and his crew of worldliness and sin, but also all the cargo of our own strength, faith and religious experience, and made room for Christ to be our All and in all always? Do we habitually cease from ourselves in everything and thus make it necessary for God to assume the responsibility and supply the proficiency, and in this spirit of self-renunciation and absolute dependence are we growing poorer and richer every day?

3. The open heart shall be filled. "Open thy mouth wide and I will fill it." We know what it is for the flower-cup to close its petals and also to open to the sunlight, the dew and the refreshing shower. The heart has its susceptibilities and receptive sensibilities, but often it is so tightened up with unbelief, doubt, fear, and self-consciousness that it cannot take in the love which God is waiting to pour out. Do we not know what it is to meet people, with a heart full of love, and find them all tightened up and heart-bound? We become conscious at once of the repulsion and feel all the fountains of our love obstructed and rolled back again upon our own aching hearts. They cannot receive us. It is like the mother who found her

long-lost child after years of separation, but the child could not recognize the mother, and as she tried to awaken its response and to pour out the full tides of her bursting heart and found no recognition, but only the dull stare of strangeness and suspicion, and all her caresses and tender overflowings of affection rejected and met with cold indifference and even recoil, her heart broke in grief and disappointment, and she wept and sobbed in agony.

The heart of God is pouring out His love to many a soul who cannot, will not, take it in. It does not know its Father. His face is strange. There seems no avenue to the dull earthly heart, and even the love of God has cause to exclaim, "How often would I have gathered you as a hen gathereth her brood under her wings, and ye would not!" I have seen a man dying for months simply because he could not swallow more than a single grain of food or spray of moisture. Many a Christian's spiritual larynx is just as shrunken, and millions are starving to death in the midst of plenty, because their hearts are not open to receive God. There must be confidence, trust, the love that draws near and takes the faith that accepts and receives, and the quietness of spirit that stays long enough open to be wholly filled.

4. Again, we are filled by waiting upon the Lord in prayer, and especially in continued and persevering prayer. It was after they had waited upon the Lord that they were all filled with the Holy Ghost. Prayer is not only an asking but also a receiving. Many of us do not wait long enough before the Lord to get filled. You can take your breakfast in half an hour, but you cannot be filled with the Holy Spirit as quickly. There should be seasons of special waiting upon the Lord for this very purpose, and then there should be a ceaseless abiding in the Lord for the quiet replenishing, moment by moment. The one may be compared to the great rain storms that flood

the river, and the other to the ceaseless moisture of the air and the morning and evening dews. No child of God who, in a proper spirit, and with an entire self-surrender and trust, waits upon God for the full baptism of His Holy Ghost, will ever be disappointed, but we shall surely go forth from such seasons refreshed and overflowing with the love and life of God, and will find that special influences of power and blessing will follow such seasons, both in our own lives and the lives of others.

5. Service for God and for others is perhaps the most effectual condition of receiving continually the fullness of the Spirit. As we pour out the blessing God will pour it in. We have a pump in one of our institutions which is worked by steam. We have a way of always knowing when the reservoir on the roof is full. There is a little tell-tale downstairs which begins to run and a little bell to ring. Then we know that the overflow has begun, and the signal has sounded. As long as the pump is silent we know that it is not full, but that little signal and the accompanying stream running from the open tap are as good as a telegram from the distant roof. So we can always tell in the Church of God when it is not full. There are some Christians whose bell only rings once in a very long time and whose overflow is so feeble and infrequent that it would scarcely furnish one good drink to a poor thirsty wayfarer.

Beloved, let us keep pouring out more of God's blessing and see if He will not more abundantly pour in the floods of His grace. Let us be very practical about this. Every blessing that we have received from God is a sacred trust, and it will be continued only as we use it for Him. Our salvation is not our own; it belongs to every perishing soul on the face of the globe who has not yet had the opportunity of accepting Jesus. Our sanctification and our great secret of the fullness of Jesus is a sacred trust for every Christian who has not yet received the fullness of God, and if we do not let this light shine, it will surely become obscure and we will not be able to tell out the story of our blessing. Our healing belongs to some sufferer. Our every experience is adjusted to some heart, and will enable us to meet some brother's need if we are but faithful to the opportunities of God's providence. Oh, how clear a truth becomes to us when we are trying to tell it to others! Oh, how real the baptism of the Holy Ghost when we are kneeling by another's side to claim it for them! Oh, how the streams of Christ's healing flow through our very flesh as we are leading some poor sufferer into the truth! Oh, how the joy of our salvation swells as we see it spring in the heart that we have just led to the fountain! Oh, the fullness that God is longing to share with every vessel that has room to receive it and readiness to give! As we have therefore received His fullness let us pass it on, drinking as the living waters flow through our hands, until we shall realize in some measure, the largeness and blessedness of the great promise of the Lord, "If any man thirst, let him come unto Me and drink. He that believeth on Me (as the Scripture saith), out of his inmost being shall flow rivers of. living water."

Chapter 4.
THE LARGER LIFE

"Be ye also enlarged." 2 Cor. vi: 11.

The law of growth is a fundamental principle of all nature and redemption. Whatever ceases to grow begins to die; stagnancy brings corruption; the corpse belongs to the worm; a self-contained pool becomes a malarious swamp. Vegetation springs from a seed, the seed grows into a tree, and the tree into a forest. Human life commences in infancy and develops to maturity. The word of God has all unfolded from a single promise. The great plan of redemption has been a ceaseless progression, and will be through the ages upon ages that are yet to come.

The experience of the soul is a growth. True, it must have a starting point. We cannot grow into Christianity we must be born from above and then grow. And so sanctification is progressive, and yet it has a definite beginning. Christ is completely formed within us, but He is the infant Christ, and grows up to the maturity of the perfect man in us just as He did in His earthly life.

It is here that the enlargement of our text meets us. It is only the truly consecrated Christian that grows. The other treads the ceaseless circle of the wilderness. But he has crossed the Jordan and begun the conquest of the land and the progressive experience of which it was the beautiful pattern and symbol. No book in the Bible has more progress in it than the book of Joshua, and yet from the very beginning it is the life of one who has wholly died to self and sin and has taken Christ for full salvation and is walking in the heavenly places in Him.

And even the book of Joshua only begins its highest advance when it is almost ended. It is after the whole land is subdued, that the call comes, "How long are ye slack to go up and possess all the land? There remaineth yet very much land to be possessed." And then it is that old Caleb, who has the weight of

A Larger Christian Life

eighty-four years on his honored head, steps forth and claims the privilege of entering upon the boldest and hardest campaign of his life, the conquest of Hebron and the Anakim. It is to us then, who know the Lord Jesus in His fullness, that He is saying, "Be ye also enlarged."

I. WHAT IT MEANS TO BE ENLARGED.

1. We need a larger vision. All great movements begin in great ideas. There is no progress without a new thought as its embryo. China has remained the same for three thousand years because China has not accepted a new idea. Her teacher is a man who lived long before Christ, and for nearly thirty centuries she has followed the ideas of Confucius and is just the same to-day as she was thirty centuries ago. Let China receive the American idea or the Christian idea, and she will be revolutionized at once.

   So the first step in our advance must be a new conception of the truth as it is in Jesus and a larger view of His word and will for us. We do not need a new Bible, but we need new eyes to read our Bible and brighter light to shine upon its deep and pregnant pages. We need to see, not simply a system of exegesis or a system of Biblical exposition and criticism; a thorough knowledge of the letter and its wondrous framework of history; geography, antiquities and ancient languages; but a vivid, large and spiritual conception of what it means for us and what God's thought in it for each of us is. We want to take it as the message of heaven to the nineteenth century and the last decade, nay, the living voice of the Son of God to us this very hour, and to see in it the very idea which He Himself has for our life and work; to take in the promises as He understands them, the commandments as He intends them to be obeyed, and the hopes of the future as He unfolds them upon the nearer horizon of their approaching fulfillment. How little have we grasped the length and breadth and depth and height of this heavenly message! How little have we realized its authority and its personal directness to us! "Open thou my eyes, 0 Lord, that I may behold wondrous things out of thy law!" "I will run in the way of thy commandments when thou shalt enlarge my heart." That ye may be filled with "the spirit of wisdom and revelation in the knowledge of Him; the eyes of your heart being enlightened; that ye may know what is the hope of His calling, and what the riches of the glory of His inheritance in the saints." May the Lord grant it to each of us in the largest possible measure in accordance with His will!

2. We need a larger faith. What is the use of light if we do not use it? We need a faith that will personally appropriate all that we understand, and a faith so large that it will reach the fullness of God's great promises; so large that it will rise to the level of each emergency as it comes into our life. Do we not often feel that a promise has been brought to us with a light and power that we have been unable to claim and a need has arisen that we are persuaded God is able to meet but for which we are conscious our faith is not grasping the victory, at least according to the full measure of the exigency? This ought not so to be. If all things are possible to him that believeth we ought to have all things in His will for every moment of life's need. The Divine pattern of faith is the faith of God. Oh, let us be enlarged to this high measure!

3. We need a larger love. We need a love that will meet God's claim of perfect love, that we shall "love the Lord our God with all our soul and with all our mind and with all our strength." We need a love that will love one another " even as He has loved us." We need a love that will "love our enemies and pray for them that despitefully use us and persecute us." We need a love that will love the lost as He loves them, over-

coming our repugnance to every personal condition, and delighting to suffer or sacrifice for their salvation with the joy that counts it no sacrifice. We need a love that will take our brother's need and pain as if it were our own, and "remember those in bonds as bound with them, and them that suffer adversity as being also in the body." We need a love that "suffers long and is kind; that envieth not: that vaunteth not itself, is not puffed up, seeketh not her own, is not provoked, thinketh no evil, rejoiceth not in iniquity but rejoiceth in the truth; beareth all things, believeth all things, hopeth all things, endureth all things; that never faileth."

4. We need a larger joy. We need a joy that will not only rejoice in the gifts of God, but will rejoice in God Himself and find in Him our portion and our boundless and everlasting delight. We need a joy that will not only rejoice in the sunshine but in the hour of darkness and apparent desertion, when men misunderstand us, when circumstances are against us and when even God seems to have forgotten us. We need a joy that will not only rejoice in all things, but rejoice evermore. We need a joy that even when we do not feel the joy, will "count it all joy," and rejoice by faith. We need a joy so large, so deep, so divine that it will not feel its sacrifices, will not talk about its trials, but will "endure the cross, despising the shame," "for the joy set before us."

5. We need a larger experience. We do not mean by this any mere state of emotional feeling, but a larger range of Christian living, a bringing of Christ more into everything; an experience that will prove Him in all situations, amid secular business, exasperating circumstances, baffling perplexities, extreme vicissitudes; and, going all round the circle of human life, will be able to say, "I have learned the secret, in every state in which I am therewith to be content. I know how to be abased and how to abound; I know how to be full

and to be hungry, to abound and to suffer need. I can do all things through Christ who strengtheneth me." That is a large experience. That is a degree in the school of Christ that will outweigh all the D.D.'s of all the colleges.

6. We need a larger work. We do not mean by this that we need a larger sphere. That may not be. That certainly is not the case if we are not filling our present; but we need a better quality of work. We need to finish our unfinished work. We need to do the things that we have thought of doing, intended to do, talked about doing, and are abundantly able to do. We need to do the work that can be done in the intervals and interstices of life, the work that can be done on the way and on the wing, *between* times as well as *in* times of special service and appointment; the word that can be spoken as we casually meet people; the work that can be done by the wayside and on the crossroads of life, where souls meet that never meet again. Sometimes the ministry that can be performed at such a moment becomes the pivot for hundreds of souls and eternal ages to turn upon. We need a work that is larger in its *upward* direction, more wholly for God, more singly devoted to His glory, and more satisfied with His approval whether men are pleased or not. And we need a larger conception and realization of the work that He expects of us in the special line in which He has been developing our Christian life. Most of those who read these lines or hear these words have been called to know Christ in a measure unknown to the great mass of the people of God, and we have not yet realized what God expects of us in spreading these special truths and extending this blessed movement, of which Christ is the centre and substance, over all the land and over all the world. God is calling us at this time to a larger faith for this special work-the testimony of Jesus in all His fullness to all the world.

A Larger Christian Life

7. We need a larger hope. We need to realize more vividly, more personally, more definitely, what the coming of the Lord means, and means to us, until the future shall become alive with the actual expectation and ever immanent prospect of His Kingdom and His reward. Oh, how little this great hope has been to the hearts and lives of most of us until within a few years! How utterly blind the majority of Christians are to it as an actual experience! How much inspiration is it fitted to afford to the heart that truly realizes it! May the Lord enlarge our hopes and intensify them until this becomes, next to the love of Jesus, the most inspiring, stimulating, quickening motive of our Christian life and work!

8. We need a larger baptism of the Holy Spirit, for this is the true summing up of all that we have said. It is one thing, not many things, that we need; and, filled with the Spirit in still larger measure, the fruit of the Spirit shall expand and increase in proportion. We need more room for His indwelling, more scope for His expanding, more channels for His outflow. We are not straitened in Him, we are straitened in ourselves. "He giveth not the Spirit by measure," but we receive Him in very confined and small capacities. He wants more room; He wants our entire being, and He wants so to fill it that we shall be expanded into larger possibilities for His inworking and His outflowing.

Beloved, "be ye enlarged." And not only in all these senses and directions, which no doubt have searched us and made us realize the limitations of our present lives, but we want to be enlarged in the quality of our life; we want not only more breadth and length, but we want depth and height, a more spiritual, a more mellow, a more mature fruition, and a more established, settled and immovable standing in and for Him.

II. CONSIDERATIONS AND DIRECTIONS WITH A VIEW TO OUR ENLARGEMENT.

1. In order to our being enlarged we must be delivered from and lifted above our old conceptions, ideas and experiences. In a word, we must be delivered from our past. Old things must pass away before all things can be made new. We must die to our religious self as well as to our sinful self. It was when he was far on in the spiritual life that Paul uttered the sublime aspiration, "Forgetting those things that are behind, and reaching forth unto those things which are before, I press towards the mark for the prize of the high calling of God in Christ Jesus." In the strata of our globe we find traces of the wreck of former conditions of organic life. There was a creation and then there was a disintegration, and on its ruins a new and higher development. So in the spiritual world, we come to the place where we are conscious that the old experience fails to satisfy. The old "Rephidims" are dry, and we must open some new rock of Horeb and receive supplies from a higher source than before. When you find your old nest ceasing to rest you, be willing to leave it, and like the eaglets, be hurled into space, that you may be taught to fly. Let the old things pass away. They are but the basis of something better. Let the old turnpike be broken up. The King's Highway is to be built above it, and God's great elevated railway carry us where formerly we trod with weary feet.

There is nothing that keeps us from advancement more than ruts and drifts, wheel-tracks into which our chariots roll and then move on in the narrow line with unchanging monotony, currents in life's stream on which we are borne in the old direction until the law of habit almost makes advance impossible. The true remedy for all this is to commence each day anew and to commence at nothing; taking Christ afresh to be the Alpha and Omega for a deeper, higher, diviner experience, waiting even for His Conception of thought, desire, prayer, and afraid lest our highest thought should be below His great plan of wisdom and love.

Are there not some of us, beloved, who have been trying a good while to get back an old experience? If we succeeded we should only be where we were, and if we are only going to get where we were, we have abandoned the law of progress and begun the downward retrogression. God has Himself withered by His own consuming breath the flower and fragrance of your former joys, that He may lead you into something better. Let your old experience go, and take the living, everlasting Christ instead. Be willing to be enlarged according to His thought, and exceeding abundantly above all that you have yet been able to ask or think.

2. If we would be enlarged according to the thought of God, we must be delivered from all human standards, opinions and patterns, and accept nothing less than God's own divine ideal. Multitudes are kept from spiritual progress by cast-iron systems of doctrine which have settled forever the fact that holiness is impossible in the present life, and that "no mere man, since the fall, is able to keep the commandments of God, but doth daily break them in word, thought and deed." And then a row of human characters is set before us to prove the impossibility of sanctification, and to show the satisfying and humbling influence of human imperfection. Multitudes have made up their minds in advance that they never can have the fullness of Jesus beyond certain narrow limits, and, of course, they cannot advance beyond their standards. Now we quite agree with the statement that no mere man can be holy or blameless, but the Lord Jesus is no mere man, and when He owns and keeps the heart it is a divine holiness and a divine keeping; and we do assert that what no mere man can do the living Christ can do and does do for those who

abide in Him. Let us take the divine measure, whatever man may think or say.

Many also are ever looking to some human example, and, "measuring themselves by themselves and comparing themselves among themselves, are not wise." Either we shall find ourselves as good as somebody else and be content, or we shall be satisfied to be as some human ideal, and so shall stop short of the only perfect pattern. We shall never grow up to the measure of the Lord until we take the Lord's own word and character as our standard and ideal; until we take our stand upon the sure and immutable ground that He who commands holiness expects us to be holy, and that He who promises His own grace and all-sufficiency to enable us to meet his demands, will not excuse us if we fail. He has offered us Himself as the life and power of our obedience and holiness, and nothing less than His own perfect example should ever satisfy our holy ambition. Looking unto Him and pressing ever closer to His side and foot-prints, we shall be transformed into the same image, from glory to glory, and shall thus go from strength to strength.

3. If we would be enlarged we must accept all that God sends us as His own divinely appointed means of developing and expanding our spiritual life. We are so content to abide on the old plane that God has often to compel us to rise to a higher level by bringing us face to face with situations which we cannot meet without greatly enlarged measures of His grace. To use a suggestive figure, He has to send the tidal wave to flood the lowlands where we dwell that we may be compelled to move to the hills beyond; or, to take a more scriptural and beautiful figure, like the mother bird, He has to break up our downy nest and to hurl us into empty space, where we must either learn to use an entirely new and higher method of support or sink into destruction. Thus He al-

lowed the crisis of His terrible peril to close around Jacob on the night when he bowed at Peniel in supplication, in order to bring him to the place where he could take hold of God as he never would have done; and forth from that narrow pass of peril Jacob came enlarged in his faith and knowledge of God, and in the power of a new and victorious life. He had to suffer Israel to be shut in at the Red Sea that they might be compelled to take hold of God for their supernatural help, or perish. He had to compel David, by a long and painful discipline of years, to learn the almighty power and faithfulness of his God, and to grow up into the established principles of faith and godliness, which were indispensable for his subsequent and glorious career as the king of Israel. Nothing but the extremities in which Paul was constantly placed could ever have taught him, and taught the church through him, the full meaning of the great promise he so learned to claim, "My grace is sufficient for thee." And nothing but our trials and perils would ever have led some of us to know Him as we do, to trust Him as we have, and to draw from Him the measures of grace which our very extremities made indispensable.

Often He calls us to a work far beyond our natural strength or endowments, but the emergency only throws us upon Him, and we always find Him equal to the need which His wisdom and providence have brought in our way. It is said that good Mrs. Booth, the great associate leader of the Salvation Army, and perhaps the most gifted Christian woman in England, was led into all her public work by being compelled unexpectedly to face a large congregation and fill an appointment of which she had not dreamed. Two courses were open-one to shrink and evade the unexpected issue, the other to throw herself upon God for larger resources of wisdom, utterance and power. She was astonished at the answer which her Father gave as she went forward in simple confidence, and from that hour she dwelt in the large place of divine sufficiency and worldwide usefulness, into which she had almost been forced.

Many of us can remember how in the beginning of our Christian work we ventured to accept positions of responsibility for which we felt we were inadequate, but, as we threw ourselves upon God and dared to go forward, His grace was sufficient. When a young minister of twenty-one, and just leaving my theological seminary, I had the choice of two fields of labor-one an extremely easy one, in a delightful town with a refined, affectionate and prosperous church, just large enough to be an ideal field for one who wished to spend a few years in quiet preparation for future usefulness; the other, a large, absorbing city church, WITH many hundred members, and overwhelming and heavy burdens, which were sure to demand the utmost possible care, labor and responsibility. All my friends, teachers and counsellors advised me to take the easier place. But an impulse, which I now believe to have been, at least indirectly, from God, even though there must have been some human ambition in it, led me to feel that if I took the easier place I should probably rise to meet it and no more, and if I took the harder I should not rest short of all its requirements. I found it even so. My early ministry was developed and the habit of venturing on difficult undertakings was largely established, by the grace of God, through the necessities of this difficult position.

Let us then, beloved, be willing to be enlarged, although it may involve many a sacrifice, many a peril, many a hazardous undertaking.

4. If we would be enlarged let us take the Holy Ghost Himself to enlarge us by filling us with His fullness. The highest enlargement is by the power of expansion. It is the incoming

wave which enlarges the little pool as it fills it, and then rolls back to the sea to return with still larger fullness and make yet ampler room. Nothing so sweeps away the littleness of our conceptions of God, the pettiness of our faith, the narrowness of our love, the meanness of our self-consciousness, the insignificance of our work, as to be filled with His glorious presence, to look in His face, to feel the tides of His love, and to be thrilled with the touch of His own heart and its mighty thoughts and purposes for us and for the world for which He died. We need not say that the place to receive Him is the mercy seat. Waiting before Him in prayer, receiving Him in communion, drinking deeper and deeper of His life and love, the vessel is not only filled but expanded, until we know something of the prayer of the apostle in the third chapter of Ephesians, "that ye might be strengthened with might by His Spirit in the inner man; that Christ may dwell in your hearts by faith; that ye, being rooted and grounded in love, may be able to comprehend with all saints what is the length and breadth and depth and height, and to know the love of God which passeth knowledge, that ye might be filled with all the fullness of God."

5. If we would be enlarged to the full measure of God's purpose, let us endeavor to realize something of our own capacities for His filling. We little know the size of the human soul and spirit. Never, until He renews, cleanses and enters the heart can we have any adequate conception of the possibilities of the being whom God made in His very image, and whom He now renews after the pattern of the Lord Jesus Himself. When we remember that God has made the human soul to be His temple and abode, and that He knows how to make the house that can hold His infinite fullness, we may be very sure that there are capacities in the human spirit which none of us have ever yet begun to realize. We know some-

thing of them as all our nature quickens into spring-tide life at the coming of the Holy Spirit, and as from time to time new baptisms awaken the dormant powers and susceptibilities that we did not know we possessed.

But all this is but the beginning of an infinite possibility. Oh, how He has sometimes taken a low, coarse, brutal nature, that for "years has seemed to possess no capacity except for crime and sensuality, and made it not only as pure but as bright as an angel's mind, and brought forth from that brain, that voice, that tongue, that taste, that imagination, when illuminated and vivified by the Holy Ghost, such glorious fruitions as the life work of a Harry Moorhouse, the eloquence of a Richard Weaver, the marvelous allegory of a John Bunyan, and the exquisite hymns and poems of a Newton.

Oh, let us give Him the right to make the best of us, and, with wonder filled, we shall some day behold the glorious temple which He has reared, and shall say, "Lord, what is man that thou hast set thine heart upon Him?"

6. If we would rise to the full measure of God's standard for us, let us realize the magnitude of God as well as of our own being, for it is with nothing less than Himself that He means to fill us. Let us take in the full dimensions of His resources of grace, their length, their breadth, their depth, their height; and then let us measure, if we can, the magnitude of God who is the living substance and personal source of all this grace, and we shall have some approximation at least to what the apostle means when He exclaims, "Now unto Him that is able to do exceeding abundantly above all that we ask or think, according to the power that worketh in us, unto Him be glory in the church by Christ Jesus, throughout all ages, world without end. Amen."

7. And, finally, let us remember that we have eternal years in which to develop all this divine ideal. Oh, could we see our-

selves as we shall some day be, could we behold this morning that glorious creature that the universe shall some day come to behold in the image of the Son of God, could we see our faces shining as the sun in the kingdom of our Father, and hear the songs of rapture that will yet burst from our lips in higher notes than angels ever sung, we would wonder at the littleness of our faith to-day and our fear to ask our Father for the merest fraction in advance of our great inheritance.

This is no picture of the imagination. This is no soaring dream of hope or fancy, for He has told us that we shall be like Him when He shall appear. Oh, could we take you up to heaven this morning and let you gaze a single moment on the face of Jesus, shining "as the sun shineth in his strength;" could we comprehend the infinite wisdom that this very moment is taking in the whole sweep of the universe in the grasp of His thought, listening to a thousand prayers at once, administering the government of innumerable worlds, and yet at leisure to listen to our faintest cry; could we measure His omnipotence as He holds in His hands the reins of universal power and dominion; could we stand the vision of His beauty and feel the thrill of His love in all its ecstatic power-we would have some conception of what we are ourselves yet to be: for "we shall know even as we are known;" we shall share the work of His omnipotence; we shall shine in all His beauty; we shall reflect His moral perfections; we shall sit with Him upon His throne; we shall be invested with His transcendent glory; and all we receive of Him to-day is a mere instalment in advance of that which is already our own by right of inheritance, and which shall be actually realized as fast as we can take it in. We have eternity before us. Beloved, let us rise to the height of such a prospect even here; let us walk as those who dwell in heavenly places and share the resurrection and ascension life of their loving Head.

A. B. SIMPSON

Rise with thy risen Lord,
Ascend with Christ above,
And in the heavenlies walk with Him
Whom seeing not, you love.

Look on your trials here
As He beholds them now,
Look on this world as it will seem
When glory crowns your brow.

Walk as a heavenly race,
Princes of royal blood;
Walk as the children of the Lord,
The sons and heirs of God.

Fear not to take your place
With Jesus on the throne,
And bid the powers of earth and hell
His sovereign sceptre own.

Your full redemption rights
With holy boldness claim,
And to its utmost fullness prove
The power of Jesus' name.

Your life is hidden now,
Your glory none can see,
But when He comes His bride will shine
All glorious as He.

Chapter 5.
ISHMAEL AND ISAAC; OR, THE DEATH OF SELF

"Not I, but Christ." Gal. ii: 20.

The story of Abraham, Ishmael and Isaac is a parable, illustrating this text. The casting out of Ishmael is most clearly declared in this very epistle to be an allegory setting forth the spiritual experience of the believer when he dies to the law and sin through the cross of Jesus Christ, and comes into the resurrection life of his Risen Lord. But there is something more than the experience of Ishmael and our deliverance from the power of indwelling sin. In the patriarchal story, this was followed by the offering up of Isaac on Mount Moriah, and there can be no doubt that this sets forth the deeper spiritual experience into which the fully consecrated heart must come, when even the sanctified self is laid upon the altar like Isaac upon the mount, and we become dead henceforth, not only to sin, but to that which is worse than sin, even self.

> There is a foe whose hidden power
> The Christian well may fear;
> More subtle far than inbred sin
> And to the heart more dear.
>
> It is the power of selfishness,
> The proud and wilful I;
> And ere my Lord can live in me,
> My very self must die.

This is the lesson of Isaac's offering and Paul's experience. "I have been crucified with Christ," that is the death of sin; "nevertheless I live," that is the new life in the power of His resurrection; "yet not I, but Christ liveth in me," that is the offering of Isaac, the deliverance from self, and the substitution of Christ Himself for even the new self; a substitution so complete that even the faith by which this life is maintained is no longer our self-sustained confidence but the very "faith of the Son of God who loved me and gave Himself for me, that is, instead of me, and as my Substitute.

I. THE FORMS OF SELF.

We read in the book of Joshua of the three sons of Anak, who formed the Anakim, the race of giants who held the city of Hebron before Caleb's conquest, and were the terror of the Israelites. Literally Anak means long-necked, and represents pride, confidence, willfulness, and self-sufficiency. The first of the Anakim may be called,

1. Self-will, the disposition to rule, and especially to rule ourselves; the spirit that brooks no other will and is its own law and god. Therefore the first step in the consecrated life is unconditional surrender. This is indispensable to break the power of self at the centre, and to establish forever the absolute sovereignty of the will of God in the heart and life of the Christian. We cannot abide in holiness and we cannot be wholly used for God until self-will is so utterly crucified that we could not even think for an instant of acting contrary to His will or without His orders. This is obedience, and obedience is the law of the Christian life and must be absolute, unquestioning, and without any possible exception. "Ye are my friends if ye do whatsoever I command you."

It is true that God requires of us in the life of faith the exercise of a very strong will continually, and there is no doubt that faith itself is largely the exercise of a sanctified and intensified will, but in order to this it is necessary that our will be wholly renounced and God's will invariably accepted instead, and then we can put into it all the strength and force of our being, and will it even as God wills it, and because He wills it. In short, it is an exchanged will; the despotic tyranny of Anak exchanged for the wise, beneficent yet still more absolute sovereignty of God.

2. Self-confidence is the next of Anak's race. It is the spirit that draws its strength from self alone and disdains the arm of God and the help of His grace. In a milder form it is the spirit that trusts its own spiritual graces or virtues, its morality perhaps, its courage, its faith, its purity, its steadfastness, its joy, and its transitory emotions of hope, enthusiasm, or zeal. It is just as necessary to die to our self-sufficiency as to our self-will. If we do not we shall have many a fall and failure until we learn, with the most triumphant and successful laborer that ever followed the footsteps of his Lord, that "we are not sufficient of ourselves to think anything as of ourselves, but our sufficiency is of God." The sanctified heart is not a self-constituted engine of power, but is just a set of wheels and pulleys that are absolutely dependent upon the great central engine whose force is necessary continually to move them. It is just a capacity to hold God; just a vessel to be filled with His goodness, held and used by His hand; just a possibility of which He, in His abiding life, is constantly the motive power and impelling force. The word "consecrate "in Hebrew means "to fill the hand," and beautifully suggests the idea of an empty hand which God Himself must continually fill.

3. Self-glorying is the last and most impious of these Canaanitish tribes. He takes the very throne of Jehovah and claims the glory due unto Him alone. Sometimes it is a desire for human praise. Sometimes it is more subtle, the pride so proud that it will not stoop to care for the approval of others, and its supreme delight is in its own self-consciousness and superiority, ability or goodness. Metaphysicians have sometimes made this happy distinction, that vanity is an inferior vice to

pride. Vanity only seeks the praise of others, but pride disdains the opinions of others and rests back in the complacent consciousness of its own excellency. Whatever its phase may be, the root and principle is the same. It is impious self, sitting on the throne of God, and claiming the honor and glory that belong to Him alone.

These three forms of self are illustrated by three very solemn examples in the word of God. Saul the first king of Israel is a fearful monument of the peril of self-will. His downward career began in a single act of disobedience, a disobedience which seemed to have respect to a mere question of detail, but which was really an act of self-will, a substitution of his choice for God's express command. The prophet Samuel characterizes his sin in these very expressive words, "To obey is better than sacrifice, and to hearken than the fat of rams. For rebellion is as the sin of witchcraft (or devil worship), and stubbornness is as iniquity and idolatry. Because thou hast rejected the word of the Lord, He hath also rejected thee from being king." It is evident from these words that the very essence of Saul's sin lay in this element of willfulness and stubbornness which had dared to substitute his own ideas and preferences for the word of Jehovah. From this moment his obedience was necessarily qualified and of course worthless, and God sent His prophet to choose another king, who, although full of human imperfections, had this one thing on which God could fully depend, namely, a purpose to obey God when he fully understood His will. Therefore God calls David "a man after my own heart who shall perform all my will." David made many mistakes and committed many dark and terrible sins, but they were when under strong temptation and when blinded by passion and haste, but never with the purpose of disobeying God, or, at the time, with the consciousness that he was transgressing. The sad, sad story of Saul's downward descent and final and

A Larger Christian Life

tragic ruin should be enough to make us tremble at the peril which lies before the willful soul, and to lead us to cry, "Not my will but thine be done."

We have just as marked an instance of the peril of self-confidence in Simon Peter. Strong in his transitory enthusiasm, and ignorant of the real weakness of his own heart, he honestly meant what he said, when he exclaimed, "Though all men should deny thee yet will I never deny thee." But alas! the shameful denial, the upbraiding look of Jesus, the bitter tears of penitence and the sad days of the crucifixion that followed had to teach him the lesson of his nothingness, and the necessity of walking henceforth with downward head in the strength of the Lord alone.

We are not left without as vivid and impressive an object lesson of the last form of self-will-the pride that glories in its own achievements or excellencies. "Is not this great Babylon that I have built?" cries Nebuchadnezzar, in the hour of his triumph, as he looks upon that splendid city, which was indeed a paragon of human glory, and surveys in his imagination the mightier empire of which it was the metropolis, an empire which literally comprised the world. If mortal could ever have cause to glory in earthly magnificence, Nebuchadnezzar had, for God Himself had compared him and his kingdom to a majestic head of gold and had symbolized his power under the figure of a winged lion, combining the majesty and sovereignty of the eagle and the lion in one splendid image. But the very instant that vain-glorious word reached the ears of God, the answer fell from heaven like a knell of judgment, "The kingdom is departed from thee. And they shall drive thee from men, and thy dwelling shall be with the beasts of the field, till thou know that the Most High ruleth in the kingdom of men, and giveth it to whomsoever He will." This is the glorying of the carnal heart, but even the follower of God may mingle his own self-seeking and his own honor with his work for God and thus impair his usefulness and lose his own recompense.

There is not a more pitiful picture in the long panorama of the Bible than that morbid and grumbling prophet, sitting outside the gates of Nineveh under a withered gourd, his face blistered and swollen with the scorching sun and his eyes red with useless weeping; asking God that he might die, because his ministry had been dishonored; and presenting a spectacle of ridiculous melancholy and chagrin while all around him millions were rejoicing and praising God for the mercy which had just delivered them from an awful catastrophe. Poor Jonah! God had given him the most honorable ministry ever yet accorded to a human being. The first foreign missionary, he had been sent to preach to the mightiest empire on the face of the globe and the imperial city of the world, proud Nineveh! His preaching had been successful as no mortal ever had succeeded. The whole city was lying prostrate on their faces at the footstool of mercy in penitence and prayer through his words, and the nation's heart, for a moment at least, was turned to God. And yet so full of himself had all his work been, so utterly was he absorbed in his own credit, reputation and honor, that when God listened to the penitent cries of the Ninevites and revoked the sentence which Jonah himself had uttered, and rendered his prophecy null and void, so that instead of his word coming to pass he himself would probably be afterwards ridiculed as a fanatic and idle alarmist, poor Jonah became disgusted and exasperated and like a petted child went out and threw himself upon his face on the ground and asked God to kill him, just because He had by His mercy spoiled his reputation as a true prophet. He could not see, as God did, the unspeakable horror and anguish that had been averted. He could not see the joy of the divine heart in exercising mercy and in hearing the penitent cries of the people. He could not see the great principle of grace which underlies the divine threatenings. He could not see that great-souled pity, that felt for the one hundred and twenty thousand infant children of the great capital, or the dumb brutes, which would have moaned in their dying agony, if Nineveh had fallen.

All he could see was Jonah's reputation as a true prophet or what people might say when they found that his word had not come to pass; and with that one little worm gnawing at the root, his peace and happiness, like his own gourd, withered away, and God had to set him up as a sort of dried specimen of selfishness, to show the meanness and misery of the self-life that mingles its own glory with the sacred work of the glorious God, and which, ever since the days of Jonah, has rendered it impossible for God to use many a gifted man, and has blighted the church of Christ and rendered vain the ministry of thousands because God could not use them without giving to men the glory which He will never give to another. God had tried to kill Jonah before He sent him to Nineveh, for He knew the secret bane of his heart, and so He immersed him for three days and nights in the sea and buried him in the bowels of a whale; but out of that Jonah came, as a great many other people come out of the experience of sanctification with a big self, supreme even in the sin-cleansed soul. Oh let us lift up the heart-felt prayer,

O to be saved from myself, dear Lord,
O to be lost in Thee!
O that it may be no more!
But Christ that lives in me!

II. THE EFFECTS OF SELF.

1. It dishonors God and sets up a rival on His throne. The devil was not altogether a liar when he said to our first parents, "Ye shall be as gods." This is just what fallen man tries to be, a god unto himself. This is the essence of the sin of selfishness,

that it puts man in the place of God by making him a law and an end unto himself. Whenever, any person acts, either because it is his own selfish will, or for his own self-interest, purely as an end, he is claiming to be his own god and directly disobeying the first commandment, "Thou shalt have no other gods besides Me." Moreover, in assuming the place of God, he is doing it in a spirit the very opposite of God's, for God is love, and love is the very opposite of selfishness. He is thus mimicking God and proving, at the same time, his utter unfitness to occupy His throne by his unlikeness to Him.

2. It leads to every other sin and brings back the whole power of the carnal nature. For while self alone attempts to keep the heart it finds sin and Satan too strong. A self- perfection is not possible for any man. There must be more than "I" before there can be victory. In the seventh of Romans the apostle tells us what "I, myself" can do and that is, ineffectually struggle. In the eighth it is what "Christ in me" can do, and that is victory and everlasting love. The man or woman who only goes so far as to receive Adamic purity, if such a thing be included in the Gospel at all, will soon have the next chapter of Adamic history, and that is the temptation and fall. But the man who receives Christ to dwell within and keep the heart by His mighty power, shall rise "to the measure of the stature of the fullness of Christ."

3. The self-life leads back to the dominion of Satan. Satan's own fall began probably in a form of self-love. Made to be dependent on God every moment, probably he became independent; and contemplating his own perfection, and thinking it was something that was his own, he became separated from God, and then inevitably fell into rebellion against Him and eternal rivalry, disobedience and all that can be the opposite of the divine and the holy. And so still, any soul that becomes self-constituted or occupied with its own virtues,

and tries to be independent of Jesus, either as the source of its strength or the supreme end of its being, will fall under the power of Satan and share his awful descent. Where can we find a sadder illustration of the end of self than in the story of Saul? He began with Saul and ended with Satan. The first chapter is self-will, the last is the awful night at Endor and the bloody day of death and ruin on Mount Gilboa.

4. It is fatal to the spirit of love and harmony. It is the opposite of love and the source of strife, bigotry, suspicion, sectarianism, envy, jealousy and the whole race of social sins and grievances that afflict the Christian life and the church of God. It is the mother of the strifes and sectarianisms of the church from the very beginning. Where it prevails there can be no true unity, no happy co-operation. You never can have a harmonious church or a happy family where self is predominant in the hearts of the people. The very secret of Christian co-operation and happy church life is "forbearing one another in love," endeavoring to keep the unity of the Spirit in the bond of peace, "in honor preferring one another."

5. It mars our work for God. Self-will will try to force the chariots of God's power and grace upon our own side-tracks, and that God will never permit. Self-confidence will seek to build up the kingdom of Christ by human means and unsanctified instrumentalities, and presume to go where God has not sent and to do what God has not qualified us by His Holy Spirit to do. The result is, it is but crude work, defiled by worldliness and sin, impermanent and unfruitful, as much of the Christian work of to-day is, in all the churches of Christ. And above all others, the spirit of self-glorying will try to use the pulpit, the organ gallery, the subscription books, the religious paper, the charitable scheme, the very mission for winning souls, as a channel for developing some brilliant character, or to glorify some rich man or woman, or minister to the

spiritual self-sufficiency of some successful worker; and God is disgusted with the spirit of idolatry, and His Holy Spirit turns away grieved for the honor of Jesus. Until we are so yielded to our Master that He and He alone can be glorified in our work, the Lord cannot trust us with much service for Him or it will simply become the pinnacle of the temple from which the devil will hurl us down.

6. Self makes us unhappy. It is a root of bitterness in every heart where it reigns. The secret of joy is hidden in the bosom of love, and the arms of self are too short ever to reach it. Not until we dwell in God and God in us, and learn to find our happiness in being lost in Him and living for His glory and for His people, shall we ever know the sweets of divine blessedness. All the world cannot fill this hungry heart. All our spiritual treasures only corrupt if we hoard them for ourselves. Only water that runs is living water. And only when it is poured into other empty vessels does it become wine. The self-willed man is always a miserable man. He gets his own way and does not enjoy it, and wishes after he has had it, that he had never got it, for it usually leads him over a precipice. The self-sufficient man can never know the springs which lie outside his own little heart, and the self-glorying man, like poor Herod, is eaten of the worms of corruption and remorse with which God always feeds the impious soul that dares to claim the honors due to Him alone.

7. Self-love always leads to a fall. The boasted wisdom must be proved to be foolishness. The proud arm must be laid, like Pharaoh's, in the dust. The self-sufficient boast, like Peter's, must be answered by his own failure. The disobedient path which refuses God's wise and holy will, must be proved to be a false way. Every idol must be abolished, every high thing brought low, and no flesh glory in His presence. Oh, beloved, if you are going on in your own will, your own strength, for

your own gratification and glory, beware! Thorns lie in your pathway, serpents lurk beneath your feet, yawning abysses, perilous precipices, angry tempests, midnight darkness, many a sorrow, many a tear, many a fall, await you. "He that trusteth in his own heart is a fool." "There is a way that seemeth right unto a man, but the ends thereof are the ways of death."

Oh, let us ask our faithful God to save us from this tyrant that dishonors God, that leads us into captivity to Satan, that withers love, mars the work of God, poisons all our happiness; and plunges us into failure and ruin; and so to show us that we are nothing, that we shall be glad to have Christ live in us, our "all in all."

III. THE REMEDY FOR SELF.

1. God often has to let self have its way until it cures us effectually by showing us the misery and failure which it brings. This is the only good there is in our own struggling, that it shows us the vanity of the struggle and prepares us the more quickly to surrender to God. And so sometimes even our disobedience is overruled to make us fear to repeat the experiment or to venture again one step beyond our Father's will. Let us beware, however, how we attempt the experiment ourselves, for there is always one step too far ever to return.

2. God has placed around us the blessed restraints of other hearts and lives as checks upon our selfishness, and links, which almost compel us to reach beyond ourselves and, work with and live for others. He has made no man independent of his brethren. "We are fitly framed together" and so grow into a holy temple in the Lord. We are adjusted, one to His bone, and, by that which every joint supplieth, the body is ministered unto and groweth into the fullness of His stature. The church of Christ is no autocracy where one man can be a dictator or a judge, but a fellowship where

One alone is Master. Any work which develops into a one-man despotism becomes withered. It is true that God has ranks of workers, but they are all harmonious and linked in heavenly love. The man who cannot work with his brethren in mutual comfort and harmony has something yet to learn in his own Christian life. True, God does not require us to work with unsanctified men; but there are plenty of sanctified ones, thank God, to-day, where any earnest heart can find a congenial fellowship of service; and while He will teach any of us by ourselves, and wants us to be independent of our brethren in the sense of leaning on them instead of' God, yet He does require that we should be able to co-operate with them for God, submitting ourselves one to another in the fear of God, one sowing and another reaping, and both rejoicing together, "bearing one another's burdens and so fulfilling the law of Christ," "true yoke-fellows." And so by innumerable phrases and figures He has taught us the blessed truth of Christian cooperation in the spirit of self-renunciation and mutual confidence and love. Let us receive these blessed lessons and helps, and let Him so slay in us the self-asserting "I" that we can be true yoke-fellows, and like David's men, be able to "keep rank" in the great host of God.

3. The love of Jesus is the divinely appointed prescription for the death of self. Paul expresses it beautifully, "We thus judge that if one died for all then were all dead. And that He died for all that they which live should not henceforth live unto themselves, but unto Him that died for them and rose again." Many of us have seen at some time a young, beautiful, petted, luxurious and selfish girl, growing up surrounded with wealth, affection, admiration, adulation, until she was wholly spoiled, and became the centre of the circle in which she lived, her whole being perverted by her selfishness. But we have seen that girl years afterwards, and we would not have

known her had we not traced the intermediate steps. She was now a self-denying, loving wife and mother, her whole being devoted to the happiness of that husband whose fortunes she had followed amid poverty, obscurity and separation from all her former friends; sharing his penury, toiling for his comfort, and nursing as a faithful and loving mother, the little children who had come into her arms, with the love that never wearied, that felt no task too hard, and no work too menial. What has made all the difference? What has cast out that idol, self, from its throne? Nothing but love. That man has won her heart. He has come in and taken the place that it had occupied; it is cast out and he reigns. That is the simple story of the death of self in the Christian life. It is the love of Jesus that has excluded it, and never, until we become fascinated with His affection, and won in complete captivity to His love, shall we cease to live unto ourselves. Then, like that girl, we will follow Him anywhere. We will toil and suffer with Him. We will be content without many things that before we thought we must have, because His smile is our sunshine, His presence is our joy, His love, shed abroad in our hearts, is our heaven, and we cannot speak or think of sacrifice or suffering, our heart is so satisfied with Him.

Beloved, if you would die to self you must fall in love with Jesus and let Him become to you the personal reality of Solomon's sweet Song in which the whole heart summers into a land of Beulah and a "Hephzibah" of joy.

4. But it is not the love of Christ merely that we want; it is the living Christ Himself. Many people have touches of the love of Christ, but He is a Christ away up in heaven. The apostle speaks of something far mightier. It is Christ Himself who lives inside and who is big enough to crowd out and keep out the little "I." There is no other that can truly lift and keep the heart above the power of self but Jesus, the Mighty Lord,

the stronger than the strong man armed, who taketh away his armour wherein he trusted and spoileth all his goods and then takes forever the heart that has given him its goods. Blessed Christ! He is able not only for sin, sorrow and sickness, put He is able for you and me-able so to be our very life, that moment by moment we shall be conscious that He in us fills us with Himself and conquers the self that ruled before. The more you try to fight a self-thought the more it clings to you. The moment you turn away from it and look to Him, He fills all the consciousness and disperses everything with His own presence. Let us abide in Him, and we shall find there is nothing else to do.

5. It is almost the same thing, but another way of saying it, that the baptism and indwelling of the Holy Ghost within us will deliver and keep us from the power of self. When the cloud of glory entered the tabernacle there was no room for Moses to remain; and when filled with the heavenly presence of the blessed Spirit we are lost in God and self hides away, and like Job we can say, "Now mine eye seeth Thee. Wherefore I abhor myself and repent in dust and ashes."

Beloved, these temples were reared for Him. Let Him fill them so completely that like the oriental temple of glass in the ancient legend, the temple shall not be seen, but only the glorious sunlight, which not only shines into it, but through it, and the transparent walls are all unseen.

It is not a new, but it is an appropriate thought, that all the things that God has used have first been sacrificed. It is a sacrificed Saviour, One who emptied Himself, and made Himself of no reputation, that God has so highly exalted, and given Him a name that is above every name, "that at the name of Jesus every knee should bow, of things in heaven and things in earth and things under the earth." It was a sacrificed Isaac that God made the promised seed and the progenitor of Israel's tribes. And it was on that very Mount Moriah where Isaac was sacrificed, that God afterwards reared His glorious temple. And so it is only when our Isaac is on the altar and our whole being lost in God that He can lay the deep foundations and rear the everlasting walls of the living temple of which He is the Supreme and eternal glory.

I look back to-day with unutterable gratitude to the lonely and sorrowful night, when, mistaken in many things, and imperfect in all, my heart's first full consecration was made, and not knowing but that it would be death in the most literal sense before the morning light, yet with unreserved surrender I first could say,

«Jesus, I my cross have taken,
All to leave and follow thee;
Destitute, despised, forsaken,
Thou from hence my All shalt be."

Never, perhaps, has my heart known quite such a thrill of joy as when the following Sabbath morning I gave out those lines and sung them with all my heart. And if God has been pleased to make my life in any measure a little temple for His indwelling and for His glory, and if He ever shall be pleased to use me in any fuller measure, it has been because of that hour, and it will be still in the measure in which that hour is made the key-note of a consecrated, crucified and Christ-devoted life.

Oh, beloved, come and let Him teach you the superlative degree of joy, the joy that has learned to say not only, "My Beloved is mine," but better even, "I am my Beloved's;" and we shall find as one of our dear missionaries in China used to say, "He is willing to come into the heart of every one of us and love us to death."

Chapter 6.
"MORE THAN CONQUERORS"

> "Nay, in all these things we are more than conquerors through Him that loved us."-Rom. viii : 37.

It is a great thing to be a conqueror in Christian life and conflict. It is a much greater thing to be a conqueror "in all these things" which the apostle names, a perfect host of trials, troubles and foes. But what does it mean to be "more than conqueror"?

1. It means to have a decisive victory. There are some victories that cost nearly as much as defeats, and a few more such triumphs would annihilate us. There are some battles which have to be renewed again and again until we are exhausted with the ceaseless strife. Many a Christian is kept in constant warfare through lack of courage to venture on a bold and final contest and end the strife by a decisive victory. It is blessed so to die that we are dead indeed; so to yield that the last strand of the heart's reluctance is severed; so to say "no" to the enemy that he will never repeat the solicitation. There are decisive battles in the world's history, conflicts whose issues settle the future of an empire or of a world, and the soul has such battles too. God is able to give us the grace so to win in a few en-counters that there shall be no doubt about the side on which the victory falls and no danger of the contest ever being renewed again. Other battles we may have and shall have, but surely it is possible for us to settle the questions that meet us, one by one, and settle them forever.

    Beloved, are not some of you weakened by this indecisiveness in your views of truth, in your steps of faith, in your refusals of temptation, in your surrender to God, in your consecration to His service and your obedience to His special call? You have been just uncertain enough to keep the question open and tempt the adversary to renew the conflict evermore. We sometimes read in God's word after one of David's hardest conflicts, or one of Joshua's boldest triumphs, "the land had rest from war!" Thus we have rest by becoming "more than conquerors through Him that loved us."

2. It is to have such a victory as will effectually break the adversary's power and not only defend us from his attacks but effectually weaken and destroy his strength. This is one of the purposes of temptation, that we may be workers together with God in destroying evil. We read of Joshua's battles that "it was of the Lord that these kings should come against Joshua in battle for this very purpose, that they might be utterly destroyed." It was not enough for Israel to beat them off and be saved from their attacks, but God wanted them exterminated. And so when God allows the enemy to appear in our lives it is that we may do him irreparable and eternal injury, and thus glorify God and be workers with Christ in destroying the works of the devil. For this purpose God frequently brings to light in our own lives and in our work for God, evils that were concealed, not that they might crush us, but that we might put them aside. But for their discovery and resistance they might still have remained unrevealed and some day have broken out with fatal effectiveness. But God allows them to be provoked into activity in order to challenge our resistance and lead to our aggressive and victorious advance against them. Therefore when we find anything in our own hearts and lives, or in connection with the work of our Master committed to our hands, which seems to threaten our triumph or His work, let us remember that God has allowed it to confront us, that, in His name, it might be forever put aside and rendered powerless to injure or oppose again.

Beloved, are we thus fighting the good fight of faith, resisting the devil and rising up for God against them that do wickedly? Are we looking upon our adversaries and our obstacles as things that have come, not to crush us, but to be put aside and become tributary to our successes and our Master's glory? Thus shall we be "more than conquerors through Him that loved us," and as the prophet beautifully expresses it, "Behold, all they that were incensed against thee shall be ashamed and confounded: they shall be as nothing; and they that strive with thee shall perish. Thou shalt seek them and shalt not find them, even them that contended with thee: they that war against thee shall be as nothing and as a thing of naught."

3. It is to have such a victory as brings actual benefit out of the battle and makes it tributary to our own and our Master's cause. It is possible in a certain sense to take our enemies prisoners and make them fight in our ranks, or at least do the menial work of our camp. It is possible to get such good out of Satan's assaults that he shall actually become our ally without intending it and shall find with eternal chagrin that he has been doing us real service. Doubtless he thought, when he stirred up Pharaoh to murder the little children of the Hebrews, that he was exterminating a race of which he was afraid. But that very act of his brought Moses into Pharaoh's house and raised up a deliverer for Israel and the destroyer of Pharaoh. Surely that was being "more than conqueror!" The devil was not only beaten but made to work in the Lord's chain-gang as a galley slave. Again, he overmatched himself when he instigated Haman to build his lofty gallows and send forth the decree for Israel's extermination, for he had the misery of seeing Haman hang on those gallows and Israel delivered. So again, no doubt, he put the Hebrew children into the furnace and Daniel into the den of lions hoping to destroy the last remnant of godliness on the earth, but lo! these heroes were "more than conquerors." Not only did they escape their destroyer, but their deliverance

led to the proclamation of Nebuchadnezzar, magnifying the truth of God through the entire Babylonian empire, and to the similar confession of Darius, recognizing God throughout all the confines of the still greater Persian empire. Surely Satan was more than beaten that time!

His most audacious attempt was the crucifixion of our Lord, and all hell, no doubt, held high jubilee on that dark afternoon when Jesus sank to death; but lo! the cross has become the weapon by which Satan's head is already bruised and his kingdom is yet to be exterminated. So God makes him forge the weapons of his own destruction, and hurl the thunderbolts that fall back upon his own head. So may we ever thus turn his fiercest assaults to our advantage, and to the glory of our King.

It is very interesting to look at the old frontispiece in Wickliffe' s Bible, where a group of figures are gathered round a fire which is bursting through the open pages of a holy Bible. Their countenances all wear a look of consternation, and with one consent they are gathered round the fire, trying to blow it out. There are bishops and archbishops of the church of Rome, and the devil at the head of the crowd, all blowing lustily with swollen cheeks and strained countenances. But lo! the more they blow the more it burns, until at last the fierce blaze leaps up so high and out so far and wide that they are obliged to shrink back, and even Satan himself, though used to such an atmosphere, is glad to escape from its consuming flame. So let us overcome and more than overcome our spiritual foes.

The best thing they do for us often is the discipline they bring us in our spiritual life. In this way, and in this alone, do we learn to exercise victorious faith and endure hardness as good soldiers of Jesus Christ. The two things that the Christian needs most are the power to believe and the power to suffer, and these the enemy often comes to teach us. Not until we are ready to sink beneath the pressure do we often learn the secret of triumph. It was a great thing for the American nation that she had the Mexican War before she had the War of the Rebellion. It was there that her officers were trained and fitted to lead the armies of the greater struggle. So the Lord lets the devil act as drill sergeant in His army, and teach His children the use of His spiritual weapons. So we may "count it all joy when we fall into divers temptations; knowing that the trying of our faith worketh patience."

This, indeed, is to be "more than conqueror," to learn such lessons from the enemy as will fit us for his next assaults and prepare us to meet him without fear of defeat. There are some things that cannot easily be learned. Our spiritual senses seem to require the pressure of difficulty and suffering to awaken all their capacities and to constrain us to prove the full resources of heavenly grace. God's school of faith always is trial, and God's school of love is provocation and wrong. Instead therefore of murmuring against our lot and wondering why we are permitted to be so tried, let us glorify God and put our adversary to shame by wringing a blessing from Satan's hate and hell's hostility, and we shall find, after a while, that the enemy will be glad to let us alone for his own sake if not for ours.

4. To be " more than conqueror" is not only to have the victory, but the spoils of victory. When Jehoshaphat's army won their great deliverance from the hordes of Moab and Ammon, it took them three days to gather all the spoils of their enemies camps. When David captured the camp of Ziklag' s destroyers he won so vast a booty that he was able to send rich presents over all Israel among his brethren. When the lepers found their way to the deserted camp of the Syrians they found such abundance that in a single hour the famine of Samaria was turned into satiety. And so our spiritual con-

flicts and conquests have their rich reward in the treasures recovered from the hands of the enemy. How many things there are which Satan possesses which we might and should enjoy! Oh, the rich delight which fills the heart when we expel the giants of ill-temper, irritation, haste, hatred, malice and envy who long have ravaged and preyed upon all the sweetness of our life. What a luxuriant land we now enter into, when we overcome these foes, and how delightfully the spoils of peace and love and sweetness and heavenly joy are enriching us in the very things where once they reigned! How rich the spoils recovered from the cruel adversary when through the name of Jesus he is driven from our body, and the suffering frame which had groaned and trembled under his oppression springs into health and freedom and yields all the fullness of its strength to the service of God and the joy of a victorious life. Oh, the rich reward that comes to the home that has been rescued from the dominancy of the devil, perhaps in the form of drunkenness in a husband and father, or of shameful lust, or sinful vanity, or empty frivolity, or heartless worldliness, or bitter strife, evil speaking and anger in some other heart, and life once more becomes a happy Eden, with love and peace enthroned by the hearth and altar of a Christian home. Oh, the rich spoils that are to come from a world rescued from the hand of its cruel usurper. How it will bloom again in beauty, fruitfulness and blessedness, and yield its riches to its benignant and rightful King and to those who dare to conquer it for Him and shall share with Him its happy Millennial sway!

God takes special delight in making that a blessing to us which has been recovered from Satan's power. The two mightiest strongholds of ancient Canaan were Hebron and Zion. The former was the seat of the Anakim, the giant chieftains of Canaan; but the brave, heroic Caleb dared to challenge them in their lair, and in the strength of God was "more than conqueror" over their terrific strength, and won the heights of Hebron as his special inheritance. But not only did he receive the dear old city of Abraham as his portion and spoil, but God took peculiar delight in subsequently blessing and honoring this very place, it would seem, just because it had been snatched from the very jaws of the enemy; for Hebron was the chosen seat where David's throne was subsequently established, and where God began the kingdom of Israel which He Himself is yet to rule in the coming age of Israel's restoration.

Still more defiant was the strength of the citadel of Zion. It was the last stronghold that the Canaanites relinquished. All through the days of Joshua and his successors they succeeded in holding it; all through the centuries of the Judges, all through the days of Saul, all through the early days of even David's kingdom. The fortress was impregnable so that the haughty Canaanites told their enemies in scorn that they would only deign to garrison it with the blind and the lame and they challenged them to capture it from its feeble and crippled defenders. But David met the challenge and Joab executed it by a glorious assault and took by storm the heights of Zion from the last chieftains of Canaan. Then it was that Israel found its true metropolis and the rescued stronghold was set apart by God Himself to be the very seat of the sacred kingdom and the monument of the glorious victory which had been achieved. There it was that David reigned; there it was that Solomon in all his glory swayed his glorious sceptre; there it was that the temple rose from the adjoining heights of Moriah full in view of Zion; there it is that Jesus is coming soon to reign once more. Oh, how rich and glorious the recompense of a single victory! How different the world's history if the old Canaanites had still been permitted to hold the heights of Jebus!

Beloved, the richest treasure of your life is held by Satan. He is too shrewd to waste his strength upon what is worthless. He has put his hand upon the sweetest, dearest and most precious things of life, and whether in your heart, in your home, or in your circle of acquaintance, there you may be sure there is a Hebron or a Zion that God wants you to overcome, and in overcoming which you shall find the richest inheritance of your life and your eternity, and shall forever say with rejoicing, as you realize the full meaning of your victory, "more than conqueror through Him that loved us."

5. "More than conquerors" means not only the spoils of war and triumph over all the assaults of our foes, but it means new territory, aggressive warfare, and positive and even larger conquests for the glory of our Lord and the salvation of others. Merely to beat back your foes is but a small part of the great commission of the Christian soldier. He is called not only to wield the shield of faith but also the sword of the Spirit by which he moves against the conquered foe and claims new territory with each advance. We have the armor of righteousness on the right hand and on the left. The armor on the left is for defense, but the armor on the right is for aggression. We are called, not only to "withstand in the evil day," but to go forth and reclaim the world for Christ. Such conflicts meet us in our Christian work at every step, in the souls we seek to win for Jesus, in the progress of truth, the spread of the gospel, the awakening and reviving of the church of God, the elevation of Christian life and holiness, the suppression of evil in all its myriad and gigantic forms around us, the evangelization of the world and the hastening of our Master's Kingdom and Coming. Surely we should not be ever occupied in holding our own salvation. Indeed, we shall hold it best by leaving it with God and pressing on to claim the salvation of others.

In the last great European war the aggressors were the victors. If Germany had waited to be attacked and simply defended herself, probably she might have failed. But with wise and prompt aggression she hurled her hosts across the Rhine and into the battlefields of France and marched from victory to victory, her recompense being not only the conquest of her enemy's country, but the security of her own as well and her citizens, from even the touch of the enemy.

This is the best way to keep the devil off our territory; keep him busy on his own, defending his kingdom from our bold attacks. Beloved, have we settled the question of our own salvation and Christian life, and are we at leisure for the battles of the Lord and thus "more than conquerors through Him that loved us"?

6. "More than conquerors" means not only to win your battle and save your territory, but to do honor to your Captain and your God, to be a credit to your cause and so to acquit yourself in the campaign that God shall be glorified. Many of our battles are fought in view of heaven alone. That is a strange picture that the apostle gives of his trials, "We are made a gazing-stock to angels and principalities." Have you not felt, beloved, in some quiet hour, in the secret of your closet, that you were going through a decisive battle which no mortal saw. Within the silent walls of your chamber an issue was being decided which would affect all eternity. The question was, should you be true to God, should you trust Him, should you obey God, or should you compromise? It was a great thing for you that you gained the victory, but it was a greater thing for your Lord. Oh, how intently He watches these spectacles! How the ranks of hell and heaven look on as some David and Goliath fight alone amidst the gaze of other worlds! How your Saviour's brow flushes with shame if you betray Him, or even shrink! How the ranks of

hell shout with satisfaction when you betray the slightest weakness! And how your Master smiles with glad approval and sees of the travail of His soul with satisfaction, as like some ancient hero you dare to answer, "Our God is able to deliver us, but if not we will not bow down to the graven image which thou hast set up."

Do you know, beloved, that Christ's greatest victories were alone with God and the devil? No human eye saw that victory in the wilderness, but God saw it and was glorified. Shall we stand for Him, and so stand that He can count us, as He did His ancient prophet, His very towers and fortresses behind which He can intrench Himself and His cause, and say to us, "I have made thee this day a defenced city and an iron pillar and brazen walls against the whole land. They shall fight against thee, but they shall not prevail against thee. I have made thy face strong against their faces and thy forehead against their foreheads. As an adamant, harder than flint have I made thy forehead; fear them not, neither be dismayed at their looks though they be a rebellious house." God wants men and women today, on whom He can depend, to stand as bulwarks and battlements against the shocks of hell's artillery. Men and women of whom he can say, "upon this rock have I built my church and the gates of hell shall not prevail against it." Shall we, beloved, be not only conquerors, but trusted soldiers whom God can use as His battle-axes and His weapons of war, as His mighty ironclads, to carry the battle to the very ships of the enemy, not fearing their hardest blows, and hurling against them the thunder-bolts of His victorious power?

7. "More than conquerors" means not only victory but final triumph and eternal reward. How Heaven will recompense her victors some glorious day! Two cities today are struggling for the tomb of the man who was honored in this land as the

leader of the victorious army that won the battle of the Rebellion. He is honored simply because he was a conqueror. How little these earthly victories will seem some day in the light of the triumph of a Stephen, a Paul, a David Livingstone, or some gentle woman or lowly man, who stood faithful to God on some quiet battlefield which decided the issues of life, perhaps the future of nations and ages!

For four things Paul expected a crown, but the first of them was because he had fought the good fight of faith. Among the special recompenses of the Day of His Appearing there is a crown, not only for the martyr, not only for the faithful minister, not only for those who love His appearing, but for "the man that endureth temptation." "Blessed is the man that endureth temptation, for when he is tried he shall receive the crown of life which the Lord hath promised to them that love Him." There is a chance for all of you. There is a chance for you who think that you have the hardest time of any human being.

Beloved, it is but an opportunity for coronation. Will you not only triumph, but so triumph that you shall wear a crown of life in which these tears which you shed today shall flash as crystal diamonds, and these scars of battle shall be transformed into marks of eternal beauty and everlasting honor?

But mere enthusiasm or even high and glorious purpose will not accomplish this great result. It is "through Him that loved us" that we must overcome. Thank God that is possible for us all! He whom Joshua saw as Captain of the Lord's Host and whom Joshua took as his Great Commander-in-chief waits to lead your battle and claim your victory too. "I have overcome for thee," He stands exclaiming by thy side. Commit thy conflict to His hands, take Him into thy heart as strength, "be strong in the Lord and the power of

His might," and "put on the whole armor of God that ye may stand against the wiles of the devil." "The battle is not yours but God's." "The Lord shall fight for you, and ye shall hold your peace," and when all is accomplished and the banner waves in triumph and the crown is bestowed, we shall drape our battle-flags around His throne, and lay our diadems at His feet, and cry, not the old version, "Thanks be unto God which always causeth us to triumph," but "thanks be unto God which leadeth us in triumph through Jesus Christ our Lord." "In all these things we are more than conquerors through Him that loved us."

Chapter 7.
GRACE ABOUNDING

"Where sin abounded grace did much more abound."
Rom. v: 20.

We find in nature a beautiful approximation to the truth declared in this verse, a sort of parable and symbol of the glory of redemption. It is this. Go into the woods and cut a wound in the side of a living tree, and then go back again a few years later and see how the tree has endeavored to heal its wound and restore the breach by a very beautiful reproductive force. The notch in the trunk is all grown up again. Not, however, with the old fibres, but with far stronger materials; and you will find the grain of the wood interlaced and twisted across the old fibres in a sort of tangle, which all your efforts would frequently be found unable to cleave asunder. In fact, the healed breach is much stronger than any other part of the tree, and nature has not only made good the loss, but far more abundantly brought good out of it.

So, it is said, a broken bone heals much more strongly than the natural bone, as though nature were determined to fortify herself against a second attack, and to turn to account, in double strength, the assault made upon her.

Very beautifully is this illustrated in the formation of the pearl. A little grain of sand or a piercing thorn in the sensitive side of the pearl oyster, irritating its nerves, provokes him, not to retaliate and thus inflict upon himself a greater wound, but to throw around the intruding element a crystalline liquid and to bury it out of sight in a smooth and beautiful gem; so that out of the thorn and the wound come beauty and victory, and the value of the little mollusk is enhanced a thousand-fold by the very incident that threatened his destruction.

This is what the apostle means in a sublimer measure when he sums up his splendid antithesis between sin and salvation,

Adam and Christ, the fall and the redemption, with the magnificent declaration, "where sin abounded grace did much more abound." Out of the terrible attack which the powers of darkness hurled against the world, the wisdom and grace of heaven have brought the victory which is to prove the triumph of the ages. Out of the catastrophe which threatened man's eternal destruction, God has evolved a new creation transcendently greater and more glorious than the old. Out of the ocean depths of sin, Christ has brought the Pearl of Great Price, the church, which shall shine amid the glories of eternity with a lustre reflecting His own. Let us endeavor by the help of God to realize a little more fully this elevating and transporting truth.

1. It is illustrated in the salvation of the most abandoned sinners and the grace which is often so magnified in their conversion and subsequent usefulness. God seems to love to take the worst materials for His greatest triumphs. He chose a Jacob and a David in the Old Testament, both weak and wicked men in many a terrible sense and measure, to become the respective heads of the patriarchal and the kingly periods. He saved a Manasseh after half a century of bloody crimes. He took a Rahab from the slums of Jericho, to be a mother in the line of the Messiah's ancestry. And when He would choose His most illustrious apostle to found the glorious work of the gospel among the infamous Gentile races, He took "the chief of sinners." There is no doubt that Paul's calm estimate of his own wickedness, given by the inspiration of the Holy Spirit, was not exaggerated. Moral though he was, yet even his own testimony leaves sufficient evidence of the atrocity of his religious crimes. Not satisfied with insulting the name of Jesus and abetting the murderers of Stephen His faithful martyr, he devoted himself to exterminating the followers of Christ; and with a fiendish excess of cruelty he feared not to destroy their souls as well as their bodies by committing the

most fearful crimes and compelling them to blaspheme the Name of Him on whom they believed. He must have known full well the awfulness of the crimes he required of them, and that although they might even be mistaken in their faith, yet to sin against their conscience by profaning the name of Christ was, to them, the height of impiety, and on his part the very extreme of refined and Satanic cruelty.

And yet he, "the chief of sinners," tells us that he obtained mercy for this very purpose, that he might become the pattern of the principle on which God was to act in the economy of grace, namely, to "show forth all long-suffering unto them that should hereafter believe on the name of Jesus Christ to life everlasting." And this does not merely mean that God will save the most guilty, but that He will take peculiar pleasure in making more of their redeemed lives just because of their former wickedness. And so Paul can say "the grace of God was exceeding abundant towards me, with faith and love which is in Christ Jesus our Lord." "Where sin abounded grace did much more abound," not only in forgiving the sin but in making the sinner a vessel of the riches of divine grace and love, and an instrument in the hands of God for greater usefulness than ever was permitted perhaps to a mortal.

So still, through all these succeeding centuries has He loved to take the thorn and the thistle and turn them into the fir tree, and the myrtle and make it unto himself "for an everlasting sign that shall not be cut off." And, therefore, a wicked Bunyan, a degraded Newton, a contemptible, thieving Moorhouse, a polluted and criminal McAuley, yes, and many a woman whose name is written upon His hands, if not on the tablets of Christian fame, has been in like manner made an especial monument of this cardinal principle of divine redemption, "where sin abounded grace did much more abound."

Oh, is there a soul reading these lines that conscience and the tempter have conspired to discourage on account of aggravated sin? It matters not how great the sin, how strange the aggravations, and how long the story of impenitence and even of unbelief. To you is this message spoken and you may echo back to the throne of grace the deep petition which inspiration long ago breathed from the lips of David, "For thine own sake, 0 Lord, pardon mine iniquity, for it is great."

But we, the people of God, must also fully realize this principle if we would stand prepared to fulfill the purpose of our Master. In this age the messengers have passed out with the last invitations to the gospel feast. No longer are they to be chiefly addressed to the first invited guests, but it is from the highways and from the hedges and from the streets and lanes of the city that they are coming in today in great multitudes, and not only coming, but becoming the brightest trophies of redeeming grace and the most useful and honored instruments in the salvation of others. Shall we, beloved, fully realize the significance of this truth that the more lost, degraded and hopeless the soul may be to which we bring this precious gospel, the more willing is our Master to welcome it and the more glorious may be the issues of the redeemed life? As our faith in man decreases, thank God our faith in God rises to sublimer heights, that "where sin abounded grace shall much more abound."

2. This text is illustrated in the sanctification of believers and especially in their sanctification from qualities and tendencies naturally the most unholy and contrary to their new and sanctified lives. Still it is literally true in the deeper life of the soul that "where sin abounded grace much more abounds." It is not that God will make the good better, but that He will make the bad good, and the utterly and hopelessly bad divinely pure and holy. Sanctification is not the refining and

elevating of the naturally pure, but the transforming of darkness into light, a selfish soul into a living sacrifice of love, and a heart all steeped in corruption into the glorious counterpart of Christ's own holiness. In the work of grace God takes peculiar delight in contradicting natural probabilities and tendencies. He took a shrinking Jeremiah to be a bold and courageous reprover of Israel's prophets, priests and kings. He took a cowardly Peter to be the courageous and defiant apostle of Pentecost. He took a Son of Thunder to be the gentle, loving disciple of love. He took a raging persecutor to be the long-suffering apostle who could say, "I beseech you by the meekness and gentleness of Christ." He can make the weakest things in you the strongest, the worst things in you the occasions for the grace which will magnify in you the best and divinest qualities of the Christian life.

Beloved, shall we therefore cease to think and speak of the Christian life as a mere matter of education, and fully realize that it is all a new creation and a miracle of infinite and omnipotent grace? All that God requires in each of us is an opportunity to show what He can do, and to prove over and over again that "where sin abounded grace shall much more abound."

3. The text is illustrated in the fact that divine grace not only saves and sanctifies but counteracts the consequences of his sins and more than triumphs over the sad and hurtful effects of the sin. Many a poor fellow thinks, and many a sermon we fear has helped him to think, that though he has been forgiven and saved yet he need never expect to be delivered from the fruits of his life in harvests of sorrow and shame. He must not expect the consequences to be obviated but cheerfully endure them in patience and humility, thanking God that he has been saved from so much, and counting this but a reasonable reminder of the past and a very small retribu-

tion compared with what he deserved. He quotes, or others quote to him, a passage in Galatians vi: 7. "Whatsoever a man soweth that shall he also reap," and so they expect to reap in their bodies the physical infirmities and diseases which are the legitimate fruit of a life of dissipation and sin. They expect that their social and secular life may be embarrassed and impeded by the issues of their past, and that only after a long and patient endurance can they expect to recover themselves from the entanglement of the sins of their youth which encompassed them about.

Now we believe that grace is able to do something better than this, and that our blessed Lord has borne the bitter fruit of sin as our Substitute, and that His atonement has power to cancel all the effects of sin and even turn the curse into a blessing. The great Augustine, one of the fathers of the Christian Church, found himself at his conversion a physical wreck in his early youth. Every drop of his blood was poisoned by the virus of sin, and his frame was literally dropping into corruption through every abominable excess. But the grace of God not only saved his soul, but restored his body and gave him nearly half a century of almost unparalleled usefulness in physical health and strength and glorious service for his Master and the church.

Many a redeemed drunkard today can tell the same story of physical forces perfectly restored and every trace of a degraded life removed, not only from the physical energies but even from the very countenance. And so the grace of Christ can take the social life and counteract the innumerable currents of evil that have gone forth from us to return in our own life in entanglements and embarrassments and to work their lasting influences in the lives of others. In proportion to our faith, God can undo these influences and give us back all that we have lost and more. "I will restore to you," He says, "the years that the locust hath eaten, the cankerworm and the caterpillar, my great army which I sent among you." Sometimes the very life that the sinner has lived in the service of Satan is made an opportunity for greater usefulness, as he is enabled to reach classes to which the moral and respectable cannot even have access. And so God is constantly taking men out of the dives and slums, out of the saloons and dance-halls, out of the great lost world, that He may send them back again to their own former sphere as messengers of redeeming love. Fear not, then, poor trembling disciple, that you shall be drawn into the vortex that your own past life has created. Reckon yourself dead indeed unto it in all its issues, and go forth claiming the full redemption of your risen Lord and walking with Him as though you were not even the same person who once lived the life of sin and misery.

4. The text is illustrated most sublimely of all in the work of redemption. In a word its deep significance is simply this, that the work of Christ's redemption has more than counteracted and will ultimately transcend all the effects of the Fall. We believe that it has brought more glory to God than if the human race had kept their first estate. It has led to a new revelation of the divine character, which, but for sin, might never have been known. Creation revealed God in His power, wisdom and purity, but only redemption has revealed Him in His attitude of grace, that is, divine goodness dealing with the sinful and the lost. Had man never fallen, God would certainly have been known as a holy Being, through the terrible retribution which He visited upon the angels which kept not their first estate; but the wreck of the human race has exhibited Him in the most beautiful and attractive of all attitudes, as the God of mercy and love to the unworthy and wicked. Heaven would often have heard the song, "Alleluia! for the Lord God Omnipotent reigneth," even if Christ never had died, but only redemption has given the key-note of the new song, "Worthy is the Lamb that was slain!"

But it is not only an exhibition of His love and grace, but of that transcendent wisdom that could still vindicate His righteousness and guard the sanctity of His holy will, and yet devise a way by which mercy could have free exercise and God could be just and yet a Saviour. The cross of Jesus Christ becomes a monument of God's infinite wisdom, righteousness and love, and through all the ages to come will exhibit "the exceeding riches of His grace in His kindness towards us by Jesus Christ." Take out of the coming eternity the song of redemption, the millennial kingdom, the glory of Jesus and the prospects of His redeemed people, and heaven will seem annihilated and the universe a dreary waste, while even God Himself shall become enveloped in clouds of thickest, darkest and remotest distance, and the Bible will be obliterated from existence.

The benefits that come to men are still more manifest and deeply interesting. The redemption of our fallen race brings us to a far higher place than the first creation ever gave us. Unfallen man was only a creature made in the image of God, but a little lower than the angels. Redeemed man has been raised above the rank of angels to partake of the very nature of God, to be a joint-heir with the Son of God and to share eternally the throne of his Creator and the attributes of the eternal Son, our glorious Head. Redemption is therefore not the restoration of Adamic holiness, happiness or honor, but it is the uniting of man with the Son of God and the exalting of the redeemed sinner to kindred fellowship with a higher Being, so that, eternally like his Lord; the redeemed man shall be, not only a man, but a man united with God and possessing in the depths of his being the very spirit and nature of the eternal Jehovah.

This is so sublime that we would fear to boldly state it, had we not the unmistakable language of the Holy Scriptures. "Behold what manner of love the Father hath bestowed upon us that we should be called the sons of God. Beloved, now are we the sons of God, and it doth not yet appear what we shall be, but we know that when He shall appear we shall be like Him, for we shall see Him as He is," "Whereby are given unto us exceeding great and precious promises that by these ye might be partakers of the divine nature." "Your life is hid with Christ in God, but when Christ, who is your life, shall appear, then shall we also appear with Him in glory." Yes, the day is coming when Satan shall gaze upon the consummated work of the Great Restorer and see everything his hand has touched transformed into a monument of the grace and power of the Redeemer, and even he shall bow the knee and bitterly confess like one of his ancient disciples, "Oh, Nazarene! Thou hast conquered."

We may not be able to understand all sides of this great problem. Of course it would not be right to say that God intended or desired the sin and fall of His creatures and the sad train of still greater sin and misery that has followed. But we can surely believe that while He discountenanced the disobedience of Adam, as He does all disobedience, while He desires His children to walk in His will in holy obedience, and while He still is deeply grieved with every transgression and something is lost by it inevitably, yet the resources of His grace and power are such that, being committed, He has ample expedients to counteract its effects; and while all the consequences are not averted, yet enough good is brought out of it to result, in the end, in a higher aggregate of blessing, to turn the evil to the best possible account, and to show that God's all-sufficiency is more than a match for every emergency that can ever arise.

For ourselves, surely, the practical lessons are not hard to find. If there be a discouraged life within reach of this message, if there is a heart that has been held back by the iron fetters of the past and to whom Satan has been whispering, "There is no hope, but we will go on in the imagination of our hearts," oh, beloved, surely we have seen enough in this passage to answer the unworthy thought and ignoble fear, and to encourage us just because of the extremity of our situation, to claim more boldly the interposition of our Almighty Friend and the over-ruling power of His grace and love. The very hardest case is the one which He most loves to take. The most hopeless situation is the one through whose relief He is most glorified. If everything in your life seems against you, and if, worst of all, you feel that you alone are to blame for everything that is against you; if it has been, not only sorrow but sin, and every aggravation of sin-beloved, the grace of Jesus Christ was prepared for you and such as you. Only prove its all-sufficiency and you shall be among all that we have already specified, the crowning illustration of this most blessed truth, that "where sin abounded grace did much more abound."

God's great ultimate purpose for His redeemed people is the key to all the "exceeding great and precious promises." This, and this alone, explains the strong language in which He speaks to us of the provisions of His grace for our needs. These promises are out of all proportion to our importance or worth, and it is not strange that naturally we should hesitate to accept such boundless and stupendous assurances of love and care, and that our faith should be as narrow and paltry as it often is. It is not strange that the beggar child should be content with rags and crumbs, and almost think it is mocked when you talk to it about palaces and offer it the costly robes and the princely treasures of royalty. The truth is, we are the children naturally of low and shameful birth and spiritual destitution, but we have been adopted into a higher rank, nay, we have been born into a heavenly life and a divine sonship, and we are destined, as the very children of God, to share the exceeding riches of His glory through all the ages to come; and, therefore, we are recognized by Him now and treated in the manner befitting our future glory. We are like the children of wealthy parents who are at school in a foreign land, not having yet come into their inheritance, but being supplied by their father, even in their minority, with boundless wealth for every need. And so, although we have not entered upon our eternal inheritance, yet God has given us a cheque book on the bank of heaven, and on the back of every cheque He has Himself endorsed the vast and illimitable guarantee, "My God shall supply all your need according to His riches in glory by Jesus Christ."

And so this word "abound" has come to be a sort of a keynote to the New Testament promises. Even of His promises He says, "God willing MORE ABUNDANTLY to shew unto the heirs of promise the immutability of His counsel confirmed it by an oath" (Heb. vi: 17). His word is abundant, His promises boundless, His loving, faithful heart struggles to express in ever ampler language and larger utterance, the immeasurable and unspeakable fullness of His love, so that His great promises are like mountains piled upon mountains until His faithfulness truly reacheth unto the clouds.

So, again, His mercy and grace to the sinful are as abundant. "The grace of our Lord," says the Apostle, "was EXCEEDING ABUNDANT with faith and love which is in Christ Jesus." And again in Rom. v: 17, he speaks of those who "receive ABUNDANCE OF GRACE and the gift of righteousness, who shall reign in life by one, Jesus Christ." The life that Jesus brings to us is not only life, but "life MORE ABUNDANTLY" (Jno. x: 10). Redemption and forgiveness are declared in Eph. 1: 7, 8, to be "according to the riches of His grace wherein HE HATH ABOUNDED toward us in all wisdom and prudence," that is, in all the variety of the love and care that adapts and adjusts His mercy and His grace to every shade of guilt and need, and which anticipates every future emergency; for this is the meaning of "prudence," literally, foresight and providence.

His purpose in our salvation is that "in the ages to come He might show the EXCEEDING RICHES OF HIS GRACE in His kindness toward us by Christ Jesus" (Eph. ii: 7). All the dispensations of His providence are destined to give occasion for still larger manifestations of His grace, "For all things are for your sakes that the ABUNDANT GRACE might through the thanksgiving of many redound to the glory of God" (2 Cor. iv: 15). Even in our deepest sorrows He has made provision for such overflowing abundance of comfort and joy that the sorrow shall be lost in the joy, for, "As the sufferings of Christ abound in us, so our CONSOLATION ALSO ABOUNDETH by Christ" (2 Cor. i: 5). The provisions of grace for our Christian life and work are equally boundless, for "God is able to make ALL GRACE ABOUND toward you that ye always having all-sufficiency in all things, MAY ABOUND to every good work" (2 Cor. ix: 8). And like a mountain-top, high above all the rest and lost in the clouds, it is all summed up in the sublime hyperbole, "Now unto Him that is ABLE TO DO EXCEEDING ABUNDANTLY above all that we ask or think, according to the power that worketh in us, unto Him be glory in the church by Christ Jesus, throughout all ages, world without end. Amen" (Eph. iii: 20, 21.)

This is the divine measure of redeeming grace, and, so on our side we are called upon to meet God's high measure with corresponding fullness. We are to abound in faith. "Rooted and built up in Him, and stablished in the faith, as ye have been taught, ABOUNDING therein with thanksgiving" (Col. ii: 7). We are to abound in love. "And this I pray, that your LOVE MAY ABOUND yet more and more in knowledge and in all judgment" (Phil. i: 9). "And the Lord make you to increase and ABOUND IN LOVE one toward another, and toward all men, even as we do toward you" (1

Thess. iii: 12). We are to abound in holiness. "Furthermore then we beseech you, brethren, and exhort you by the Lord Jesus, that as ye have received of us how ye ought to walk and to please God, so ye WOULD ABOUND MORE AND MORE " (1 Thess. iv: 1). We are to abound in joy. "That your rejoicing may be more ABUNDANT in Christ Jesus" (Phil. i: 29); and in hope, "Now the God of hope fill you with all joy and peace in believing, that ye may ABOUND IN HOPE, through the power of the Holy Ghost" (Rom. xv: 13). We are to abound in liberality, even in the depths of poverty. "The abundance of their joy and their deep poverty ABOUNDED unto the riches of their liberality." "Therefore as ye abound in everything, in faith and utterance, in knowledge, and in all diligence, and in your love to us, see that ye ABOUND IN THIS GRACE ALSO" (2 Cor. viii: 2, 7).

And our spiritual experience is to be not a strained but an ample one, ever growing in breadth, depth, height and symmetry, through the abundant grace of the divine nature in our heart. "And besides this, giving all diligence, add to your faith virtue; and to virtue, knowledge; and to knowledge, temperance; and to temperance, patience; and to patience, godliness; and to godliness, brotherly kindness; and to brotherly kindness, charity. For if these things be in you, AND ABOUND, they make you that ye shall neither be barren nor unfruitful in the knowledge of our Lord Jesus Christ" (2 Pet. i: 5-8). And finally if we thus enter into His abundant grace we shall have His glorious recompense in like proportion, and "So an entrance shall be ministered unto you ABUNDANTLY into the everlasting kingdom of our Lord and Saviour Jesus Christ."

Beloved, shall we so receive "His fullness, even grace for grace," and so enter in at last, not like a battered ship, with masts and sails all gone and banner torn to shreds, and slowly drawn by some old tug boat across the bar into the harbor or the dry-dock; but shall we rather, with flags all flying, and sails swelling in the gales of heaven, and myriads on the shore waiting to welcome us, shall we have an entrance ministered unto us abundantly into the everlasting kingdom of our Lord and Saviour Jesus Christ, while wondering angels, looking back to the past and gazing in amazement on our present glory, shall turn to each other and say, "where sin abounded, grace did much more abound."

A. B. SIMPSON

Chapter 8.
FROM STRENGTH TO STRENGTH

"From strength to strength." - Psalm lxxxiv 7.

This is a chapter of the "Pilgrim's Progress" through the valley of Baca, of which this beautiful psalm is a picture. It is the story of the life of trust, and its two keynotes are the fifth and twelfth verses of the psalm, "O Lord of hosts, blessed is the man that trusteth in thee." "Blessed is the man whose strength is in thee." To him the valley of Baca, the valley of weeping, at once becomes a well of living waters, and every low and dry place a pool for the heavenly rain to fill with floods of deeper blessing; and drinking from the living waters the pilgrims go "from strength to strength," and all at last go home, for "every one of them in Zion appeareth before God."

"From strength to strength!" But there is a previous chapter, from weakness to strength. For man is naturally the weakest creature in the universe. He comes into life with the wail of a helpless infant, weaker than the tiger's cub or the birdling in its nest. But his physical frailty is but a figure of his spiritual helplessness. When we were yet without strength in due time Christ died for the ungodly." But the grace of God in the conversion of the soul brings its first spiritual strength, enabling it to choose and trust the Lord, to turn from sin and walk in holy obedience. Then it sings the new song, "O Lord, I will praise thee; though thou wast angry with me thine anger is turned away and thou comfortest me. Behold, God is my salvation; I will trust and be not afraid, for the Lord Jehovah is my strength and my song; He also is become my salvation."

Very strong is the new-born trust and love of the converted soul; very strong its purpose, its joy and its holy enthusiasm. It truly seems as if it never could be tempted to doubt or disobey, and, like Peter, it is ready to cry, "Though all men should deny thee, yet will I never deny thee." And God meets us on this plane and helps our strength, although He has something far better for us further on. Speaking to such a heart in the forty-first of Isaiah and the ninth verse, He says, "Thou art my servant; I have chosen thee, and not cast thee away." It is the experience of the soul that has just come to God. And then He adds, "Fear thou not, for I am with thee; be not dismayed, for I am thy God; I will strengthen thee; yea, I will help thee; yea, I will uphold thee with the right hand of my righteousness."

These last three clauses describe three very distinct experiences of our early Christian life. The first comes when we begin to feel our strength insufficient and cry to God for increased strength, and He strengthens us. It is the old kind of strength, but He gives us more of it. But soon even this is not sufficient, and, as we still sink, He comes and adds His help to our strength. "I will help thee," He says. It is now the strengthened heart with the strong Lord helping. But still you will notice that we are in front and not the Lord. It is our battle, and He is simply reinforcing us with His auxiliaries. But now a greater crisis comes. Even this is not sufficient, and we sink in the conflict and are ready to fall in utter exhaustion and discouragement, when lo! our Mighty Helper comes upon the field Himself, takes the battle in His own almighty hands, lifts up our sinking form as a mother would a babe, bids us no longer to stand even in His help, but takes us bodily in His arms and carries us with His own almighty strength as He cries, "Yea, I will uphold thee with the right hand of my righteousness." Oh, that is from strength to strength! From our own strength to His increased strength, and now from even this to the absolute all-sufficiency of God Himself.

Now we notice in the vivid imagery of the prophet a sudden and complete change upon the battlefield, and looking round, we find that all our foes have already fled before His face. Our almighty Captain has taken the field, and "lo! all they that were incensed against thee shall be ashamed and confounded, and they that strive with thee shall perish. Thou shalt seek them and not find them, even them that contended with thee; they that war against thee shall be as nothing, and as a thing of nought."

In the third chapter of Revelation we see the little church of Philadelphia going through something like this experience. "Thou hast a little strength," the Master says, "and hast kept my word and not denied my name." But in the tenth verse we find a mightier strength coming to the faithful in Philadelphia. "Because thou hast kept the word of my patience I also will keep thee." It is God's keeping now, not our own; and in the twelfth verse it reached its climax. The one who had "a little strength" has now become "a pillar," with strength enough not only to uphold its own weight, but to support the edifice under which it stands. But when Philadelphia becomes a pillar its own individuality passes away, and it becomes identified with God Himself, for He says, "I will write upon him the name of my God, and the name of the city of my God, which is New Jerusalem, which cometh down out of Heaven from my God; and I will write upon him my new name." This is not now mere human strength, but the strength of Jehovah.

We have now got to the great theme which we desire to impress as the Lord enables us.

1. It is divine, not human strength, and it is strength which is wholly divine and in no sense or measure human. It is an exchange of strength in which we have surrendered all our fancied power and received instead the divine power and enabling. This glorious exchange of strength is vividly set forth in the animated language of the sublime Isaiah, chapter xl: "He giveth power to the faint, and to them that have no might He increaseth strength. Even the youths shall faint and be weary, and the young men shall utterly fall, but they that wait upon the Lord shall exchange their strength." That is to say, the strongest human strength, the manhood of young

men, the vigor and vitality of youth, shall be wholly inadequate for the exigencies of Christian life and conflict, and it is not until these have failed that God has room to display the resources of His omnipotence. When we become "faint," then He giveth His power, and when we have "no might," then He "increaseth strength," that is; gives yet more because of our utter helplessness. Waiting on the Lord, we let our strength go and take His instead, and so renew or exchange our strength.

A simple figure may help to illustrate the thought. Look at that man trying to ford a river, and with all his might struggling with the deep flood, and, by dint of tremendous physical exertions, stemming its mighty waters, and panting and exhausted reaching the other shore. That is strength matched with the strength of the elements. But look at another. Wading out a little distance into the deep flood by the exercise of his own strength, he now lets go, and falls and sinks upon the bosom of the river. Lo! it bears him without a struggle and carries him down in its swift current. He has let go his strength, and he is now carried by the strength of the stream.

So there are many of us who are trying to ford the stream by our own strong will and efforts. There is a sweeter way, by ceasing from our strength and falling into the mighty current of God's infinite life and love and being borne by a power superior to ours without a struggle. Many people never reach their true development until their difficulties become so great that they break down in the struggle and fall into the arms of God. This is what the apostle meant when he exclaimed, "I take pleasure in infirmities; when I am weak then am I strong." And this was but an echo of the Master's own assurance, "My grace is sufficient for thee, for my strength is made perfect in weakness."

Beloved, have you exchanged your strength for the Lord's? Have you gone "from strength," that is yours, "to strength," that is the strength divine?

2. It is strength for a higher spiritual plane. "They shall mount up with wings as eagles." It is a strength which enables us to mount to a higher element of life and communion with God. It brings us into the divine life and raises us up to dwell in heavenly places with Christ. It resists and overcomes the natural direction of earth, to draw us downward, and, like the buoyant wing of the fowls of the firmament, it bears us and holds us on high, in a calm and heavenly atmosphere where the world lies beneath our feet, and we are lifted above the things which once encompassed and entangled us. We are not now fighting the wild waves, but flying far above them in another element. The mightiest human strength cannot lift us up to this. Only the strong pinions of the Heavenly Dove can bear us aloft to, and hold us supremely in, this heavenly region. This is God's true deliverance from most of our troubles; not to change them, but to rise above them. Oh, how we need these seasons of spiritual elevation and heavenly inspiration to strengthen us for the practical sphere of common life, and enable us to "run and not be weary," and to "walk and not faint."

> Yes, we need these times of waiting,
> When their strength our souls renew:
> Drinking at the heavenly fountain,
> Bathing in the heavenly dew;
>
> Yes, we need these heights of rapture,
> When we mount on eagles' wings,
> Then returning to earth's duties,
> All our heart exultant springs.
>
> Oh, how every labor lightens!
> As with swift divine constraint,
> We can "run and not be weary,"
> We can walk and never faint.

3. Strength for the practical duties of life. For they that thus "renew their strength" "shall run and not be weary; and they shall walk and not faint." It is not all for heights of rapture or hours of vision, but these experiences reach their true fruition in the consecration of our common life and the triumph of faith and patience in the routine of daily duty. This is the pathway where we have often to run the strong race of peculiar difficulty, strenuous exertion and sudden and severe emergency, but God's strength does not grow weary under the most extreme tests. Then there are the long protracted strains, the almost interminable delays, the endless minutiae of trial, irritation and care, that need the sustained strength which holds on its way and carries us through all the details of life's experiences as victoriously as through its greater battlefields. These are the things that exhaust mere human strength, but the strength of God can "walk and not faint." Beloved, have we thus exchanged our strength and are we victoriously pursuing our onward way with calm victorious spirit, unwearied and unfainting?

4. It is strength to "withstand in the evil day and having done all to stand." Dr. Mackay of Hull once said that Isaiah had left out one of the things which God's strength enables us to do, for it is harder to run than to fly, and harder to walk than to run, but there is something harder than walking, and that is to stand. Now Paul has supplied this omission, if it be one, in his superb picture of the Christian conqueror in the sixth chapter of Ephesians. This chapter, by the way, is the very chapter of the life that has mounted up with wings as eagles and is dwelling on high. Its keynote is, "Dwelling in heavenly places in Christ Jesus," and, like the picture in Isaiah, the apostle ends with a very practical conclusion. The outcome of all this strength is to "put on the whole armor of God that ye may be able to stand against the wiles of the devil. For

we wrestle not against flesh and blood, but against principalities, against powers, against the rulers of the darkness of this world, against spiritual wickedness in high places. Wherefore take unto you the whole armor of God that ye may be able to stand in the evil day and having done all to stand." This is the only strength which will enable you to stand. The sooner we discover the better, that the strongest of us is no match for Satan, and that our highest and holiest resolutions will be surely broken and our souls trodden down in defeat and despair beneath our conqueror's scornful feet, unless we meet our spiritual foes in the very presence and power of Jesus.

For this is just what all this picture means. The shield of faith is the faith of God; the sword of the Spirit is the Word of God, wielded by the Holy Ghost within us; the very prayer in which we are to overcome is to be prayed in the Spirit; the armor is the armor of God; the strength is to "be strong in the Lord and the power of His might." In a word, it is to confront the devil with the living God within us and so possessing us that the battle is not ours but God's, and the enemy, from the beginning, understands that he has challenged, not a poor unequal man, but his own Almighty Conqueror, the Son of God. This is to be "more than conqueror through Him that loved us;" this is to say, "Thanks be unto God who always leadeth us in triumph through our Lord Jesus Christ."

5. It is strength to endure. Let us read attentively Col. i: 11. "Strengthened with all might, according to His glorious power, unto all patience and longsuffering with joyfulness." Here is one of the advanced stations of the pilgrim's progress "from strength to strength." We may well pause and ask if we have reached this place of strength. Is this then the goal of Pentecost? Is this the great objective point contemplated by the mighty baptism of the Holy Ghost? Is this the meaning of the power from on high? "Strengthened with all might

according to His glorious power!" One would surely look for a sublimer battlefield to follow such a splendid parade of the armies of God. But lo! we behold an entirely different spectacle. A solitary soldier on an obscure and weary pathway, battling with a thousand petty hardships, difficulties and trials, or standing through all the day of battle without a single opportunity of advancing, and seemingly called to nothing else but to stand under the fire of the enemy and to "endure hardness as a good soldier of Jesus Christ." His whole business seems to be "patience and longsuffering;" the first, with reference to the trials which God is pleased to send upon him; the second, the annoyances and injuries of men. Ah! these are the very things human strength cannot endure. Many a brave man can stand under a cannon's fire more calmly than he can endure the taunts of a fellow creature. The highest victory of the Son of God was, that, "when He was reviled He reviled not again; when He suffered He threatened not:" and the mightiest triumphs of the strength of God in us are realized when we can receive the hiding of our Father's face and even the weight of His mighty hand without a doubt or murmur, and accept the misconceptions, opprobriums, reproaches and wrongs of our fellow men, not only with longsuffering, but with joyfulness; not only unruffled and unretaliating, but sweetly realizing and fully believing that they are to us the pledges of some richer blessing from our heavenly Father, and the guarantees of something so glorious that we cannot but thank God for giving us the opportunity of thus winning another blessing.

Beloved, have we any room for progress here "from strength to strength"?

6. It is strength that carries us in victory through the whole range of our Christian experience with all its extremes, and enables us to say, "I can do all things through Christ which

strengtheneth me." The apostle had tested it in the heights and depths of human circumstances and found it equal to all vicissitudes, variations and exigencies. The force of his glorious confession lies in the "all things." Human strength can accomplish some things, but the strength of God is equally adequate for all. It is equal in its uniformity, immutability, unvariableness. Over every opening morning it inscribes the promise, "As thy day so shall thy strength be." It has such an infinite reserve of all-sufficiency that we need not question whether our strength is adequate to the duty. All we need to know is, does God require it? for if He does He will abundantly enable us. The great ships of ocean, and especially the ships of today, are scarcely affected by the storms or the elements. They are so strong that they move on with equal facility through the glassy sea or the rolling waves. The strength of God in a human life will carry it thus steadily through all life's changes.

> «Calm as the ray of sun or star,
> Which storms assail in vain,
> Moving unruffled through life's war,
> The eternal calm to gain."

7. It is strength which enables us to receive Christ's indwelling in all its fullness, and to enter into all the meaning of His mystical life. "For this cause I bow my knees unto the Father of our Lord Jesus Christ, of whom the whole family in heaven and earth is named, that He would grant you, according to the riches of His glory, to be strengthened with might by His Spirit in the inner man, that Christ may dwell in your hearts by faith, that ye, being rooted and grounded in love, may be able to comprehend with all saints what is the breadth, and length, and depth and height; and to know the love of Christ which passeth knowledge, that ye might be filled with all the fullness of God. Now unto Him that is

able to do exceeding abundantly above all that we can ask or think, according to the power that worketh in us, unto Him be glory in the church by Christ Jesus throughout all ages, world without end. Amen."

The apostle is speaking here of the indwelling of God in the heart; "That ye might be filled with all the fullness of God," is the crowning statement of this great truth and experience. This is possible in a measure "exceeding abundantly above" all that we are enabled to ask or think. It is to be realized through Christ dwelling in our hearts, and Christ's indwelling will bring us into an experience of love in which we shall know and comprehend the height and depth and length and breadth of His love which passeth knowledge. But this indwelling of Christ is to come through simple faith. Now all this looks extremely easy on paper and in theory, but the apostle tells us that in order to enter into it we must be "strengthened with might by His Spirit in the inner man." This divine filling requires a vessel that can hold it, and a vessel supernaturally strengthened. You cannot put a charge of dynamite or a hundred-pound shot into a pocket pistol or a vessel of clay. You want the mightiest ordnance, the strongest barrel and breech, to bear the enormous strain of so much concentrated power. And God has to prepare us as the vessels of His power, and, in order to do so, He must take us out of our own strength into the strength of Christ. Our mere natural capacities cannot receive Jesus. The loftiest intellect, the strongest brain, is unequal to this experience; but the humblest capacity, when strengthened by the Holy Ghost, may know God as no angel ever knew Him, and exult in His immeasurable love, as only His loved ones can.

And even after we have received Christ's indwelling through the Holy Ghost enabling us, there are depths and heights in "all the fullness of God" in which we more perfectly enter, in proportion as we allow the Holy Ghost to fit us for the deeper and higher experience. This is often what our severest trials are meant for, to give to our spirit a vigor and capacity which will enable us to rise to a higher place in the fellowship.

8. It is strength which is established and perfected by spiritual discipline. "But the God of all grace, who hath called us unto His eternal glory by Christ Jesus, after that ye have suffered a while, make you perfect, stablish, strengthen, settle you" (1 Pet. v: 20). Every new experience of Christ's grace must be confirmed by some new discipline in the school of trial, and even after we have come to know God as "the God of all grace, who hath called us unto His eternal glory," we must suffer a while, that even this knowledge and experience of His grace may be established, strengthened, settled.

And so we are ever passing on "from strength to strength," and finding, like the giant oak, that the wildest tempests, instead of tearing us from our foundation, only plant us deeper and root us the more securely to the Rock of Ages.

Chapter 9.
GOD'S MEASURELESS MEASURES

"But they measuring themselves by themselves, and comparing themselves among themselves are not wise. But we will not boast of things without our measure, but according to the measure of the rule which God hath distributed to us, a measure to reach even unto you." 2 Cor. x:12, 13.

"With what measure ye mete it shall be measured to you; and unto you that hear shall more be given." Mark iv 24.

We have here two sorts of measures contrasted, the human and the divine. There is a great deal in a measure. Half an inch off the draper's yard stick makes a good many yards difference when the goods are delivered. The division of a hair line in a carpenter's rule might destroy all the calculations of the architect in the construction of a building. A little boy told his mother that he was six feet high, and when she doubted the statement he assured her that he had just measured himself by his own little rule. His calculations would have been all right if his rule had been right, but when examined, it was found to be a little less than six inches long. This is the sort of rule that a great many Christians measure by.

There are two sorts of human measures; the one is when we are "measuring ourselves by ourselves;" the other, when we are "comparing ourselves among ourselves;" that is, measuring by others. Both are equally "unwise," for both come equally short of the divine rule. Many persons are always trying to measure up to their ideal and their aspirations and to the out-reaching of their poor souls, and the lofty ideals of humanity, as they are pleased to call them. They will tell us that they have lived up to their light and to their conscience and are satisfied with their opinions and content with their lives, and that it is nobody's business but their own. They are measuring themselves by themselves. Some who have come upon a higher plane are measuring themselves by a past experience, by some memory of blessing, some little Mizar or some lofty mount to which they have risen in the distant past, and this, to them, is the type and ideal of all their life. And so, we find thousands trying to hold on to their experience or to get it back again, instead of remembering that God is "able to do exceeding abundantly above all we ask or think."

Others again are ever comparing themselves with others, congratulating themselves that they are as good as some of their standard, or aiming to resemble some human ideal. The result of this is to be seen in the human traditions and the stereotyped patterns of Christian living, according to which so many are moulding their dwarfed and wretched lives. All this is but human measuring; all this is most unwise. From all this Paul turned to reach up to God's measure, and, "forgetting the things that were behind he pressed forward to the mark for the prize of the high calling of God in Christ Jesus;" striving that he might "apprehend that for which he was apprehended of Christ Jesus." It is a great thing to have a worthy ideal or pattern. It is better to aim high and miss it than it is to aim low and reach it. The famous artist was wise when he wept with bitter tears because he had reached his ideal. He could dream of nothing higher than he had achieved with his brush and to him the charm and inspiration of life had gone.

We find a number of God's standards and measures referred to in the Holy Scriptures, rising like the rounds of Jacob's ladder from earth to heaven. There is a simple phrase oft repeated in the New Testament and often overlooked, which expresses these measures and steppings. It is the phrase "ACCORDING TO," two words which rise like the uprights of Jacob's ladder to the heavens, and across which many of the precious promises may be seen in the vision of faith firmly fastened as heavenly steps leading higher and higher up to all the good and perfect will of God. Let us glance at some of these heavenly measures.

I. THE WILL OF GOD.

This is at once the limitation and the inspiration of our faith and prayer. "If we ask anything ACCORDING TO His will He heareth us." "The Spirit maketh intercession for the saints ACCORDING TO the will of God." Beyond this our desires and our aspirations cannot go, but beyond it they need not desire to go, for within it lie all the probabilities of blessing which a human and immortal life can receive; and God's chief desire is to get us to see how much it means of blessing for us. As we have often said, there is no vaster prayer within the reach of faith than the simple sentence, "Thy will be done." This will must mean for each of us our highest possible good. We know it includes our salvation, if we will accept salvation, for "God will have all men to be saved." We know it includes our sanctification, for "this is the will of God, even your sanctification." We know it includes our deliverance from physical evil if we will receive it in His Name in faith and obedience, for He has said, "I will. Be thou clean." We know it includes every needed blessing that the obedient can require, for He has said "He will withhold no good thing from them that walk uprightly." The apostle's prayer for his beloved friends was that they might have fulfilled in them "all the good pleasure of His goodness;" and that they might "prove that good and acceptable and perfect will of God."

Beloved, are you measuring up to this divine rule? Are you meeting all your Father's will? Are you walking "worthy of Him to all pleasing," and having fulfilled the benediction and prayer that "He may make you perfect in all things to do His will, working in you, that which is pleasing in His sight through Jesus Christ to whom be glory forever and ever? Amen."

II. HIS WORD.

"Behold the handmaid of the Lord!" is the sublime response of Mary to the angel's astonishing message, "be it unto me ACCORDING TO thy word." Never was faith put to a harder test.

Never was woman asked to stand in so delicate a place of peril and possibility, of humbling shame and glorious everlasting honor. Realizing, perhaps, with every instinct of her maiden heart all that this might cost her, she meekly, unhesitatingly, without one question, one faltering breath, accepted the stupendous promise and responsibility and rose to meet the divine measure, "ACCORDING TO Thy word," and like an echo came back the heavenly benediction, "Blessed is she that believed, for there shall be a performance of those things that were told her from the Lord."

Beloved, are you living up to this great measure? Is faith resting and claiming, not according to signs and seemings, frames and feelings, but according to His word? Is obedience walking, not according to the course of this world, or the moods of our capricious hearts, or the standards of men, or the example of others, or the traditions even of the church, but according to His word? Are we Bible Christians and determined to believe and obey every word within these inspired and heavenly pages? Then we shall be found in "the way everlasting," for "the grass withereth and the flower fadeth, but the word of our God shall stand forever," and "he that doeth the will of God abideth forever.

III. THE RICHES OF HIS GRACE.

"In whom we have redemption through His blood, even the forgiveness of sins AC-CORDING TO the riches of His grace, wherein He hath abounded towards us in all wisdom and prudence." Peter has used a parallel expression. "ACCORDING TO His abundant mercy He hath begotten us again unto a lively hope." This is God's standard and measure of salvation. He works and saves according to the riches of His grace. He abounds towards us in all wisdom and prudence, that is, He adapts His mercy to every variety of guilt, and He anticipates, in His prudence and foresight, every future emergency. He sees Peter from the beginning to the end of his career and accepts him "for better or for worse;" and when the hour of his shameful fall is near, He can say, "I have prayed for thee." So He takes every one of us and adjusts His infinite grace to all the minutiae of our sin and its worst aggravations, our corrupt and ruined nature and all its wreck, our weak and helpless will and all its inability to stand, our circumstances, our temptations and all that besets us. Knowing and anticipating all, He just encompasses us in His everlasting arms and saves and keeps us, "ACCORDING to the riches of His grace."

Beloved, have you entered into the fullness of this measure, and have you understood it in all its all sufficiency for a lost world and the most wretched and ruined lives over whom you pray and love? Oh, let our faith look up from lost humanity, to the mighty love of God and "the exceeding riches of His grace." And if there be a discouraged and guilty soul within reach of this message, may God help you, beloved one, to put your sins with all their aggravations side by side with God's immeasurable grace, until you shall realize something of the Psalmist's sublime figure when he sang, "As far as the east is from the west, so far has God removed our transgressions from us. As high as the heaven is above the earth so great is His mercy toward them that fear Him." Our sins may have reached to the clouds until they have become like thick cloud" but, thank God, "His mercy is in the heavens," and far above the clouds.

IV. THE RICHES OF HIS GLORY.

Can we form any conception of the riches of His glory? Moses asked to see that glory but was told it was too bright for human gaze, and only in the distance and from behind could he dare to look upon it. A little glimpse of it the disciples beheld on the Mount of Transfiguration, but they were afraid of its brightness and their eyes were overcome with slumber under its spell. "The heavens declare His glory, and the firmament showeth His handiwork," and some conception of the riches of His power and majesty may be gathered from these glorious constellations and worlds of light which science is more fully exploring in these wondrous days. Sometimes we have sat down and allowed our minds to dwell on the multitude of these discoveries and calculations. We have tried to take in the magnitude of yonder planet many hundred times larger than our world, and yonder sun outweighing the world many thousandfold, and stars beyond stars,

«where system into systems runs
And other planets circle other suns,"

until our brain whirls and threatens to collapse under the pressure of the sublimity; and "lo! these are part of His ways, but the full thunder of His power who can comprehend?" His hand holds all these orbs; His will commands all these forces; His wisdom poises all these spheres and directs them in their course without a jar or catastrophe; His sceptre sways this mighty empire; His creating word called every portion of it into being; His providence upholds it every moment; His taste and goodness have adorned it with beauty and loveliness and enriched it with happiness and blessing. There is not a creature among its inhabitants from the highest archangel to the lowest insect but owes its being to His power and goodness. And all this is but "the hiding of His power," for His omnipotence could call millions of such universes into being in a moment. Nay, all this is but a scaffolding for the glory which He is preparing for the abode of His redeemed. The riches of His glory will not be complete until the new heavens and earth shall have emerged from the flames of a dissolving world and the New Jerusalem descended from heaven in the glory of God with streets of gold and gates of pearl and foundations of precious gems, and all the thrones are reared, and crowns are set, and the mansions are completed, and the glorified are shining "as the sun in the Kingdom of their Father," and we ourselves are crowned with all "the riches of His glory."

Oh beloved! we shall then understand something of the meaning of such verses as these, "I pray that God would grant you ACCORDING TO the riches of His glory, to be strengthened by His spirit in the inner man, that Christ may dwell in your hearts by faith." Or again, "Strengthened with all might ACCORDING TO His glorious power unto all patience and long-suffering with joyfulness." Or again, "My God shall supply all your need ACCORDING TO the riches of His glory by Christ Jesus." It is according to the riches of His glory that He is working out the new creation in our hearts and preparing the more glorious temple of the soul for His own eternal abode. It is according to the riches of His glory that He is willing to strengthen the heart for all patience and long-suffering. And it is according to the riches of His glory that He is able and ready to supply all our need. There is nothing too hard for such a God, too rich and glorious for His wisdom, grace and love. He looks at the littleness of our faith and cries, "Hast thou not known, hast thou not heard, that the everlasting God, the Lord, the Creator of the ends of the earth, fainteth not neither is weary? There is no searching of His understanding. He giveth power to the faint and to them that have no might he increaseth strength."

Beloved, let us lift up our eyes and behold the glory of our God and begin to walk as sons and heirs, and claim, even in our minority, something of the riches of His glory.

V. THE RESURRECTION AND ASCENSION OF JESUS CHRIST.

"That ye may know what is the hope of His calling and what the riches of the glory of His inheritance in the saints, and what is the exceeding greatness of His power to us-ward that believe, ACCORDING TO the working of His mighty power, which He wrought in Christ, when He raised Him from the dead, and set Him at His own right hand in the heavenly places, far above all principality and power and might and dominion, and every name that is named, not only in this world, but also in that which is to come; and hath put all things under His feet, and gave Him to be the Head over all things to the church, which is His body, the fullness of Him that filleth all in all."

The resurrection and ascension of Jesus Christ have become for us the pledge and pattern of all our faith and hope can claim. The power that God hath wrought in Christ in raising Him from the dead and setting Him upon His own right hand is the very same power which we may expect Him to exercise to us-ward who believe. "The riches of the glory of this inheritance in the saints" is the standard of what we may share in our spiritual experience now. God has performed for us the most stupendous miracle of grace and power, and nothing can ever be too hard or too high for us to expect from "the God and Father of our Lord Jesus Christ." The picture is a very definite as well as a very glorious one. Step by step we can ascend its transcendent and celestial heights with our ascending Lord, as we see Him rise, first above the mighty power of earth, and then above and far above all principality and power and might and dominion and every name that is named, not only in this world but in that which is to come, until all things are beneath His feet. And then as we gaze upon His lofty preeminence we are permitted to sit down by His side and claim all the fullness of His glory as our own. For all His ascension power and majesty are not for His own personal exaltation, but that He might become the Head over all things for His body the church, and He takes His high preeminence as our Representative and recognizes us as already seated with Him in the heavenly place. His resurrection, therefore, involves ours, His triumphs ours, His ascension ours, His rights are shared with us.

Do we require in our behalf the exercise of an authority that transcends all other authority? We have but to remember that He, our exalted Head, is sitting far above all principalities. Do we require a force to be exercised for us over-matching the mightiest forces of nature or of evil? He is sitting far above all power and might. Do we ask something which even natural law would seem to hinder? God already has done something in His resurrection which is superior to all law, for that is what "dominion" means. Are we confronted with imposing names and despised by human pride? We are sitting side by side with one who is exalted above every name that is named both in this world and that which is to come. Indeed, the whole economy of human life, the whole system of providence is a framework for the accomplishment of God's purposes for His redeemed people. Nations rise and fall, human society exists, great cities swarm with their inhabitants and move with the mighty currents of commerce and social life. All the events of the great world as they pass are but movements of Christ's mighty hand, primarily designed for those who immediately take part in them, but ultimately for the good of His church and the building up of His kingdom; and men and nations are but puppets in the hands of our anointed King, whom He uses for His wise purposes even when they are fulfilling their own pleasure, and then drops them when He pleases. After the resurrection of Christ, and in view of His enthronement there is nothing we need fear to claim according to this mighty measure, as part of the riches of our inheritance.

VI. CHRIST HIMSELF.

We read in Romans xv: "ACCORDING TO Christ Jesus." This is the highest of all standards, higher even than His resurrection, ascension and glory. As He is, so shall we be when He appears but, "As He is so are we," even here. "Ye are not of the world even as I am not of the world." "Love one another as I have loved you." "As I live by the Father so he that eateth me even he shall live by me." "As Thou hast sent me into the world even so send I them into the world." "When He shall appear we shall be like Him, for we shall see Him as He is." Such are some of the touches of heavenly light which reveal our identity with Jesus and unfold the mystery of His life in us. Not only is He our example, but He is our life. Miniatures of Christ, God expects us to be, receiving and reflecting Him in all His fullness, our life His life, our love His love, His riches ours. We represent Him, we dwell among men not as citizens of earth, but dead to our old citizenship and walking like Him as if we had been sent specially from heaven on a mission from another world.

Beloved, is Christ our Pattern, our Type, our living Head, our Divine Standard and Measure? Are we determined to have nothing less and to be nothing less than even as He? Shall we cease to copy men, and follow only Him?

And even though we oft are conscious of very imperfect resemblance to the Great Original, are we still holding our standard as high as Christ? I have often noticed the artists in the great gallery copying the paintings of the masters. I have sometimes come back weeks afterwards and found them still working on the copy of some great painting. Their work was not complete, but their copy was, and while it hung upon the wall with its perfect form and tints their copy was constantly reaching closer approximation to the great object lesson. But if they had begun to copy the works of the artists around them or to complete the picture from their own recollection or conception of it, it would have soon become a cheap and worthless daub.

So let us always keep our eye upon the heavenly standard and be satisfied with nothing less than "ACCORDING TO Christ Jesus." Sometimes in Kindergarten schools a picture is held before the children for a little and then it is removed and they are required to tell from memory some of its features. Then it is held again and they are again required to tell or draw some of the features that they have noticed and marked until, at length, the whole object lesson is imprinted like a copy upon their minds. So God holds Jesus before us and bids us, not only follow our conception of Him, or the copies we see in others, but again and again contemplate the Original and hold Him constantly in view that even our conception of Christ shall be ever corrected, enlarged, vivified, until it shall be transformed to our inmost being, not only as the Pattern but as the very life of our life.

"Christ men," as one has said, "are the men God wants today." It would not hurt if this word became coined into Christian phraseology, and its meaning stamped upon all our life. A poor heathen Kroo boy came on board a ship, hundreds of miles from the Congo, and finding a party of missionaries going up the river, eagerly sought an interview with them and sent a message by them to one of the missionaries in the far interior. "Tell him," he said in his rude speech, "that when I left him two years ago I promised to be Christ's man. Tell him that I am Christ's man still." Rude and simple as the heathen conception was it was the truest and the highest that mortal thought can reach. It is God's own divine measure of Christian life, to be a "Christ man," living, loving, trusting, serving, suffering, overcoming, "ACCORDING TO Christ Jesus."

VII. ACCORDING TO THE POWER THAT WORKETH IN US.

"Now unto Him that is able to do exceeding abundantly above all that we ask or think, ACCORDING TO the power that worketh in us" (Eph. iii: 20).

"Whereinto I also labor, striving ACCORDING TO the power that worketh in me mightily" (Col. i: 29).

"ACCORDING TO the working whereby He is able to subdue all things unto Himself" (Phil iii: 21).

In these passages we have God's present working referred to in two directions; namely, in the believer's heart and in the sphere of providence and government. The one must ever keep pace with the other. God does work mightily in the forces around us, but we must allow Him to work within us or all the might of His providence shall be ineffectual for us. "He is able to do exceeding abundantly," but it must be wrought in us. It is "ACCORDING TO the power that worketh in us." All the forces of that mighty engine in the factory yonder are limited and measured by the attachment of the little pulley of each particular machine. It can drive a hundred printing presses if they are in contact, but its power is ACCORDING TO the measure in which each one will receive it and co-operate. God is waiting to work in each of us, indeed He is already working up to the full measure of our yieldedness, and we may have all which we are willing to have inwrought in our own being. The Holy Spirit is always in advance of us, pressing us on to more than we have yet wholly received and we may be very sure that ACCORDING TO the measure of His inward pressure will always be the external workings of God's Almighty hand. Whenever we find the wheels within in motion we may be very sure that the wheels of providence are moving in accord, even to the utmost bounds of the universe and to the utmost limits of God's Almighty power and supreme authority.

Let us then yield to the power that worketh in us to its full measure. Let our being be responsive to its slightest touch, so responsive that, like the Eolian harp, it will answer to the faintest breath of the Holy Spirit as He moves upon the chords of our inmost being.

VIII. ACCORDING TO OUR FAITH.

"ACCORDING TO THY FAITH be it unto thee" was Christ's great law of healing and blessing in His earthly ministry. This was what He meant when He said "with what measure ye mete it shall be measured to you again." All these mighty measures that we have been holding up are limited by the measures that we bring. God deals out His heavenly treasures to us in these glorious vessels, but each of us must bring our drinking cup and according to its measure we shall be filled. But even the measure of our faith may be a divine one. Thank God, the little cup has become enlarged through the grace of Jesus, until from its bottom there flows a pipe into the great ocean, and if that connection is kept open we shall find that our cup is as large as the ocean and never can be drained to the bottom. For He has said to us "Have the faith of God," and surely this is an illimitable measure.

A few weeks ago a noble band of missionaries landed upon the coast of Sierra Leone, filled with faith and holy enthusiasm. Before many days however three of their number had fallen victims to the dreadful African fever. Shortly afterwards one of these dear brothers was to us a very touching and wonderful message. He said that on his way across the Atlantic he had been led to see the truth of divine healing and had taken the Lord Jesus as his healer. Soon after, the death of these friends came upon him like a bewildering shock and for a few hours his faith seemed to be wholly paralyzed. Then he threw himself at the feet of Jesus and to his surprise there came upon him such a baptism of rest and confidence, with which he seemed to have nothing to do, that he rose not only comforted, but so established in His confidence, so assured that the Lord was his healer and keeper that he had no fear even of the failure of his faith, but was able to say with humble and holy confidence that come what might he would trust the Lord alone, and was confident that his life and faith would be upheld until his work was done. His old faith had died, and out of its grave had come the faith of God. His little drinking cup had broken, and all the water had leaked out, but lo! a hand divine had opened through that broken cup a connection with that heavenly fountain, and henceforth his cup was not only full but full forevermore with all the fullness of God. He had passed out of himself into Christ, and was now able to meet the immeasurable promises with a trust as measureless and divine.

So let us, beloved, rise unto the fullness of Jesus and sweetly
«Find His fullness round our incompleteness,
Round our restlessness His rest."

Chapter 10.
SPIRITUAL GROWTH

"But grow in grace and in the knowledge of our Lord and Saviour Jesus Christ." - 2 Peter iii 18.

I have heard of a little boy being found by his mother in one of the garden beds with his feet buried in the soil, and standing beside a tall sunflower, to which he was eagerly looking up. When his mother asked him what it all meant, he said that he was trying to grow to be a man, and wanted to be as tall as the sunflower. How truly has our Master said of all our struggles to grow taller, "Which of you by taking thought can add one cubit to his stature?" All the little fellow's stretching did not increase his height. No doubt his mother told him to go inside and eat a good hearty supper, and day by day drink plenty of fresh milk and eat his meals with heartiness, and run about and play for wholesome exercise and be a happy, thoughtless child, and thus he would grow to be a man without trying. His desire to grow would not really help him to grow unless he took the proper means.

It is just so in our spiritual life. Fretting and straining will not enlarge our spiritual manhood. God has Himself revealed the secret of growth, and it is not very different from the mother's counsel to her little boy.

Let us look at some principles of spiritual progress.

I. THE RELATION OF SPIRITUAL GROWTH TO SANCTIFICATION.

The apostle who has given us our text had already laid down the principles of spiritual growth in the opening chapter of his epistle with great fullness and marvelous clearness and power. There is no single paragraph in the Scriptures which more profoundly unfolds the depths and heights of Christian life than the first eleven verses of the first chapter of 2nd Peter. And the very point we are now referring to is made perfectly plain in these verses. The fifth verse is an injunction to grow in grace, but the preceding verses give us the standpoint from which this growth is to start. It is nothing less than the experience of sanctification. The persons to whom this is addressed are recognized as having already "escaped the corruption that is in the world through lust," and having already "become partakers of the divine nature."

These two facts constitute the whole of sanctification. It is that experience by which we become united to Christ in so divine and personal a sense that we become partakers of His nature, and the very person of Christ, through the Holy Ghost, comes to dwell in our hearts, and by His indwelling becomes to us the substance and support of our spiritual life. The converted soul is a human spirit born from above by the power of the Holy .Spirit. The sanctified soul is that human spirit wholly yielded to and wholly possessed and occupied by God's indwelling presence, so as to be able to say, "Not I, but Christ liveth in me." The effect of this is to deliver from "the corruption that is in the world through lust." God's indwelling excludes the power of sin and evil desire, which is just what the word lust means. The Greek tenses here leave no room to doubt the question of time and the order of events. This deliverance from corruption precedes the command to grow, and is the very ground of that command. For the word translated "besides this," as Alford so happily shows, means something entirely different namely, "for this very reason," that is, because God hath provided for our sanctification, and imparted to us His nature and delivered us from the power of sin, for this very reason we are to grow.

It is very evident, therefore, that we do not grow into sanctification, but grow from sanctification into maturity. This corresponds exactly with the description of the growth of Christ Himself in the opening of the gospel of Luke. "The child grew and waxed strong in spirit filled with wisdom, and the grace of God was upon Him." Surely no one will dare to say that He grew into sanctification. He was sanctified from the very first. But He was a sanctified child and grew into manhood. And so still later, in Luke ii: 5, it is added that, at the age of twelve years, "Jesus grew in wisdom, and stature, and in favor with God and man."

And so the same Christ is formed in each of us; is formed as a babe and grows, as He did on earth, into maturity in our spiritual life, and we grow into a closer union with Him, and a more habitual and intimate dependence upon Him for all our life and actions.

Beloved, have we come to the starting point of spiritual growth by receiving Christ as our indwelling sanctifier and life?

II. THE RELATION OF GROWTH TO THE PROVISIONS AND RESOURCES OF DIVINE GRACE.

The same beautiful passage brings this out also in great fullness and definiteness. "According as His divine power hath given unto us all things that pertain to life and godliness, through the knowledge of Him that hath called us to His glory and virtue. Whereby are given unto us exceeding great and precious promises." Here we are taught that God hath provided all the resources necessary for a holy and mature Christian life. These resources are provided for us through the graces and virtues of our Lord Jesus Christ, which we are called to receive and share. "He hath called us," not to our glory and virtue, but "to His glory and virtue." It is the same thought which the same apostle expresses in his first epistle, ii: 9, "That ye should show forth the excellencies of Him who hath called you out of darkness into His marvelous light." Not, "the praises of Him," which is obviously a bad translation, but "the excellencies." We are to display the excellencies of Jesus to the world, or, as it is here, "The glory and virtue of Jesus." He clothes us with His character and in His garments, and we are to exhibit them to men and to angels. And these provisions of grace are brought within our reach through all "the exceeding great and precious promises," which we may claim and turn into heavenly currency for every needed blessing.

This is the conception of Christian life given in the first chapter of the gospel of John, in that wonderful little expression "grace for grace." That is to say, every grace that we need to exercise already exists in Christ, and may be transferred into our life from Him, as we "receive of His fullness, even grace for grace." Up in yonder mount Moses was called to see and study a model of the Tabernacle, corresponding in a higher degree to the models which you may see in the Patent Office in Washington of all the different machines that have been patented and built. A few weeks later the same Tabernacle might be seen going up piecemeal in the valley below, and, when completed, was an exact facsimile of the other shown to Moses in the mount; for God's explicit command was, "See that thou make all things according to the pattern which was shewed thee in the mount." Corresponding to this is the tabernacle which God is building in each of our lives. It is just as heavenly a structure as the other and far more important, and is meant to be, as it is, the dwelling place of God. It, too, has its model in the mount, and we may see, by the eye of faith, the model of our life, the pattern, the plan of all the graces which we exemplify and the life which is to be built up, worked out, and established. All the materials for our spiritual building are there now, already provided, and the whole design fully wrought out in the purpose of God and the provisions of His grace. But we have to take these resources and materials moment by moment, step by step, and transfer them into our lives. We have not to make the graces ourselves, but take them, wear them, live them, and exhibit them. "Of His fullness we receive grace for grace," His graces for our graces, His love for our love, His trust for our trust, His power for our strength.

Over in an English factory you can find numerous models of iron cottages, composed of hundreds of sections screwed to-

A Larger Christian Life

gether, and standing just as they would appear when erected on their permanent site. The purchaser from a distant colony, where wood is scarce and metal has to be used instead, comes along and purchases one of these cottages, and orders it to be shipped to Australia, with the understanding that it shall correspond in every particular to the model in the London yard. The order is fulfilled, and a few months later you may see the identical facsimile in a pleasant lawn in Melbourne or Sydney, or a few weeks sooner you may see the sections arrive piece by piece, and the different pieces screwed together until the building is complete, and corresponds in every particular to the London model. All the materials have been sent from the distant city, and the structure reared according to the model, piece for piece. This will illustrate what John meant by "grace for grace." Christ has, in Himself, the pattern of your life and mine, and all the materials. Our part is simply to receive, live out and exemplify them before the world.

III. RELATION OF SPIRITUAL GROWTH TO OUR OWN RESPONSIBILITY AND EFFORTS.

While it is true, on the one hand, that all the resources are divinely provided, this does not justify, on our part, a spirit of passive negligence, but summons us all the more to diligence and earnestness in pressing forward in our spiritual career. And so the apostle adds, after this strongly emphasized enumeration of the resources of God's grace, "Giving all diligence, add to your faith," etc. There is to be no languid leaning upon God's grace, no dreamy fatalism, based upon His almighty purpose and power, but a strenuous and unceasing energy on our part in meeting Him with the co-operation of our faith, vigilance and obedience. In fact, the very provisions of God's grace are made, by the apostle, the ground of his exhortation to give earnest attention to this matter. For this very reason, that is, because God has so abundantly provided for us, and is so mightily working in our lives and hearts, and developing us from the power of sin, for this very reason, "Add to your faith," etc.

It is the same thought which Paul has expressed in Philippians, "Work out your own salvation with fear and trembling. For it is God that worketh in you to will and to do of His good pleasure." This does not mean that we are to work for our salvation, for we are represented as already saved, otherwise it could not be "our own salvation." But it is yet in embryo and infancy, an inward principle of life which must be worked out into its full development and maturity in every part of our life, and to this we are "to give all diligence," a diligence, indeed, which often reaches the extent of fear and trembling," a holy and solemn sense of responsibility to make the most of our spiritual resources and opportunities, because "it is God that worketh in us." It is as if, with the finger of solemn warning raised, He were standing and looking into our eyes and saying, "God has come. The Almighty has taken this matter in hand. The Eternal Jehovah has undertaken the work, therefore, mind what you do! Let there be no laxness, no negligence, and no failure on your part to meet Him and afford Him the utmost opportunity to fulfill in you all the good pleasure of His will, and the accomplishment of His high and mighty purpose for your soul."

In our Sunday school lesson, within the last few weeks, we have had a very solemn thought, whose most impressive point has perhaps escaped the thought of some of us. It is in connection with the parable of the pounds, and the thought we refer to is the obvious truth there unfolded, that to every servant is given, at the beginning of his spiritual life, an equal measure of spiritual resource, and that the difference in the issues of human lives is not to be found in the unequal measure of grace and power afforded from on high, but in the unequal measure in which they have improved the power given. One pound is given to each servant, but in the end, one servant has so traded with his pound that it has grown to ten, while his neighbor has the same little pound wrapped up in a napkin, unchanged, unimproved. The difference lies wholly in the diligence of the two men. The one "giving all diligence" added to his faith virtue, knowledge, temperance. The other simply tried to keep what he got and probably took excellent care of it, wrapping it in a costly handkerchief maybe, or putting it into a secret drawer or worthy place, but doing nothing to increase it. "The manifestation of the Spirit is given to every man," the apostle says, "to profit withal." This expression, "to profit," carries the same idea with it as the trading in the parable of the pounds and the "all diligence" of Peter's epistle.

Beloved, are we "giving all diligence" to make the most of God's divine resources, of "the exceeding great and precious promises," of " the divine nature" within us?

IV. THE RELATION OF THE VARIOUS DETAILS AND THE RESPECTIVE GRACES OF OUR CHRISTIAN LIFE.

The verse employed to describe our spiritual progress is a very unusual one and full of exquisite suggestiveness. It is a musical figure, and we all know that there is nothing that so perfectly expresses the idea of harmony and adjustment as music. Paraphrased into the English meaning of the figure the passage might thus be read, "Add to your faith, virtue, knowledge, temperance, etc., just as in a perfect musical harmony one note is added to another until the majestic Hallelujah Chorus swells to heaven without a discordant part or measure wanting.

In the Greek national festivals it was customary for some prominent and gifted individual to get up a chorus or special musical entertainment, and the one to whom this high trust was committed was called the *"Choregos."* From this our word choir has been derived. He was really the choirmaster and his business was to combine together the voices, the instruments and the musical compositions in such a manner as to produce the most perfect effect and the most complete harmony. So the Greek verb based on this word, *"Epichorego,"* just means to combine together as a musical harmony, or as a choir-master would combine the notes, the instruments, the voices and all the parts in a splendid performance. This is the beautiful verb imperfectly translated. A dry figure of arithmetic is unhappily substituted for a suggestive musical metaphor.

Perhaps we have already anticipated the fine thought lying back of this figure, viz.: that God wishes our Christian growth to be like the growth of a sublime oratorio, a growth in which all the parts are so blended and the entire effect so harmonious that our life will be like a heavenly song or a Hallelujah Chorus. Faith is the melody, but to this is added all the other parts, courage which reaches the high tenor, temperance perhaps the medium alto, patience the deep bass, and knowledge, godliness and love, the song itself, to which all the music is but the accompaniment. It is easy to grow in one direction and to be strong in one peculiarity, but only the grace of God and the power of the Divine nature within can enable us to grow up to Him in all things, "unto the measure of the stature of the fullness of Christ." It is one thing to have faith and courage, but it is another thing to have that blended with temperance and love. It is one thing to have self-restraint, but it is another thing to have it combined with knowledge. It is one thing to have brotherly kindness, but it is quite another to have charity to all men. It is one thing to have godliness, but it is another to have it in perfect adjustment with love. It is the harmony with all the parts which constitutes the perfection of the song and the completeness of the Christian life.

Beloved, perhaps God has educated you in each of the graces, but He is now educating you in the blending of these graces in perfect proportion, so that your love will be rendered mellow and like a perfectly proportioned face, not so marked in any of its single features as in the whole expression of the countenance. Indeed, the most beautiful faces are sometimes so proportioned that we can scarcely remember a single feature, and perhaps the best musical compositions are those which leave the simplest effects and are less striking for any particular measure than for the exquisite sweetness and simplicity of the whole. This is the heavenly meaning brought out in the preposition *"in"* all through this progression. It is not *add to* your faith courage, but *"in* your faith courage, knowledge, temperance, etc." It is in the intermingling and the tempering of one grace with another that the power of the whole consists. It is the addition of courage along with the faith which renders the faith effectual. It is the addition of self-restraint along with patience which keeps it from becoming fanaticism, and zeal without knowledge. It is in the quality of temperance and self-control combined with knowledge that the elements of discretion and wisdom are developed. But self-control and self-denial need patience to save them from being transitory outbursts and to give them permanence and stability. All these qualities without godliness would leave us on a low plane, but this lifts them all to heaven and makes them all a living sacrifice upon the altar of His glory. But even godliness alone would leave us narrow and cold, and so God requires of us the inner linking with our brethren and the culture of these social qualities, which brings us into loving fellowship with one another and lifts us out of ourselves into brotherly kindness, that is the love of the brethren, the love of Christ's people. And yet even this would not be complete if the circle were not widened far beyond the range of Christ's people and our brethren in the Lord, to comprehend the whole world in the sweep of a charity which can love even as God loves, the unworthy, the unattractive and even those that hate us and repel us.

It is very beautiful to notice the fine shades of holy character which the New Testament expresses. For example, what a multitude of words the Holy Spirit has given us for the various forms of love and patience. Here are some of them: love, charity, brotherly kindness, tenderness, meekness, long-suffering, patience, forbearance, unity, peace, courtesy, gentleness, considering one another, in honor preferring one another, kindly affectioned one to another, etc. They are like so many fine shades of color, all of the same class, yet no two exactly the same. Thus God is tempering our lives and this is a very large part of Christian growth.

It is said that a great sculptor was visited by a friend twice, at an interval of several months. The friend was astonished to find that his work seemed no further on. "What have you been doing?" "Why," he said, "I have been touching this feature, rounding that, raising that." "Why, but these are all trifles, mere touches!" "Yes," said the artist, "but these make perfection and perfection is no trifle." It is an old story but a spiritual lesson which is very far from wornout. God keeps us sometimes years learning a few touches of heavenliness, which constitutes the difference between the image of Christ and the blundered and broken image of an imperfect man.

V. THE RELATION OF GROWTH TO OUR SECURITY AND STEADFASTNESS IN CHRISTIAN LIFE.

It is not a matter of personal preference whether we shall grow or not. It is a matter of vital necessity, for only thus can we be kept from retrograding. This the apostle hints in our text, "Beware lest ye also, being led away with the error of the wicked, fall from your own steadfastness. But grow in grace and in the knowledge of our Lord and Saviour Jesus Christ." Growth is the remedy for declension and we must ever grow or go backward. So in 1 Peter ii: the same truth is expounded. "If ye do these things ye shall never fall. He that lacketh these things is blind and cannot see afar off, and hath forgotten that he was purged from his old sins." That is the very experience of conversion-it fades away and becomes but a dim recollection unless we press on to deeper and higher things.

Alas! have we not all sometimes seen men truly and wonderfully converted and much used of God for the conversion even of others, and yet men who refused to go on to higher experiences, and sometimes even have scouted the doctrine and experience of sanctification as an affectation or fanaticism. Alas! the day came when even their experience of conversion faded, at least for a time, and they were plunged in some deep and bitter fall to compel them to see the need of something higher. It is not possible for us to remain with safety in any stereotyped experience. Indeed, it is necessary for us to grow with an accelerated motion and to make more rapid progress the longer we continue in the Christian life.

And so we have a very strong figure even in this passage expressing this thought. The word translated "abound" in our version, in the Greek is "multiply." "If these things be in you and multiply, they shall make you that ye shall neither be barren nor unfruitful in the knowledge of our Lord Jesus." Let us not fail to notice the striking antithesis of the "add" in verse 3, and the "multiply" of verse 8. We all know in arithmetic the difference between addition and multiplication. The addition of nine to nine makes eighteen, but the multiplication of nine into nine reverses the figures and makes eighty-one, or nearly five times as much. Everything depends upon the size of the multiplier. In the spiritual arithmetic the multiplier is God and infinitely higher than the highest digits of human calculation. God simply takes the surrendered heart and unites Himself with it, and the result is as many times greater than itself as God is greater than man.

Beloved, shall we meet God's expectation and provision and press on from grace to grace and from grace to glory?

VI. THE RELATION OF GROWTH TO REWARD.

The apostle carries on the thought to the sublime consummation when the struggles and trials of time shall all have passed and we shall be entering the eternal port and coming into the eternal issues of our present lives. Then no struggle will be regarded as too severe, no self-denial will be regretted, no toilsome patient victory will be remembered as too trying, but these very things will constitute the exquisite joy and recompense of our eternal homecoming. "For so," he says, "an entrance shall be ministered unto you abundantly into the everlasting kingdom of our Lord and Saviour Jesus Christ." How it lights up this whole passage with a wondrous glory to remember that the Greek word used here to describe our entrance into the kingdom is the very same Greek word used with respect to the "adding" to our faith virtue, knowledge, temperance, godliness, and all the train of heavenly graces. It is the beautiful metaphor of the *"choregos."* It is not that an abundant entrance merely shall be ministered unto us, but the idea is that a whole chorus of heavenly voices and harmonies will sing us home, and that we shall enter like warriors returning in triumphal procession from a hard won and glorious victory. It is not merely that a chorus will meet us, but it is the very same choir that we ourselves gathered around us in our earthly conflict. The graces, the virtues, the victories, the triumphs of patience and love that we won and perhaps had quite forgotten will all be waiting yonder like troops of angels, and all shall gather round us and fit into the chorus of joy that shall celebrate our homecoming.

Sometimes God has given us a little taste on earth of this ecstatic joy, when some ministry of love that we had long ago forgotten comes back to our recollection through the friend whom we had been the means of saving, or some word or deed is recalled by the testimony of one to whom we were made a blessing through an act of self-denial or faithfulness; and we find, a quarter of a century afterwards, that the little service has been travelling round the world and blessing hundreds on the way. We are melted into grateful wonder and adoring praise.

But these are but approximations of what it will be then, when all that we have been permitted to suffer and do for Jesus will be found awaiting us on the threshold of glory, and shall usher us in triumphal procession into the eternal kingdom of our Lord and Saviour Jesus Christ. Oh, how we shall rejoice that we were permitted once to suffer and sacrifice for Jesus! Oh, how some will wish that they might have once more the opportunity of winning such a welcome and gaining such a great reward. Beloved, nothing that we gain for God can ever be lost. Oh, may the Master help us, "giving all diligence," to make the most of life and all its opportunities and resources of grace and lay up for ourselves treasures on high which shall never fade away.

Chapter 11.
ENLARGED WORK

"Enlarge the place of thy tent." Isa. liv: 2a

About one hundred years ago a humble Baptist preacher stood in an English pulpit and announced this text at the opening of what was perhaps the first Missionary Convention of modern times. He then proposed the two following divisions as the themes of his discourse. 1. Attempt great things for God. 2. Expect great things from God. And then from these two propositions, themselves inspiring enough to impel the whole missionary movement, he proceeded to preach a sermon which became the watchword of the greatest Christian movement, since Apostolic days. That was the birthday of modern missions. Soon he himself was a missionary in Calcutta, and today an army of missionaries is girdling the world and about to multiply more and more every year until the Master comes. The preacher had been one of those whom the Lord delights to use-one of the weak things, and the things that are despised. A humble cobbler, he had supported himself by toiling all day long at his last, but while his hands were busy, his heart was out upon the world, and his eyes were often upon the maps that lined the walls of his workshop, and the calculations and plans for the world's evangelization. Deep down in his heart had grown up a mighty faith for the lost millions of mankind, and his great sermon was but the outbreaking of the pent-up fires that had long been burning in his breast. It was the voice of God to his generation. It is the voice of God to another generation, the generation of today. It is the voice of God to us, beloved. Fresh from the hallowed influences that have so deeply moved our hearts and blessed so many here, God is pointing to a world where a thousand millions still are lost, and saying to us-"Enlarge the place of thy tent, fear not, lengthen thy cords and strengthen thy stakes, let them stretch forth the curtains of thine habitations on the right hand and on the left. For thy Maker is thy husband, the Lord of Hosts is His name, and thy Redeemer the Holy One of Israel, the God of the whole earth shall He be called."

Three thoughts are here suggested.

I. ENLARGEMENT.

God's plan for all His work is to begin in feebleness and expand and develop to maturity. He first makes a perfect sample and then multiplies it. So the work He has done for us is but a sample of what He can do, and wants to do for all the world. The blessing that has filled and thrilled our hearts these past days may be multiplied as many times as there are cities in the world, and reproduced wherever there are hungry hearts to fill and messengers to tell of the grace and the fullness of Jesus. That gospel of the Saviour's fullness that has filled your heart can fill a thousand million hearts. That faith which has brought you deliverance can deliver all the captives of the great oppressor and set the whole world free. That humble work which has grown up out of "a handful of corn on the top of the mountains" can become a mighty forest on all the mountains and "shake like Lebanon, and they of the city flourish like the grass of the field."

God has simply been making samples, but He can multiply them by millions. Will we let Him use us for their reproduction, for they are multiplied by reproduction. They are not made as the machines in yonder factory, but they grow as seeds multiply, as yonder geraniums by culturings, as that oak by the seeds it drops into the ground, or that single grain of wheat that sometimes sends up twenty stalks from a single seed, and each stalk bears half a hundred seeds. God has given us in this blessed work a gospel so full that it needs a world for its field. He is showing us the plan of a Christian church, that is much more than an association of congenial friends to listen once a week to an intellectual and musical entertainment and carry on by proxy a mechanism of Christian work; but rather a church that can be at once the mother and the home of every form of help and blessing which Jesus came to give to lost and suffering men, the birthplace and the home of souls, the fountain of healing and cleansing, the sheltering home for the orphan and distressed, the school for the culture and training of God's children, the armory where they are equipped for the battle of the Lord and the army which fights those battles in His name. Such a centre of life and power Christ wants in every centre of population in this sad and sinful world.

The figure of enlargement is that of a tent; its curtains are to be stretched forth and its cords are to be lengthened. These curtains are surely the promises and provisions of the Gospel, and they will stretch as wide as the needs of human lives and the multitudes that seek their shelter. The cords are cords of prayer, cords of faith, cords of love, cords of holy effort and service. He bids us lengthen the cords of prayer. Let us ask more, but let the strands of faith be as long and strong. Let us believe more fully, more firmly, and for a wider circle than we have dared before. Let the cords of love be lengthened until we shall draw men to Christ with the very cords of our hearts. Let our efforts for His kingdom reach a wider circle. Let each of us make the world our parish, and as the Bride of the Lamb realize that all that concerns our Lord's kingdom concerns our hearts, "For our Maker is our husband, the Lord of Hosts is His name, the God of the whole earth shall He be called."

God has committed to our trust the gospel in its fullness. Let us never rest until in all its fullness it is known in every hamlet of this great land and in every land and tongue.

And we must lengthen the cords of our liberality. The Lord is asking for millions today to spread His gospel in its fullness over the world, and we to whom this full gospel has been such a blessing are especially called to take it as our trust for Him and send it everywhere. The world is open today and the workers are being prepared as never before, men and women full of faith and the Holy Ghost. Never was there a time when a little money would go so far in spreading Christ's Word. Less than ten millions today would evangelize all the world before the close of the century.

When I think of the opportunity of using money for God today, I could almost envy the men who have the opportunities of successful business. God is going to send very large amounts into the treasuries of consecrated work, and if we are but true to this trust we shall yet see tens of millions spent in sending the fourfold gospel to every corner of the globe.

II. CONSOLIDATION.

But the wider our work the stronger it must be at the centre. And therefore as the cords are lengthened the stakes must also be strengthened. What are these stakes?

1. Surely God's Word is the first. The more widespread the work God gives us to do the more important is it that we be true to the great standard of truth, the Bible and the gospel of Jesus Christ. This is the day of new theologies and loose views of evangelical truth. More sacredly than ever does the Master require us to stand faithful to the cross of Jesus Christ, the doctrine of man's sin and ruin, the great atonement, the inspiration of the Holy Scriptures, the person and work of the Holy Ghost and the certainties of future retribution and reward. Thank God we do not have to resort to the novelties of rationalism to attract the multitudes. Give them the Living Bread, the atoning blood, the old and ever new story of Jesus and His love.

2. Personal holiness. This is the next safeguard of the Lord's work. God cannot trust an unsanctified people or an uncon-

secrated man with much service for Him. Poor Jonah is sure to mar his most successful work with a touch of himself. The more God entrusts to our hands the more humbly let us lie at His feet and the more faithfully use our trust for His glory. This is one of the wise things the Salvation Army has done. It has required all its officers to be sanctified men and women. Such a work can afford to be successful. God grant us wisdom to see to it that all who bear the vessels of the Lord are clean. So shall He give us the world itself for our inheritance.

3. The spirit of self-sacrifice. No work can ever be glorious without the martyr spirit. Luxury is killing the churches today, and the only remedy for it is the red blood of sacrifice. Great faith and great sacrifice will always be found together. This must be the spirit of this work if it is to cover the world. We must be willing to endure hardness as good soldiers of Jesus Christ. We must be indifferent to popularity, and human praise or blame, we must be willing to live with great simplicity and rigid economy, we must be willing to be misunderstood and persecuted, we must be glad to be the companions of the lowly and despised, we must gladly face toil, hardship and even death, and count all things but loss for Christ and His kingdom. Such a people only can possess the world for Christ, and such soldiers shall march to worldwide victory while the splendid brigades of rank and luxury shall fail in the day of battle and prove but a splendid pageant and a dress parade.

God give us the spirit of Scriptural faith, personal consecration and true self-sacrifice, and then He can give us the world for Christ.

The figure of the tent suggests the idea of constant vicissitudes and humility. This is no proud architectural pile but a simple tent, ever changing and oft taken down and moved forward. It is the figure of the changing wilderness, the pilgrim life and constant movement. This is not our rest. This is no place for great cathedrals and splendid establishments and ecclesiastical states but continual advance and ceaseless aggression. It is to be feared that splendid churches have been the greatest curse of the church. As long as the early Christians met in humble upper rooms, they had the power of God and godliness, but when they began to imitate the splendor of the world and vie with the architecture of imperial palaces and heathen temples, the Holy Spirit took His flight, and the world and the devil became paramount. The days of the Jewish tabernacle were better days than those of Solomon's temple. The beginning of this work was in a humble tent; let us never forget the tent spirit or lose the pilgrim spirit. "Enlarge the place of thy tent." He does not say get a temple, but a bigger tent. Lord, help us to enlarge but never leave our tents.

III. DIVINE RESOURCES.

"For thy Maker is thy Husband; the Lord of Hosts is His name, the God of the whole earth shall He be called." This is the secret of it all. We have back of us one who has infinite resources, and He is not only our King and our Friend, He is our Husband. He has given us all His heart and all His glory, and He will surely give us all the world for our dowry and our inheritance. This is the secret of successful work, to know Christ in this blissful and intimate relation, and to receive our work, by virtue of our union with Him, as the very fruit of our marriage with the King of Kings. So may He reveal Himself to us all, and then, as His very bride, standing at the threshold of His home and inviting in His lost and wandering children, it shall be true of us, "The Spirit and the bride say, Come," and the world will come to Him.

"How knowest thou whether thou be come to the kingdom for such a time as this?" Like Esther on Ahasuerus' throne, we have been called to the kingdom that we might use our place of right and power to save a world. God help us so to win them back to our beloved Husband, so to bear them for Him as His very children and ours, that "the God of the whole earth shall He be called."

It has been the experience of some of God's children, and it was mine, to be called by His Spirit, in years of loneliness and sorrow, to learn very deeply the Song of Solomon in its true spiritual significance, and then, in this deep, sweet love-life with Christ, to be led into precious service for Him, and to find the life filled with most gracious fruitfulness and blessing. O beloved, He is calling you to His bosom and then to His work, "Hearken, O daughter, and consider, forget also thy kindred and thy father's house; so shall the King greatly desire thy beauty: for He is thy Lord; and worship thou Him." And then, "Instead of thy fathers shall be thy children, whom thou mayest make princes in all the earth."

"Enlarge the place of thy tent." Isa. liv: 2a

About one hundred years ago a humble Baptist preacher stood in an English pulpit and announced this text at the opening of what was perhaps the first Missionary Convention of modern times. He then proposed the two following divisions as the themes of his discourse. 1. Attempt great things for God. 2. Expect great things from God. And then from these two propositions, themselves inspiring enough to impel the whole missionary movement, he proceeded to preach a sermon which became the watchword of the greatest Christian movement, since Apostolic days. That was the birthday of modern missions. Soon he himself was a missionary in Calcutta, and today an army of missionaries is girdling the world and about to multiply more and more every year until the Master comes. The preacher had been one of those whom the Lord delights to use-one of the weak things, and the things that are despised. A humble cobbler, he had supported himself by toiling all day long at his last, but while his hands were busy, his heart was out upon the world, and his eyes were often upon the maps that lined the walls of his workshop, and the calculations and plans for the world's evangelization. Deep down in his heart had grown up a mighty faith for the lost millions of mankind, and his great sermon was but the outbreaking of the pent-up fires that had long been burning in his breast. It was the voice of God to his generation. It is the voice of God to another generation, the generation of today. It is the voice of God to us, beloved. Fresh from the hallowed influences that have so deeply moved our hearts and blessed so many here, God is pointing to a world where a thousand millions still are lost, and saying to us-"Enlarge the place of thy tent, fear not, lengthen thy cords and strengthen thy stakes, let them stretch forth the curtains of thine habitations on the right hand and on the left. For thy Maker is thy husband, the Lord of Hosts is His name, and thy Redeemer the Holy One of Israel, the God of the whole earth shall He be called."

Three thoughts are here suggested.

I. ENLARGEMENT.

God's plan for all His work is to begin in feebleness and expand and develop to maturity. He first makes a perfect sample and then multiplies it. So the work He has done for us is but a sample of what He can do, and wants to do for all the world. The blessing that has filled and thrilled our hearts these past days may be multiplied as many times as there are cities in the world, and reproduced wherever there are hungry hearts to fill and messengers to tell of the grace and the fullness of Jesus. That gospel of the Saviour's fullness that has filled your heart can fill a thousand million hearts. That faith which has brought you deliverance can deliver all the captives of the great oppressor and set the whole world free. That humble work which has grown up out of "a handful of corn on the top of the mountains" can become a mighty forest on all the mountains and "shake like Lebanon, and they of the city flourish like the grass of the field."

God has simply been making samples, but He can multiply them by millions. Will we let Him use us for their reproduction, for they are multiplied by reproduction. They are not made as the machines in yonder factory, but they grow as seeds multiply, as yonder geraniums by culturings, as that oak by the seeds it drops into the ground, or that single grain of wheat that sometimes sends up twenty stalks from a single seed, and each stalk bears half a hundred seeds. God has given us in this blessed work a gospel so full that it needs a world for its field. He is showing us the plan of a Christian church, that is much more than an association of congenial friends to listen once a week to an intellectual and musical entertainment and carry on by proxy a mechanism of Christian work; but rather a church that can be at once the mother and the home of every form of help and blessing which Jesus came to give to lost and suffering men, the birthplace and the home of souls, the fountain of healing and cleansing, the sheltering home for the orphan and distressed, the school for the culture and training of God's children, the armory where they are equipped for the battle of the Lord and the army which fights those battles in His name. Such a centre of life and power Christ wants in every centre of population in this sad and sinful world.

The figure of enlargement is that of a tent; its curtains are to be stretched forth and its cords are to be lengthened. These curtains are surely the promises and provisions of the Gospel, and they will stretch as wide as the needs of human lives and the multitudes that seek their shelter. The cords are cords of prayer, cords of faith, cords of love, cords of holy effort and service. He bids us lengthen the cords of prayer. Let us ask more, but let the strands of faith be as long and strong. Let us believe more fully, more firmly, and for a wider circle than we have dared before.

Let the cords of love be lengthened until we shall draw men to Christ with the very cords of our hearts. Let our efforts for His kingdom reach a wider circle. Let each of us make the world our parish, and as the Bride of the Lamb realize that all that concerns our Lord's kingdom concerns our hearts, "For our Maker is our husband, the Lord of Hosts is His name, the God of the whole earth shall He be called."

God has committed to our trust the gospel in its fullness. Let us never rest until in all its fullness it is known in every hamlet of this great land and in every land and tongue.

And we must lengthen the cords of our liberality. The Lord is asking for millions today to spread His gospel in its fullness over the world, and we to whom this full gospel has been such a blessing are especially called to take it as our trust for Him and send it everywhere. The world is open today and the workers are being prepared as never before, men and women full of faith and the Holy Ghost. Never was there a time when a little money would go so far in spreading Christ's Word. Less than ten millions today would evangelize all the world before the close of the century.

When I think of the opportunity of using money for God today, I could almost envy the men who have the opportunities of successful business. God is going to send very large amounts into the treasuries of consecrated work, and if we are but true to this trust we shall yet see tens of millions spent in sending the fourfold gospel to every corner of the globe.

II. CONSOLIDATION.

But the wider our work the stronger it must be at the centre. And therefore as the cords are lengthened the stakes must also be strengthened. What are these stakes?

1. Surely God's Word is the first. The more widespread the work God gives us to do the more important is it that we be true to the great standard of truth, the Bible and the gospel

of Jesus Christ. This is the day of new theologies and loose views of evangelical truth. More sacredly than ever does the Master require us to stand faithful to the cross of Jesus Christ, the doctrine of man's sin and ruin, the great atonement, the inspiration of the Holy Scriptures, the person and work of the Holy Ghost and the certainties of future retribution and reward. Thank God we do not have to resort to the novelties of rationalism to attract the multitudes. Give them the Living Bread, the atoning blood, the old and ever new story of Jesus and His love.

2. Personal holiness. This is the next safeguard of the Lord's work. God cannot trust an unsanctified people or an unconsecrated man with much service for Him. Poor Jonah is sure to mar his most successful work with a touch of himself. The more God entrusts to our hands the more humbly let us lie at His feet and the more faithfully use our trust for His glory. This is one of the wise things the Salvation Army has done. It has required all its officers to be sanctified men and women. Such a work can afford to be successful. God grant us wisdom to see to it that all who bear the vessels of the Lord are clean. So shall He give us the world itself for our inheritance.

3. The spirit of self-sacrifice. No work can ever be glorious without the martyr spirit. Luxury is killing the churches today, and the only remedy for it is the red blood of sacrifice. Great faith and great sacrifice will always be found together. This must be the spirit of this work if it is to cover the world. We must be willing to endure hardness as good soldiers of Jesus Christ. We must be indifferent to popularity, and human praise or blame, we must be willing to live with great simplicity and rigid economy, we must be willing to be misunderstood and persecuted, we must be glad to be the companions of the lowly and despised, we must gladly face toil, hardship and even death, and count all things but loss

for Christ and His kingdom. Such a people only can possess the world for Christ, and such soldiers shall march to worldwide victory while the splendid brigades of rank and luxury shall fail in the day of battle and prove but a splendid pageant and a dress parade.

God give us the spirit of Scriptural faith, personal consecration and true self-sacrifice, and then He can give us the world for Christ.

The figure of the tent suggests the idea of constant vicissitudes and humility. This is no proud architectural pile but a simple tent, ever changing and oft taken down and moved forward. It is the figure of the changing wilderness, the pilgrim life and constant movement. This is not our rest. This is no place for great cathedrals and splendid establishments and ecclesiastical states but continual advance and ceaseless aggression. It is to be feared that splendid churches have been the greatest curse of the church. As long as the early Christians met in humble upper rooms, they had the power of God and godliness, but when they began to imitate the splendor of the world and vie with the architecture of imperial palaces and heathen temples, the Holy Spirit took His flight, and the world and the devil became paramount. The days of the Jewish tabernacle were better days than those of Solomon's temple. The beginning of this work was in a humble tent; let us never forget the tent spirit or lose the pilgrim spirit. "Enlarge the place of thy tent." He does not say get a temple, but a bigger tent. Lord, help us to enlarge but never leave our tents.

III. DIVINE RESOURCES.

"For thy Maker is thy Husband; the Lord of Hosts is His name, the God of the whole earth shall He be called." This is the secret of it all. We have back of us one who has infinite resources, and He is not only our King and our Friend, He is our Husband. He has given us all His heart and all His glory, and He will surely give us all the world for our dowry and our inheritance. This is the secret of successful work, to know Christ in this blissful and intimate relation, and to receive our work, by virtue of our union with Him, as the very fruit of our marriage with the King of Kings. So may He reveal Himself to us all, and then, as His very bride, standing at the threshold of His home and inviting in His lost and wandering children, it shall be true of us, "The Spirit and the bride say, Come," and the world will come to Him.

"How knowest thou whether thou be come to the kingdom for such a time as this?" Like Esther on Ahasuerus' throne, we have been called to the kingdom that we might use our place of right and power to save a world. God help us so to win them back to our beloved Husband, so to bear them for Him as His very children and ours, that "the God of the whole earth shall He be called."

It has been the experience of some of God's children, and it was mine, to be called by His Spirit, in years of loneliness and sorrow, to learn very deeply the Song of Solomon in its true spiritual significance, and then, in this deep, sweet love-life with Christ, to be led into precious service for Him, and to find the life filled with most gracious fruitfulness and blessing. 0 beloved, He is calling you to His bosom and then to His work, "Hearken, 0 daughter, and consider, forget also thy kindred and thy father's house; so shall the King greatly desire thy beauty: for He is thy Lord; and worship thou Him." And then, "Instead of thy fathers shall be thy children, whom thou mayest make princes in all the earth."

www.ingramcontent.com/pod-product-compliance
Lightning Source LLC
Chambersburg PA
CBHW060449090426
42735CB00011B/1949